Praise for Building Embedded Linux Systems

"This book is the most thorough and proper treatment of embedded Linux in existence. Yaghmour is simply a must-have for anyone doing serious ~~embedded Linux~~ development."

> —Bill Gatliff, Independent Consultant, E~~mbedded~~
> regular contributor to *Embedded Syste~~ms~~*

"Employing Linux for embedded systems requires intimate ~~knowledge of~~ topics, and Yaghmour manages to give a comprehensive view of all the relevant ones in his book. His focus on Open Source Software and explanations how to build everything that is needed from pristine sources allows the reader to get an in-depth understanding of the whole system. This book is a must for all developers and users of Embedded Linux systems."

> —Wolfgang Denk, Embedded Linux Expert, founder and CEO of
> DENX Software Engineering, and maintainer of the U-Boot open
> source bootloader

"In general, I'm very impressed with *Building Embedded Linux Systems*. While reviewing it I found it to be well laid-out and comprehensive; it'll be a very useful guide both to newcomers to embedded Linux and to more experienced hands."

> —David Woodhouse, Main author and maintainer of the MTD kernel
> subsystem

"*Building Embedded Linux Systems* demonstrates its author's impressive grasp of the book's subject matter. Embedded system designers will appreciate the book's detailed descriptions of the procedures unique to building systems based on Linux."

> —Jerry Epplin, Technical Editor, LinuxDevices.com

"Karim has done an excellent job of describing all the components of an embedded Linux project and has managed not to short-change any one particular area. One thing I especially like about the book is its lack of source code filler. Another thing I liked is that it's obvious that Karim did his homework. He goes out of his way to show that there are many options when considering boot firmware, file systems, C libraries, and the other portions of an embedded Linux system. I'd recommend this book to any experienced programmer considering an embedded Linux project. The project checklist/worksheets in the back are worth the price alone!"

> —Clark Williams, Senior Architect, Red Hat Custom Engineering,
> embedded Linux group

"Karim Yaghmour delivers a complete and thorough description of everything that you will need to set up a custom embedded Linux system."

> —Greg Kroah-Hartman, Linux kernel developer

Building Embedded
LINUX
SYSTEMS

Related titles from O'Reilly

Building Secure Servers with Linux

Essential System Administration

Learning Red Hat Linux

Linux Device Drivers

Linux in a Nutshell

Linux Network Administrator's Guide

LPI Linux Certification in a Nutshell

Programming Embedded Systems in C and C++

Running Linux

Understanding the Linux Kernel

Also available

The Linux Web Server CD Bookshelf

Building Embedded
LINUX
SYSTEMS

Karim Yaghmour

O'REILLY®

Beijing · Cambridge · Farnham · Köln · Paris · Sebastopol · Taipei · Tokyo

Building Embedded Linux Systems
by Karim Yaghmour

Copyright © 2003 O'Reilly Media, Inc. All rights reserved.
Printed in the United States of America.

Published by O'Reilly Media, Inc., 1005 Gravenstein Highway North, Sebastopol, CA 95472.

Editor:	Andy Oram
Production Editor:	Linley Dolby
Cover Designer:	Emma Colby
Interior Designer:	Bret Kerr

Printing History:

April 2003:	First Edition.

 This book uses RepKover™, a durable and flexible lay-flat binding.

ISBN-10: 0-596-00222-X
ISBN-13: 978-0-596-00222-0
[M]   [12/07]

*To Mom, whose courage and determination
are an everyday guiding light,
and to Dad, whose foresight and engineering spirit
are an everlasting source of inspiration.*

—Karim Yaghmour

Table of Contents

Preface

When I first suggested using Linux in an embedded system back in 1997 while working for a hardware manufacturer, my suggestion was met with a certain degree of skepticism and surprise. Today, the use of Linux in embedded systems is no laughing matter. Indeed, many industry giants and government agencies are increasingly relying on Linux for their embedded software needs.

The widespread interest and enthusiasm generated by Linux's successful use in a number of embedded applications has led to the creation of a plethora of articles, web sites, companies, and documents all pertaining to "embedded Linux." Yet, beyond the flashy announcements, the magazine articles, and the hundreds of projects and products that claim to ease Linux's use in embedded systems, professional developers seeking a useful guide are still looking for answers to fundamental questions regarding the basic methods and techniques required to build embedded systems based on the Linux kernel.

Much of the documentation currently available relies heavily on the use of a number of prepackaged, ready-to-use cross-platform development tools and target binaries. Yet other documents cover only one very precise aspect of running Linux on an embedded target.

This book is a radical departure from the existing documentation in that it makes no assumptions as to the tools you have at hand or the scope of your project, other than your desire to use Linux. All that is required for this book is an Internet connection to download the necessary packages, browse specific online documentation, and benefit from other developers' experiences, as well as share your own, through project mailing lists. You still need a development host and documentation regarding your target's hardware, but the explanations I outline do not require the purchasing of any product or service from any vendor.

Besides giving the greatest degree of freedom and control over your design, this approach is closest to that followed by the pioneers who have spearheaded the way for Linux's use in embedded systems. In essence, these pioneers have *pulled* on Linux to fit their applications by stripping it down and customizing it to their purposes. Linux's penetration of the embedded world contrasts, therefore, with the approach followed by many software vendors to *push* their products into new fields of applications. As an embedded system developer, you are likely to find Linux much easier to pull towards your design than to adapt the products being pushed by vendors to that same design.

This book's approach is to allow you to pull Linux towards your design by providing all the details and discussing many of the corner cases encountered in using Linux in embedded systems. Though it is not possible to claim that all embedded designs are covered by this book, the resources provided here allow you to easily obtain the rest of the information required for you to customize and use Linux in your embedded system.

In writing this book, my intent has been to bring the embedded system developers who use open source and free software in their designs closer to the developers who create and maintain these open source and free software packages. Though a lot of mainstream embedded system developers, many of whom are high-caliber programmers, rely on third-party offerings for their embedded Linux needs, there is a clear opportunity for them to contribute to the open source and free software projects on which they rely. Ultimately, this sort of dynamic will ensure that Linux continues to be the best operating system choice for embedded systems.

Audience of This Book

This book is intended first and foremost for the experienced embedded system designer who wishes to use Linux in a future or current project. Such a reader is expected to be familiar with all the techniques and technologies used in developing embedded systems, such as cross-compiling, BDM or JTAG debugging, and the implications of dealing with immature or incomplete hardware. If you are such a reader, you may want to skip some of the background material about embedded system development presented early in some sections. There are, however, many early sections (particularly in Chapter 2) that you will need to read, because they cover the special implications of using the Linux kernel in an embedded system.

This book is also intended for the beginning embedded system developer who would like to become familiar with the tools and techniques used in developing embedded systems based on Linux. This book is not an introduction to embedded systems, however, and you may need to research some of the issues discussed here in an introductory text book. Appendix B contains a list of books and other resources to help you.

If you are a power user or a system administrator already familiar with Linux, this book should help you produce highly customized Linux installations. If you find that distributions install too many packages for your liking, for example, and would like to build your own custom distribution from scratch, many parts of this book should come in handy, particularly Chapter 6.

Finally, this book should be helpful to a programmer or a Linux enthusiast who wants to understand how Linux systems are built and operated. Though the material in this book does not cover how general-purpose distributions are created, many of the techniques covered here apply, to a certain extent, as much to general purpose distributions as they do to creating customized embedded Linux installations.

Scope and Background Information

To make the best of Linux's capabilities in embedded systems, you need background in all the following topics, which in many books are treated distinctly:

Embedded systems
> You need to be familiar with the development, programming, and debugging of embedded systems in general, from both the software and hardware perspectives.

Unix system administration
> You need to be able to tend to various system administration tasks such as hardware configuration, system setup, maintenance, and using shell scripts to automate tasks.

Linux device drivers
> You need to know how to develop and debug various kinds of Linux device drivers.

Linux kernel internals
> You need to understand as much as possible how the kernel operates.

GNU software development tools
> You need to be able to make efficient use of the GNU tools. This includes understanding many of the options and utilities often considered to be "arcane."

In this book, I assume that you are familiar with at least the basic concepts of each topic. On the other hand, you don't need to know how to create Linux device drivers to read this book, for example, or know everything about embedded system development. As you read through this book and progress in your use of Linux in embedded systems, you are likely to feel the need to obtain more information regarding certain aspects of Linux's use. In addition to the references to other books scattered through this book, take a look at Appendix B for a list of books you may find useful for getting more information regarding the topics listed above.

Though this book discusses only the use of Linux in embedded systems, part of this discussion can certainly be useful to developers who intend to use one of the BSD variants in their embedded system. Many of the explanations included here will, however, need to be reinterpreted in light of the differences between BSD and Linux.

Organization of the Material

There are three major parts to this book. The first part is composed of Chapters 1 through 3. These chapters cover the preliminary background required for building any sort of embedded Linux system. Though they describe no hands-on procedures, they are essential to understand many aspects of building embedded Linux systems.

The second part spans Chapters 4 through 9. These important chapters lay out the essential steps involved in building any embedded Linux system. Regardless of your systems' purpose or functionality, these chapters are required reading.

The final part of the book is made up of Chapters 10 and 11, and covers material that, though very important, is not essential to building embedded Linux systems.

Chapter 1, *Introduction*, gives an in-depth introduction to the world of embedded Linux. It lays out basic definitions and then introduces real-life issues about embedded Linux systems, including a discussion of open source and free software licenses from the embedded perspective. The chapter then introduces the example system used in other parts of this book and the implementation method used throughout the book.

Chapter 2, *Basic Concepts*, outlines the basic concepts that are common to building all embedded Linux systems.

Chapter 3, *Hardware Support*, provides a thorough review of the embedded hardware supported by Linux, and gives links to web sites where the drivers and subsystems implementing this support can be found. This chapter discusses processor architectures, buses and interfaces, I/O, storage, general purpose networking, industrial grade networking, and system monitoring.

Chapter 4, *Development Tools*, covers the installation and use of the various development tools used in building embedded Linux systems. This includes, most notably, how to build and install the GNU toolchain components from scratch. It also includes sections discussing Java, Perl, and Python, along with a section about the various terminal emulators that can be used to interact with an embedded target.

Chapter 5, *Kernel Considerations*, discusses the selection, configuration, cross-compiling, installation, and use of the Linux kernel in an embedded system.

Chapter 6, *Root Filesystem Content*, explains how to build a root filesystem using the components introduced earlier in the book, including the installation of the C library and the creation of the appropriate */dev* entries. More importantly, this chapter covers the installation and use of BusyBox, TinyLogin, Embutils, and System V *init*.

Chapter 7, *Storage Device Manipulation*, covers the intricacies of manipulating and setting up storage devices for embedded Linux systems. The chapter's emphasis is on solid-state storage devices, such as native flash and DiskOnChip devices, and the MTD subsystem.

Chapter 8, *Root Filesystem Setup*, explains how to set up the root filesystem created in Chapter 6 for the embedded system's storage device. This includes the creation of JFFS2 and CRAMFS filesystem images, and the use of disk-style filesystems over NFTL.

Chapter 9, *Setting Up the Bootloader*, discusses the various bootloaders available for use in each embedded Linux architecture. Special emphasis is put on the use of GRUB with DiskOnChip devices, and U-Boot. Network booting using BOOTP/DHCP, TFTP, and NFS is also covered.

Chapter 10, *Setting Up Networking Services*, focuses on the configuration, installation, and use of software packages that offer networking services, such as SNMP, SSH, and HTTP.

Chapter 11, *Debugging Tools*, covers the main debugging issues encountered in developing software for embedded Linux systems. This includes the use of *gdb* in a cross-platform development environment, tracing, performance analysis, and memory debugging.

Appendix A, *Worksheet*, introduces a worksheet that can be used in conjunction with this book to provide a complete specification of an embedded Linux system.

Appendix B, *Resources*, provides resources you may find useful when building embedded Linux systems.

Appendix C, *Important Licenses and Notices*, includes important postings by Linus Torvalds and other kernel developers regarding the kernel's licensing and the issue of non-GPL binary kernel modules.

Though Chapters 7 through 9 are independent, note that their content is highly interrelated. Setting up the target's storage device as discussed in Chapter 7, for example, requires a basic knowledge about the target filesystem organization as discussed in Chapter 8, and vice versa. So, too, does setting up storage devices require a basic knowledge of bootloader set up and operation as discussed in Chapter 9, and vice versa. I therefore recommend that you read Chapters 7 through 9 in one breath a first time before carrying out the instructions of any of these chapters. When setting up your target thereafter, you will nevertheless follow the same sequence of operations outlined in these chapters.

Hardware Used in This Book

As we'll see in Chapter 3, Linux supports a very wide range of hardware. For this book, I've used a few embedded systems to test the various procedures. Table P-1 contains the complete list of systems I used.

Some of these systems, such as the iPAQ or the Dreamcast, are commercial products available in the mainstream market. I included these intentionally, to demonstrate that any willing reader can find the materials to support learning how to build embedded Linux systems. Sega Dreamcast consoles, for instance, are available for less than $50 on eBay. Though they boot using a specially formatted CD-ROM, they are one of the cheapest ways for learning cross-platform development with Linux. You can, of course, still use an old x86 PC for experimenting, but you are likely to miss much of the fun given the resemblance between such systems and most development hosts.

Table P-1. Target systems used throughout this book

Architecture	System type	Processor clock speed	RAM size	Storage size and type
PPC	TQ components TQM860L	80 MHz	16 MB	8 MB flash
SuperH	Sega Dreamcast	200 MHz	16 MB	CD-ROM (see text)
ARM	Compaq iPAQ 3600	206 MHz	32 MB	16 MB flash
x86	Kontron Teknor VIPer 806	100 MHz	40 MB	32 MB CompactFlash
x86	COTS[a] Pentium	100 MHz	8 MB	32 MB DiskOnChip

[a] Commercial Off-The-Shelf.

Apart from running on a slew of embedded systems, Linux also runs on a wide variety of workstations. Throughout this book, I used the hosts presented in Table P-2. Though the Apple PowerBook served as my main development host for the book, I had to use an x86 host for some aspects of building x86-based embedded targets, because some software components cannot be cross-compiled for an x86 target on a non-x86 host. Both GRUB and LILO, for example, have to be built on an x86 host. I can report, nevertheless, that I wrote this entire book on a PowerBook host running the Yellow Dog Linux distribution. This is yet another sign that Linux changes the computing world's landscape by providing one standard operating environment across a very fragmented world of hardware.

Table P-2. Host systems used throughout this book

Architecture	System type	Processor clock speed	RAM size	Storage size
PPC	Apple PowerBook	400 MHz	128 MB	> GB hard disk
x86	Pentium II	350 MHz	128 MB	> GB hard disk

To illustrate the range of target architectures on which Linux can be used, I varied the target hardware I used in the examples between chapters. Table P-3 lists the target architecture used in each chapter. Though each chapter is based on a different architecture, the commands given in each chapter apply readily to other architectures as well. If, for instance, an example in a chapter relies on the *arm-linux-gcc* command, which is the *gcc* compiler for ARM, the same example would work for a PPC target by using the *powerpc-linux-gcc* command instead. Whenever more than one architecture is listed for a chapter, the main architecture discussed is the first one listed. The example commands in Chapter 5, for instance, are mainly centered around the ARM, but there are also a few references to PPC commands.

Though Table P-3 lists the target being used in example for each chapter, it provides no indication as to the host being used, because it makes no difference to the discussion. Instead, unless specific instructions are given to the contrary, the host's architecture is always different from the target's. In Chapter 4, for example, I used a PPC host to build tools for an x86 target. The same instructions could, nevertheless, be carried out on a SPARC or an S/390 with little or no modification. Note that most of the content of the early chapters is architecture independent, so there is no need to provide any architecture-specific commands.

Table P-3. Main target architectures used for commands examples

Chapter	Target architectures
Chapter 1	N/A
Chapter 2	N/A
Chapter 3	N/A
Chapter 4	x86
Chapter 5	ARM, PPC
Chapter 6	PPC
Chapter 7	x86, PPC
Chapter 8	ARM
Chapter 9	PPC, x86
Chapter 10	ARM
Chapter 11	PPC

Software Versions

The central software on which an embedded Linux system depends, of course, is the Linux kernel. This book concentrates on Version 2.4 of the Linux kernel, and on Release 2.4.18 in particular. Changes within 2.4 will probably have only a benign effect on the information in the book. That is, new releases will probably support more hardware than Chapter 3 lists. But the essential tasks described in this book are unlikely to change in 2.4. As the kernel evolves past Version 2.4, however, some of the steps described in this book are likely to require updating.

In addition, this book discusses the configuration, installation, and use of over 40 different open source and free software packages. Each package is maintained independently and is developed at a different pace. Because these packages change over time, it is likely that the package versions covered in this book may be outdated by the time you read it. In an effort to minimize the effect of software updates on the text, I have kept the text as version independent as possible. The overall structure of the book and the internal structure of each chapter, for example, are unlikely to vary regardless of the various software changes. Also, many packages covered by this book have been around for quite some time, so they are unlikely to change in any substantial way. For instance, the commands to install, set up, and use the different components of the GNU development toolchain, which is used throughout this book, have been relatively constant for a number of years, and are unlikely to change in any substantial way in the future. This statement applies equally to most other software packages discussed.

Book Web Site

Given that many of the software packages discussed in this book are in continuous development that may cause some of the explanations included here to change, I set up a web site for providing updates and links related to this book:

http://www.embeddedtux.org/

The worksheet presented in Appendix A, for example, is available for download in both PDF and OpenOffice formats from the book's web site.

Typographical Conventions

The following is a list of typographical conventions used in this book:

Constant width

> Is used to show the contents of code files or the output from commands, and to indicate source code keywords that appear in code.

Constant width bold

> Is used to indicate user input.

Italic

> Is used for file and directory names, program and command names, command-line options, URLs, and for emphasizing new terms.

This icon indicates a tip, suggestion, or general note.

This icon indicates a warning or caution.

Contact Information

Please address comments and questions concerning this book to the publisher:

O'Reilly & Associates, Inc.
1005 Gravenstein Highway North
Sebastopol, CA 95472
(800) 998-9938 (in the United States or Canada)
(707) 829-0515 (international or local)
(707) 829-0104 (fax)

We have a web page for this book, where we list errata, examples, or any additional information. You can access this page at:

http://www.oreilly.com/catalog/belinuxsys/

To comment or ask technical questions about this book, send email to:

bookquestions@oreilly.com

For more information about our books, conferences, Resource Centers, and the O'Reilly Network, see our web site at:

http://www.oreilly.com

Acknowledgments

E quindi uscimmo a riveder le stelle.[*] It is with these words that Dante ends *Inferno*, the first part of his *Devine Comedy*. Though it would be misleading to suggest that writing this book wasn't enjoyable, Dante's narrative clearly expresses the feeling of finishing a first iteration of the book you now hold in your hands. In particular, I have to admit that it has been a challenging task to pick up the bits and pieces of information available on the use of Linux in embedded systems, to complete this information in as much as possible, and put everything back together in a single straightforward manuscript that provides a practical method for building embedded Linux systems. Fortunately, I was aided in this task by very competent and willing people.

First and foremost, I would like to thank Andy Oram, my editor. Much like Virgil assisted Dante in his venture, Andy shepherded me throughout the various stages of writing this book. Among many other things, he patiently corrected my non-idiomatic phrases, made sure that my text actually conveyed the meaning I meant for it to convey, and relentlessly pointed out the sections where I wasn't providing enough detail. The text you are about to read is all the much better, as it has profited from Andy's input. By the same token, I would like to thank Ellen Siever with whom I initially started working on this book. Though our collaboration ended earlier than I

---

[*] "And from there we emerged to see the stars once more."

wished it had, many of the ideas that have made their way into this final version of the book have profited from her constructive feedback.

I have been extremely fortunate to have an outstanding team of reviewers go over this book, and am very greatful for the many hours they poured into reading, correcting, and pointing out problems with various aspects of this book. The review team was made up of Erik Andersen, Wolfgang Denk, Bill Gatliff, Russell King, Paul Kinzelman, Alessandro Rubini, David Schleef, and David Woodhouse. I'd like to especially thank Alessandro for his dogged pursuit of perfection. Any remaining errors you may find in the following pages are without a doubt all mine.

Writing about the use of Linux in embedded systems requires having access to a slew of different hardware. Given that embedded hardware is often expensive, I would like to thank all the companies and individuals who have stepped forward to provide me with the appropriate equipment. In particular, I would like to thank Stéphane Martin of Kontron for providing a Teknor VIPer 806 board, Wolfgang Denk of DENX Software Engineering for providing a TQ components TQM860L PPC board, and Steve Papacharalambous and Stuart Hughes of Zee2 for providing a uCdimm system.

I have found much of the incentive and thrust for writing this book from being a very satisfied open source and free software user and contributor who has profited time and again from the knowledge and the work produced by other members of this community. For this, I have many people to thank. Primarily, I'd like to thank Michel Dagenais for his trust, his guidance, and for giving me the chance to freely explore uncharted terrain. My work on developing the Linux Trace Toolkit, as part of my masters degree with Michel, got me more and more involved in the open source and free software community. As part of this involvement, I have met a lot of remarkable individuals whose insight and help I greatly appreciate. Lots of thanks to Jacques Gélinas, Richard Stallman, Jim Norton, Steve Papacharalambous, Stuart Hughes, Paolo Mantegazza, Pierre Cloutier, David Schleef, Wolfgang Denk, Philippe Gerum, Loic Dachary, Daniel Phillips, and Alessandro Rubini.

Last, but certainly not least, I owe a debt of gratitude to Sonia for her exceptional patience as I spent countless hours testing, writing, testing some more, and writing even more. Her support and care has made this endeavour all the more easy to carry out. *La main invisible qui a écrit les espaces entre les lignes est la sienne et je lui en suis profondément reconnaissant.**

---

* "The invisible hand that wrote the spaces between each line is hers, and I am profoundly grateful to her for this."

## CHAPTER 1

Introduction

Since its first public release in 1991, Linux has been put to ever wider uses. Initially confined to a loosely tied group of developers and enthusiasts on the Internet, it eventually matured into a solid Unix-like operating system for workstations, servers, and clusters. Its growth and popularity accelerated the work started by the Free Software Foundation (FSF) and fueled what would later be known as the open source movement. All the while, it attracted media and business interest, which contributed to establishing Linux's presence as a legitimate and viable choice for an operating system.

Yet, oddly enough, it is through an often ignored segment of computerized devices that Linux is poised to become the preferred operating system. That segment is embedded systems, and the bulk of the computer systems found in our modern day lives belong to it. Embedded systems are everywhere in our lives, from mobile phones to medical equipment, including air navigation systems, automated bank tellers, MP3 players, printers, cars, and a slew of other devices about which we are often unaware. Every time you look around and can identify a device as containing a microprocessor, you've most likely found another embedded system.

If you are reading this book, you probably have a basic idea why one would want to run an embedded system using Linux. Whether because of its flexibility, its robustness, its price tag, the community developing it, or the large number of vendors supporting it, there are many reasons for choosing to build an embedded system with Linux and many ways to carry out the task. This chapter provides the background for the material presented in the rest of the book by discussing definitions, real-life issues, generic embedded Linux systems architecture, examples, and methodology.

Definitions

The words "Linux," "embedded Linux," and "real-time Linux" are often used with little reference to what is being designated. Sometimes, the designations may mean something very precise. Other times, a broad range or category of applications is meant. Let us look at these terms and what they mean in different situations.

What Is Linux?

Linux is interchangeably used in reference to the Linux kernel, a Linux system, or a Linux distribution. The broadness of the term plays in favor of the adoption of Linux, in the large sense, when presented to a nontechnical crowd, but can be bothersome when providing technical explanations. If, for instance, I say: "Linux provides TCP/IP networking." Do I mean the TCP/IP stack in the kernel or the TCP/IP utilities provided in a Linux distribution that are also part of an installed Linux system, or both? This vagueness actually became ammunition for the proponents of the "GNU/Linux" moniker, who pointed out that Linux was the kernel, but that the system was mainly built on GNU software.

Strictly speaking, Linux refers to the kernel maintained by Linus Torvalds and distributed under the same name through the main repository and various mirror sites. This codebase includes only the kernel and no utilities whatsoever. The kernel provides the core system facilities. It may not be the first software to run on the system, as a bootloader may have preceded it, but once it is running, it is never swapped out or removed from control until the system is shut down. In effect, it controls all hardware and provides higher-level abstractions such as processes, sockets, and files to the different software running on the system.

As the kernel is constantly updated, a numbering scheme is used to identify a certain release. This numbering scheme uses three numbers separated by dots to identify the releases. The first two numbers designate the version, and the third designates the release. Linux 2.4.20, for instance, is version number 2.4, release number 20. Odd version numbers, such as 2.5, designate development kernels, while even version numbers, such as 2.4, designate stable kernels. Usually, you should use a kernel from the latest stable series for your embedded system.

This is the simple explanation. The truth is that far from the "official" releases, there are many modified Linux kernels that you may find all over the Internet that carry additional version information. 2.4.18-rmk3-hh24, for instance, is a modified kernel distributed by the Familiar project. It is based on 2.4.18, but contains an extra "-rmk3-hh24" version number controlled by the Familiar development team. These extra version numbers, and the kernel itself, will be discussed in more detail in Chapter 5.

Linux can also be used to designate a hardware system running the Linux kernel and various utilities running on the kernel. If a friend mentions that his development team is using Linux in their latest product, he probably means more than the kernel. A Linux system certainly includes the kernel, but most likely includes a number of other software components that are usually run with the Linux kernel. Often, these will be composed of a subset of the GNU software such as the C library and binary utilities. It may also include the X window system or a real-time addition such as RTAI.

A Linux system may be custom built, as you'll see later, or can be based on an already available distribution. Your friend's development team probably custom built their own system. Conversely, when a user says she runs Linux on the desktop, she most likely means that she installed one of the various distributions, such as Red Hat or Debian. The user's Linux system is as much a Linux system as that of your friend's, but apart from the kernel, their systems most likely have very different purposes, are built from very different software packages, and run very different applications.

Finally, Linux may also designate a Linux distribution. Red Hat, Mandrake, SuSE, Debian, Slackware, Caldera, MontaVista, Embedix, BlueCat, PeeWeeLinux, and others are all Linux distributions. They may vary in purpose, size, and price, but they share a common purpose: to provide the user with a shrinkwrapped set of files and an installation procedure to get the kernel and various overlaid software installed on a certain type of hardware for a certain purpose. Most of us are familiar with Linux distributions through CD-ROMs, but there are distributions that are no more than a set of files you retrieve from a web site, untar, and install according to the documentation. The difference between mainstream, user-oriented distributions and these distributions is the automated installation procedure in the mainstream ones.

Starting with the next chapter and in the rest of this book, I will avoid referring to the word "Linux" on its own. Instead, I will refer directly to the object of discussion. Rather than talking about the "Linux kernel," I will refer to the "kernel." Rather than talking about the "Linux system," I will refer to the "system." Rather than talking about a "Linux distribution," I will refer to a "distribution." In all these circumstances, "Linux" is implied but avoided to eliminate any possible confusion. I will continue, however, to use the term "Linux," where appropriate, to designate the broad range of software and resources surrounding the kernel.

What Is Embedded Linux?

Again, we could start with the three designations Linux suggests: a kernel, a system, and a distribution. Yet, we would have to take the kernel off the list right away, as there is no such thing as an embedded version of the kernel distributed by Linus. This doesn't mean the kernel can't be embedded. It only means you do not need a special kernel to create an embedded system. Often, you can use one of the official kernel releases to build your system. Sometimes, you may want to use a modified kernel distributed by a third party, one that has been specifically tailored for a special hardware configuration or for support of a certain type of application. The kernels provided with the various embedded distributions, for example, often include some optimizations not found in the main kernel tree and are patched for support for some debugging tools such as kernel debuggers. Mainly, though, a kernel used in an embedded system differs from a kernel used on a workstation or a server by its build configuration. Chapter 5 covers the build process.

An embedded Linux system simply designates an embedded system based on the Linux kernel and does not imply the use of any specific library or user tools with this kernel.

An embedded Linux distribution may include: a development framework for embedded linux systems, various software applications tailored for usage in an embedded system, or both.

Development framework distributions include various development tools that facilitate the development of embedded systems. This may include special source browsers, cross-compilers, debuggers, project management software, boot image builders, and so on. These distributions are meant to be installed on the development host.

Tailored embedded distributions provide a set of applications to be used within the target embedded system. This might include special libraries, executables, and configuration files to be used on the target. A method may also be provided to simplify the generation of root filesystems for the target system.

Because this book discusses embedded Linux systems, there is no need to keep repeating "embedded Linux" in every name. Hence, I will refer to the host used for developing the embedded Linux system as the "host system," or "host," for short. The target, which will be the embedded Linux system will be referred to as the "target system," or "target," for short. Distributions providing development frameworks will be referred to as "development distributions."* Distributions providing tailored software packages will be referred to as "target distributions."

What Is Real-Time Linux?

Initially, real-time Linux designated the RTLinux project released in 1996 by Michael Barabanov under Victor Yodaiken's supervision. The goal of the project was to provide deterministic response times under a Linux environment.

Nonetheless, today there are many more projects that provide one form or another of real-time responsiveness under Linux. RTAI, Kurt, and Linux/RK all provide real-time performance under Linux. Some projects' enhancements are obtained by inserting a secondary kernel under the Linux kernel. Others enhance the Linux kernel's response times by means of a patch.

The adjective "real-time" is used in conjunction with Linux to describe a number of different things. Mainly, it is used to say that the system or one of its components is supposed to have fixed response times, but if you use a strict definition of "real-time," you may find that what is being offered isn't necessarily "real-time." I will discuss "real-time" issues and further define the meaning of this adjective in "Time constraints."

---

* It would be tempting to call these "host distributions," but as you'll see later, some developers choose to develop directly on their target, hence the preference for "development distributions."

Real Life and Embedded Linux Systems

What types of embedded systems are built with Linux? Why do people choose Linux? What issues are specific to the use of Linux in embedded systems? How many people actually use Linux in their embedded systems? How do they use it? All these questions and many more come to mind when pondering the use of Linux in an embedded system. Finding satisfactory answers to the fundamental questions is an important part of building the system. This isn't just a general statement. These answers will help you convince management, assist you in marketing your product, and most of all, enable you to evaluate whether your initial expectations have been met.

Types of Embedded Linux Systems

We could use the traditional segments of embedded systems such as aerospace, automotive systems, consumer electronics, telecom, and so on to outline the types of embedded Linux systems, but this would provide no additional information in regard to the systems being designated, because embedded Linux systems may be structured alike regardless of the market segment. Rather, let's classify embedded systems by criteria that will provide actual information about the structure of the system: size, time constraints, networkability, and degree of user interaction.

Size

The size of an embedded linux system is determined by a number of different factors. First, there is physical size. Some systems can be fairly large, like the ones built out of clusters, while others are fairly small, like the Linux watch built by IBM. Most importantly, there are the size attributes of the various electronic components of the system, such as the speed of the CPU, the size of the RAM, and the size of the permanent storage.

In terms of size, I will use three broad categories of systems: small, medium, and large. Small systems are characterized by a low-powered CPU with a minimum of 2 MB of ROM and 4 MB of RAM. This isn't to say Linux won't run in smaller memory spaces, but it will take you some effort to do so. If you plan to run Linux in a smaller space than this, think about starting your work from one of the various distributions that put Linux on a single floppy. If you come from an embedded systems background, you may find that you could do much more using something other than Linux in such a small system. Remember to factor in the speed at which you could deploy Linux, though.

Medium-sized systems are characterized by a medium-powered CPU with around 32 MB or ROM and 64 MB of RAM. Most consumer-oriented devices built with Linux belong to this category. This includes various PDAs, MP3 players, entertainment systems, and network appliances. Some of these devices may include secondary storage in the form of solid-state drives, CompactFlash, or even conventional hard drives.

These types of devices have sufficient horsepower and storage to handle a variety of small tasks or can serve a single purpose that requires a lot of resources.

Large systems are characterized by a powerful CPU or collection of CPUs combined with large amounts of RAM and permanent storage. Usually, these systems are used in environments that require large amounts of calculations to carry out certain tasks. Large telecom switches and flight simulators are prime examples of such systems. Typically, such systems are not bound by costs or resources. Their design requirements are primarily based on functionality while cost, size, and complexity remain secondary issues.

In case you were wondering, Linux doesn't run on any processor below 32 bits. This rules out quite a number of processors traditionally used in embedded systems. Actually, according to traditional embedded system standards, all systems running Linux would be classified as large systems. This is very true when compared to an 8051 with 4K of memory. Keep in mind, though, current trends: processors are getting faster, RAM is getting cheaper and larger, systems are as integrated as ever, and prices are going down. With growing processing demands and increasing system requirements, the types of systems Linux runs on are quickly becoming the standard. In some cases, however, it remains that an 8-bit microcontroller might be the best choice.

16-Bit Linux?

Strictly speaking, the above statement regarding Linux's inability to run on any processor below 32 bits is not entirely true. There have been Linux ports to a number of odd processors. The *Embeddable Linux Kernel Subset* (ELKS) project found at *http://elks. sourceforge.net/*, for example, aims at running Linux on 16-bit processors such as the Intel 8086 and 286. Nevertheless, it remains that the vast majority of development done on the kernel and on user-space applications is 32-bit-centric. Hence, if you choose to use Linux on a processor lower than 32 bits, you will be on your own.

Time constraints

There are two types of time constraints for embedded systems: stringent and mild. Stringent time constraints require that the system react in a predefined time frame. Otherwise, catastrophic events happen. Take for instance a factory where workers have to handle materials being cut by large equipment. As a safety precaution, optical detectors are placed around the blades to detect the presence of the specially colored gloves used by the workers. When the system is alerted that a worker's hand is in danger, it must stop the blades immediately. It can't wait for some file to get swapped or for some task to relinquish the CPU. This system has stringent time requirements; it is a *hard real-time* system.

Streaming audio systems would also qualify as having stringent requirements, because any transient lagging is usually perceived as bothersome by the users. Yet, this later example would mostly qualify as a *soft real-time* system because the failure of the application to perform in a timely fashion all the time isn't catastrophic as it would be for a hard real-time system. In other words, although infrequent failures will be tolerated, the system should be designed to have stringent time requirements.

Mild time constraints vary a lot in requirements, but they generally apply to systems where timely responsiveness isn't necessarily critical. If an automated teller takes 10 more seconds to complete a transaction, it's generally not problematic. The same is true for a PDA that takes a certain number of seconds to start an application. The extra time may make the system seem slow, but it won't affect the end result.

Networkability

Networkability defines whether a system can be connected to a network. Nowadays, we can expect everything to be accessible through the network, even the refrigerator. This, in turn, places special requirements on the systems being built. One factor pushing people to choose Linux as an embedded OS is its proven networking capabilities. Falling prices and standardization of networking components are accelerating this trend. Most Linux devices have one form or another of network capability. You can attach a wireless network card in the Linux distribution built for the Compaq iPAQ, for instance, simply by inserting the adapter in the PCMCIA jacket. Networking issues will be discussed in detail in Chapter 10.

User interaction

The degree of user interaction varies greatly from one system to another. Some systems, such as PDAs, are centered around user interaction, while others, such as industrial process control systems, might only have LEDs and buttons for interaction. Some other systems, have no user interface whatsoever. For example, some components of an autopilot system in a plane might take care of wing control but have no direct interaction with the human pilots.

Examples

The best way to get an idea of what an embedded Linux system might do is to look at examples of such systems. Trouble is, if you try to look for example embedded systems whose details are publicly available on the Internet, you will mostly find consumer devices. Very few examples of Linux in aerospace, industrial control, telecom, or automotive systems are publicly detailed. Yet, it isn't as if Linux wasn't used in those types of applications. Rather, in contrast to consumer devices, the builders of such devices see little advantage in advertising their designs. For all they know, they may be providing critical information to competitors who may decide to switch to Linux to catch up with them. Consumer device builders, on the other hand, leverage the "hype" factor into promoting their consumer products. And given the different market dynamics between consumer products and industrial products, they can afford to play to the crowd.

Surprisingly (or maybe not so surprising after all), some of the best examples of Linux in critical systems are provided in the pages of *Linux Journal* magazine. Digging back a few years, I was able to uncover a treasure of non–consumer-oriented embedded applications based on Linux. This, combined with the consumer devices detailed on the Internet and the statistics we shall see below, provide a fair image of Linux's capabilities and future as an embedded operating system. Table 1-1 contains a summary of the example embedded Linux systems discussed below. The first column is a brief description of the system. The second column details the type of the embedded system. The next four columns characterize the system based on the criteria outlined in the previous section.

Table 1-1. Example embedded Linux systems' characteristics

Description	Type	Size	Time constraints	Networkability	Degree of user interaction
Accelerator control	Industrial process control	Medium	Stringent	Yes	Low
Computer-aided training system	Aerospace	Large	Stringent	No	High
Ericsson "blip"	Networking	Small	Mild	Yes	Very low
SCADA protocol converter	Industrial process control	Medium	Stringent	No	Very low
Sharp Zaurus	Consumer electronics	Medium	Mild	Yes	Very high
Space vehicle control	Aerospace	Large	Stringent	Yes	High

Accelerator control

The accelerator control system was built at the European Synchrotron Radiation Facility and is described in issue 66 of *Linux Journal*. The accelerator equipment is built of many hardware and software components that control all the aspects of experimentation. While not all software was transferred to Linux, some interesting parts have been. This includes the serial line and stepper motor controllers. Many instances of these devices are employed to control various aspects of the system. Serial lines, for instances, control vacuum devices, power supplies, and programmable logic controllers (PLCs). Stepper motors, on the other hand, are used in positioning goniometers, slits, and translation stages. Serial lines are controlled via serial boards running on PC/104.

The PC/104 single board computer (SBC) controlling the serial boards has a Pentium 90 MHz with 20 MB of RAM and a 24 MB solid-state hard disk. A standard workstation distribution, SuSE 5.3, was trimmed down to fit in the limited permanent storage space. Some stepper motor controllers run on a similar configuration, while others run on VME boards that have 8 to 32 MB of memory and load the operating system from a Unix-type server using BOOTP/TFTP. These boards run a modified version of Richard Hirst's Linux for 680x0-based VME boards. All the equipment is network accessible and controllable through a TCP/IP network. Here, Linux, in the broad sense, was chosen because it is configurable, stable, free, and well supported, contains support for many standards, and its source code is accessible.

Computer-aided training system

The computer-aided training system (CATS) was built at CAE Electronics and is described in issue 64 of *Linux Journal*. Unlike full flight simulators, which include visual, sound, and motion simulation, CATS provides only a visual representation of the various aircraft panels. A CATS isn't a cheap version of a flight simulator. Instead, it complements a flight simulator by providing entry-level training. Conventional CAE CATS were built on IBM RS/6000 workstations running AIX. A port to Linux was prompted by the low cost of powerful x86 systems and the portability of Linux itself.

The CATS come in three different versions: one-, three-, and seven-screen systems. Development and testing was done on a workstation equipped with a Pentium II 350 MHz processor, 128 MB of RAM, and Evolution4 graphic cards from Color Graph ics Systems, which provide for control of four displays each. Xi Graphics' Accelerat-edX X server was used to control the Evolution4 and provide adequate multiheaded display. A single-screen version could still run easily on a Linux system equipped with the standard XFree86 X server.

Because of customer requirements, the system was provided on a bootable CD-ROM to avoid local installation. Hence, the complete CATS is run from the CD-ROM using a RAM filesystem. The end system has been found to be reliable, predictable, dependable, stable, and in excess of performance requirements. Work on prototype flight simulators running Linux began in April 2000. Having had very positive results, most full flight simulators currently shipped run Linux.

Ericsson "blip"

The Ericsson "blip" is a commercial product. Details of the product can be found on Ericsson's blip web site at *http://www.ericsson.com/about/blipnet/* and on LinuxDevices. com. "blip" stands for "Bluetooth Local Infotainment Point" and enables Bluetooth devices to access local information. This product can be used either in public places to provide services or at home for accessing or synchronizing with local information.

The blip houses an Atmel AT91F40816 ARM7TDMI paced at 22.5 MHz with 2 MB of RAM, 1 MB of system flash, and 1 MB of user flash. The Atmel chip runs the uClinux distribution, with kernel 2.0.38 modified for MMU-less ARM, provided by Lineo along with uClibc, the miniature C library, and talks via a serial link to a standalone Bluetooth chip. Access to the device is provided by a proprietary Bluetooth stack, an Ethernet interface, and a serial port. Custom applications can be developed for the blip using an SDK provided by Ericsson and built using customized GNU software. Linux was chosen, because it provided an open and inexpensive development environment both for the host and the target, hence encouraging and stimulating the development of third-party software.

SCADA protocol converter

The System Control and Data Acquisition (SCADA) protocol converter is detailed in issue 77 of *Linux Journal*. Here, an existing Digital Control System (DCS) controlling a turbocompressor in an oil extraction plant had to be integrated into a SCADA system to facilitate management of the plant. Converting the complete DCS for better integration would have been expensive, hence the choice was made to build a conversion gateway that interfaced between the existing DCS and the SCADA system.

Linux was chosen because it is easy to tailor, it is well documented, it can run from RAM, and development can be done directly on the target system. An 8 MB DiskOn-Chip (DOC) from M-Systems provides a solid-state drive for the application. To avoid patching the kernel with the binary drivers provided by M-Systems, the DOC's format is left in its shipped configuration as a DOS filesystem.* The kernel and root filesystem are compressed and placed in the DOC along with DOS. Upon bootup, the batch files invoke *Loadlin* to load Linux and the root filesystem. The system files are therefore read-only and the system is operated using a RAM root filesystem. The root filesystem was built using Red Hat 6.1 following the BootDisk HOWTO instructions. The system is an industrial PC with 32 MB of RAM.

Sharp Zaurus

The Sharp Zaurus is a commercial product sold by Sharp Electronics. Details on the Zaurus can be found on its web site at *http://www.myzaurus.com/* and on Linux-Devices.com. The Zaurus is a Personal Digital Assistant (PDA) completely based on Linux. As such, it comes equipped with all the usual PDA applications, such as contacts, to do list, schedule, notes, calculator, email, etc.

The original Zaurus, the SL-5500, was built around an Intel StrongARM 206 MHz processor with 64 MB of RAM and 16 MB of flash. A newer version, the SL-5600, is built around an Intel XScale 400 MHz processor with 32 MB of RAM and 64 MB of flash. The system is based on Lineo's Embedix embedded Linux distribution and uses QT's Palmtop GUI. Independent development of the Zaurus software is encouraged by Sharp who maintains a developer web site at *http://developer.sharpsec.com/*.

Space vehicle control

The space vehicle control was built at the European Space Agency (ESA) and is detailed in issue 59 of *Linux Journal*. The Automatic Transfer Vehicle (ATV) is an unmanned space vehicle used in the refueling and reboosting of the International

---

* Though this project used M-Systems' binary drivers, there are GPL'd drivers for the DOC, as we'll see in Chapter 7.

Space Station (ISS). The docking process between the ATV and the ISS requires the ATV to catch up to the ISS and dock with precision. This process is governed by complex mathematical equations. Given this complexity, monitoring systems are needed to ensure that all operations proceed as planned. This is the role of the Ground Operator Assistant System (GOAS) and the Remote ATV Control at ISS (RACSI).

The GOAS runs on the ground and provides monitoring and intervention capabilities. It used to run on a Sun UltraSPARC 5–based workstation with 64 MB of RAM and 300 MB of disk space. It was ported to a Pentium 233 MHz system with 48 MB of RAM running Linux.

The RACSI runs on the ISS and provides temporary mission interruption and collision avoidance. It runs on an IBM ThinkPad with 64 MB of RAM and uses 40 MB of the available disk space. The system runs the Slackware 3.0 distribution. Moo-Tiff libraries are used to provide Motif-like widgets.

Linux was chosen, because it provides the reliability, portability, performance, and affordability needed by space applications. Despite these benefits, the ESA finally decided to run the RACSI and GOAS on Solaris, using the same equipment, for operational reasons.

As these examples show, Linux can be put to use in many fields in many ways, using different hardware and software configurations. The fastest way to build an embedded system with Linux is often to look at similar projects that have used Linux in their systems. There are many more examples of embedded systems based on Linux that I have not discussed. A search through the various resources listed in Appendix B may yield fruitful leads. Keep in mind, though, that copying other projects may involve copying other people's mistakes. In that case, the best way to guard yourself from chasing down other people's problems is to ensure that you have an understanding of all the aspects of the system or, at least, have a pointer where you can find more information regarding the gray areas of your system.

Survey Findings

Since Linux started being used as an embedded operating system, many surveys have been published providing information regarding various aspects of Linux's use in this way. Though the complete results of many of the surveys are part of commercial reports, which are relatively expensive, there are a few interesting facts that have been publicized. Let's look at the findings of some of these surveys.

In 2000, *Embedded Systems Programming* (ESP) magazine conducted a survey on 547 subscribers. The survey found that, though none considered it in 1998 and 1999, 38% of readers were considering using Linux as the operating system for their next design. This is especially interesting, as Linux came in only second to VxWorks, WindRiver's flagship product. The survey also found that, though none were using it in 1998 and 1999, 12% of respondents were already using Linux in their embedded systems in 2000.

As part of reporting on embedded Linux, LinuxDevices.com set up a web-based survey in 2000 and 2001 that site visitors could fill to provide information regarding their use of Linux in embedded systems. Both years, a few hundred respondents participated in the survey. Though there were no control mechanisms to screen respondents, the results match those of other more formal surveys. Both surveys contained a lot of information. For the sake of simplicity, I will only mention the surveys' most important findings.

In 2000, the LinuxDevices.com survey found that most developers considering the use of Linux in embedded systems were planning to use an x86, ARM, or PPC target with a custom board. The survey shows that most developers plan to boot Linux from a DiskOnChip or from a native flash device, and that the main peripherals included in the system would be Ethernet and data acquisition cards. The most important reasons developers have for choosing Linux are the superiority of open source software over proprietary offerings, the fact that source availability facilitates understanding the operating system, and the elimination of the dependency on a single operating system vendor. Developers reported using Red Hat, Debian, and MontaVista as their main embedded Linux distributions.

In 2001, the LinuxDevices.com survey found that developers plan to use Linux in embedded systems mostly based on x86, ARM, and PPC systems with custom boards. As in the previous survey, most developers plan to boot their system from some form of flash storage. In contrast with the previous survey, this survey provides insight regarding the amount of RAM and persistent storage developers intend to use. The majority of developers seem to want to use Linux with system having more than 8 MB of RAM and 8 MB of persistent storage. In this survey, developers justify their choice of Linux based on source code availability, Linux's reliability and robustness, and its high modularity and configurability. Developers reported that Red Hat and Debian were their main embedded Linux distributions. Combined with the 2000 survey, the results of the 2001 LinuxDevices.com survey confirm a steady interest in Linux.

Another organization that has produced reports on Linux's use in embedded systems is the *Venture Development Corporation* (VDC). Though mainly aimed at companies selling products to embedded Linux developers, the VDC's reports published in 2001 and 2002 provide some interesting facts. First, the 2001 report states that the market for embedded Linux development tools products was worth $20 million in 2000 and would be worth $306 million by 2005. The 2001 report also finds that the leading vendors are Lineo, MontaVista, and Red Hat. The report finds that the key reasons developers have for selecting Linux are source code availability and the absence of royalties.

The 2002 VDC report included a web-based survey of 11,000 developers. This survey finds that the Linux distributions currently used by developers are Red Hat, Roll-Your-Own, and non-commercial distributions. Developers' key reasons for choosing Linux are source code availability, reduced licensing, reliability, and open source development community support. Interestingly, the report also lists the most important factors inhibiting Linux's use in embedded applications. The most important factor is real-time limitations, followed by doubts about availability and quality of support, and fragmentation concerns. In addition, the report states that respondents consult the open source community for support with technical issues regarding Linux, and that most are satisfied with the answers they get.

The *Evans Data Corporation* (EDC) has also conducted surveys in 2001 and 2002 regarding Linux's use in embedded systems. The 2001 survey conducted on 500 developers found that Linux is fourth in the list of operating systems currently used in embedded systems, and that Linux was expected to be the most used embedded operating system in the following year. In 2002, the survey conducted on 444 developers found that Linux was still fourth in the list of operating systems currently used in embedded systems, and that Linux is as likely to be used as Windows as the operating system of choice for future designs.

While these results are partial and though it is too early to predict Linux's full impact on the embedded world, it is clear that there is great interest in embedded Linux and that this interest is growing. Moreover, the results show that the interest for Linux isn't purely amateuristic. Rather, Linux is being considered for and used in professional applications and is being preferred to a lot of the traditional embedded OSes. Also, contrary to popular belief and widespread FUD (fear, uncertainty, and doubt) Linux isn't interesting only because it's free. The fact that its source code is available, is highly reliable, and can easily be tailored to the task are other important reasons, if not more important. Interestingly, the Debian distribution is one of the favorite embedded distributions, even though no vendor is pushing this distribution on the market.

Reasons for Choosing Linux

Apart from the reasons polled by the various surveys mentioned above, there are various motivations for choosing Linux over a traditional embedded OS.

Quality and reliability of code

Quality and reliability are subjective measures of the level of confidence in the code. Although an exact definition of quality code would be hard to obtain, there are properties common programmers come to expect from such code:

Modularity and structure
> Each separate functionality should be found in a separate module, and the file layout of the project should reflect this. Within each module, complex functionality is subdivided in an adequate number of independent functions.

Ease of fixing
> The code should be (more or less) easy to fix for whoever understands its internals.

Extensibility
> Adding features to the code should be fairly straightforward. In case structural or logical modifications are needed, they should be easy to identify.

Configurability

It should be possible to select which features from the code should be part of the final application. This selection should be easy to carry out.

The properties expected from reliable code are:

Predictability

Upon execution, the program's behavior is supposed to be within a defined framework and should not become erratic.

Error recovery

In case a problematic situation occurs, it is expected that the program will take steps to recover from the problem and alert the proper authorities, usually the system administrator, with a meaningful diagnostic message.

Longevity

The program will run unassisted for long periods of time and will conserve its integrity regardless of the situations it encounters.

Most programmers agree that the Linux kernel and most projects used in a Linux system fit this description of quality and reliability of their codebase. The reason is the open source development model (see note below), which invites many parties to contribute to projects, identify existing problems, debate possible solutions, and fix problems effectively. You can expect to run Linux for years unattended without problems, and people have effectively done so. You can also select which system components you want to install and which you would like to avoid. With the kernel, too, you can select which features you would like during build configuration. As a testament to the quality of the code making up the various Linux components, you can follow the various mailing lists and see how quickly problems are pointed out by the individuals maintaining the various components of the software or how quickly features are added. Few other OSes provide this level of quality and reliability.

 Strictly speaking, there is no such thing as the "open source" development model, or even "free software" development model. "Open source" and "free software" correspond to a set of licenses under which various software packages can be distributed. Nevertheless, it remains that software packages distributed under "open source" and "free software" licenses very often follow a similar development model. This development model has been explained by Eric Raymond in his seminal book, *The Cathedral and the Bazaar* (O'Reilly).

Availability of code

Code availability relates to the fact that Linux's source code and all build tools are available without any access restrictions. The most important Linux components, including the kernel itself, are distributed under the GNU General Public License (GPL). Access to these components' source code is therefore compulsory. Other components are distributed under similar licenses. Some of these licenses, such as the BSD license, for instance, permit redistribution of binaries without the original source code or the redistribution of binaries based on modified sources without requiring publication of the modifications. Nonetheless, the code for the majority of projects that contribute to the makeup of Linux is readily available without restrictions.

When source access problems arise, the open source and free software community seeks to replace the "faulty" software with an open source version providing similar capabilities. This contrasts with traditional embedded OSes, where the source code isn't available or must be purchased for very large sums of money. The advantages of having the code available are the possibility of fixing the code without exterior help and the capability of digging into the code to understand its operation. Fixes for security weaknesses and performance bottlenecks, for example, are often very quickly available once the problem has been publicized. With traditional embedded OSes you have to contact the vendor, alert them of the problem, and await a fix. Most of the time, people simply find workarounds instead of waiting for fixes. For sufficiently large projects, managers even resort to purchasing access to the code to alleviate outside dependencies.

Hardware support

Broad hardware support means that Linux supports different types of hardware platforms and devices. Although a number of vendors still do not provide Linux drivers, considerable progress has been made and more is expected. Because a large number of drivers are maintained by the Linux community itself, you can confidently use hardware components without fear that the vendor may one day discontinue that product line. Broad hardware support also means that Linux runs on dozens of different hardware architectures, at the time of this writing. Again, no other OS provides this level of portability. Given a CPU and a platform, you can reasonably expect that Linux runs on it or that someone else has gone through a similar porting process and can assist you in your efforts. You can also expect that the software you write on one architecture be easily ported to another architecture Linux runs on. There are even device drivers that run on different hardware architectures transparently.

Communication protocol and software standards

Linux also provides broad communication protocol and software standards support as we'll see throughout this book. This makes it easy to integrate Linux within existing frameworks and to port legacy software to Linux. You can easily integrate a Linux system within an existing Windows network and expect it to serve clients through *Samba*, while clients see little difference between it and an NT server. You can also use a Linux box to practice amateur radio by building this feature into the kernel. Likewise, Linux is a Unix clone, and you can easily port traditional Unix programs to it. In fact, most applications currently bundled with the various distributions were first built and run on commercial Unixes and were later ported to Linux. This includes all the software provided by the FSF. Most traditional embedded OSes are, in this regard, very limited and often provide support only for a limited subset of the protocols and software standards available.

Available tools

The variety of tools existing for Linux make it very versatile. If you think of an application you need, chances are others felt the need for this application before you. It is also likely that someone took the time to write the tool and made it available on the Internet. This is what Linus Torvalds did, after all. You can visit *Freshmeat* (*http://www.freshmeat.net*) and *SourceForge* (*http://www.sourceforge.net*) and browse around to see the variety of tools available.

Community support

Community support is perhaps one of the biggest strengths of Linux. This is where the spirit of the free software and open source community can most be felt. As with application needs, it is likely that someone has encountered the same problems as you in similar circumstances. Often, this person will gladly share his solution with you, provided you ask. The development and support mailing lists are the best place to find this community support, and the level of expertise found there often surpasses what can be found over expensive support phone calls with proprietary OS vendors. Usually, when you call a technical support line, you never get to talk to the engineers who built the software you are using. With Linux, an email to the appropriate mailing list will often get you straight to the person who wrote the software. Pointing out a bug and obtaining a fix or suggestions is thereafter a rapid process. As many programmers experience, seldom is a justified plea for help ignored, provided the sender takes the care to search through the archives to ensure that her question hasn't already been answered.

Licensing

Licensing enables programmers to do with Linux what they could only dream of doing with proprietary software. In essence, you can use, modify, and redistribute the software with only the restriction of providing the same rights to your recipients. This, though, is a simplification of the various licenses used with Linux (GPL, LGPL, BSD, MPL, etc.) and does not imply that you lose control of the copyrights and patents embodied in the software you generate. These considerations will be discussed in "Copyright and Patent Issues." Nonetheless, the degree of liberty available is quite large.

Vendor independence

Vendor independence, as was demonstrated by the polls presented earlier, means that you do not need to rely on any sole vendor to get Linux or to use it. Furthermore, if you are displeased with a vendor, you can switch, because the licenses under which Linux is distributed provide you the same rights as the vendors. Some vendors, though, provide additional software in their distributions that isn't open source, and you might not be able to receive service for this type of software from other vendors. Such issues must be taken in account when choosing any distribution. Mostly, though, you can do with Linux as you would do with a car. Since the hood isn't welded shut, as with proprietary software, you can decide to get service from a mechanic other than the one provided by the dealership where you purchased it.

Cost

The cost of Linux is a result of open source licensing and is different from what can be found with traditional embedded OSes. There are three components of software cost in building a traditional embedded system: initial development setup, additional tools, and runtime royalties. The initial development setup cost comprises the purchase of development licenses from the OS vendor. Often, these licenses are purchased for a given number of "seats," one for each developer. In addition, you may find the tools provided with this basic development package to be insufficient and may want to purchase additional tools from the vendor. This is another cost. Finally, when you deploy your system, the vendor will ask for a per-unit royalty. This may be minimal or large, depending on the type of device you produce and the quantities produced. Some mobile phone manufacturers, for instance, choose to implement their own OSes to avoid paying any royalties. This makes sense for them, given the number of units sold and the associated profit margins.

With Linux, this cost model is turned on its head. All development tools and OS components are available free of charge, and the licenses under which they are distributed prevent the collection of any royalties on these core components. Most developers, though, may not want to go chasing down the various software tools and components and figure out which versions are compatible and which aren't. Most developers prefer to use a packaged distribution. This involves purchasing the distribution or may involve a simple download. In this scenario, vendors provide support for their distribution for a fee and offer services for porting their distributions to new architectures and developing new drivers for a fee. This is where their money is made. They may also charge for additional proprietary software packaged with their distribution. Compared to the traditional embedded software cost model, though, this is relatively inexpensive, depending on the distribution you choose.

Players of the Embedded Linux Scene

Unlike proprietary OSes, Linux is not controlled by a single authority who dictates its future, its philosophy, and its adoption of one technology or another. These issues and others are taken care of by a broad ensemble of players with different but complementary vocations and goals.

Free software and open source community

The free software and open source community is the basis of all Linux development and is the most important player in the embedded Linux arena. It is made up of all the developers who enhance, maintain, and support the various software components that make up a Linux system. There is no central authority within this group. Rather, there is a loosely tied group of independent individuals, each with his specialty. These folks can be found discussing technical issues on the mailing lists concerning them or at gatherings such as the Ottawa Linux Symposium. It would be hard to characterize these individuals as a homogeneous group, because they come from different backgrounds and have different affiliations. Mostly, though, they care a great deal about the technical quality of the software they produce. The *quality and reliability* of Linux, as discussed earlier, are a result of this level of care.

Your author is actually part of the free software community and has made a number of contributions. Besides maintaining a presence on some mailing lists and participating in the advancement of free software in various ways, I wrote and maintain the Linux Trace Toolkit, which is a set of components for the tracing of the Linux kernel. I have also contributed to other free software and open source projects, including RTAI and Adeos.

Throughout this book, I will describe quite a few components that are used in Linux systems. Each maintainer of or contributor to the components I will describe is a player in the free software and open source community.

Industry

Having recognized the potential of Linux in the embedded market, many companies have moved to embrace and promote Linux in this area. Industry players are important because they are the ones pushing Linux as an end-user product. Often, they are the first to receive feedback from those end users. Although postings on the various mailing lists can tell the developer how the software is being used, not all users participate in those mailing lists. Vendors must therefore strike an equilibrium between assisting their users and helping in the development of the various projects making up Linux without falling in the trap of wanting to divert development to their own ends. In this regard, many vendors have successfully positioned themselves in the embedded Linux market. Here are some of them.

The vendors listed here are mentioned for discussion purposes only. Your author has not evaluated the services provided by any of these vendors for the purposes of this book, and this list should therefore *not* be interpreted as any form of endorsement.

Red Hat
> This Linux distribution is one of the most widely used, if not the most widely used. Other distributions have been inspired by this distribution or, at least, had to take it into consideration. Red Hat was one of the first Linux distributions and, as such, has an established name as a leader that has contributed time and again back to the community it took from. Through its acquisition of Cygnus, it procured some of the key developers of the GNU development toolchain. This

adds to the list of key Linux contributors already working for Red Hat. Cygnus had already been providing these tools in a shrinkwrapped package to many embedded system developers. Red Hat continued on this trajectory. Although it does not sell an embedded distribution different from its standard distribution, it provides a development package for developing embedded Linux systems using its distribution. Red Hat maintains a web site about the projects it contributes to at *http://sources.redhat.com/*.

MontaVista

Founded by Jim Ready, an embedded industry veteran, MontaVista has positioned itself as a leader in the embedded Linux market through its products, services, and promotion of Linux in industrial applications. Its main product is MontaVista Linux, which is available in two versions: Professional and Carrier Grade. MontaVista has contributed to some open source projects including the kernel, ViewML, Microwindows, and LTT. Although MontaVista does not maintain a web site for the projects it contributes to, copies of some of its contributions can be found at *http://www.mvista.com/developer/sourceforge.html*.

LynuxWorks

This used to be known as Lynx Real-Time Systems and is one of the traditional embedded OS vendors. Contrary to other traditional embedded OS providers, Lynx decided to embrace Linux early and changed its name to reflect its decision. This, combined with the later acquisition of BSDi by WindRiver* and QNX's decision to make its OS available for free to download, were signs that open source in general, and Linux in particular, are making serious inroads in the embedded arena. That said, LynuxWorks still develops, distributes, and supports Lynx. In fact, LynuxWorks promotes a twofold solution. According to LynuxWorks, programmers needing hard real-time performance should continue to use Lynx while those wanting open source solutions should use BlueCat, their embedded Linux distribution. LynuxWorks has even modified Lynx to enable unmodified Linux binaries to run as-is. The fact that LynuxWorks was already a successful embedded OS vendor and that it adopted Linux early confirms the importance of the move towards open source OSes in the embedded market.

There are also many small players who provide a variety of services around open source and free software. In fact, many open source and free software contributions are made by individuals who are either independent or work for small-size vendors. As such, the services provided by such small players are often on a par or sometimes surpass those provided by larger players. Here are some individuals and small companies who provide embedded Linux services and are active contributors to the open source and free software community: Alessandro Rubini, Bill Gatliff, CodePoet Consulting, DENX Software Engineering, Opersys, Pengutronix, System Design & Consulting Services, and Zee2.

---

* WindRiver has since changed its mind and its relationship with BSD seems to be a matter of the past.

Organizations

There are currently three organizational bodies aimed at promoting and encouraging the adoption of Linux in embedded applications: the *Embedded Linux Consortium (ELC)*, *Emblix*, the *Japan Embedded Linux Consortium*, and the *TV Linux alliance*. The ELC was founded by 23 companies as a nonprofit vendor-neutral association and now includes more than 100 member companies. Its current goals include the creation of an embedded Linux platform specification inspired by the Linux Standard Base and the Single Unix Specification. It remains unclear whether the ELC's specification will gain any acceptance from the very open source and free software developers that maintain the software the ELC is trying to standardize, given that the drafting of the standard is not open to the public, which is contrary to the open source and free software traditions. Emblix was founded by 24 Japanese companies with similar aims as the ELC but with particular emphasis on the Japanese market. The TV Linux alliance is a consortium that includes cable, satellite, and telecom technology suppliers and operators who would like to support Linux in set-top boxes and interactive TV applications.

These efforts are noteworthy, but there are other organizational bodies that influence Linux's advancement, in the broad sense, although they do not address embedded systems particularly.

First and foremost, the *Free Software Foundation* (FSF), launched in 1984 by Richard Stallman, is the maintainer of the GNU project from which most components of a Linux system are based. It is also the central authority on the GPL and LGPL, the licenses most software in a Linux system fall under. Since its foundation, the FSF has promoted the usage of free software[*] in all aspects of computing. The FSF has taken note of the recent rise in the use of GNU and GPL software in embedded systems and is moving to ensure that user and developer rights are preserved.

The *OpenGroup* maintains the *Single Unix Specification* (SUS), which describes what should be found in a Unix system. There is also the *Linux Standard Base* (LSB) effort, which aims at developing and promoting "a set of standards that will increase compatibility among Linux distributions and enable software applications to run on any compliant Linux system," as stated on the LSB web site at *http://www.linuxbase.org/*. In addition, the *Filesystem Hierarchy Standard* (FHS) maintained by the *Filesystem Hierarchy Standard Group* specifies the content of a Linux root tree. The *Free Standards Group* (FSG) maintains the *Linux Development Platform Specification* (LDPS), which specifies the configuration of a development platform to enable applications developed on conforming platforms to run on most distributions available. Finally, there is the *Real-Time Linux Foundation*, which aims at promoting and standardizing real-time enhancements and programming in Linux.

---

[*] "Free" as in "free speech," not "free beer." As Richard Stallman notes, the confusion is due to the English language, which makes no difference between what may be differentiated in other languages such as French as "libre" and "gratuit." In effect, "free software" is translated to "logiciel libre" in French.

Resources

Most developers connect to the embedded Linux world through various resource sites and publications. It is through these sites and publications that the Linux development community, industry, and organizations publicize their work and learn about the work of the other players. In essence, the resource sites and publications are the meeting place for all the people concerned with embedded Linux. A list of resources can be found in Appendix B, but there are two resources that stand out, LinuxDevices.com and *Linux Journal*.

LinuxDevices.com was founded on Halloween day* 1999 by Rick Lehrbaum. It has since been acquired by ZDNet and, later still, been purchased by a company owned by Rick. To this day, Rick continues to maintain the site. LinuxDevices.com features news items, articles, polls, forums, and many other links pertaining to embedded Linux. Many key announcements regarding embedded Linux are made on this site. The site contains an archive of actively maintained articles regarding embedded Linux. Though its vocation is clearly commercial, I definitely recommend taking a peek at the site once in a while to keep yourself up to date with the latest in embedded Linux. Among other things, LinuxDevices.com was instrumental in launching the Embedded Linux Consortium.

As part of the growing interest in the use of Linux in embedded systems, the *Embedded Linux Journal* (ELJ) was launched by Specialized System Consultants, owners of *Linux Journal* (LJ), in January 2001 with the aim of serving the embedded Linux community, but was later discontinued. Though ELJ is no longer published as a separate magazine, LJ now contains an "embedded" section every month, which contains articles that otherwise would have been published in ELJ.

Copyright and Patent Issues

You may ask: what about using Linux in my design? Isn't Linux distributed under this weird license that may endanger the copyrights and patents of my company? What are all those licenses anyway? Is there more than one license to take care of? Are we allowed to distribute binary only kernel modules? What about all these articles I read in the press, some even calling Linux's license a "virus"?

These questions and many more have probably crossed your mind. You probably even discussed some of these issues with some of your coworkers. The issues can be confusing and can come back to haunt you if they aren't dealt with properly. I don't say this to scare you. The issues are real, but there are known ways to use Linux without any fear of any sort of licensing contamination. With all the explanations provided below,

---

* The date was selected purposely in symbolic commemoration of the infamous Halloween Documents uncovered by Eric Raymond. If you are not familiar with these documents and their meaning, have a look at *http://www.opensource.org/halloween/*.

it would be important to keep in mind that this isn't legal counsel and I am not a lawyer. If you have any doubts about your specific project, consult your attorney.

OK, now that I've given you ample warning, let us look at what is commonly accepted thought on Linux's licensing and how it applies to Linux systems in general, including embedded systems.

Textbook GPL

For most components making up a Linux system, there are two licenses involved, the GPL and the LGPL, introduced earlier. Both licenses are available from the FSF's web site at *http://www.gnu.org/licenses/*, and should be included with any package distributed under the terms of these licenses.* The GPL is mainly used for applications, while the LGPL is mainly used for libraries. The kernel, the binary utilities, the gcc compiler, and the gdb debugger are all licensed under the GPL. The C library and the GTK widget toolkit, on the other hand, are licensed under the LGPL.

Some programs may be licensed under BSD, Mozilla, or another license, but the GPL and LGPL are the main licenses used. Regardless of the license being used, common sense should prevail. Make sure you know the licenses under which the components you use fall and understand their implications.

The GPL provides rights and imposes obligations very different from what may be found in typical software licenses. In essence, the GPL is meant to provide a higher degree of freedom to developers and users, enabling them to use, modify, and distribute software with few restrictions. It also makes provisions to ensure that these rights are not abrogated or hijacked in any fashion. To do so, the GPL stipulates the following:

- You may make as many copies of the program as you like, as long as you keep the license and copyright intact.
- Software licensed under the GPL comes with *no warranty whatsoever*, unless it is offered by the distributor.
- You can charge for the act of copying and for warranty protection.
- You can distribute binary copies of the program, as long as you accompany them with the source code used to create the binaries, often referred to as the "original" source code.†
- You cannot place further restrictions on your recipients than what is provided by the GPL and the software's original authors.

---

* The licenses are often stored in a file called *COPYING*, for the GPL, and a file called *COPYING.LIB*, for the LGPL. Copies of these files are likely to have been installed somewhere on your disk by your distribution.

† The specific wording of the GPL to designate this code is the following: "The source code for a work means the preferred form of the work for making modifications to it." Delivering binaries of an obfuscated version of the original source code to try circumventing the GPL is a trick that has been tried before, and it doesn't work.

- You can modify the program and redistribute your modifications, as long as you provide the same rights you received to your recipients. In effect, any code that modifies or includes GPL *code*, or any portion of a GPL'd program, cannot be distributed outside your organization under any license other than the GPL. This is the clause some PR folks refer to as being "virus"-like. Keep in mind, though, that this restriction concerns source code only. Packaging the unmodified software for the purpose of *running* it, as we'll see below, is not subject to this provision.

As you can see, the GPL protects authors' copyrights while providing freedom of use. This is fairly well accepted. The application of the modification and distribution clauses, on the other hand, generates a fair amount of confusion. To clear this confusion, two issues must be focused on: running GPL software and modifying GPL software. *Running* the software is usually the reason why the original authors wrote it. The authors of gcc, for example, wrote it to compile software with. As such, the software compiled by an unmodified gcc is not covered by the GPL, since the person compiling the program is only running gcc. In fact, you can compile proprietary software with gcc, and people have been doing this for years, without any fear of GPL "contamination." *Modifying* the software, in contrast, creates a *derived work* that is based on the original software, and is therefore subject to the licensing of that original software. If you take the gcc compiler and modify it to compile a new programming language of your vintage, for example, your new compiler is a derived work and all modifications you make cannot be distributed outside your organization under the terms of any license other than the GPL.

Most anti-GPL speeches or writings play on the confusion between running and modifying GPL software, to give the audience an impression that any software in contact with GPL software is under threat of GPL "contamination." This is not the case.

There is a clear difference between running and modifying software. As a developer, you can safeguard yourself from any trouble by asking yourself whether you are simply running the software as it is supposed to be run or if you are modifying the software for your own ends. As a developer, you should be fully capable of making out the difference.

Note that the copyright law makes no difference between static and dynamic linking. Even if your proprietary application is integrated to the GPL software during runtime through dynamic linking, that doesn't exclude it from falling under the GPL. A derived work combining GPL software and non-GPL software through any form of linking still cannot be distributed under any license other than the GPL. If you package gcc as a dynamic linking library and write your new compiler using this library, you will still be restricted from distributing your new compiler under any license other than the GPL.

Whereas the GPL doesn't allow you to include parts of the program in your own program unless your program is distributed under the terms of the GPL, the LGPL allows you to use *unmodified* portions of the LGPL program in your program without any problem. If you modify the LGPL program, though, you fall under the same restrictions as the GPL and cannot distribute your modifications outside your organization under any license other than the LGPL. Linking a proprietary application, statically or dynamically, with the C library, which is distributed under the LGPL, is perfectly acceptable. If you modify the C library, on the other hand, you are prohibited from distributing all modifications under any license other than the LGPL.

 Note that when you distribute a proprietary application that is linked against LGPL software, you must allow for this LGPL software to be replaced. If you are dynamically linking against a library, for example, this is fairly simple, because the recipient of your software need only modify the library to which your application is linked at startup. If you are statically linking against LGPL software, however, you must also provide your recipient with the object code of your application before it was linked so that she may be able to substitute the LGPL software.

Much like the running versus modifying GPL software discussion above, there is a clear difference between linking against LGPL software and modifying LGPL software. You are free to distribute your software under any license when it is linked against an LGPL library. You are not allowed to distribute any modifications to an LGPL library under any license other than LGPL.

Pending issues

Up to now, I've discussed only textbook application of the GPL and LGPL. Some areas of application are, unfortunately, less clearly defined. What about applications that run using the Linux kernel? Aren't they being linked, in a way, to the kernel's own code? And what about binary kernel modules, which are even more deeply integrated to the kernel? Do they fall under the GPL? What about including GPL software in my embedded system?

I'll start with the last question. Including a GPL application in your embedded system is actually a textbook case of the GPL. Remember that you are allowed to redistribute binary copies of any GPL software as long as your recipients receive the original source code. Distributing GPL software in an embedded system is a form of binary distribution and is allowed, granted you respect the other provisions of the GPL regarding running and modifying GPL software.

Some proprietary software vendors have tried to cast doubts about the use of GPL software in embedded systems by claiming that the level of coupling found in embedded systems makes it hard to differentiate between applications and, hence, between what falls under GPL and what doesn't. This is untrue. As we shall see in Chapters 6 and 8, there are known ways to package embedded Linux systems that uphold modularity and the separation of software components.

To avoid any confusion regarding the use of user applications with the Linux kernel, Linus Torvalds has added a preamble to the GPL license found with the kernel's source code. This preamble has been reproduced verbatim in Appendix C and stipulates that user applications running on the kernel are not subject to the GPL. This means that you can run any sort of application on the Linux kernel without any fear of GPL "contamination." A great number of vendors provide user applications that run on Linux while remaining proprietary, including Oracle, IBM, and Adobe.

The area where things are completely unclear is binary-only kernel modules. Modules are software components that can be dynamically loaded and unloaded to add functionality to the kernel. While they are mainly used for device drivers, they can and have been used for other purposes. Many components of the kernel can actually be built as loadable modules to reduce the kernel image's size. When needed, the various modules can be loaded during runtime.

Although this was intended as a facilitating and customizing architecture, many vendors and projects have come to use modules to provide capabilities to the kernel while retaining control over the source code or distributing it under licenses different from the GPL. Some hardware manufacturers, for instance, provide closed-source binary-only module drivers to their users. This enables the use of the hardware with Linux without requiring the vendor to provide details regarding the operation of their device.

The problem is that once a module is loaded in the kernel, it effectively becomes part of its address space and is highly coupled to it because of the functions it invokes and the services it provides to the kernel. Because the kernel is itself under the GPL, many contend that modules cannot be distributed under any other license than the GPL because the resulting kernel is a derived work. Others contend that binary-only modules are allowed as long as they use the standard services exported to modules by the kernel. For modules already under the GPL, this issue is moot, but for non-GPL modules, this is a serious issue. Linus has said more than once that he allows binary-only modules as long as it can be shown that the functionality implemented is not Linux specific, as you can see in some of his postings included in Appendix C. Others, however, including Alan Cox, have come to question his ability to allow or disallow such modules, because not all the code in the kernel is copyrighted by him. Others, still, contend that because binary modules have been tolerated for so long, they are part of standard practice.

There is also the case of binary-only modules that use no kernel API whatsoever. The RTAI and RTLinux real-time tasks inserted in the kernel are prime examples. Although it could be argued that these modules are a class of their own and should be treated differently, they are still linked into kernel space and fall under the same rules as ordinary modules, whichever you think them to be.

At the time of this writing, there is no clear, definitive, accepted status for binary-only modules, though they are widely used and accepted as legitimate. Linus' latest public statements on the matter, made during a kernel mailing list debate on the Linux Security Module infrastructure (reproduced verbatim in Appendix C), seem to point to the fact that the use of binary-only modules is an increasingly risky decision. In fact, the use of binary-only modules is likely to remain a legally dubious practice for the foreseeable future. If you think you need to resort to binary-only proprietary kernel modules for your system, I suggest you follow Alan Cox's advice and seek legal counsel beforehand. Actually, I also suggest you reconsider and use GPL modules instead. This would avoid you many headaches.

RTLinux patent

Perhaps one of the most restrictive and controversial licenses you will encounter in deploying Linux in an embedded system is the license to the RTLinux patent held by Victor Yodaiken, the RTLinux project leader. The patent covers the addition of real-time support to general purpose operating systems as implemented by RTLinux.

Although many have questioned the patent's viability, given prior art, and Victor's handling of the issue, it remains that both the patent and the license are currently legally valid, at least in the United States, and have to be accounted for. The U.S. Patent Number for the RTLinux patent is 5,995,745, and you can obtain a copy of it through the appropriate channels. The patent license that governs the use of the patented method is available on the Web at *http://www.fsmlabs.com/about/patent/*.

The license lists a number of requirements for gratis use of the patented method. Notably, the license stipulates that there are two approved uses of the patented process. The first involves using software licensed under the terms of the GPL, and the second involves using an *umodified version* of the "Open RTLinux" as distributed by FSMLabs, Victor Yodaiken's company. The traditional way in which these requirements have been read by real-time Linux developers is that anyone distributing non-GPL real-time applications needs to purchase a license from FSMLabs. Not so says Eben Moglen, the FSF's chief legal counsel. In a letter that was sent to the RTAI community, the original of which is available at *http://www.aero.polimi.it/~rtai/documentation/articles/moglen.html*, Moglen makes the following statement: "No application in a running RTLinux or RTAI system does any of the things the patent claims. No applications program is therefore potentially infringing, and no applications program is covered, or needs to be covered, by the license."

Though Moglen's authoritative statement is clear on the matter, it remains that FSM-Labs' continued refusal to provide explanations regarding the patent's reach has left a cloud of uncertainty regarding all real-time extensions using the patented process.

It follows from this that the only way to stay away from this mess is to avoid using the patented process altogether. In other words, another method than that covered by the patent must be used to obtain deterministic response times from Linux. Fortunately such a method exists.

Basing myself entirely on scientific articles on nanokernel research published more than one year earlier than the preliminary patent application, I wrote a white paper describing how to implement a Linux-based nanokernel to enable multiple OSes to share the same hardware. The white paper, entitled "Adaptive Domain Environment for Operating Systems," was published in February 2001 and is available from *http://www.opersys.com/adeos/* along with other papers on other possible uses of this method. Given that your author started working on this book soon after the paper's publication, there was little development effort being put on the project, and the idea lay dormant for over a year.

The situation changed in late April 2002 when Philippe Gerum, a very talented free software developer, picked up the project and decided to push it forward. By early June, we were sufficiently satisfied with the project's status to make the first public release of the Adeos nanokernel. The release made on June 3, 2002, was endorsed by several free software organizations throughout the world, including Eurolinux (*http://www.eurolinux.org/*) and April (*http://www.april.org/*), as a patent-free method for allowing real-time kernels to coexist with general purpose kernels. Though, as with any other patent, such endorsements do not constitute any guarantee against patent infringement claims, the consensus within the open source and free software community is that the Adeos nanokernel and its applications are indeed patent free. For my part, I encourage you to make your own verifications, as you should do for any patent. Among other things, review the original white paper and, most importantly, the scientific articles mentioned therein.

Already, Adeos is being used by developers around the world for allowing different types of kernels to coexist. RTAI, for instance, which previously used the patented process to take control from Linux, and was therefore subject to the patent license, has already been ported to Adeos. Though at the time of this writing Adeos runs on single processor and SMP x86 systems only, ports to other architectures should be relatively straightforward, given the nanokernel's simplicity. If you are interested in contributing to Adeos, by porting it to other architectures for example, or if you would just like to use it or get more information, visit the project's web site at *http://www.adeos.org/*.

Using Distributions

Wouldn't it be simpler and faster to use a distribution instead of setting up your own development environment and building the whole target system from scratch? What's the best distribution? Unfortunately, there are no straightforward answers to these questions. There are, however, some aspects of distribution use that might help you find answers to these and similar questions.

To use or not to use

First and foremost, you should be aware that it isn't necessary to use any form of distribution to build an embedded Linux system. In fact, all the necessary software packages are readily available for download on the Internet. It is these same packages that distribution providers download and package for you to use. This approach provides you with the highest level of control and understanding over the packages you use and their interactions. Apart from this being the most thorough approach and the one used within this book, it is also the most time-consuming, as you have to take the time to find matching package versions and then set up each package one by one while ensuring that you meet package interaction requirements.

Hence, if you need a high degree of control over the content of your system, the "do it yourself" method may be best. If, however, like most people, you need the project ready yesterday or if you do not want to have to maintain your own packages, you should seriously consider using both a development and a target distribution. In that case, you will need to choose the development and target distributions most appropriate for you.

How to choose a distribution

There are a number of criteria to help in the choice of a distribution, some of which have already been mentioned in "Survey Findings." Depending on your project, you may also have other criteria not discussed here. In any case, if you choose commercial distributions, make sure you have clear answers to your questions from the distribution vendor when you evaluate his product. As in any situation, if you ask broad questions, you will get broad answers. Use detailed questions and expect detailed answers. Unclear answers to precise questions are usually a sign that something is amiss. If, however, you choose an open source distribution,* make sure you have as much information as possible about it. The difference between choosing an open source distribution and a commercial distribution is the way you obtain answers to your questions about the distribution. Whereas the commercial distribution vendor will provide you with answers to your questions about his product, you may have to look for the answers to those same questions about an open source distribution on your own.

An initial factor in the choice of a development or target distribution is the license or licenses involved. Some commercial distributions are partly open source and distribute *value-added* packages under conventional software licenses prohibiting copying and imposing royalties. Make sure the distribution clearly states the licenses governing the usage of the value-added software and their applicability. If unsure, ask. Don't leave licensing issues unclear.

Before evaluating a distribution, make yourself a shopping list of packages you would like to find in it. The distribution may have something better to offer, but at least you know if it fits your basic requirements. A development distribution should include items covered in "Setting Up and Using Development Tools," whereas a target distribution should automate and/or facilitate, to a certain degree, items covered in "Creating a Target Linux System" and "Networking." Of course, no distribution can take away issues discussed in "Developing for the Embedded," since only the system developers know what type of programming is required for the system to fit its intended purpose.

One thing that distinguishes commercial distributions from open source distributions is the support provided by the vendor. Whereas the vendor supplying a commercial distribution almost always provides support for her own distribution, the open source

---

* An open source distribution is a distribution that is maintained by the open source community, such as Debian. Inherently, such distributions do not contain any proprietary software.

community supplying an open source distribution does not necessarily provide the same level of support that would be expected from a commercial vendor. This, however, does not preclude some vendors from providing commercial support for open source distributions. Through serving different customers with different needs in the embedded field, the various vendors build a unique knowledge about the distributions they support and the problems clients might encounter during their use, and are therefore best placed to help you efficiently. Mainly, though, these vendors are the ones who keep up with the latest and greatest in Linux and are therefore the best source of information regarding possible bugs and interoperability problems that may show up.

Reputation can also come into play when choosing a distribution, but it has to be used wisely, as a lot of information circulating may be presented as fact while being mere interpretation. If you've heard something about one distribution or another, take the time to verify the validity of the information. In the case of a commercial distribution, contact the vendor. Chances are he knows where this information comes from and, most importantly, the rational explanation for it. This verification process, though, isn't specific to embedded Linux distributions. What is specific to embedded Linux distributions is the reputation commercial distributions build when their vendors contribute to the open source community. A vendor that contributes back by providing more open source software or by financing development shows that he is in contact with the open source community and has therefore a privileged position in understanding how the changes and developments of the various open source projects will affect his future products and ultimately his clients. In short, this is a critical link and a testament to the vendor's understanding of the dynamics involved in the development of the software he provides you. In the case of open source distributions, this criterion is already met, as the distribution itself is an open source contribution.

Another precious tool commercial distributions might have to offer is documentation. In this day and age where everything is ever-changing, up-to-date and accurate documentation is a rare commodity. The documentation for the majority of open source projects is often out of date, if available at all. Linus Torvalds' words ring true here. "Use the source, Luke," he says, meaning that if you need to understand the software you should read the source code. Yet not everyone can invest the amount of time necessary to achieve this level of mastery, hence the need for appropriate documentation. Because the open source developers prefer to invest time in writing more code than in writing documentation, it is up to the distribution vendors to provide appropriately packaged documentation with their distributions. When evaluating a distribution, make sure to know the type and extent of accompanying documentation. Although there is less documentation for open source distributions, in comparison with commercial distributions, some open source distributions are remarkably well documented.

Given the complexity of some aspects of development and target setup, the installation of a development and/or target distribution can be hard. In this regard, you may be looking for easy-to-install distributions. Although this is legitimate, keep in mind that once you've installed the distributions, you should not need to reinstall them afterward. Notice also that installation does not really apply for a target distribution,

as it was defined earlier, because target distributions are used to facilitate the generation of target setups and don't have what is conventionally known as an "installation"
process. The three things you should look for in the installation process of a distribution are clear explanations (whether textually during the installation, in a manual, or
both), configurability, and automation. Configurability is a measure of how much
control you have over the packages being installed, while automation is the ability to
automate the process using files containing the selected configuration options.

With some CPU models and boards being broadly adopted for embedded systems
development, commercial distribution vendors have come to provide prepackaged
development and/or target distributions specifically tailored for those popular CPU
models and boards. If you are intending to use a specific CPU model or board, you
may want to look for a distribution that is already tested for your setup.

What to avoid doing with a distribution

There is one main course of action to avoid when using a distribution: using the distribution in a way that makes you dependent solely on this same distribution for all
future development. Remember that one of the main reasons to use Linux is that you
aren't subject to anyone's will and market decisions. If your development relies
solely on proprietary tools and methods of the distribution you chose, you are in risk
of being locked into continuous use of that same distribution for all future development. This does not mean, though, that you shouldn't use commercial distributions
with value-added software the likes of which cannot be found on other distributions. It only means that you should have a backup plan to achieve the same results
with different tools from different distributions, just in case.

Example Multicomponent System

To present and discuss the material throughout the book, this section will examine
an example embedded Linux system. This embedded system is composed of many
interdependent components, each of which is an individual embedded system. The
complete system has a set of fixed functionalities, as seen by its users, but the individual components may vary in composition and implementation. Hence, the example provides us with fertile ground for discussing various solutions, their trade-offs,
and their details. Overall, the system covers most types of embedded systems available, from the very small to the very large, including many degrees of user interaction and networking and covering various timing requirements.

General Architecture

The embedded system used as the basis of the examples in this book is an industrial
process control system. It is composed of networked computers all running Linux.
Figure 1-1 presents the general architecture of the example system.

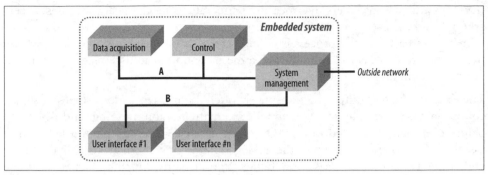

Figure 1-1. Example embedded Linux system architecture

Internally, the system is made up of four different types of machines, each fulfilling a different purpose: data acquisition (DAQ), control, system management (SYSM), and user interface (UI). The components interconnect using the most common interface and protocol available, TCP/IP over Ethernet. In this setup, the acquisition and control modules sit on a dedicated Ethernet link, while the user interface modules sit on another link. In addition to being the interface between the two links, the system control module provides an interface to the "outside world," which may be a corporate intranet, through a third link.

The process being controlled here could be part of a factory, treatment facility, or something completely different, but this is of no importance to the main design being discussed, because all process control systems have similar architectures. To control a process, the system needs to know at all times the current state of the different components of the process. This is what data acquisition is for. Having acquired the data, the system can determine how to keep the process under control. The location where the analysis is conducted may vary, but all control commands will go out through the control module. Because some aspects of the process being controlled often need human interaction and/or monitoring, there has to be a way for the workers involved to observe and modify the process. This is provided by the various user interfaces. To glue all this together and provide a central data repository and management interface, the system control module is placed at the center of all the components while providing a single access point into the system from the outside world.

Requirements of Each Component

Each component has its own set of requirements to fit in the grand scheme of things and is, therefore, built differently. Here is a detailed discussion of each component.

Data acquisition module

The first components of process measurement are transducers. Transducers are devices that convert a physical phenomenon into an electrical signal. Thermocouples, strain gauges, accelerometers, and linear variable differential transformers

(LVDTs) are all transducers that measure temperature, mechanical variations, acceleration, and displacement, respectively. The transducers are usually placed directly within the area where the process is taking place. If a furnace boils a liquid of which the temperature needs to be monitored, a thermocouple would be placed within the receptacle containing the liquid.

The electrical signals output by transducers often go through various stages of signal conditioning, which may include amplification, attenuation, filtering, and isolation, before eventually being fed to a DAQ device. The DAQ device, often a DAQ card installed in a computer, samples the analog values, converts them to digital values, and stores these values in a sample buffer. Various software components can then use these values to plot curves, detect certain conditions, or modify certain control parameters in reaction to the signal, such as in a feedback loop.

As DAQ is a vast domain discussed by a number of books, it is not the purpose of this chapter to discuss DAQ in full. Rather, we will assume that all signal retrieval and conditioning is already done. Also, rather than limiting the discussion to one DAQ card in particular, we will assume a DAQ card for which a driver exists complying with the API provided by Comedi, a software package for data acquisition and control, which I will cover later.

Hence, the DAQ module is an industrial computer containing a DAQ card controlled via Comedi to retrieve data about the process. The computer runs a medium-sized embedded system with stringent time constraints and no user interface, while being connected to the rest of the system using Ethernet.*

In a typical setup, the DAQ module stores the data retrieved in a local buffer. Analysis may be conducted on this data on site or it may be transferred to the SYSM module for analysis. In any case, important data is forwarded to the SYSM module for backup and display by the various UIs. When analysis is conducted onsite, the DAQ module will signal the SYSM module if it detects an anomaly or critical situation. Conversely, the DAQ module will carry out the DAQ commands sent by the SYSM module. These commands may dictate sample rate, analysis parameters, or even what the module should do with acquired data once analysis is over. For the SYSM module to be aware of the DAQ module's operations, the DAQ module will forward status and errors to the SYSM module whenever necessary or whenever it is asked to do so.

The DAQ module typically boots off a CompactFlash or a native flash device and uses a RAM disk or CRAMFS. This lets the module be replaced easily in case of hardware failure. Software configuration involves a kernel built for preemption running on either a PC-type system or a system based on the PowerPC architecture. The DAQ provides no outside services such as FTP, HTTP, or NFS. Instead, it runs custom daemons that communicate with the SYSM module to carry out the proper behavior of the overall system. Because it is not a multiuser system and no user ever

---

* Though they are not used in this example, off-the-shelf Ethernet-enabled DAQ devices are readily available.

interacts with it directly, the DAQ module has only minimal support for user tools. This may involve the BusyBox package. The IP address used by the DAQ is fixed and determined at design time. Hence, the SYSM module can easily check whether the DAQ module is alive and operational.

Control module

Conventional process control involves programmable logic controllers (PLCs) and similar systems that are expensive, run their own particular OSes, and have special configuration procedures. With the advent of inexpensive modern hardware on the consumer market, it is becoming more common to see mainstream hardware such as PCs used in process control. Even industrial hardware has seen its price falling because of the use of mainstream technology.

Here too, process control is a vast domain and I do not intend to cover it in full. Instead, we assume that the hardware being controlled is modeled by a state machine. The overlaying software receives feedback to its control commands based on the current state of the controlled hardware as modeled by the state machine.

The control module is an industrial computer with an interface to the hardware being controlled. The computer runs a medium-sized embedded system with stringent time-constraints and no user interface, much like the DAQ module, while being connected to the rest of the system using an Ethernet link.

The control module's main task is to issue commands to the hardware it controls, while monitoring the progression of the hardware's behavior in reaction to the commands. Typically, these commands originate from the SYSM module, which is the central decision maker, and that will make decisions according to the data it gets from the DAQ module. Because the commands provided by the SYSM module may involve many hardware operations, the control module will coordinate the hardware to obtain the final result requested by the SYSM. Once operations are complete, whenever any special situation occurs or whenever it is requested, the control module will send the SYSM module a status report on the current hardware operations.

The control module can boot off a CompactFlash or a CFI flash device and use a RAM disk or CRAMFS, much like the DAQ module. It is based on a PowerPC board, which runs a kernel configured for preemption along with a real-time kernel, such as RTAI or RTLinux, since hard real-time response times are necessary to control complex hardware. Hardware control will therefore be carried out by custom, hard real-time drivers. Here too, no outside networking services are provided. Custom daemons communicate with the SYSM to coordinate system behavior. Because the control module is not a multiuser system and has no direct user interaction, only minimal user tools will be available. BusyBox may be used. The control module also uses a fixed IP address for the same reason as the DAQ module.

System management module

The SYSM module manages and coordinates the interactions between the different components of the system, while providing a point of entry into the system to the outside world, as mentioned earlier. It is a large embedded system with stringent time constraints and no user interface. It contains three network adapters: one for DAQ and control, one for user interfaces, and one for the outside network. Each networking interface has its set of rules and services.

On link A, the SYSM module retrieves data from the DAQ module, stores all or parts of it, and forwards pertinent data to the various UIs for display. The stored data can be backed up for future reference and may form the base of a quality control procedure. The data can be backed up either by means of conventional backup or using a database that has a backup procedure. As said earlier, the SYSM module may carry out analysis on acquired data if this isn't done on the DAQ module. Whether the analysis is done locally or on the DAQ module, the SYSM module will issue commands to the control module according to that analysis and according to the current state of the controlled process. The SYSM module runs custom daemons and utilities that complement the daemons present on the DAQ module and control module to communicate with them appropriately. As with the other elements on link A, the SYSM module has a fixed IP address so the DAQ and control modules can identify it easily.

To the outside network, the SYSM module provides HTTP and SSH services. The HTTP service enables authorized users on the outside network to configure or monitor various aspects of the complete system through the use of web pages and forms. The SSH services make it possible for the embedded system's manufacturer to log into the system from a remote site for troubleshooting and upgrades. The availability of an SSH server on such a large system reduces maintenance cost for both the manufacturer and the client.

One of the configurable options of the SYSM module is the way errors are reported to the outside world. This indicates to the SYSM what it should do with an error it cannot handle, such as the failure of the DAQ or control module. The standard procedure may be to signal an alarm on a loudspeaker, or it may involve using SNMP to signal the system operator or simply sending a critical display request to the appropriate UI module. The link to the outside world is another configurable option. The SYSM module may either have a fixed IP address or retrieve its IP address using DHCP or BOOTP.

On link B, the SYSM module offers DHCP services so the UIs can dynamically allocate their addresses. Once UIs are up and have registered themselves with the SYSM, it will forward them the data they are registered to display, along with the current system state, and will react to value changes made in a UI according to the system's state. In the course of system operation, workers can modify the amount of data displayed according to their needs, and the SYSM module will react accordingly by starting or ceasing to forward certain data to the UIs.

As the SYSM module is a large embedded system, it will boot off a hard disk and use the full features made available to a conventional workstation or server including swapping. The server may be an a Sun, a PowerPC, an ARM, or a conventional PC. It makes little difference which type of architecture is actually used for the SYSM module, since most of its functionality is fairly high level. Because it needs to serve many different applications in parallel while answering rapidly to incoming traffic, the SYSM module runs a kernel configured for preemption. Also, as it serves as a central point for management, it is a multiuser system with an extensive user toolset. The root filesystem on the SYSM module will look similar to the one found on common workstations and servers. In fact, we may even install a conventional server distribution on the SYSM module and configure it to our needs.

User interface modules

The user interface modules enable workers to interact with the ongoing process by viewing values that reflect the current status and modifying variables that control the process. The user interfaces are typically small embedded systems with mild time constraints. They too are network enabled, but in various ways. In contrast to the previous system components covered earlier, user interface modules can have various incarnations. Some can be fixed and attached close to a sensitive post or process control. Others can be portable and may be used by workers to walk around the processing plant and enter or retrieve various data. After all, some aspects of the controlled process may not be automated and may need to be entered by hand into the system.

The values displayed by the various UIs are retrieved from the SYSM module by communication with the appropriate custom daemons running on it. As UIs may receive critical events to display immediately, custom daemons run on the UI devices awaiting critical events sent from the SYSM module. The user can choose which variables she wants to view, or the data set may be prefixed, all depending on the purpose and the type of worker using the UI. In any case, some messages, such as critical events, will be displayed regardless of the configuration. Some UIs may display only limited data sets, while others may display detailed information regarding the ongoing process. On some UI modules, it is possible to engage in emergency procedures to handle a critical situation.

As UI modules are small, they typically boot from native flash or through the network. In the later case, the SYSM module has to be configured to accommodate remote boot. Whether remote boot is used or not, the UI modules all obtain their IP addresses via DHCP. Portable UI modules are typically based on ARM, MIPS, or m68k architectures and run standard kernels. As the UI modules are used to interact with the user in an automated fashion, only minimal user tools are necessary, although extensive graphical utilities and libraries are required to accommodate the display and the interaction with the user. Since we assume that anyone on the premises has access to the UI modules, we do not implement any form of authentication on the UI devices, and hence all UI modules are not multi-user systems. This, though, could change depending on system requirements.

Variations in Requirements

The description of the various modules given above is only a basic scheme by which to implement the system. Many variations can be made to the different components and the architecture of the system. Here is a list of such variations in no particular order:

- Depending on the physical conditions where the system is deployed, it may be necessary to constantly verify the connectivity of the various system components. This would be achieved by a keepalive signal transmitted from the modules to the SYSM module or using watchdogs.

- Using TCP/IP over Ethernet on link A may pose some problems if reactions to some critical conditions need to be carried out in a deterministic time frame. If a certain chemical reaction being observed by the DAQ module shows signs of imminent disaster, the SYSM module may need to be notified before the chemical reaction goes out of control. In those cases, it may be a good idea to use RTNet, which provides hard real-time UDP over Ethernet.* This would necessitate running a real-time kernel on the SYSM module.

- Ethernet is not fit for all environments. Some other protocols are known to be more reliable in industrial environments. If need be, the designers may wish to replace Ethernet with one of the known industrial networking interfaces, such as RS485, DeviceNet, ARCnet, Modbus, Profibus, or Interbus.

- For compactness and speed, designers may wish to implement the DAQ, control, and SYSM modules in a single physical device, such as a CompactPCI chassis with a separate card for each module.

- For management purposes, it may be simpler to implement the UI modules as X terminals. In this configuration, the UI modules would act only as display and input terminals. All computational load would be carried out on the SYSM module, which would be the X application host.

- If the system is not very large and the process being controlled is relatively small, it may make sense to combine the DAQ, control, and SYSM modules into a single sufficiently powerful computer.

- If one network link isn't sufficient for the traffic generated by the DAQ module, it may make sense to add another link that would be dedicated to data transfers only.

- Since it is more and more frequent to keep process data for quality assurance purposes, the SYSM module may run a database. This database would store information regarding the various operations of the system along with data recorded by the DAQ module.

Other variations are also possible, depending on the system's requirements.

---

* Though UDP does not delay packet transfers as TCP does, the standard TCP/IP stack in Linux is not hard real time. RTNet provides hard real-time network communication by providing a UDP stack directly on top of RTAI or RTLinux.

Design and Implementation Methodology

Designing and implementing an embedded Linux system can be carried out in a defined manner. The process includes many tasks, some of which may be carried out in parallel, hence reducing overall development time. Some tasks can even be omitted, if a distribution is being used. Regardless of the actual tools or methodology you use, Chapter 2 is required reading for all tasks involved in building an embedded Linux system.

While designing and implementing your embedded Linux system, use the worksheet provided in Appendix A to record your system's characteristics. It includes a section to fully describe each aspect of your embedded system. This worksheet will help your team keep track of the system's components and will help future maintainers understand how the system was originally built. In fact, a properly completed worksheet should be sufficient for people outside your team to rebuild the entire system without any assistance.

Given that the details of the tasks involved in building embedded Linux systems sometimes change with the updating of the software packages involved, visit this book's web site (*http://www.embeddedtux.org/*) from time to time for updates.

Creating a Target Linux System

A target Linux system is created by configuring and bundling together the appropriate system components. Programming and development aspects are a separate subject, and are discussed later in this chapter.

There are four main steps to creating a target Linux system:

- Determine system components
- Configure and build the kernel
- Build root filesystem
- Set up boot software and configuration

Determining system components is like making a shopping list before you go to the grocery store. It is easy to go without a shopping list and wonder at all the choices you have, as many do with Linux. This may result in "featurism," whereby your system will have lots and lots of features but won't necessarily fulfill its primary purpose. Hence, before you go looking at all the latest Linux gizmos available, sit down and write a list of what you need. I find this approach helps in focusing development and avoids distractions such as: "Look honey, they actually have salami ice cream." This doesn't mean that you shouldn't change your list if you see something pertinent. It is just a warning about the quantity of software available for Linux and the inherent abundance of choices.

Chapter 3 discusses the hardware components that can be found as part of an embedded Linux system. This should provide you with enough background and maybe even ideas of what hardware you can find in an embedded Linux system. As Linux and surrounding software are ever evolving targets, use this and further research on the Net to find out which design requirements are met by Linux. In turn, this will provide you with a list of items you need to develop to complete your system. This step of development is the only one that cannot be paralleled with other tasks. Determining system requirements and Linux's compliance to these requirements has to be completed before any other step.

Because of the ever evolving nature of Linux, you may feel the need to get the latest and greatest pieces of software for your design. Avoid doing this, as new software often needs testing and may require other software to be upgraded because of the dependencies involved between packages. Hence, you may find yourself locked in a frantic race to keep up with the plethora of updates. Instead, fix the bugs with the current software you have and keep track of other advances so that the next generation projects you design can profit from these advances. If you have an important reason to upgrade a software component, carefully analyze the consequences of such an upgrade on the rest of your system before actually carrying out the upgrade. You may also want to test the upgrade on a test system before applying it to your main system.

Having determined which features are pertinent to your design, you can select a kernel version and relevant configuration. Chapter 5 covers the configuration and build process of the kernel. Unlike other pieces of software, you may want to keep updating your kernel to the latest stable version throughout your project's development up until the beta stage. Though keeping the kernel version stable throughout the development cycle may seem simple, you may find yourself trying to fix bugs that have been fixed in more recent kernels. Keeping yourself up to date with recent kernel developments, as we discuss in Chapter 5, will help you decide whether updating to the most recent kernel is best for you. Also, you may want to try newer kernels and roll back to older ones if you encounter any serious problems. Note that using kernels that are too old may cut you off from community support, since contributors can rarely afford keep answering questions about old bugs.

Regardless of whether you decide to follow kernel updates, I suggest you keep the kernel configuration constant throughout the project. This will avoid completed parts from breaking in the course of development. This involves studying the configuration options closely, though, in light of system requirements. Although this task can be conducted in parallel with other tasks, it is important that developers involved in the project be aware of the possible configuration options and agree with the options chosen.

Once configuration is determined, it is time to build the kernel. Building the kernel involves many steps and generates more than just a kernel image. Although the generated components are not necessary for some of the other development aspects of the project, the other project components tend to become more and more dependent on the availability of the kernel components as the project advances. It is therefore preferable to have the kernel components fully configured and built as early as possible, and kept up to date throughout the project.

In parallel to handling the kernel issues, you can start building the root filesystem of the embedded system, as explained in Chapter 6. The root filesystem of an embedded Linux system is similar to the one you find on a workstation or server running Linux, except that it contains only the minimal set of applications, libraries, and related files needed to run the system. Note that you should not have to remove any of the components you previously chose at this stage to obtain a properly sized root filesystem. In fact, if you have to do so, you probably did not determine system components adequately. Remember that this earlier stage should include an analysis of all system requirements, including the root filesystem size. You should therefore have as accurate as possible an estimate of the size of each component you selected during the first step of creating the target system.

If you are unable to predetermine the complete list of components you will need in your embedded system and would rather build your target root filesystem iteratively by adding the tools and libraries you need as you go along, then do so, but do not treat the result as your final root filesystem. Instead, use the iterative method to explore the building of root filesystems and then apply your experience into building a clean root filesystem for your target system. The reason behind this is that the trial and error nature of the iterative method makes its completion time nondeterministic. The structured approach may require more forethought, but its results are known and can be the basis for additional planning.

Setting up and configuring the storage devices and the bootloader software are the remaining tasks in creating a target Linux system. Chapters 7, 8, and 9 discuss these issues in full. It is during these steps that the different components of the target system come together: the bootloader, the root filesystem, and the kernel. As booting is highly dependent on the architecture, different bootloaders are involved. Within a single architecture there are also variations in the degree of debugging and monitoring provided by the bootloaders. The methodology to package and boot a system is fairly similar among the different architectures, but varies according to the permanent storage device from which the system is booted and the bootloader used. Booting a system from native flash, for instance, is different from booting a system from a DiskOnChip or CompactFlash device, and is even more different from booting from a network server.

Setting Up and Using Development Tools

Software development for embedded systems is different from software development for the workstation or server environments. Mainly, the target environment is often dissimilar to the host on which the development is conducted. Hence the need for a host/target setup whereby the developer develops his software on the host and downloads it onto the target for testing. There are two aspects to this setup: development and debugging. Such a setup, however, does not preclude you from using Linux's multiarchitecture advantage to test your target's applications on your host with little or no modification. Though not all applications can be tested in this way, testing target applications on the host will generally save you a lot of time.

Embedded development is discussed in Chapter 4. Prior to testing any code on the target system, it is necessary to establish a host/target connection. This will be the umbilical cord by which the developer will be able to interact with the target system to verify whether the applications he develops function as prescribed. As the applications cannot typically run on bare hardware, there will have to be a functional embedded Linux system on the target hardware already. Since it is often impossible to wait for the final target setup to be completed to test target applications, you can use a development target setup. The latter will be packaged much more loosely and will not have to respect the size requirements imposed on the final package. Hence, the development root filesystem may include many more applications and libraries than will be found in the final root filesystem. This also allows different and larger types of permanent storage devices during development.

Obtaining such a setup necessitates compiling the target applications and libraries. This is achieved by configuring or building the various compiler and binary utilities for cross-development. Using these utilities, you can build applications for the target and therefore build the development target setup used for further development. With this done, you can use various Integrated Development Environments (IDEs) to ease development of the project components and other tools such as CVS to coordinate work among developers.

Given the horsepower found on some embedded systems, some developers even choose to carry out all development directly on the target system. In this setup, the compiler and related tools all run on the target. This, in effect, combines host and target in a single machine and resembles conventional workstation application development. The main advantage of such a configuration is that you avoid the hassle of setting up a host/target environment.

Whatever development setup you choose, you will need to debug and poke at your software in many ways. You can do this with the debugging tools covered in Chapter 11. For simple debugging operations, you may choose to use ad hoc methods such as printing values using printf( ). Some problems require more insight into the runtime operations of the software being debugged; this may be provided by symbolic debugging. *gdb* is the most common general-purpose debugger for Linux, but symbolic debugging on embedded systems may be more elaborate. It could involve such things as remote serial debugging, kernel debugging, and BDM and

JTAG debugging tools. But even symbolic debugging may be inadequate in some situations. When system calls made by an application are problematic or when synchronization problems need to be solved, it is better to use tracing tools such as *strace* and LTT. For performance problems, there are other tools more adapted to the task, such as *gprof* and *gcov*. When all else fails, you may even need to understand kernel crashes.

Developing for the Embedded

One of the main advantages of using Linux as an embedded OS is that the code developed for Linux should run identically on an embedded target as on a workstation, right? Well, not quite. Although it is true that you can expect your Linux workstation code to build and run the same on an embedded Linux system, embedded system operations and requirements differ greatly from workstation or server environments. Whereas you can expect errors to kill an application on a workstation, for instance, leaving the responsibility to the user to restart the application, you can't afford to have this sort of behavior in an embedded system. Neither can you allow applications to gobble up resources without end or behave in an untimely manner.[*] Therefore, even though the APIs and OS used may be identical, there are fundamental differences in programming philosophies.

Networking

Networking enables an embedded system to interact with and be accessible to the outside world. In an embedded Linux environment, you have to choose networking hardware, networking protocols, and the services to offer while accounting for network security. Chapter 10 covers the setup and use of networking services such as HTTP, Telnet, SSH, and/or SNMP. One interesting aspect in a network-enabled embedded system is the possibility of remote updating, whereby it is possible to update the system via a network link without on-site intervention. This is covered in Chapter 8.

---

[*] Normal Linux workstation and server applications should not gobble up resources either. In fact, the most important applications used on Linux servers are noteworthy for their stability, which is one reason Linux is so successful as a server operating system.

CHAPTER 2
Basic Concepts

As we saw in the previous chapter, there is a rich variety of embedded Linux systems. There are nevertheless a few key characteristics that apply uniformly to most embedded Linux systems. The purpose of this chapter is to present to you the basic concepts and issues that you are likely to encounter when developing any sort of embedded Linux system.

Many of the subjects introduced here are discussed in far greater detail in other chapters. They are introduced here to give you a better sense of how the entire system comes together.

The chapter starts by discussing the types of hosts most commonly used for developing embedded Linux systems, the types of host/target development setups, and the types of host/target debug setups. These sections are meant to help you select the best environment for developing embedded Linux systems or, if the environment is already specified and can't be changed, understand how your particular setup will influence the rest of your development effort. The chapter then presents details of the structure commonly found in most embedded Linux systems. I present the generic architecture of an embedded Linux system, I explain the system startup, the types of boot configurations, and the typical system memory layout.

Types of Hosts

In Chapter 3, I cover the hardware most commonly found in embedded Linux targets. Each possible target system can be developed by a wide variety of hosts. In the following, I discuss the types of hosts most commonly used, their particulars, and how easy it is to develop embedded Linux systems using them.

Linux Workstation

This is the most common type of development host for embedded Linux systems. It is also the one I recommend, because developing embedded Linux systems requires that you become quite familiar with Linux and there is no better way of doing this than using it for your everyday work.

A standard PC is your most likely Linux workstation. Do not forget, nonetheless, that Linux runs on a variety of hardware and that you are not limited to using a PC. I, for example, regularly use an Apple PowerBook running Linux for my embedded work. It lacks an RS232 serial port, but this is easily fixed by adding a USB serial dongle.

You may use any of the standard Linux distributions such as Debian, Mandrake, Red Hat, SuSE, or Yellow Dog on your host. In fact, I assume you are running a common distribution throughout this book. As I said in Chapter 1, you do not need an embedded Linux distribution to develop embedded Linux systems. This book provides you with all the necessary information to build your own development environment.

 Though I've made an effort to keep the text host-distribution independent, the instructions in this book are slightly tilted towards Red Hat–type distributions. You may therefore need to make minor modifications to a few commands, depending on the distribution installed on your host. Wherever possible, distribution-dependent commands are presented as such.

Of course, the latest and fastest hardware is every engineer's dream. Having the fastest machine around will certainly help you in your work, but you can still use a relatively mild-powered machine with appropriate RAM for this type of development. Remember that Linux is very good at making the best of the available hardware. I, for instance, often use a Pentium II 350MHz system with 128 MB of RAM for development.

What you will need in large quantity, however, is storage space, both disk space and RAM. In addition to the space used by your distribution, you should plan for 2 to 3 GB of disk space, if not more, for your development environment and project workspace. An uncompressed kernel source tree, for example, which is one of the many components you will have in your project workspace, uses more than 100 MB of space before compilation. After compilation, this grows even further. If you are experimenting with three or four kernels at the same time, you can therefore easily use up to 500 MB of disk space for kernel work alone.

As for RAM, some of the GNU toolchain compilation steps require large amounts of it, especially during the build of the C library. I recommend 128 MB of RAM and 128 MB of swap space for the host.

Unix Workstation

Depending on your circumstances, you may be required to use a traditional Unix workstation. Solaris workstations, for instance, are very common among telecommunication solutions developers. Although the use of such workstations is much less common than the use of Linux workstations for developing embedded Linux systems, it is still feasible.

Because Linux itself is very much like Unix, most of what applies to Linux also applies to Unix. This is especially true when it comes to the GNU development tool-chain, since the main GNU tools such as the compiler, the C library, and the binary utilities (more commonly known as *binutils*) were developed and used on traditional Unix systems even before Linux existed.

Therefore, the descriptions that follow in the rest of this book should also work fine on any Unix workstation. I say "should" because there may be slight differences that you may have to resolve on your own. The recommendations I gave above for a Linux workstation in regards to storage space apply to Unix workstations as well.

Windows (2000, NT, 98, etc.) Workstation

Almost a decade ago, embedded system development shifted towards Windows workstations. Many developers have since become used to working on this platform and many new developers have been initiated to embedded systems development on it. For these and other reasons some developers would like to continue using Windows workstations for, ironically, developing embedded Linux systems.

At first glance, it would seem that the main problem with this platform is the availability and use of the GNU development toolchain. This is not a problem, because Red Hat provides the Cygwin environment, which is the Windows-compatible GNU toolchain, and some people have used it to build cross-platform tools for Linux. Mumit Khan has detailed the procedure to build a cross-platform development toolchain for an i386 Linux target on a Windows host at *http://www.nanotech.wisc.edu/~khan/software/gnu-win32/cygwin-to-linux-cross-howto.txt*. Although attempts to use this procedure for other Linux targets have not been "officially" reported, there are no obvious reasons for it to fail.

If you really need to continue using a Windows workstation and would like to have an easy way of working in a Linux environment to develop a Linux target, you may want to use emulation and virtualization software such as VMWare or Connectix. In this case, you can run Linux in a virtual environment while your main workstation is still Windows.

Remember, however, that by continuing to use Windows for your everyday work, you are not getting to know Linux's intricacies. You may, therefore, find it difficult to understand some of the problems you encounter on your Linux target. Also, you may need to get the latest in workstation power and space requirements to get an adequate work environment.

Types of Host/Target Development Setups

Three different host/target architectures are available for the development of embedded Linux systems: the linked setup, the removable storage setup, and the standalone setup. Your actual setup may belong to more than one category or may even change categories over time, depending on your requirements and development methodology.

Linked Setup

In this setup, the target and the host are permanently linked together using a physical cable. This link is typically a serial cable or an Ethernet link. The main property of this setup is that no physical hardware storage device is being transferred between the target and the host. All transfers occur via the link. Figure 2-1 illustrates this setup.

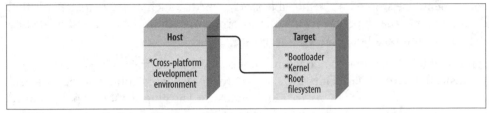

Figure 2-1. Host/target linked setup

As illustrated, the host contains the cross-platform development environment, which we will discuss in Chapter 4, while the target contains an appropriate bootloader, a functional kernel, and a minimal root filesystem.

Alternatively, the target can use remote components to facilitate development. The kernel could, for instance, be available via Trivial File Transfer Protocol (TFTP). The root filesystem could also be NFS-mounted instead of being on a storage media in the target. Using an NFS-mounted root filesystem is actually perfect during development, because it avoids having to constantly copy program modifications between the host and the target, as we'll see in "Types of Boot Configurations."

The linked setup is the most common. Obviously, the physical link can also be used for debugging purposes. It is, however, more common to have another link for debugging purposes, as we shall see in "Types of Host/Target Debug Setups." Many embedded systems, for instance, provide both Ethernet and RS232 link capabilities. In such a setup, the Ethernet link is used for downloading the executable, the kernel, the root filesystem, and other large items that benefit from rapid data transfers between the host and the target, while the RS232 link is used for debugging.

Removable Storage Setup

In this setup, there are no direct physical links between the host and the target. Instead, a storage device is written by the host, is then transferred into the target, and is used to boot the device. Figure 2-2 illustrates this setup.

As with the previous setup, the host contains the cross-platform development environment. The target, however, contains only a minimal bootloader. The rest of the

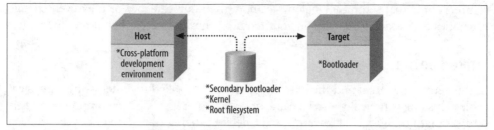

Figure 2-2. Host/target removable storage setup

components are stored on a removable storage media, such as a CompactFlash IDE device or any other type of drive, which is programmed on the host and loaded by the target's minimal bootloader upon startup.

It is possible, in fact, that the target may not contain any form of persistent storage at all. Instead of a fixed flash chip, for instance, the target could contain a socket where a flash chip could be easily inserted and removed. The chip would be programmed by a flash programmer on the host and inserted into the socket in the target for normal operation.

This setup is mostly popular during the initial phases of embedded system development. You may find it more practical to move on to a linked setup once the initial development phase is over, so you can avoid the need to physically transfer a storage device between the target and the host every time a change has to be made to the kernel or the root filesystem.

Standalone Setup

Here, the target is a self-contained development system and includes all the required software to boot, operate, and develop additional software. In essence, this setup is similar to an actual workstation, except the underlying hardware is not a conventional workstation but rather the embedded system itself. Figure 2-3 illustrates this setup.

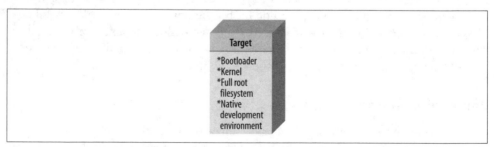

Figure 2-3. Host/target standalone setup

Contrary to the other setups, this setup does not require any cross-platform development environment, since all development tools run in their native environment.

Furthermore, it does not require any transfer between the target and the host, because all the required storage is local to the target.

This type of setup is quite popular with developers building high-end PC-based embedded systems, such as high-availability systems, since they can use standard off-the-shelf Linux distributions on the embedded system. Once development is done, they then work at trimming down the distribution and customizing it for their purposes. Although this gets developers around having to build their own root filesystems and configure the systems' startup, it requires that they know the particular distribution they are using inside out. If you are interested in this approach, you may want to take a look at *Running Linux* and, if you plan to use Red Hat, *Learning Red Hat Linux*, both published by O'Reilly.

Types of Host/Target Debug Setups

There are basically three types of interfaces that developers use to link a target to a host for debugging: a serial line, a networking interface, and special debugging hardware. Each debugging interface has its own benefits and applications. We will discuss the detailed use of some of these interfaces in Chapter 11. This section briefly reviews the benefits and characteristics of each type.

Using a serial link is the simplest way to debug a target from a host, because serial hardware is simple and is often found, in some form or another, in embedded systems. There are two potential problems in using a serial link, however. First, the speed of most serial links is rather limited. Second, if there's only one serial port in the embedded system or if the serial link is the embedded system's only external interface, it becomes impossible to debug the system and interact with it using a terminal emulator at the same time. The absence of terminal interaction is not a problem in some cases, however. When debugging the startup of the kernel using a remote kernel debugger, for example, no terminal emulator is required, since no shell actually runs on the target until the kernel has finished booting.

The use of a networking interface, such as TCP/IP over Ethernet, provides much higher bandwidth than a serial link. Moreover, the target and the host can use many networking connections over the same physical network link. Hence, you can continue to interact with the target while debugging applications on it. You can also debug over a networking link while interacting with the target using a terminal emulator over the embedded system's serial port. However, the use of a networking interface implies the presence of a networking stack. Since the networking stack is found in the Linux kernel, a networking link cannot be used to debug the kernel itself. In contrast, kernel debugging can be and is often carried out over a serial link.

Both the use of a serial link and the use of a networking interface requires that some minimal software be taking care of the most primitive I/O hardware available on the target. In some cases, such as when porting Linux to a new board or when debugging the kernel itself, this assumption does not hold. In those cases, it is necessary to use a debugging interface that provides direct hardware control over the software. There are several ways to achieve this, but most are quite expensive.

Currently, the preferred way to obtain direct control over hardware for debugging purposes is to use a BDM or JTAG interface. These interfaces rely on special BDM or JTAG functionality embedded in the CPU's silicon. By connecting a special debugger to the JTAG or BDM pins of the CPU, you can take complete control of its behavior. For this reason, JTAG and BDM are often used when bringing up new embedded boards or debugging the Linux kernel on such boards.

Though the BDM and JTAG debuggers are much less expensive and much less complicated, in terms of their technical operation, than In-Circuit Emulators (ICEs), they still require the purchase of special hardware and software.[*] Often, this software and hardware is still relatively expensive because CPU manufacturers are not keen to share the detailed information regarding the use of the JTAG and BDM interfaces included in their products. Obtaining this information often involves establishing a trust relationship with the manufacturer and signing stringent NDAs.

Though it would probably be too expensive to equip each member of an engineering team with her own BDM or JTAG debugger, I highly recommend that you have at least one such debugger available throughout your project for debugging the very difficult problems that a serial or networking debugger cannot deal with appropriately. When selecting such a debugger, however, you may want to evaluate its compatibility with the GNU development toolchain. Some BDM and JTAG debuggers, for instance, require the use of specially modified *gdb* debuggers. A good BDM or JTAG debugger should be able to deal with the standard GNU development toolchain, and the binary files generated using it, transparently.

Generic Architecture of an Embedded Linux System

Since Linux systems are made up of many components, let us take a look at the overall architecture of a generic Linux system. This will enable us to set each component in context and will help you understand the interaction between them and how to best take advantage of their assembly. Figure 2-4 presents the architecture of a generic Linux system with all the components involved. Although the figure abstracts to a high degree the content of the kernel and the other components, the abstractions presented are sufficient for the discussion. Notice that there is little difference in the following description between an embedded system and a workstation or server system, since Linux systems are all structured the same at this level of

---

[*] Have a look at some of the books listed in Appendix B if you are not familiar with the various hardware tools commonly used for debugging embedded systems, including ICEs.

abstraction. In the rest of the book, however, emphasis will be on the details of the application of this architecture in embedded systems.

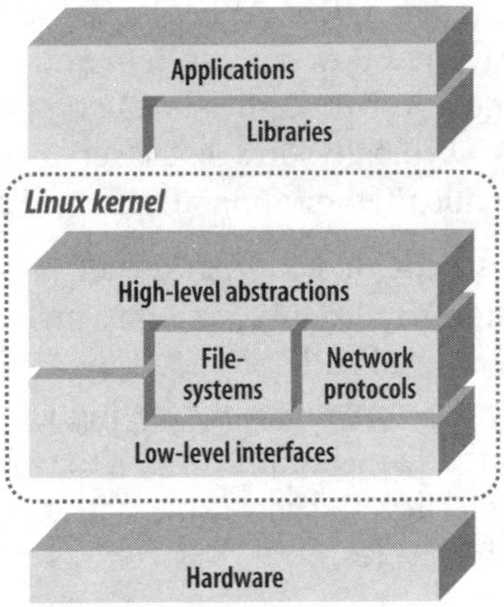

Figure 2-4. Architecture of a generic Linux system

There are some broad characteristics expected from the hardware to run a Linux system. First, Linux requires at least a 32-bit CPU containing a memory management unit (MMU).* Second, a sufficient amount of RAM must be available to accommodate the system. Third, minimal I/O capabilities are required if any development is to be carried out on the target with reasonable debugging facilities. This is also very important for any later troubleshooting in the field. Finally, the kernel must be able to load and/or access a root filesystem through some form of permanent or networked storage. See "Types of Embedded Linux Systems" in Chapter 1 for a discussion of typical system configurations.

Immediately above the hardware sits the kernel. The kernel is the core component of the operating system. Its purpose is to manage the hardware in a coherent manner while providing familiar high-level abstractions to user-level software. As with other Unix-like kernels, Linux drives devices, manages I/O accesses, controls process scheduling, enforces memory sharing, handles the distribution of signals, and tends to other administrative tasks. It is expected that applications using the APIs provided by a kernel will be portable among the various architectures supported by this kernel with little or no changes. This is usually the case with Linux, as can be seen by the body of applications uniformly available on all architectures supported by Linux.

---

* As we'll see below, a specially modified version of Linux called uClinux does run on some CPUs that aren't equipped with MMUs. The development of applications for Linux on such processors differs, however, sufficiently from standard Linux application development to require a separate discussion. I will therefore not cover the use of Linux on MMU-less architectures.

Within the kernel, two broad categories of layered services provide the functionality required by applications. The low-level interfaces are specific to the hardware configuration on which the kernel runs and provide for the direct control of hardware resources using a hardware-independent API. That is, handling registers or memory pages will be done differently on a PowerPC system and on an ARM system, but will be accessible using a common API to higher-level components of the kernel, albeit with some rare exceptions. Typically, low-level services will handle CPU-specific operations, architecture-specific memory operations, and basic interfaces to devices.

Above the low-level services provided by the kernel, higher-level components provide the abstractions common to all Unix systems, including processes, files, sockets, and signals. Since the low-level APIs provided by the kernel are common among different architectures, the code implementing the higher-level abstractions is almost constant regardless of the underlying architecture. There are some rare exceptions, as stated above, where the higher-level kernel code will include special cases or different functions for certain architectures.

Between these two levels of abstraction, the kernel sometimes needs what could be called *interpretation components* to understand and interact with structured data coming from or going to certain devices. Filesystem types and networking protocols are prime examples of sources of structured data the kernel needs to understand and interact with to provide access to data going to and coming from these sources.

Disk devices have been and still are the main storage media for computerized data. Yet disk devices, and all other storage devices for that matter, themselves contain little structure. Their content may be addressable by referencing the appropriate sector of a cylinder on a certain disk, but this level of organization is quite insufficient to accommodate the ever changing content of files and directories. File-level access is achieved using a special organization of the data on the disk where file and directory information is stored in a particular fashion so that it can be recognized when it is read again. This is what filesystems are all about. Through the evolution of OSes in time, however, many different incompatible filesystems have seen the light of day. To accommodate these existing filesystems and the new ones being developed, the kernel has a number of filesystem engines that can recognize a particular disk structure and retrieve or add files and directories from this structure. The engines all provide the same API to the upper layers of the kernel so that accesses to the various filesystems are identical even though accesses to the lower-layer services vary according to the structure of the filesystem. The API provided to the virtual filesystem layer of the kernel by, for instance, the FAT filesystem and the ext2 filesystem is identical, but the operations both will conduct on the block device driver will differ according to the respective structures used by FAT and ext2 to store data on disk.

During its normal operation, the kernel requires at least one properly structured filesystem, the root filesystem. It is from this filesystem that the kernel loads the first application to run on the system. It also relies on this filesystem for future operations such as module loading and providing each process with a working directory.

The root filesystem may either be stored and operated on from a real hardware storage device or loaded into RAM during system startup and operated on from there. As we'll see later, the former is becoming much more popular than the latter with the advent of facilities such as the JFFS2 filesystem.

You'd expect that right above the kernel we would find the applications and utilities making up and running on the OS. Yet the services exported by the kernel are often unfit to be used directly by applications. Instead, applications rely on libraries to provide familiar APIs and abstract services that interact with the kernel on the application's behalf to obtain the desired functionality. The main library used by most Linux applications is the GNU C library. For embedded Linux systems, substitutes to this library can be used, as we'll see later, to compensate for the GNU C library's main deficiency, its size. Other than the C library, libraries such as Qt, XML, or MD5 provide various utility and functionality APIs serving all sorts of purposes.

Libraries are typically linked dynamically with applications. That is, they are not part of the application's binary, but are rather loaded into the application's memory space during application startup. This allows many applications to use the same instance of a library instead of each having its own copy. The C library found on a system's filesystem, for instance, is loaded only once in the system RAM, and this same copy is shared among all applications using this library. But note that in some situations in embedded systems, static linking, whereby libraries are part of the application's binary, is preferred to dynamic linking. When only part of a library is used by one or two applications, for example, static linking will help avoid having to store the entire library on the embedded system's storage device.

System Startup

Three main software components participate in system startup: the bootloader, the kernel, and the init process. The bootloader is the first software to run upon startup and is highly dependent on the target's hardware. As we'll see in Chapter 9, there are many bootloaders available for Linux. The bootloader will conduct low-level hardware initialization and thereafter jump to the kernel's startup code.

The early kernel startup code differs greatly between architectures and will conduct initialization of its own before setting up a proper environment for the running of C code. Once this is done, the kernel jumps to the architecture-independent start_kernel( ) function, which initializes the high-level kernel functionality, mounts the root filesystem, and starts the init process.

I will not cover the details of the kernel's internal startup and initialization, because they have already been covered in detail in Chapter 16 of *Linux Device Drivers* (O'Reilly). Also, Appendix A of *Understanding the Linux Kernel* (O'Reilly) provides a lengthy description of the startup of PC-based systems from the initial power-on to the execution of the init process. That discussion covers the kernel's internal startup for the x86.

The rest of the system startup is conducted in user space by the init program found on the root filesystem. We will discuss the setup and configuration of the init process in Chapter 6.

Types of Boot Configurations

The type of boot configuration chosen for a system greatly influences the selection of a bootloader, its configuration, and the type of software and hardware found in the host. A network boot configuration, for example, requires that the host provide some types of network services to the target. In designing your system, you first need to identify the boot configurations you are likely to use during development and in the final product. Then, you need to choose a bootloader or a set of bootloaders that will cater to the different types of boot setups you are likely to use. Not all bootloaders, for example, can boot kernels from disk devices. In the following, I will cover the possible boot configurations. Let us start, nevertheless, by reviewing some boot basics.

All CPUs fetch their first instruction from an address preassigned by their manufacturer. Any system built using a CPU has one form or another of solid state storage device at that location. Traditionally, the storage device was a masked ROM, but flash chips are increasingly the norm today.* The software on this storage device is responsible for bootstrapping the system. The level of sophistication of the boot software and the extent to which it is subsequently used as part of the system's operation greatly depends on the type of system involved.

On most workstations and servers, the boot software is responsible only for loading the operating system from disk and for providing basic hardware configuration options to the operator. In contrast, there are very few agreed upon purposes, if any, for boot software in embedded systems because of the diversity in purposes of embedded applications. Sometimes, the boot software will be the very software that runs throughout the system's lifetime. The boot software may also be a simple monitor that loads the rest of the system software. Such monitors can then provide enhanced debugging and upgrading facilities. The boot software may even load additional bootloaders, as is often the case with x86 PCs.

Embedded Linux systems are as diverse as their non-Linux counterparts. Embedded Linux systems are characterized, nevertheless, by the requirement to load a Linux kernel and its designated root filesystem. How these are loaded and operated, as we'll see, largely depends on the system's requirements and, sometimes, on the state of its development, as described in "Types of Host/Target Development Setups."

There are three different setups used to bootstrap an embedded Linux system: the solid state storage media setup, the disk setup, and the network setup. Each setup

---

* Masked ROMs continue to be used when devices are produced in very large quantities. Consumer gaming devices such as consoles, for example, often use masked ROMs.

has its own typical configurations and uses. The following subsections discuss each setup in detail.

We will discuss the setup and configuration of specific bootloaders for each applicable setup described below in Chapter 9.

Solid State Storage Media

In this setup, a solid state storage device holds the initial bootloader, its configuration parameters, the kernel, and the root filesystem. Though the development of an embedded Linux system may use other boot setups, depending on the development stage, most production systems contain a solid state storage media to hold all the system's components. Figure 2-5 shows the most common layout of a solid state storage device with all the system components.

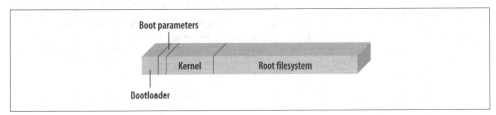

Figure 2-5. Typical solid state storage device layout

No memory addresses are shown in Figure 2-5, because the ranges vary greatly. Intuitively, you may think that addresses are lower on the left and grow towards the right. However, there are cases where it is the inverse and the bootloader is at the top of the storage device address range instead of the bottom. For this reason, many flash devices are provided in both top-boot and bottom-boot configurations. Depending on the configuration, the flash region where the bootloader is found often has special protection mechanisms to avoid damage to the bootloader if a memory write goes astray. In top-boot flash devices, this protected region is located at the top of the device's address range, and in bottom-boot flash devices, it is located in the bottom of the device's address range.

Although Figure 2-5 shows the storage device separated into four different parts, it may contain fewer parts. The boot parameters may be contained within the space reserved for the bootloader. The kernel may also be on the root filesystem. This, however, requires that the bootloader be able to read the root filesystem. Also, the kernel and the root filesystem could be packaged as a single image that is uncompressed in RAM before being used. Depending on the capabilities provided by your bootloader, there may even be other possible configurations, each with its advantages and disadvantages. Usually, a setup can be categorized using the following criteria: flash memory use, RAM use, ease of upgrading, and bootup time.

Boot storage media are initially programmed using a device programmer or the CPU's integrated debug capabilities, such as JTAG or BDM. Once the device is initially programmed, it can be reprogrammed by the system designer using the boot-loader, if it provides this capability, or using Linux's MTD subsystem. The system may also contain software that enables the user to easily update the storage device. We will discuss the programming of solid state storage media in Chapter 7.

Disk

This is the setup you are probably most familiar with because of its widespread use in workstations and servers. Here, the kernel and the root filesystem are located on a disk device. The initial bootloader either loads a secondary bootloader off the disk or fetches the kernel itself directly from the disk. One of the filesystems on the disk is then used as the root filesystem.

During development, this setup is particularly attractive if you would like to have a large number of kernel and root filesystem configurations for testing. If you plan to develop your embedded system using a customized mainstream distribution, for instance, this setup is helpful. If you are using a hard disk or a device mimicking a hard disk, such as CompactFlash, in your production system, this boot setup is prob-ably the best choice.

Because this scheme is well known and well documented, we will only discuss it briefly in Chapter 9.

Network

In this setup, either the root filesystem or both the kernel and the root filesystem are loaded via a network link. In the first case, the kernel resides on a solid state storage media or a disk, and the root filesystem is mounted via NFS. In the second case, only the bootloader resides on a local storage media. The kernel is then downloaded via TFTP, and the root filesystem is mounted via NFS. To automate the location of the TFTP server, the bootloader may also use BOOTP/DHCP. In that case, the target does not need any preset IP addresses to find either the TFTP server or the NFS server.

This setup is ideal in early stages of development, because it enables the developer to share data and software rapidly between his workstation and the target without hav-ing to reprogram the target. Software updates can then be compiled on the host and tested immediately on the target. In contrast, few production systems use this setup, because it requires the presence of a server. In the case of the control system described in Chapter 1, nevertheless, this setup actually can be used for some of the devices, because the SYSM module already provides network services.

Obviously, this setup involves configuring the server to provide the appropriate net-work services. We will discuss the configuration of these network services in Chapter 9.

System Memory Layout

To best use the available resources, it is important to understand the system's memory layout, and the differences between the physical address space and the kernel's virtual address space.* Most importantly, many hardware peripherals are accessible within the system's physical address space, but have restricted access or are completely "invisible" in the virtual address space.

To best illustrate the difference between virtual and physical address spaces, let's take a closer look at one component of the example system. The user interface modules, for instance, can be easily implemented on the StrongARM-based iPAQ PDA. Figure 2-6 illustrates the physical and virtual memory maps of an iPAQ running the Familiar distribution. Note that the regions illustrated are not necessarily proportional to their actual size in memory. If they were, many of them would be too small to be visible.

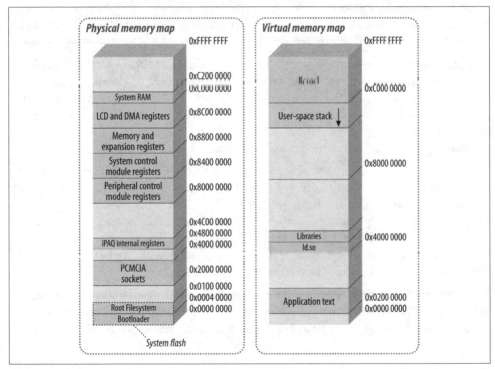

Figure 2-6. Physical and virtual memory maps for the Compaq iPAQ

The physical map of a system is usually available with the technical literature accompanying your hardware. In the case of the iPAQ, the StrongARM manual, the *SA-1110 Developer's manual*, is available from Intel's web site.

---

* What I call here "virtual address" is known in x86 jargon as "logical address" and can have other names on other architectures.

The physical map is important, because it provides you with information on how to configure the kernel and how to develop custom drivers. During the kernel's configuration, for instance, you may need to specify the location of the flash devices in your system. During development, you may also need to write a driver for a memory-mapped peripheral. You will also need to provide your bootloader with information regarding the components it has to load. For these reasons, it is good practice to take the time to establish your system's physical memory map before starting software development.

On the iPAQ, the flash storage is divided in two. The first part contains the bootloader and starts at the lowest memory address available. Given the bootloader's size, this region is rather small. The rest of the flash storage space is occupied by the system's root filesystem, which in the case of Familiar, is a JFFS2 filesystem. In this case, the kernel is actually on the root filesystem. This is possible, because the bootloader has enough understanding of JFFS2 to find the kernel on the filesystem.

Upon startup, the bootloader reads the kernel from the root filesystem into the system's RAM and jumps to the kernel's start routines. From there on, the rest of the system startup is carried out by Linux.

Once Linux is running,* the programs use virtual addresses. In contrast to the physical memory map, the layout of the virtual memory map is of secondary importance for kernel configuration or device driver development. For device driver development, for instance, it is sufficient to know that some information is located in kernel space and some other information is located in user space, and that appropriate functions must be used to properly exchange data between the two.

The virtual memory layout is mostly important in helping you understand and debug your applications. As you can see in Figure 2-6, the kernel occupies a quarter of the virtual address space starting from address 0xC0000000. This region is also known as "kernel space." The rest of the address space is occupied by application-specific text, data, and library mappings. This is also known as "user space." Whereas the kernel is always located above the 0xC0000000 mark for all applications, applications' memory maps may differ even on the same system.

To reconstruct a process' virtual memory map, you need to look at the *maps* file in the process' PID entry in the */proc* filesystem. For more details on how to get this information, see the Chapter 20 in *Understanding the Linux Kernel* (O'Reilly).

* I assume that you are using MMU-equipped hardware. This discussion does not hold if you are using a Linux variant for MMU-less processors.

CHAPTER 3
Hardware Support

Having covered the basics of embedded Linux systems, including generic system architecture, we will now discuss the embedded hardware supported by Linux. I will first cover the processor architectures supported by Linux that are commonly used in embedded systems. Next, I will cover the various hardware components involved, such as buses, I/O, storage, general-purpose networking, industrial-grade networking, and system monitoring. Although I include many different components, I have omitted components not typically used in embedded configurations.

Note that the following discussion does not attempt to analyze the pros and cons of one hardware component or another. Use it, rather, as a starting point for your research in either identifying the components to include in your system or judging the amount of effort needed to get Linux to run on the hardware you have already chosen.

Also, the following does not cover the software made available by the various hardware vendors to support their hardware. It covers only hardware supported by the open source and free software communities. Some vendors may provide closed-source drivers for their hardware. If you intend to use such hardware, keep in mind that you will have no support from the open source and free software development community. You will have to refer to the vendor for any problems related or caused by the closed-source drivers. Open source and free software developers have repeatedly refused to help anyone that has problems when using closed-source drivers.

Processor Architectures

Linux runs on a large number of architectures, but not all these architectures are actually used in embedded configurations, as I said above. The following discussion looks at each architecture in terms of the support provided by Linux to the CPUs belonging to that architecture and the boards built around those CPUs. It also covers the intricacies of Linux's support and any possible caveats. I will not cover the MMU-less architectures supported by uClinux, however. Though the code maintained by this project has been integrated late in the 2.5 development series, it remains that the development of the uClinux branch and the surrounding software has its own particularities. If you are interested in an MMU-less architecture to run Linux, you are invited to take a closer look at the uClinux project web site at *http:// www.uclinux.org/*. uClinux currently supports Motorola MMU-less 68K processors, MMU-less ARM, Intel's i960, Axis' Etrax, and other such processors.

x86

The x86 family starts with the 386 introduced by Intel in 1985 and goes on to include all the descendants of this processor, including the 486 and the Pentium family, along with compatible processors by other vendors such as AMD and National Semiconductor. Intel remains, though, the main reference in regards to the x86 family and is still the largest distributor of processors of this family. Lately, a new trend is to group traditional PC functionality with a CPU core from one of the 386 family processors to form a System-on-Chip (SoC). National Semiconductor's Geode family and ZF Micro Devices' ZFx86 are part of this SoC trend.

Although the x86 is the most popular and most publicized platform to run Linux, it represents a small fraction of the traditional embedded systems market. In most cases, designers prefer ARM, MIPS, and PowerPC processors to the i386 for reasons of complexity and overall cost.

That said, the i386 remains the most widely used and tested Linux platform. Thus, it profits from the largest base of software available for Linux. Many applications and add-ons start their lives on the i386 before being ported to the other architectures supported by Linux. The kernel itself was in fact written for the i386 first before being ported to any other architecture.

Since most, if not all, i386 embedded systems are very similar, or identical to the workstation and server counterparts in terms of functionality and programmability, the kernel makes little or no difference between the various x86 CPUs and related boards. When needed, a few *#ifdef* statements are used to accommodate the peculiarities of a certain CPU or board, but these are rare.

The i386-based PC architecture is the most widely documented architecture around. There are many different books and online documents in many languages discussing the intricacies of this architecture. This is in addition to the documents available from the various processor vendors, some of which are very complete. To get an idea of the scope of the existing documentation, try searching for "pc architecture" in the book section of Amazon.com. It would be hard to recommend a single source of information regarding the i386 and PC architecture. *Intel Architecture Software Developer's Manual, Volume 1: Basic Architecture*, *Volume 2: Instruction Set Reference*, and *Volume 3: System Programming Guide* published by Intel are traditionally rich sources of information about how to program the i386s, albeit limited to Intel's products. The availability of these documents may vary. At some point, hardcopies were not available from Intel's literature center. During that time, however, the documents were available in PDF format online. At the time of this writing, the manuals are available in hardcopy from Intel's literature center.

Regarding the PC architecture itself, a source I've found useful over time is a package of DOS shareware called *HelpPC*,[*] which contains a number of documents describing the intricacies and operations of various components of the PC architecture. Another useful manual with similar information is *The PC Handbook* by John Choisser and John Foster (Annabooks). Note that your particular setup's technical configuration may differ slightly from the information provided by the various sources. Refer to your hardware's documentation for exact information.

ARM

The ARM, which stands for *Advanced RISC Machine*, is a family of processors maintained and promoted by ARM Holdings Ltd. Contrary to other chip manufacturers such as IBM, Motorola, and Intel, ARM Holdings does not manufacture its own processors. Instead, ARM designs the CPU cores for its customers based on the ARM core, charges customers licensing fees on the design, and lets them manufacture the chip wherever they see fit. This offers various advantages to the parties involved, but it does create a certain confusion to the developer approaching this architecture for the first time, as there does not seem to be a central producer of ARM chips on the market. There is, though, one unifying characteristic that is important to remember: all ARM processors share the same ARM instruction set, which makes all variants fully software compatible. This doesn't mean that all ARM CPUs and boards can be programmed and set up in the same way, only that the assembly language and resulting binary codes are identical for all ARM processors. Currently, ARM CPUs are manufactured by Intel, Toshiba, Samsung, and many others. The ARM architecture is very popular in many fields of application and there are hundreds of vendors providing products and services around it.

At the time of this writing, Linux supports 10 distinct ARM CPUs, 16 different platforms, and more than 200 related boards. Given the quantity and variety of information involved, I refer you to the complete and up-to-date list of ARM systems supported and their details at *http://www.arm.linux.org.uk/developer/machines/*. Suffice it to say that Linux supports most mainstream CPUs and boards, such as Intel's SA1110 StrongARM CPUs and Assabet development boards. In case you need it, there is a method to add support for new hardware. Generally, for any information regarding the Linux ARM port, consult the project's web site at *http://www.arm.linux.org.uk/*.

In addition to the kernel port to the ARM, many projects have geared up for ARM support. First, hard real-time support is available from the RTAI project and a

---

[*] A search on the web for "HelpPC" should rapidly point you to an appropriate URL where you can download the package. Although the document files included with the shareware have a special format allowing them to be read by the DOS HelpPC utility, these documents are plain text files that can be read with any usual editor in Linux.

StrongARM RTLinux port is available at *http://www.imec.be/rtlinux/*. In addition, Java support is available from the Blackdown project.[*] There is however no kernel debugger, since most developers who need to debug the kernel on an ARM system use a JTAG debugger.

For any information regarding the ARM architecture and its instruction set, consult the *ARM Architecture Reference Manual* edited by David Seal (Addison Wesley), and Steve Furber's *ARM System-on-Chip Architecture* (Addison Wesley). Contrary to other vendors, ARM does not provide free manuals for its chips. These are the only reference manuals currently available for the ARM. Although the *ARM Architecture Reference Manual* isn't as mature as technical documentation provided by other processor vendors, it is sufficient for the task. Because individual chip manufacturers are responsible for developing the chips, they provide specific information such as timing and mechanical data regarding their own products. Intel, for example, provides online access to manuals for its StrongARM implementation.

IBM/Motorola PowerPC

The PowerPC architecture is the result of a collaboration between IBM, Motorola, and Apple. It inherited ideas from work done by the three firms, especially IBM's Performance Optimization With Enhanced RISC (POWER) architecture, which still exists. The PowerPC is mostly known for its use in Apple's Macs, but there are other PowerPC-based workstations from IBM and other vendors as well as PowerPC-based embedded systems. The popular TiVo system, for instance, is based on an embedded PowerPC processor.

Along with the i386 and the ARM, the PowerPC (PPC) is a very well supported architecture in Linux. This level of support can be partly seen by looking at the large number of PPC CPUs and systems on which Linux runs.

To provide compatibility with the various PPC hardware, each type of PPC architecture has its own low-level functions grouped in files designated by architecture. There are such files, for example, for CHRP, Gemini, and PReP machines. Their names reflect the architectures, such as *chrp_pci.c* or *gemini_pci.c*. In a similar fashion, the kernel accounts for the embedded versions of the PPC, such as IBM's 4xx series and Motorola's 8xx series.

In addition, a great number of applications that run on the i386 are available for the PPC. Both RTLinux and RTAI, for instance, support the PPC. There is also support for Java, and OpenOffice has been ported to the PPC. The PPC Linux community is

---

[*] The Blackdown project is the main Java implementation for Linux and is located at *http://www.blackdown.org/*. When evaluating the level of Java support provided for the other architectures, it is the level of support provided by the Java run-time environment packages available from the Blackdown project that will be my main reference. There may be commercial Java solutions other than the Blackdown project for any of the architectures discussed, but they are not considered here as they aren't open source. A more in-depth discussion of Linux's Java support is carried out in Chapter 4.

active in many areas of development ranging from workstation to embedded systems. The main PPC Linux site is *http://penguinppc.org/*. This site is maintained by community members and is not affiliated with any particular vendor. It contains valuable documentation and links and should be considered the starting point for any Linux development on the PPC. There is also *http://www.linuxppc.org/*, which is affiliated with the LinuxPPC distribution. This site was the initial home of the efforts to port Linux to to the PPC. While I'm discussing distributions, it is worth noting that there are a number that support the PPC, some exclusively. LinuxPPC and Yellow Dog Linux, for example, provide Linux only for PPC machines. There are also traditional mainstream distributions that provide support for the PPC as part of their support for other architectures. These include Mandrake, Debian, and SuSE.

If you intend to use the PPC in your embedded application and want to be in touch with other folks using this architecture in their systems, be sure to subscribe to the very active linuxppc-embedded list. Most problems are recurring, so there is probably someone on that list that has had your problem before. If not, many people will be interested to see your problem solved, as they may encounter it, too. The list is hosted on linuxppc.org, which hosts many other PPC-related lists.

Early on, the companies behind the PPC agreed upon a standard system architecture for developing boards based on the chip. This was initially provided through the *PowerPC Reference Platform* (PReP), which was eventually replaced by the *Common Hardware Reference Platform* (CHRP). Documentation on CHRP is available in the book entitled *PowerPC Microprocessor Common Hardware Reference Platform: A System Architecture guide* (Morgan Kaufmann Publishers), available online at *http://www.rs6000.ibm.com/resource/technology/chrp/*. Documentation on the 32-bit versions of the PowerPC is available from both IBM and Motorola through a manual entitled *PowerPC Microprocessor Family: Programming Environments for 32-bit Microprocessors*. This manual is available online in the technical documentation sections of both companies' web sites and in hardcopy for free from Motorola through the literature center section of its web site.

MIPS

The MIPS is the brain child of John Hennessey, mostly known by computer science students all over the world for his books on computer architecture written with David Patterson, and is the result of the Stanford *Microprocessor without Interlocked Pipeline Stages* project (MIPS). MIPS is famed for having been the basis of the workstations and servers sold by SGI and of gaming consoles such as Nintendo's 64-bit system and Sony Playstations 1 and 2. But it is also found in many embedded systems. Much like the ARM, the company steering MIPS, MIPS Technologies Inc., licenses CPU cores to third parties. Unlike the ARM, however, there are many instruction set implementations, which differ from each other to various degrees. 32-bit MIPS implementations are available from IDT, Toshiba, Alchemy, and LSI. 64-bit implementations are available from IDT, LSI, NEC, QED, SandCraft, and Toshiba.

The initial port of Linux to MIPS was mainly done to support MIPS-based workstations. Eventually, the port also came to include development boards and embedded systems based on MIPS. To accommodate the various CPUs and systems built around them, the layout of the MIPS portion of the kernel is divided into directories based on the type of system the kernel will run on. Similarly, kernel configuration for a given MIPS system is mainly influenced by the type of board being used. The actual type of MIPS chip on the board is much less important.

Looking around, you will find that support for Linux on MIPS is limited when compared to other architectures such as the i386 or the PowerPC. In fact, few of the main distributions have actually been ported to MIPS. When available, commercial vendor support for MIPS is mostly limited to embedded architectures. Nevertheless, there is a Debian port to both big endian and little endian MIPS, and a port of Red Hat 7.1 is also available. Also, many PDA and development board manufacturers actively support Linux ports on their MIPS-based hardware. As with some other ports, MIPS lacks proper Java support. Hard real-time support is however available for some MIPS boards from the RTAI project.

In addition to conventional MIPS-based machines, an entirely different set of processors is based on NEC's VR chips for the purpose of running WindowsCE. A number of developers were interested in having Linux running on these devices, and hence started new projects for the purpose. These projects have advanced rapidly and have come to occupy a large portion of the Linux-on-MIPS development.

For more information regarding the MIPS port of Linux in general, take a look at the official home of the Linux MIPS port at *http://www.linux-mips.org/*. The web site contains a list of supported systems, documentation, links, and other useful resources. For information on the VR and other PDA-related efforts on MIPS, check out the Linux VR page at *http://linux-vr.org/*. If you're looking into working with Linux on MIPS, I suggest you take a look at both sites. There are also commercial embedded distributions that provide extensive support for some MIPS boards. Depending on the board you choose and your development model, that may be a practical way to get Linux up and running on a MIPS system.

Because MIPS is divided into multiple platforms, you will need to refer to the data provided by your system's manufacturer to evaluate and/or implement Linux support. One general resource that is recommended on MIPS Technologies Inc.'s own web site is *See MIPS run* by Dominic Sweetman (Morgan Kaufmann Publishers). You can also get PDFs on MIPS's web site. MIPS provides 32- and 64-bit editions of their *MIPS Architecture for Programmers* three volume series, made up of *Volume I: Introduction to the MIPS Architecture*, *Volume II: The MIPS instruction set*, and *Volume III: The MIPS Privileged Resource Architecture*.

Hitachi SuperH

In an effort to enhance its 8- and 16-bit H8 line of microcontrollers, Hitachi introduced the SuperH line of processors. These manipulate 32-bit data internally and offer various external bus widths. Later, Hitachi formed SuperH Inc. with STMicroelectronics (formerly SGS-Thomson Microelectronics). SuperH Inc. licenses and heads the SuperH much the same way ARM Holdings Ltd. steers the ARM and MIPS Technologies Inc. steers the MIPS. The early implementations of the SuperH, such as the SH-1, SH-2, and their variants, did not have an MMU. Starting with the SH-3, however, all SuperH processors include an MMU. The SuperH is used within Hitachi's own products, in many consumer-oriented embedded systems such as PDAs, and the Sega Saturn and Dreamcast game consoles.

As the early SuperH (SH) processors did not include MMUs, they are not supported by Linux. Currently, both the SH-3 and SH-4 are supported by Linux. However, not all SH-3 and SH-4 systems are supported by Linux, as there are many variations with various capabilities. Linux supports the 7707, 7708, and 7709 SH-3 processors and the 7750, 7751, and ST40 SH-4 processors. Accordingly, Linux supports a number of systems that use these processors, including the Sega Dreamcast. Although discontinued, this system is a great platform to practice with to become familiar with non i386 embedded Linux systems. An SH-5 port is also in the works, though it is not yet part of the main kernel tree. For more information on this port, visit the project's web site at *http://www.superh-software.com/linux/*.

Support for the SH outside the kernel is rather limited for the moment. There is no support for Java, for instance, although the architecture has a kernel debugger. There is also an RTLinux port to the SH-4 created by Masahiro Abe of A&D Co. Ltd., but this port is not part of the main Open RTLinux distributed by FSMLabs. The port can be found at *ftp://ftp.aandd.co.jp/pub/linuxsh/rtlinux/current/*. There are no SH distributions either. There are, however, many developers actively working to increase the level of support provided for this architecture by Linux, including a Debian port. Accordingly, there are a number of web sites that host Linux SH–related documentation, resources, and software. The two main ones are *http://linuxsh.sourceforge.net/* and *http://www.m17n.org/linux-sh/*.

As there is no standard SH architecture, you will need to refer to your hardware's documentation for details about the layout and functionality of the hardware. There are, nonetheless, manuals that describe the operations and instruction set of the various processors. The SH-3's operation is described in *Hitachi SuperH RISC engine SH-3/SH-3E/SH3-DSP Programming Manual*, and the SH-4's operation is described in *SuperH RISC engine SH-4 Programming Manual*. Both resources are available through Hitachi's web site.

Motorola 68000

The Motorola 68000 family is known in Linux jargon as m68k and has been supported in its MMU-equipped varieties for quite some time, and in its MMU-less varieties starting with the 2.5 development series. The m68k came in second only to the x86 as a popular 1980s architecture. Apart from being used in many popular mainstream systems by Atari, Apple, and Amiga, and in popular workstation systems by HP, Sun, and Apollo, the m68k was also a platform of choice for embedded systems development. Recently, though, interest has drifted away from the m68k to newer architectures such as ARM, MIPS, SH, and PowerPC for embedded systems design.

Linux supports many systems based on the m68k, starting with the mainstream and workstation systems already mentioned and including VME systems from Motorola and BVM. Because these systems are completely different from each other, the kernel tree is built to accommodate the variations and facilitate the addition of other m68k-based systems. Each system has its own set of specific modules to interface with the hardware. An example of this is the interrupt vector tables and related handling functions. Each system has a different way of dealing with these, and the kernel source reflects this difference by having a different set of functions to deal with interrupt setup and handling for each type of system.

Since the MMU versions of the m68k are seldom used nowadays in new, cutting-edge designs, they lag behind in terms of software support. There is, for instance, no hard real-time support and no Java support. Nor is the processor architecture listed among supported architectures for other user-level applications such as OpenOffice. For up-to-date information regarding the port, the supported hardware, and related resources, refer to the m68k Linux port homepage at *http://www.linux-m68k.org/*. One distribution that has done a lot work for the m68k is Debian. Check out their documentation and mailing lists if you plan to deploy an m68k-based embedded Linux system.

Since there is no standard m68k-based platform such as the PC for the i386, there is no single reference covering all m68k-based systems. There are, however, many textbooks and online resources that discuss the traditional use of the m68k and its programming. Motorola provides the *68000 Family Programmer's Reference Manual* and the *M68000 8-/16-/32-Bit Microprocessors User's Manual* free through its literature center. Other, more elaborate, texts that include examples and applications can be found by looking for "68000" on any online bookstore.

Buses and Interfaces

The buses and interfaces are the fabric that connects the CPU to the peripherals that are part of the system. Each bus and interface has its own intricacies, and the level of support provided by Linux to the different buses and interfaces varies accordingly. The following is a rundown of the buses and interfaces found in embedded systems and a discussion of their support by Linux. Linux supports many other buses, such as SBus, NuBus, TurboChannel, and MCA, but these are workstation or server-centric.

ISA

The *Industry Standard Architecture* (ISA) bus was designed for and occupied the core of PC-AT architecture. It was odd even for its time, as it did not provide many of the facilities other buses offered, including ease of mapping into normal processor physical address space. Its simplicity, however, favored the proliferation of many devices for the PC, which, in turn, favored the use of PCs in embedded applications.

ISA devices are mostly accessed through the I/O port programming already available in the x86's instruction set. Therefore, the kernel does not need to do any work to enable device drivers to use the bus. Instead, the various device drivers access the appropriate I/O ports directly using the in/out assembly functions. Although the kernel provides support for *Plug and Play* (PNP) devices, this capability is of little use for embedded applications. Instead, embedded systems that do need to support hardware variations will be based on buses that support runtime hardware addition and removal, such as CompactPCI, PCMCIA, and USB. The kernel also supports *Extended ISA* (EISA) devices, but this bus has not been very popular and has been superseded by the PCI bus.

Information regarding the ISA bus can be found in many places. *The PC Handbook* and *HelpPC* mentioned above are good quick references for port numbers and their operation. *ISA System Architecture* by Anderson and Shanley (Addison Wesley) is an in-depth explanation of the operation of the ISA bus and related hardware. Also, *Linux Device Drivers* by Rubini and Corbet (O'Reilly) contains details about ISA programming in Linux.

PCI

The *Peripheral Component Interconnect* (PCI) bus, managed by the *PCI Special Interest Group* (PCI-SIG), is arguably the most popular bus currently available. Designed as a replacement for ISA, it is used in combination with many different architectures, including the PPC and the MIPS, to build different types of systems, including embedded devices.

Unlike ISA, PCI requires software support to enable it to be used by device drivers. The first part of this support is required to initialize and configure the PCI devices upon bootup. On PC systems, this is traditionally done by the BIOS. However, the kernel is capable of carrying out this task itself. If the BIOS has carried out the initialization, the kernel will browse the BIOS's table to retrieve the PCI information. In both cases, the kernel provides device drivers with an API to access information regarding the devices on the PCI bus and act on these devices. There are also a number of user tools for manipulating PCI devices. In short, the level of support for PCI in Linux is fairly complete and mature.

The *Linux Device Drivers* book mentioned above provides very good insight about PCI development in Linux and how the PCI bus operates in general. The *PCI System Architecture* book by Shanely and Anderson (Addison Wesley) gives in-depth information on the PCI bus for software developers. Of course, you can always get the official PCI specification from the *PCI-SIG*. Official specifications, however, tend to make for very dry reading material. Finally, there is the Linux PCI-HOWTO, available from the *Linux Documentation Project* (LDP) at *http://www.tldp.org/*, which discusses the caveats of using certain PCI devices with Linux and the support provided to PCI devices by Linux in general.

PCMCIA

Personal Computer Memory Card International Association (PCMCIA) is both the common name of a bus and the name of the organization that promotes and maintains related standards. Since the publication of the initial standard, which supported only 16-bit cards, other standards have been published, including the 32-bit *CardBus* and the USB *CardBay* specifications. When part of an embedded system, PCMCIA renders it flexible and easy to extend. On the iPAQ, for instance, it enables users to connect to a LAN using a wireless networking card. In other systems, it makes large permanent storage space available through the use of CompactFlash cards.

The extent of Linux support for PCMCIA can be confusing. First and foremost, there is the main Linux PCMCIA project, which is hosted on SourceForge at *http://pcmcia-cs.sourceforge.net/* and is maintained by David Hinds. The package made available by this project supports a large number of cards, listed at *http://pcmcia-cs.sourceforge.net/ftp/SUPPORTED.CARDS*. Linux support for PCMCIA is quite mature for the i386 architecture and available in part for the PPC, but unfortunately, it's still in its infancy for other chips at the time of this writing. Apart from the package maintained by Hinds, the official kernel contains support for a portion of the PCMCIA cards supported by the Hinds' package. The developers' intent is to have the official kernel become the main source for PCMCIA support. Until then, the best choice is to use Hinds' distribution for production systems. It includes the necessary system tools to configure the automatic loading and unloading of the appropriate PCMCIA device drivers when a card is inserted or removed from a PCMCIA slot.

Apart from the official *PC Card Standard* available from the PCMCIA association itself, there are a number of books on PCMCIA. However, before investigating those works, you should read the *Linux PCMCIA Programmer's Guide* written by Hinds and available on the PCMCIA project's web site. This guide includes references to books that provide more information regarding PCMCIA.

PC/104

Although simple, the ISA bus is not well adapted to the rugged environments where embedded systems are deployed. The PC/104 form factor was introduced to address the shortcomings of ISA's mechanical specification. PC/104 provides a bus whose electrical signals are identical to those of the ISA bus, but with a different mechanical specification that is more adapted to embedded system development by providing ease of extensibility and ruggedness. Instead of using slots where cards are inserted, as in a regular ISA setup, PC/104 specifies the use of pin connectors. When PCI became popular, the PC/104+ specification was introduced to provide a PCI-signal-compatible bus as an addition to the PC/104 specification. Both PC/104 and PC/104+ are managed by the *PC/104 Consortium*, which includes more than a 100 member companies.

The PC/104 is identical to ISA and the PC/104+ is identical to both ISA and PCI from the signal perspective and, therefore, from the software's perspective. Therefore, Linux requires no special functionality to support these buses. However, this does not mean that Linux supports all PC/104 and PC/104+ devices. As with any other ISA or PCI device, you should seek exact information about Linux compatibility with the PC/104 device you are evaluating.

VME

The VME* bus is largely based on Motorola's VERSA backplane bus, which was developed specifically for the 68000 in 1979. At the time, VERSA was competing with buses such as Multibus, STD, S-100, and Q-bus, although it is rarely used today. Striving to provide a new bus that would be microprocessor independent, Motorola, Mostek, and Signetics agreed that the three companies would support a new bus. This came to be the VME bus based on the VERSA's electrical signals and the Eurocard mechanical form factor. In the Eurocard form factor, VME boards are loaded vertically into a VME chassis and connected to its backplane using pin connectors, unlike common computer boards that use edge connectors inserted into slots. Since its introduction, the VME bus has become widely adopted as the preferred bus for building powerful and rugged computers. One factor that has helped the VME bus' popularity is that it is an open standard that isn't controlled by any single organization.

As the VME bus can accommodate multiple VME boards, each with its own CPU and OS, no central OS controls the bus. Instead, arbitration is used to permit a board to become bus master momentarily to conduct its operations. The job of Linux on a VME board is therefore to interact properly with its VME hardware interface to obtain the appropriate functionality.

There are currently two active Linux VME projects. The first aims at providing Motorola 68K-based boards with Linux support and can be found at *http://www.sleepie.demon.co.uk/linuxvme/*. Although the work of this project has since largely been integrated into the main kernel tree, the project's site is still the main resource for recent developments and news. The second project aims at providing Linux support for all VME boards, regardless of their CPU. It is called the VMELinux Project and can be found at *http://www.vmelinux.org/*. In each case, support is provided for

---

* Although "officially" the letters VME mean nothing, it has been revealed by an engineer taking part in the discussions between the three companies that it is short for "VERSA Module Eurocard."

each board individually. The supported boards are listed on each project's web site. So, when assessing whether your VME board is supported by Linux, you should look for support for the exact model you have. If the board you've chosen isn't supported yet, support for other board models will help provide you with examples on how to implement support for your VME board in Linux.

In addition to these two projects, a couple of software and hardware vendors provide Linux support for additional VME hardware within their own distributions. The kernel maintained by DENX Software Engineering and available from their web site using CVS, for example, provides support for various PPC-based boards not supported by the VMELinux project.

From the Linux perspective, the Linux VME HOWTO is available on the LDP's web site. The *VMEbus International Trade Association* (VITA) web site contains a number of recommended publications regarding the VME bus in general and the related standards. Missing from this list, though of interest, is John Black's *The Systems Engineer's Handbook: A guide to building VMEbus and VXIbus systems*.

CompactPCI

The CompactPCI specification was initiated by Ziatech and was developed by members of the *PCI Industrial Computer Manufacturer's Group* (PICMG), which oversees the specification and promotes the use of CompactPCI. The CompactPCI specification provides an open and versatile platform for high-performance, high-availability applications. Its success is largely based on the technical choices made by its designers. First, they chose to reuse the Eurocard form-factor popularized by VME. Second, they chose to make the bus PCI-compatible, hence enabling CompactPCI board manufacturers to reuse low-cost PCI chips already available in the mainstream market.

Technically, the CompactPCI bus is electrically identical to the PCI bus. Instead of using slot connections, as found in most workstations and servers, pin connectors are used to connect the vertically loaded CompactPCI boards to the CompactPCI backplane, much like VME. As with PCI, CompactPCI requires a single bus master,* in contrast with VME, which could tolerate multiple bus masters, as explained earlier. Consequently, CompactPCI requires the permanent presence of a board in the system slot. It is this board that arbitrates the CompactPCI backplane, just as a PCI chipset would arbitrate a PCI bus in a workstation or a server.

In addition, the CompactPCI specification allows for the implementation of the *Hot Swap* specification, which describes methods and procedures for runtime insertion and removal of CompactPCI boards. This specification defines three levels of hot

---

* The term "bus master" can mean different things in different contexts. In this particular instance, "bus master" designates the device that sets up and configures the PCI bus. There can be only one such device on a PCI bus, though more than one device on a PCI bus may actually be able to access the memory regions exported by other PCI devices.

swapping. Each level implies a set of hardware and software capabilities. Here are the available levels and their requirements:

Basic hot swap

This hot swap level involves console intervention by the system operator. When a new card is inserted, she must manually inform the OS to power it up and then configure and inform the software of its presence. To remove a card, she must tell the OS that the board is about to be removed. The OS must then stop the tasks that are interacting with the board and inform the board to shut down.

Full hot swap

In contrast to basic hot swap, full hot swap does not require console intervention by the operator. Instead, the operator flips a microswitch attached to the card injector/ejector to notify the OS of the impending removal. The OS then performs the necessary operations to isolate the board and tell it to shut down. Finally, the OS lights an LED to notify the operator that the board can now be removed. On insertion, the OS carries out the inverse operations when it receives the appropriate insertion signal.

High Availability

In this level, CompactPCI boards are under complete software control. A hot swap controller software manages the state of all the boards in the system and can selectively reverse these individual boards according to the system's state. If a board fails, for example, the controller can shut it down and power up a duplicate board that is present within the same chassis for this very purpose. This hot swap level is called "High Availability," because it is mostly useful in what are known as high-availability applications,* such as telecommunications, where downtime must be minimal.

Linux accommodates the basic CompactPCI specification, through the PCI support it already provides. Support for dynamic insertion and removal of devices in Linux also exists in different forms. Primarily, Version 2.4 of the kernel includes the required kernel functionality. The associated user tools are available through the *Linux Hotplugging* project at *http://linux-hotplug.sourceforge.net/*.

That said, this level of support is insufficient to accommodate all the complexities of CompactPCI systems. In addition, there are few drivers within the main kernel tree for mainstream CompactPCI boards, although CompactPCI board manufacturers may provide Linux drivers. This caveat has led to the emergence of a number of commercial solutions that provide high-availability Linux solutions on CompactPCI, including Availix's HA Cluster and MontaVista's High Availability Framework. The ongoing *High-Availability Linux Project*, found at *http://linux-ha.org/*, aims at providing the open source components needed to build high-availability solutions

---

* To avoid any confusion, I will refer to this hot swap level as "High Availability hot swap level" and will continue to use the "high-availability" adjective to refer to applications and systems who need to provide a high level of availability, regardless of whether they use CompactPCI or implement the "High Availability hot swap level."

using Linux. The project isn't restricted to a specific hardware configuration and is, therefore, not centered around CompactPCI.

In the future, we may see more open source software accommodating the various complexities of CompactPCI-based systems, both in terms of hot swap capabilities and in terms of software support for communication, resource monitoring, cluster management, and other software components found in high-availability systems. For now, however, if you want to use Linux for a CompactPCI-based high-availability application, you may need to work with one of the existing commercial solutions to obtain all the features described by the CompactPCI specification.

Documentation regarding Linux's hotplug capabilities, including how to write hot-plug-aware drivers and how to configure the hotplug management tools, is available through the Linux Hotplugging project web site. The web site also includes a number of links to relevant information. Information regarding CompactPCI specifications can be purchased from PICMG.

Parallel Port

Although not a bus in the traditional sense, the parallel port found in many computers can be used to connect a wide range of peripherals, including hard drives, scanners, and even network adapters. Linux support for parallel port devices is extensive, both in terms of the drivers found in the kernel and the ones provided by supporting projects. There is no central authority or project, however, that directs Linux's support for parallel port devices, since the parallel port is a ubiquitous component of computer systems. Instead, there are good resources that describe which devices are supported. These include the Hardware Compatibility HOWTO found at the LDP and the *Linux Parallel Port Home Page* found at *http://www.torque.net/linux-pp.html*. It is worth noting that Linux supports the IEEE1284 standard that defines how parallel port communication with external devices is carried out.

As the parallel port can be used for many purposes besides attaching external devices, I will discuss parallel port programming when explaining the use of the parallel port as in an I/O interface in "I/O."

SCSI

The *Small Computer Systems Interface* (SCSI) was introduced by Shugart Associates and eventually evolved into a series of standards developed and maintained by a series of standard bodies, including ANSI, ITIC, NCITS, and T10. Although mainly thought of as a high-throughput interface for hard drives for high-end workstations and servers, SCSI is a general interface that can be used to connect various hardware peripherals. Only a small segment of embedded systems ever use SCSI devices, though. These systems are typically high-end embedded systems such as the CompactPCI-based high-availability systems discussed earlier. In those cases, a CompactPCI SCSI controller inserted in the CompactPCI backplane provides an interface to the SCSI devices.

If you consider using SCSI in an embedded system, note that although Linux supports a wide range of SCSI controllers and devices, many prominent kernel developers believe that the kernel's SCSI code requires major work or even a complete rewrite. This doesn't mean that you shouldn't use SCSI devices with Linux. It is only a warning so that you plan your project's future updates in light of such possible modifications to the kernel's SCSI layer. At the time of this writing, work on the SCSI code has not yet started. It is expected that such work would be undertaken during the 2.5 development series of the kernel. For now, the SCSI hardware supported by Linux can be found in the Hardware Compatibility HOWTO from the LDP. As with the parallel port, there is no single reference point containing all information regarding Linux's support for SCSI, since the SCSI interface is an established technology with a very large user base.

Discussion of the kernel's SCSI device drivers architecture can be found at *http://www.torque.net/sg/*, at *http://www.andante.org/scsi.html*, and in the Linux 2.4 SCSI subsystem HOWTO from the LDP. Information regarding SCSI programming in Linux is available in the Linux SCSI Programming HOWTO from LDP. This should be the starting point for the development of any SCSI driver for Linux, along with the *Linux Device Drivers* book by O'Reilly. For a broad discussion about SCSI, *The Book of SCSI: I/O For The Millennium* by Gary Field and Peter Ridge (No Starch Press) is a good start. As with other standards, there are always official standards documents provided by the standard bodies, but again, such documentation often makes for dry reading material.

USB

The *Universal Serial Bus* (USB) was developed and is maintained by a group of companies forming the *USB Implementers Forum* (USB-IF). Initially developed to replace such fragmented and slow connection interfaces as the parallel and serial ports traditionally used to connect peripherals to PCs, USB has rapidly established itself as the interface of choice for peripherals by providing inexpensive ease of use and **high** speed throughput. Although mainly a mainstream device-oriented bus, USB is increasingly appearing in hardware used in embedded systems, such as SBCs and SoCs from several manufacturers.

USB devices are connected in a tree-like fashion. The root is called the *root hub* and is usually the main board to which all USB devices and nonroot hubs are connected. The root hub is in charge of all the devices connected to it, directly or through secondary hubs. A limitation of this is that computers cannot be linked in any form of networking using direct USB cabling.[*]

---

[*] Some manufacturers actually provide some form of host-to-host link via USB, but the standard was not intended to accommodate this type of setup. There are also USB network adapters, including Ethernet adapters, that can be used to connect the computers to a common network.

Support within Linux for behaving as a USB root hub[*] is quite mature and extensive, comparing positively to the commercial OSes that support USB. Although most hardware vendors don't ship Linux drivers with their USB peripherals, many have helped Linux developers create USB drivers by providing hardware specifications. Also, as with other hardware components, many Linux drivers have been developed in spite of their manufacturers' unwillingness to provide the relevant specifications. The main component of Linux's support for USB is provided by the USB stack in the kernel. The kernel also includes drivers for the USB devices supported by Linux. User tools are also available to manage USB devices. The user tools and the complete list of supported devices is available through the *Linux USB* project web site at *http://www.linux-usb.org/*.

Support within Linux for behaving as a USB *device*[†] is limited in comparison to its support for behaving as a USB root hub. While some systems running Linux, such as the iPAQ, can already behave as devices, there is no general agreed-upon framework yet for adding USB device capabilities to the Linux kernel.

Development of USB drivers is covered by the *Programming Guide for Linux USB Device Drivers* by Detlef Fliegl, available through the Linux USB project web site. The *Linux Device Drivers* book also provides guidelines on how to write Linux USB drivers. There are a number of books that discuss USB, which you can find by looking at the various online bookstores. However, the consensus among developers and online book critics seems to indicate that the best place to start, as well as the best reference, is the original USB specification available online from the USB-IF.

IEEE1394 (FireWire)

FireWire is a trademark owned by Apple for a technology they designed in the late 80s/early 90s. They later submitted their work to the IEEE and it formed the basis of what eventually became IEEE standard 1394. Much like USB, IEEE1394 enables devices to be connected using simple and inexpensive hardware interfaces. Because of their similarities, IEEE1394 and USB are often considered together. In terms of speed, however, it is clear that IEEE1394's architecture is much more capable than USB of accommodating throughput-demanding devices, such as digital cameras and external hard drives. Recent updates to the USB standard have reduced the gap, but IEEE1394 still has a clear advantage in regards to currently existing high-throughput devices and future capabilities. Although only a small number of embedded systems actually use IEEE1394, it is likely that the need for such a technology will increase with the demand in throughput.

---

[*] Whereby Linux is responsible for all USB devices connected to it.

[†] Whereby Linux is just another USB device connected to a USB root hub, which may or may not be running Linux.

In contrast to USB, IEEE1394 connections do not require a root node. Rather, connections can be made either in a daisy-chain fashion or using an IEEE1394 hub. Also, unlike SCSI, connections do not need any termination. It is also possible to connect two or more computers directly using an IEEE1394, which isn't possible with USB. To take advantage of this capability, there is even an RFC specifying how to implement IP over IEEE1394. This provides an inexpensive and high-speed network connection for IEEE1394-enabled computers.

Linux's support for IEEE1394 isn't as extensive as that provided by some commercial OSes, but it is mature enough to enable the practical, every day use of quite a number of IEEE1394 hardware devices. The kernel sources contain the code required to support IEEE1394, but the most up-to-date code for the IEEE1394 subsystem and the relevant user utilities can be found at the *IEEE1394 for Linux* project web site at *http://www.linux1394.org/*. The list of supported devices can be found in the compatibility section of the web site. The number and types of devices supported by Linux's IEEE1394 can only increase in the future.

Support for running an IP network over IEEE1394 in Linux is currently in its infancy. In due time, this may become a very efficient way of debugging embedded Linux systems because of the quantity of data that can be exchanged between the host and the target.

Documentation on how to use the IEEE1394 subsystem under Linux with supported hardware can be found on the IEEE1394 for Linux project web site. The web site also includes links to documentation regarding the various specifications surrounding IEEE1394. The main standard itself is available from the IEEE and is therefore expensive for a single individual to purchase. Although the standard will be a must for any extensive work on IEEE1394, the *FireWire System Architecture* book by Don Anderson (Addison Wesley) is a good place to start.

GPIB

The *General-Purpose Interface Bus* (GPIB) takes its roots in HP's HP-IB bus, which was born at the end of the 1960s and is still being used in engineering and scientific applications. In the process of maturing, GPIB became the IEEE488 standard and was revised as late as 1992. Many devices that are used for data acquisition and analysis are, in fact, equipped with a GPIB interface. With the advent of mainstream hardware in this field of application, many GPIB hardware adapters have been made available for such mainstream hardware and for PCs in particular.

GPIB devices are connected together using a shielded cable that may have stackable connectors at both ends. Connectors are "stackable" in the sense that a connector on one end of a cable has the appropriate hardware interface to allow for another connector to be attached to it, which itself allows another connector to be attached. If, for instance, a cable is used to connect a computer to device *A*, the connector attached to *A* can be used to attach the connector of another cable going from *A* to device *B*.

Though the kernel itself does not contain drivers for any GPIB adapter, there is a Linux GPIB project. The project has had a troubled history, however. It started as part of the Linux Lab Project* found at *http://www.linux-lab.org/*. After some initial development and a few releases, which are still available at *ftp://ftp.llp.fu-berlin.de/LINUX-LAB/IEEE488/*, development stopped. The package remained unmaintained for a number of years, until Frank Mori Hess recently restarted the project in a new location, *http://linux-gpib.sourceforge.net/*, and updated the package to the 2.4.x kernel series. The package currently provides kernel drivers, a user-space library compatible with National Instrument's own GPIB library, and language bindings for Perl and Python. The package supports hardware from HP, Keithley, National Instruments, and other manufacturers. The complete list of supported hardware is included in the *devices.txt* file found in the package's sources and on the project's web site.

Using this package, GPIB buses are visible from user space as */dev/gpib0*, */dev/gpib1*, and so on. Programming the bus to interface with the attached devices involves knowing their GPIB addresses. The */etc/gpib.conf* file makes it easier to configure the addresses used by the attached devices. The file must be tailored to match your configuration. The installation and the operation of the package components are documented along with the GPIB library functions in the *Linux-GPIB User's Guide* included with the package.

I²C

Initially introduced by Philips to enable communication between components inside TV sets, the *Inter-Integrated Circuit* (I²C) bus can be found in many embedded devices of all sizes and purposes. As with other similar small-scale buses such as *SPI†* and *MicroWire*, I²C is a simple serial bus that enables the exchange of limited amounts of data among the IC components of an embedded system. There is a broad range of I²C-capable devices on the market, including LCD drivers, EEPROMs, DSPs, and so on. Because of its simplicity and its hardware requirements, I²C can be implemented either in software or in hardware.

Connecting devices using I²C requires only two wires, one with a clock signal, serial clock (SCL), and the other with the actual data, serial data (SDA). All devices on an I²C bus are connected using the same wire pair. The device initiating a transaction on the bus becomes the bus master and communicates with slaves using an addressing scheme. Although I²C supports multiple masters, most implementations have only one master.

---

* The Linux Lab Project is actually much more broad than GPIB. Its aim, as stated on their site, is to provide a comprehensive set of GPL software tools for all "Linux users dealing with automation, process control, engineering and scientific stuff."

† Though there is some SPI support in Linux, it is limited to a few boards. There is, in fact, no framework providing architecture-independent SPI support.

The main kernel tree includes support for I2C, a number of devices that use I2C, and the related *System Management Bus* (SMBus). Due to the heavy use of I2C by hardware monitoring sensor devices, the I2C support pages are hosted on the Linux hardware monitoring project web site at *http://www2.lm-sensors.nu/~lm78/*. The site includes a number of links, documentation, and the most recent I2C development code. Most importantly, it contains a list of the I2C devices supported along with the appropriate driver to use for each device.

Apart from the documentation included with the kernel about I2C and the links and documentation available on the hardware sensors web site, information regarding the bus and related specification can be obtained from Philips' web site at *http://www.semiconductors.philips.com/buses/i2c/*. Also of interest in understanding the bus, the protocol, and its applications is the I2C FAQ maintained by Vincent Himpe, found at *http://www.ping.be/~ping0751/i2cfaq/i2cfaq.htm*.

I/O

Input and output (I/O) are central to the role of any computerized device. As with other OSes, Linux supports a wide range of I/O devices. The following does not pretend to be a complete run-down of all of them. For such a compilation, you may want to read through the Hardware Compatibility HOWTO available from LDP. Instead, the following concentrates on the way the different types of I/O devices are supported by Linux, either by the kernel or by user applications.

Some of the I/O devices discussed are supported in two forms by the kernel, first by a native driver that handles the device's direct connection to the system, and second through the USB layer to which the device may be attached. There are, for instance, PS/2 keyboards and parallel port printers and there are USB keyboards and USB printers. Because USB has already been discussed earlier, and in-depth discussion of Linux's USB stack would require a lengthy text of its own, I will cover only the support provided by Linux to the devices directly attached to the system. Note, however, that USB drivers for similar devices tend to rely on the infrastructure already available in Linux to support the native devices. A USB serial adapter driver, for example, relies on the same facilities as the traditional serial driver, in addition to the USB stack.

Serial Port

The serial port is arguably every embedded system developer's best friend (or her worst enemy, depending on her past experience with this ubiquitous interface). Many embedded systems are developed and debugged using an RS232 serial link between the host and the target. Sometimes, PCBs are laid out to accommodate a serial port, but only development versions of the boards ever include the actual connector, while production systems are shipped without it. The simplicity of the RS232 interface has encouraged its wide-spread use and adoption, even though its bandwidth is rather limited compared to other means of transmission. Note that there are other serial interfaces besides RS232, some of which are less noise-sensitive and therefore more adapted to industrial environments. The hardware serial protocol, however, isn't as important as the actual programming interface provided by the serial device's hardware.

Since RS232 is a hardware interface, the kernel doesn't need to support RS232 itself. Rather, the kernel includes drivers to the chips that actually enact RS232 communication, Universal Asynchronous Receiver-Transmitters (UARTs). UARTs vary from one architecture to another, although some UARTs, such as the 16550, are used on more than one architecture.

The main serial (UART) driver in the kernel is *drivers/char/serial.c*. Some architectures, such as the SH, have other serial drivers to accommodate their hardware. Some architecture-independent peripheral cards also provide serial interfaces. As with other Unix systems, nonetheless, serial devices in Linux are uniformly accessed as terminal devices, regardless of the underlying hardware and related drivers. The corresponding device entries start with */dev/ttyS0* and can go up to */dev/ttyS191*. In most cases, however, there are only a handful of serial device entries in a system's */dev* directory.

Serial port basics, setup, and configuration are discussed in the Serial HOWTO available from LDP. Programming the serial port in Linux is discussed in the Serial Programming HOWTO from LDP. Since serial port programming is actually terminal programming, any good reference on Unix systems programming would be a good start. Worthy of note is Richard Stevens' *Advanced Programming in the UNIX Environment*, which is one of the most widely recognized works on the subject of Unix systems programming, including terminal I/O.

Parallel Port

In comparison to the serial port, the parallel port is seldom an important part of an embedded system. Unless the embedded system is actually a PC-style SBC, the parallel port is, in fact, rarely even part of the system's hardware. In some cases, a parallel port is used because the embedded system has to drive a printer or some sort of external device, but with the advent of USB and IEEE1394, this use is bound to diminish.

One area of embedded systems development where the parallel port fits quite nicely, however, is simple multibit I/O. When debugging, for instance, you can easily attach a set of LEDs to the parallel ports' pins and use those LEDs to indicate a position in the code. The trick is to insert a set of parallel port output commands in different portions of the code and to use the LEDs to identify the last position reached prior to machine lockup. This is possible, because the parallel ports' hardware keeps the last value output to it unchanged regardless of the state of the rest of the system. The *Linux Device Drivers* book provides a more detailed description of how to use the parallel port as a simple I/O interface and how to set up an LED array to display the parallel port's output.

Linux supports parallel port I/O through a set of three layers. At the middle level is the architecture-independent parport driver. This driver provides a central management facility for the parallel port resources. This middle-level driver is not visible from user space and is not accessible as an entry in the */dev* directory. Low-level drivers that control the actual hardware register their presence with this driver to make their services accessible to higher-level drivers. The latter may provide a number of different functions. Both low- and middle-level drivers are found in the *drivers/parport* directory of the kernel sources.

The most common high-level driver is the line printer driver, which enables user applications to use a printer directly attached to the system's parallel port. The first line printer device is visible in user space as */dev/lp0*, the second as */dev/lp1*, and so on. Some other high-level drivers use the parallel port as an extension bus to access an external device attached to the system, as discussed in "Parallel Port." They all use the parallel port middle-level driver and are visible, in one way or another, as entries in */dev*. Finally, the parallel port itself is accessible natively from user space via the user-space parallel port driver, which is seen as */dev/parportX*, where X is the number of the parallel port. This latter driver is in the *drivers/char/ppdev.c* file in the kernel sources.

Apart from the usual PC architecture references mentioned earlier and the device drivers book, Linux parallel port subsystem and API are documented in *The Linux 2.4 Parallel Port Subsystem* document available from *http://people.redhat.com/twaugh/parport/* and in the *Documentation* directory of the kernel sources.

Modem

Embedded systems that use a modem to call a data center are quite common. Alarm systems, bank machines, and remote-monitoring hardware are all examples of embedded systems that need to communicate with a central system to fulfill their primary purposes. The goals are different, but all these systems use conventional modems to interface with the POTS (plain old telephone system) to access a remote host.

Modems in Linux are seen as serial ports, which is very much the same way they are seen across a variety of OSes, including Unix. As such, they are accessible through the appropriate serial device */dev* entry and are controlled by the same driver as the native serial UARTs, regardless of whether they are internal or external. This support, however, applies only to real modems.

Recently, a sort of modem called a WinModem has appeared in the PC market. WinModems contain only the bare minimal hardware that make up a modem and are capable of providing real modem services only because of software that runs on the OS. As the name implies, these modems are mainly targeted to systems running Windows. They work fine with that OS, because their vendors provide the appropriate drivers. With Linux, however, they do not work, because they don't contain real modem hardware and the kernel can't use its serial driver to operate them.

To provide support for these types of (handicapped) devices, a number of projects have sprung up to develop the necessary software packages. A central authority on these projects is the Linmodems web site at *http://www.linmodems.org/*. The site provides documentation, news, and links to the various WinModem support projects. At the time of this writing, however, there is no body of code that provides uniform support for the various WinModems.

Real modem setup and operation is described in the Modem HOWTO from the LDP. Linmodem setup and operation is described in the Linmodem HOWTO from the LDP. Since modems are serial ports, the documentation mentioned above regarding serial ports also applies to modems.

Data Acquisition

As described in "Data acquisition module" in Chapter 1, DAQ is at the basis of any process automation system. Any modern factory or scientific lab is filled with DAQ equipment linked, in one way or another, to computers running data analysis software. Typically, as described earlier, the events occurring in the real world are measured by means of transducers, which convert a physical phenomenon into an electrical value. These values are then sampled using DAQ hardware and are thereafter accessible to software.

There is no standard interface in Unix, or any other OS for that matter, for interfacing with data acquisition hardware.* Comedi, the Linux control and measurement device interface, is the main package for interfacing with DAQ hardware. Comedi is found at *http://www.comedi.org/* and contains device drivers for a great number of DAQ boards. The complete list of boards supported is found in the *Supported hardware* section of the web site.

Along with providing drivers for DAQ hardware, the Comedi project includes Comedilib, a user-space library that provides a unified API to interface with all DAQ hardware, regardless of model or manufacturer. This is very useful, because it allows you to develop the analysis software independently of the underlying hardware, and avoid being locked in to a particular vendor.

Similarly, Kcomedilib, a kernel module providing an API similar to Comedilib, enables other kernel modules, which could be real-time tasks, to have access to the DAQ hardware.

No discussion about DAQ would be complete without covering some of the most well-known commercial (proprietary) packages used along with DAQ, such as LabVIEW, Matlab, and Simulink. Given the popularity of Linux in this field, all three packages have been made available for Linux by their respective vendors. Note, however, that

---

* DAQ hardware may actually take a number of forms. It can be an Ethernet-enabled device, a PCI card, or use some other type of connection. However, most DAQ devices used with workstations connect through some standard interface such as ISA, PCI, or PCMCIA.

there are a number of packages in development that aim at providing open source replacements for these packages. *Scilab* and *Octave*, for instance, are Matlab replacements found at *http://www-rocq.inria.fr/scilab/* and *http://www.octave.org/*, respectively.

Documentation regarding the installation and configuration of Comedi can be found on the project's web site along with examples. The site also includes a number of useful links to other Linux DAQ–related sites. Documentation regarding the closed-source packages can be found on their vendors' web sites.

Although I haven't covered them, some DAQ hardware vendors do provide drivers for their hardware, either in open source form or under a proprietary license. When evaluating whether to use such drivers, it is important to ponder future vendor support so you don't find yourself trapped with dead and unmaintained code. Even when source is available under an open source or free software license, be sure to evaluate its quality to ensure that you can actually maintain it if the vendor decides to drop its support.

Process Control

As with DAQ, process control is at the basis of any process automation system. As I said in "Control module" in Chapter 1, there are many ways to control a process, the most common being the use of PLCs. More recently, mainstream hardware such as PCs have been used for process automation and control.

Linux can be used for control in many ways. First, you can use serial or parallel ports to drive external hardware such as step motors. This involves serial and parallel port programming, which I covered earlier. There is no standard software package to interface with externally controlled hardware in this manner, such packages or APIs are specific to the application being designed.

Examples of serial or parallel ports for control are readily available both in print and online. Sometimes these examples are oriented towards the PC running DOS or Windows. In that case, they need to be adapted to Linux and the facilities it provides. If you need such a port, you will find the *Linux Device Drivers* book to be helpful.

Second, external processes can be controlled using specialized boards attached to the computer through a peripheral bus. In this case, you need a driver specific to the board being used. The Comedi package mentioned earlier provides support for some control boards. Also, control board manufacturers are becoming increasingly aware of the demand for Linux drivers for their hardware and are providing them accordingly.

Last, there is an effort underway to let a standard Linux system replace traditional PLCs. The project, *Machine Automation Tools LinuxPLC* (MAT LPLC), located at *http://mat.sourceforge.net/*, provides PLC language interpreters, hardware drivers, a PLC module synchronization library, example modules, and a GUI interface to visualize the controlled process. Building a PLC using LPLC consists of programming independent modules, either in C or an interpreted language such as "ladder logic," that are synchronized through LPLC facilities such as shared memory. Because each module is an independent process, you can add and remove control modules with ease.

The LPLC team provides information regarding the use and programming of their package on their project's web site. Although the project is still in its early stages, the development team lists practical examples showing the package's usability in real scenarios.

Home Automation

As with DAQ and process control, home automation is a vast domain. I will not attempt to cover the basics of home automation or the required background, because other authors have documented them. If you are new to home automation or would like to have more information about this field, you can find an extensive list of links and reference material in Dan Hoehnen's Home Automation Index located at *http:// www.homeautomationindex.com/*.

One technology often used in home automation is X10 Power Line Carrier (PLC)* developed in the 1970s by Pico Electronics in Scotland. Although other protocols have been put forward by manufacturers, X10 remains the dominant protocol in home automation.

Pico later formed X10 corporation as a joint venture with BSR. To this day, X10 corporation still sells X10 technology components. In the meantime however, the original X10 patent expired in 1997. Hence, many manufacturers currently provide X10-compatible equipment. The X10 PLC protocol enables transmitters and receivers to communicate using short RF bursts over power line wiring. There is therefore no need for additional wiring, because all communication occurs on the house's existing electrical wiring.

Unlike other fields in which Linux is used, there is no central open source home automation project for Linux. Instead, there are a number of active projects being developed independently. Furthermore, there is no particular home automation driver within the kernel. The required software components are all part of the various packages distributed by the home automation projects.

The following is a list of Linux-compatible open source home automation projects:

MisterHouse
> MisterHouse is a complete home automation solution. It includes a user interface and X10 interface software, can be controlled using a variety of voice recognition packages, and can interface with voice synthesis software. MisterHouse is entirely written in Perl and can therefore be used with a number of OSes, including Linux. MisterHouse is available for download under the terms of the GPL from the project's web site with complete documentation at *http://misterhouse. sourceforge.net/*.

---

* X10 PLC should not be confused with the PLCs used in process automation. These are actual control devices unrelated to the X10 PLC hardware protocol.

ALICE

The *Automation Light Interface Control Environment* (ALICE) provides a user interface and software to interact with X10 devices. ALICE is written in Java and runs on any appropriate JVM, including the Linux JVM available from the Blackdown project. ALICE is distributed under the terms of the GPL with documentation from the project's web site at *http://jhome.sourceforge.net/*.

HEYU!

HEYU! is a command-line utility that enables the control of X10 devices. It is available from the project's web site at *http://heyu.tanj.com/heyu/*. HEYU! is distributed under a special license similar to other open source licenses. You will find the exact wording of the license in the source files' headers.

Neil Cherry has put together an impressive repertoire of resources and links about home automation and Linux home automation projects. His Linux Home Automation web site is located at *http://mywebpages.comcast.net/ncherry/*. Neil also maintains the Linux Home Automation project at *http://linuxha.sourceforge.net/*. It provides a number of links and documentation related to Linux home automation.

Keyboard

Most embedded systems are not equipped with keyboards. Some may have a limited input interface, but keyboards are usually considered a luxury found only on traditional workstation and server configurations. In fact, the idea that an embedded system may have a keyboard would be viewed as awkward by most traditional embedded system designers. Nonetheless, recent breeds of web-enabled and consumer-oriented embedded systems have some form of keyboard attached to them.

As with other Unix-like systems, communication with the user in Linux is done by means of a terminal, in the Unix tty sense, where a keyboard is used for input and a console for output. This is of course a simplification of the very complex world of Unix terminal I/O, but it will suffice for the current discussion. Hence, all keyboard input is considered by the kernel as input to a terminal. The conversion from the actual data inputted by the user to actual terminal input may involve many different layers of kernel drivers, but all keyboard input is eventually fed to the terminal I/O driver.

In a PC, for instance, keyboard input is processed sequentially by the code found in the following files of the *drivers/char* directory of the kernel sources: *pc_keyb.c*, *keyboard.c*, and *tty_io.c*. The last file in the sequence is the terminal I/O driver. For systems based on other architectures, the *Input layer* mechanism is usually used. This mechanism specifies a standard way for input devices such as keyboards, mice, and joysticks to interface with the system. In the case of USB keyboards, for instance, the input processing sequence is the following, starting from the *drivers* directory of the kernel: *usb/usbkbd.c*, *input/keybdev.c*, *char/keyboard.c*, and again, *char/tty_io.c*.

There are other ways to provide input to a terminal, apart from the use of a physically connected keyboard. Terminal input is also possible through remote login, serial-linking between computers, and in the case of PDAs, hand-writing recognition software. In each case, accessing the character input programmatically requires terminal I/O programming.

Mouse

Embedded systems that have a user interface often offer some form of touch-based interaction. Whether it be a bank terminal or a PDA, the input generated by the user's touch of a screen area is treated the same way as input from a conventional workstation mouse. In this sense, many embedded systems have a "mouse." In fact, there are many more embedded systems that provide a mouse-like pointer interface than there are that provide a keyboard interface.

Since traditional Unix terminals do not account for mouse input, information about the pointer device's input doesn't follow the same path as data about keyboard activity. Instead, the pointer device is seen on most Linux systems as */dev/mouse*, which itself is often a symbolic link to the actual pointer device. The device can be polled and read to obtain information regarding the pointer device's movements and events. Although the name of the entry in */dev* where the pointer is found is usually constant, the format of the data retrieved from the device varies according to the type of device. There are, in fact, many mouse *protocols* that define different input formats. Note that the protocol used by a mouse is not directly tied to its manufacturer or even the type of physical connection used to link it to the system. This is why the configuration of the X server, for example, requires the user to specify a protocol for the mouse device. The kernel, on the other hand, has drivers that manage the actual physical link between the mouse and the system.

Any programming that involves a pointer device would require an understanding of the protocol used by the device. Fortunately, a number of libraries and environments already have this level of decoding implemented, and easy-to-use APIs are provided to obtain and react to pointer input.

Display

Blinking lights, LEDs, and alpha-numeric LCDs are the traditional visual apparel of embedded systems. With the growing incursion of embedded devices in many facets of our daily lives, including service automation, there is a push to replace such traditional display methods with visually rich interfaces. In other areas of embedded systems deployment, such as factory automation or avionics, visually rich interfaces have been the norm for quite a while.

As I mentioned above, traditional Unix systems provide output in the form of terminal consoles. This, however, is too rudimentary of an interface for today's demands. If nothing else, consoles can output only text. Other more elaborate interfaces are needed when building graphic interfaces, which may include some form of windowing system.

With Linux there are many ways to control and program a display. Some of these involve kernel support, but most rely mainly on code running in user space, hence favoring system stability and facilitating modularity. The most common way to provide a graphical interface with Linux is, of course, the X Window System, but there are other packages that may be preferable in certain circumstances.

Sound

Beep, Beep, Beep... that's what Sputnik emitted and that's pretty similar to what most embedded systems still sound like. Even the very graphic-rich avionics and factory automation systems don't have more sound output, except maybe in terms of decibel. Sound-rich embedded systems are, however, becoming more and more popular with the proliferation of consumer and service-oriented devices.

Unix, however, was never designed to accommodate sound. Over the years, a number of schemes appeared to provide sound support. In Linux, the main sound device is usually */dev/dsp*. Other audio-hardware related devices are also available for other sound capabilities such as */dev/mixer* and */dev/sequencer*.

Contrary to many other parts of development in Linux, audio is an area that has yet to mature. There are two independent projects that provide both support for sound hardware and an API to program the hardware.

The first, and oldest, is the *Open Sound System* (OSS) introduced by Hannu Savolainen. Most sound card drivers found in kernel releases prior to 2.5 are based on the OSS architecture and API put forth by Hannu. Over the years, these APIs changed and have been "cleaned up" by Alan Cox. Nonetheless, many consider them to be ill-adapted for modern audio hardware. The OSS drivers and API are actually a publicly available subset of a commercial product from Hannu's company, 4Front Technologies, which has broader support for hardware and a richer API. Documentation regarding OSS programming can be found at *http://www.opensound.com/pguide/*.

The second audio project is the *Advanced Linux Sound Architecture* (ALSA). ALSA's aims are to provide a completely modularized sound driver package and offer a superior environment to OSS, both in terms of the API and in terms of management infrastructure. In terms of hardware support, the ALSA project supports hardware not supported by the OSS. Since the ALSA project and all its components have always been open source, all documentation and source is available online at the project's web site, *http://www.alsa-project.org/*.

It was expected that the ALSA project would at some point replace the OSS content in the kernel. Starting with Linux 2.5, ALSA has indeed been integrated in the kernel, although the OSS drivers have been kept for the time being. As with other areas of Linux support, audio support varies with the target architecture. The more mainstream the architecture, the better the support.

Printer

As with many mainstream peripherals, printers don't usually grace embedded systems. There are, however, exceptions. An embedded web server that supports printing is an example of an embedded system that needs an OS with printer support. Traditional embedded system developers would usually consider "embedded web server" to be an oxymoron, but devices that provide these types of packaged services are more and more common and involve development methods similar to those of more constrained embedded devices.

Conventional Unix printer support is rather outdated in comparison to the support provided by many other OSes. Linux's printer support is, unfortunately, largely based on other Unix printing systems. There are, nonetheless, a number of projects that aim at facilitating and modernizing printing services in Linux and Unix in general.

To understand how document printing and printer support is implemented in Linux, let us review the steps a document generally goes through, starting from the user's print request to the actual printing of the document by the printer:

1. A user submits a document for printing. This may be done either at the command line or via a menu in a graphical application; there is little difference between them in Linux. Usually, printable output of Unix programs is in *PostScript* (PS) format and is sent as such to the printer. As not all printers available on the market are PS capable, PS output has to be converted to a format understandable by the actual printer being used. This conversion is done at a later stage, if necessary.

2. The document, along with the user's print options, is stored in a queue dedicated to a single printer. This queue may be either local, if the printer is directly attached to the system, or remote, if the printer is attached to a server on the network. In both cases, the process is transparent to the user.

3. A spooling system takes care of the print queue and queues the document for printing whenever the printer becomes available. It is at this stage that the conversion of the document from PS or another format to the actual format recognized by the printer takes place. The conversion is done using a set of filters, each taking care of the conversion of one type of format to another. The most important of these is the PS-to-printer filter, which is specific to each type of printer.

Depending on the print-management software being used, these steps may vary slightly. There are currently five different print-management packages available for Linux: LPD, PDQ, LPRng, CUPS, and PPR. LPD is the traditional package found on most distributions. The other packages are making inroads and are slowly replacing LPD. Whichever package is used, however, the final conversion from PS to printer format is usually done by GhostScript,* a very important package that enables the viewing

---

* GhostScript has a large memory footprint and may not be suitable for some small-sized embedded Linux systems.

and manipulation of PS files. Once this conversion is done, the output is finally fed to the actual printer device, whether it be a parallel port printer or a USB printer.

Keep in mind that all the work is done in user space. The kernel drivers get involved only at the very end to feed the filtered output to the actual printer.

If you intend to add printer support to your embedded system, I suggest you read up on Unix printer management from any of the good conventional Unix or Linux systems management books available. *Running Linux* by Welsh, Dalheimer, and Kaufman (O'Reilly) provides a good description of how printer setup is done in Linux when using LPD. For bleeding edge information regarding Linux printing, take a look at *http://www.linuxprinting.org/*, the main resource on the subject. On that same web site, you will find the Printing HOWTO, which contains extensive information about the different print-management packages, their operation, and relevant links.

Storage

All embedded systems require at least one form of persistent storage to start even the earliest stages of the boot process. Most systems, including embedded Linux systems, continue to use this same initial storage device for the rest of their operation, either to execute code or to access data. In comparison to traditional embedded software, however, Linux's use imposes greater requirements on the embedded system's storage hardware, both in terms of size and organization.

The size requirements were discussed in Chapter 1, and an overview of the typical storage device configurations was provided in Chapter 2. We will discuss the actual organization further in Chapters 7 and 8. For the moment, let us take a look at the persistent storage devices supported by Linux. In particular, we'll discuss the level of support provided for these devices and their typical use with Linux.

Memory Technology Devices

In Linux terminology, memory technology devices (MTDs) include all memory devices, such as conventional ROM, RAM, flash, and M-Systems' DiskOnChip (DOC). As explained by Michael Barr in *Programming Embedded Systems in C and C++* (O'Reilly), such devices have their own capabilities, particularities, and limitations. Hence, to program and use an MTD device in their systems, embedded system developers traditionally use tools and methods specific to that type of device.

To avoid, as much as possible, having different tools for different technologies and to provide common capabilities among the various technologies, the Linux kernel includes the MTD subsystem. This provides a unified and uniform layer that enables a seamless combination of low-level MTD chip drivers with higher-level interfaces called *user modules*, as seen in Figure 3-1. These "user modules" should not be confused with kernel modules or any sort of user-land software abstraction. The term "MTD user module" refers to software modules within the kernel that enable access to the low-level MTD chip drivers by providing recognizable interfaces and abstractions to the higher levels of the kernel or, in some cases, to user space.

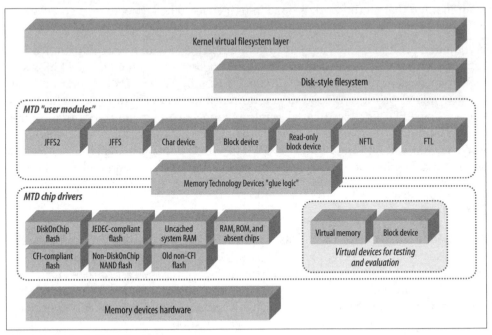

Figure 3-1. The MTD subsystem

MTD chip drivers register with the MTD subsystem by providing a set of predefined callbacks and properties in the `mtd_info` structure to the `add_mtd_device( )` function. The callbacks an MTD driver has to provide are called by the MTD subsystem to carry out operations such as erase, read, write, and sync. The following is a list of MTD chip drivers already available:

DiskOnChip

These are the drivers for M-Systems' DOC technology. Currently, Linux supports the DOC 1000, DOC 2000, and DOC Millennium.

Common Flash Interface (CFI)

CFI is a specification developed by Intel, AMD, and other flash manufacturers. All CFI-compliant flash components have their configuration and parameters stored directly on the chip. Hence, the software interfaces for their detection, configuration, and use are standardized. The kernel includes code to detect and support CFI chips.

As the CFI specification allows for different commands to be made available by different chips, the kernel also includes support for two types of command sets implemented by two different chip families, Intel/Sharp and AMD/Fujitsu.

JEDEC

The JEDEC Solid State Technology Association (*http://www.jedec.org/*) is a standardization body. Among its standards are a set of standards for flash chips. It is also responsible for handing out identification numbers for such devices. Although the JEDEC flash standard is rendered obsolete by CFI, some chips still feature JEDEC compliance. The MTD subsystem supports the probing and configuration of such devices.

Non-DOC NAND flash

The most popular form of packaging for NAND flash is M-Systems' DOC devices. There are, however, other types of NAND flash chips on the market. The MTD subsystem supports a number of such devices using a separate driver from the DOC drivers. For a complete list of the devices supported by this driver, look in the *include/linux/mtd/nand-ids.h* file in the kernel sources.

Old non-CFI flash

Some flash chips are not CFI compliant, and some aren't even JEDEC compliant. The MTD subsystem therefore provides drivers that manipulate such devices according to their manufacturers' specifications. The devices supported in this fashion are non-CFI AMD-compatible flash chips, pre-CFI Sharp chips, and non-CFI JEDEC devices. Keep in mind, however, that these drivers are not updated as frequently as the drivers for more commonly used devices such DOC or CFI memory devices.

RAM, ROM, and absent chips

The MTD subsystem provides drivers to access conventional RAM and ROM chips, mapped in a system's physical address space, as MTD devices. Since some of these chips may be connected to the system using a socket or some similar connector that lets you remove the chip, the MTD subsystem also provides a driver that can be used to preserve the registration order of the MTD device nodes in case one of the devices is removed and is therefore *absent* from the system.

Uncached RAM

If there is any system RAM that your CPU cannot cache, you can use this memory as an MTD device during normal system operation. Of course, the information stored on such a medium will be lost when the system's power is turned off.

Virtual devices for testing and evaluation

When adding or testing MTD support for your board's devices, you may sometimes want to test the operation of the user modules independently from the chip drivers. To this end, the MTD subsystem contains two MTD drivers that emulate real MTD hardware: a driver that emulates an MTD device using memory from the system's virtual address space, and another that emulates an MTD device using a normal block device.

Since there is no universally agreed upon physical address location for MTD devices, the MTD subsystem requires customized *mapping drivers*[*] to be able to see and manage the MTD devices present in a given system. As some systems and development boards have known MTD device configurations, the kernel contains a number of specific mapping drivers for a variety of such systems. It also contains a generic driver for accessing CFI flash chips on systems that have no specific mapping driver. If there are no appropriate mapping drivers for your system's memory devices, you may need to create a new one using existing ones as examples. The existing mapping drivers are found in the *drivers/mtd/maps/* directory of the kernel sources.

As with other kernel device drivers, an MTD chip driver can manage many instances of the same device. If you have two identical AMD CFI-compliant flash chips in your system, for instance, they might be managed as separate MTD devices by a single instance of the CFI driver, depending on their setup.[†] To further facilitate customization of the storage space available in MTD devices, the MTD subsystem also allows for memory devices to be divided into multiple partitions. Much like hard disk partitions, each MTD partition is then accessible as a separate MTD device and can store data in formats entirely different from those of other partitions on the same device. In practice, as we saw in Chapter 2, memory devices are often divided in many partitions, each serving a specific purpose.

Once the MTD chip drivers are properly configured for a system's memory devices, the storage space available on each MTD device can be managed by an MTD user module. The user module enforces a storage format on the MTD devices it manages, and it provides, as I said above, interfaces and abstractions recognized by higher-level kernel components. It is important to note that MTD user modules are not fully interoperable with all MTD drivers. In fact, certain MTD user modules may not be usable with certain MTD drivers because of technical or even legal limitations. At the time of this writing, for example, development is still under way to enable the JFFS2 user module to be used with NAND flash devices. Until recently, it was impossible to use the JFFS2 user module with any form of NAND flash, including DOC devices, because JFFS2 did not deal with NAND flash chip particularities. Work is underway to fix the situation, however, and JFFS2 may actually be usable with NAND devices by the time you read this. The following list describes the existing MTD user modules and their characteristics:

JFFS2

JFFS2 is a successor and a complete rewrite by Red Hat of the JFFS discussed below. As its name implies, the *Journalling Flash File System Version 2* (JFFS2) implements a journalling filesystem on the MTD device it manages. In contrast

---

[*] A mapping driver is a special kind of MTD driver whose main task is to provide MTD chip drivers with the physical location of the MTD devices in the system and a set of functions for accessing these physical devices.

[†] Identical chips placed on system buses are often arranged to appear as a single large chip.

with other memory device storage schemes, it does not attempt to provide a translation layer that enables the use of a traditional filesystem with the device. Instead, it implements a log-structured filesystem directly on the MTD device. The filesystem structure itself is recreated in RAM at mount time by JFFS2 through a scan of the MTD device's log content.

In addition to its log-structured filesystem, JFFS2 implements wear leveling and data compression on the MTD device it manages, while providing power down reliability.

Power down reliability is crucial to embedded systems, because they may lose power at any time. The system must then gracefully restart and be capable of restoring a filesystem's content without requiring outside intervention. If your Linux, or even Windows, workstation has ever lost power accidently, you probably had to wait for the system to check the filesystems' integrity upon rebooting and may have even been prompted to perform some checks manually. Usually, this is a situation that is not acceptable for an embedded system. JFFS2 avoids these problems; it can gracefully recuperate regardless of power failures. Note, however, that it does not guarantee rollback of interrupted filesystem operations. If an application had called write( ) to overwrite old data with new data, for example, it is possible that the old data may have been partially overwritten and that the new data was not completely committed. Both data sets are then lost. Your system should be built to check on startup for this type of failure.

Wear leveling is necessary, because flash devices have a limited number of erases per block, which is often 100,000 but may differ between manufacturers. Once this limit is reached, the block's correct operation is not guaranteed by the manufacturer. To avoid using some blocks more than others and thereby shortening the life of the device, JFFS2 implements an algorithm that ensures uniform usage of all the blocks on the flash device, hence leveling the wear of its blocks.

Because flash hardware is usually more expensive and slower than RAM hardware, it is desirable to compress the data stored on flash devices and then decompress it to RAM before using it. This is precisely what JFFS2 does. For this reason, *eXecute In Place* (XIP)* is not possible with JFFS2.

JFFS2 has been widely adopted as the filesystem of choice for MTD devices. The Familiar project, *http://familiar.handhelds.org/*, for instance, uses JFFS2 to manage the flash available in Compaq's iPAQ.

As I said earlier, though JFFS2 cannot currently be used with NAND devices, including DOC devices, this is under construction and may be available by the time your read this. Meanwhile, JFFS2 can be used with other types of MTD devices and is even sometimes used with CompactFlash devices, which actually behave as IDE hard drives connected to the system's IDE interface.

---

* XIP is the ability to execute code directly from ROM without copying it to RAM.

NFTL

The *NAND Flash Translation Layer* (NFTL) implements a virtual block device on NAND flash chips. As seen in Figure 3-1, a disk-style filesystem, such as FAT or ext2, must then be used to store and retrieve data from an NFTL-managed MTD device.

It is important to note that M-Systems holds patents on the algorithms implemented by NFTL and, as such, permits the use of these algorithms only with licensed DOC devices. Though NFTL is itself reliable in case of power failure, you would need to use a journalling filesystem over NFTL to make your system's storage power-failure proof. An embedded system that crashes while running ext2 over NFTL, for example, would require a filesystem integrity check on startup, much like a normal Linux workstation.

JFFS

The *Journalling Flash File System* (JFFS) was originally developed by Axis Communications AB in Sweden and was aimed at embedded systems as a crash/power down–safe filesystem. Though JFFS has reportedly been used with NAND devices—a feature likely to be available in JFFS2 by the time you read this—it has largely been replaced by JFFS2.

FTL

The *Flash Translation Layer* implements a virtual block device on NOR flash chips. As with NFTL, a "real" filesystem must then be used to manage the data on the FTL-handled device.

FTL, too, is subject to patents. In the U.S., it may be used only on PCMCIA hardware. Instead of using FTL on NOR flash chips, you may want to go with JFFS2 directly, as it is not hampered by any patents and is a better fit for the task.

Char device

This user module enables character device–like access to MTD devices. Using it, each MTD device can be directly manipulated as a character device, in the Unix sense. It is mostly useful for the initial setup of an MTD device. As we'll see in Chapter 7, there is a specific way in which reading and writing to this char device must be done for the data involved to be valid. Before writing to the char device, for example, it usually must be erased first.

Caching block device

This user module provides a block device interface to MTD devices. The usual workstation and server filesystems can then be used on these devices. Although this is of little use for production embedded systems, which require features such as those provided by JFFS2, this module is mainly useful for writing data to flash partitions without having to explicitly erase the content of the partition beforehand. It may also be used for setting up systems whose filesystems will be mounted read-only in the field.

This module is called the "caching" block device user module, because it works by caching blocks in RAM, modifying them as requested, erasing the proper MTD device block, and then rewriting the modified block. There is, of course, no power failure reliability to be found here.

Read-only block device

The read-only block device user module provides the exact same capabilities as the caching block device user module, except that no RAM caching is implemented. All filesystem content is therefore read-only.

As you can see, the MTD subsystem is quite rich and elaborate. Even though its use is complicated by the rules that govern the proper matching of MTD user modules with MTD chip drivers, it is fairly flexible and is effective in providing a uniform and unified access to memory devices. The Memory Technology Device Subsystem project web site is found at *http://www.linux-mtd.infradead.org/* and contains documentation regarding the programming API for implementing MTD user modules and MTD chip drivers. It also contains information regarding the MTD mailing list and a fairly elaborate MTD-JFFS-HOWTO by Vipin Malik.

In Chapter 7, we will continue our discussion of the MTD subsystem and will detail the setup and configuration instructions for using MTD devices in your embedded system.

ATA-ATAPI (IDE)

The *AT Attachment* (ATA)* was developed in 1986 by three companies: Imprimis, Western Digital, and Compaq. It was initially used only by Compaq but eventually became quite popular when Conner Peripherals began providing its IDE drives through retail stores. By 1994, ATA was an ANSI standard. Different versions of the standard have since been developed allowing faster transfer rates and enhanced capabilities. Along the way, the *ATA Packet Interface* (ATAPI) was developed by CD-ROM manufacturers with the help of Western Digital and Oak Technology. ATAPI allows for CD-ROM and tape devices to be accessible through the ATA interface using SCSI-like command packets. Today ATA and ATAPI are developed and maintained by ANSI, NCITS, and T13.

Although only a fraction of traditional embedded systems ever need a permanent storage media providing as much storage space as an IDE hard disk can, many embedded systems use a very popular ATA-compliant flash device, CompactFlash. Contrary to the flash devices discussed in "Memory Technology Devices," the CompactFlash's storage space can be accessed only using the ATA interface. Hence, from the software's perspective, and indeed from the hardware's perspective, it is indistinguishable from a small-sized IDE drive. Note that CompactFlash cards can also be

---

* Although it is often referred to as "IDE," which stands for *Integrated Drive Electronics*, "ATA" is the real name of this interface.

accessed through CompactFlash-to-PCMCIA adapters. We will discuss the use of CompactFlash devices with Linux further in Chapter 7. Meanwhile, keep in mind that not all CompactFlash devices have the proper characteristics for use in embedded systems. In particular, some CompactFlash devices do not tolerate power failure, and may be permanently damaged following such a failure.

In embedded Linux systems, IDE and most other types of disks are usually set up as in a workstation or server. Typically, the disk holds the OS bootloader, the root filesystem, and possibly a swap partition. In contrast to most workstations and servers, however, not all embedded system monitors and bootloaders are ATA-capable. In fact, as we'll see in Chapter 9, most bootloaders are not ATA/IDE-capable. If you want to use an IDE disk in your system and an ATA-capable monitor or bootloader is not present in your system's flash, you need to have the kernel present in flash or in ROM with the boot monitor so that it may be accessible at system startup. You then have to configure your boot monitor to use this kernel on startup in order to have access to the IDE disk. In this case, you can still configure your root filesystem and swap partition to be on the IDE disk.

Linux's support for the ATA interface is quite extensive and mature. The ATA subsystem, located in the *drivers/ide* directory of the kernel sources, includes support, and sometimes bug fixes, for many chipsets. This support spans many architectures. In addition, the kernel supports PCMCIA IDE devices and provides a SCSI-emulation driver for use with ATAPI devices. The latter can be used in conjunction with a SCSI driver to control an ATAPI device for which there is still no existing ATAPI native driver. Though it is no longer necessary since the 2.5 kernel development series, this functionality was mostly useful to users with workstations equipped with CD-RW drives, since the tools available to operate these devices in Linux used to require that the underlying hardware be SCSI.

Given the importance of ATA/IDE support, most modifications and updates posted to the kernel mailing list are directly integrated into the kernel. This contrasts with other subsystems where maintainers provide a separate up-to-date version through the subsystem's project web site, while the kernel contains a stable version that is updated every so often when the maintainers send a patch or, more commonly, a set of patches to Linus. There are, however, ATA/IDE-related tools, primarily *hdparm* and *fdisk*, maintained outside the kernel, mainly because they are user tools and are not required for the kernel's normal operation. *hdparm* gets and sets IDE hard disk parameters using the ioctl( ) commands supported by ATA/IDE drivers in the kernel. *fdisk* is used to view and modify disk partitions. If you have ever installed Linux on a workstation, you are probably already familiar with *fdisk*. Note that this utility is not limited to IDE hard disks and can be used with SCSI disks, too.

The main starting point for information on Linux's ATA/IDE capabilities is the *Linux ATA Development Project* web site located at *http://www.linux-ide.org/*. In addition to providing access to the ATA-related user tools, it provides links to many resources relevant to ATA. Also of importance is the *ide.txt* file located in the *Documentation* directory of the kernel sources, which contains information on the kernel's support for IDE devices and how to configure the kernel to properly access such devices.

Several non–Linux-specific ATA/IDE resources are available both online and in print. *PC Hardware in a Nutshell* by Robert Bruce Thompson and Barbara Fritchman Thompson (O'Reilly) contains a full chapter on IDE and SCSI hard disk interfaces, including a comparison of these interfaces. Although the discussion centers on high-level issues, it is a good introduction to the world of ATA/IDE and may be helpful in choosing a hard disk interface. For a more in-depth discussion, you may want to have a look at the *Enhanced IDE FAQ*, available from *http://www.faqs.org/*, which contains tips and tricks resulting from the cumulative knowledge available on the *comp.sys.ibm.pc.hardware.storage* newsgroup. Finally, if you really want to know all the ins and outs of the ATA interface, purchase the relevant standards documents from ANSI. Before you do so, however, be sure to read the relevant portions of the kernel's sources, as they too often contain hard-to-find information.

SCSI

As described in the "SCSI" subsection of the "Buses and Interfaces" section, the use of SCSI storage devices in embedded Linux systems is limited. When used, these devices are set up and configured in much the same way they would be used in a server. You may therefore follow the instructions and recommendations provided in any appropriate system administration book or online manual. The documentation and resources mentioned in the earlier "SCSI" section are, of course, still recommended. As an introduction to SCSI storage devices, *PC Hardware in a Nutshell* (O'Reilly) contains a brief discussion of SCSI storage devices and a comparison with ATA/IDE.

General Purpose Networking

An increasing number of embedded systems are attached to general purpose networks. These devices, although more constrained than other computerized systems in many ways, are often expected to provide the very same network services found in many modern servers. Fortunately, Linux lends itself quite well to general purpose networks, since it is itself often used in mainstream servers.

The following discussion covers the networking hardware most commonly found in embedded systems. Linux supports a much wider range of networking hardware than I will discuss, but many of these networking interfaces are not typically used in embedded systems and are therefore omitted. Also, as many of these networking interfaces have been extensively covered elsewhere, I will limit the discussion to the topics relevant to embedded Linux systems and will refer you to other sources for further information.

Network services will be discussed further in Chapter 10.

Ethernet

Initially developed at Xerox's PARC research center in Palo Alto, California, Ethernet is currently the most pervasive, best documented, and least expensive type of networking available. Its speed has kept up with the competition, growing geometrically over the decades. Given Ethernet's popularity and the increasing demand for embedded systems to be network enabled, many embedded development boards and production systems have been shipping with Ethernet hardware.

Linux supports a slew of 10 and 100 Megabit Ethernet devices and chips. It also supports a few Gigabit Ethernet devices. The kernel build configuration menu is probably the best place to start to see whether your particular hardware is supported, since it contains the latest drivers list.* The Ethernet HOWTO, available from the LDP, also contains a list of supported hardware, and a lot of information regarding the use of Ethernet with Linux. Finally, Donald Becker, who wrote quite a few Linux Ethernet drivers, maintains a web site with information regarding Linux's network drivers at *http://www.scyld.com/network/*.

A number of resources discuss the use and internals of Ethernet. Charles Spurgeon's *Ethernet: The Definitive Guide* (O'Reilly) is a good starting point. Charles also maintains a web site containing Ethernet resources at *http://wwwhost.ots.utexas.edu/ethernet/*. One of these resources is the Ethernet FAQ based on postings made on the *comp.dcom.lans.ethernet* newsgroup. If you need to write your own Ethernet driver for your hardware, you will find the *Linux Device Drivers* book useful.

IrDA

The *Infrared Data Association* (IrDA) was established in 1993 by 50 companies with the mandate to create and promote a standard for low-cost interoperable infrared data interconnections. The first IrDA specification was released in 1994 and continues to be maintained and developed by the association from which the specification takes its name. Today, IrDA hardware and software can be found in many consumer devices, including PDAs, cellular phones, printers, and digital cameras, to name a few. In comparison to other wireless schemes, such as Bluetooth, IrDA is inexpensive. This, in turn, favors its widespread adoption.

There are two main types of protocols within the IrDA specification: mandatory and optional. A device must at least implement the mandatory protocols in order to be able to interoperate properly with other IrDA devices. The mandatory protocols are the physical signaling layer (IrPHY), the link access protocol (IrLAP), and the link management protocol (IrLMP). The last protocol also includes the Information Access Service (IAS), which provides service discovery capabilities.

---

* You may also want to use this list as the basis of your hardware design, as I suggested earlier.

IrDA devices can exchange data at rates of up to 4 Mbps within a one meter range. Unlike other wireless technologies, IrDA requires directional pointing of the devices involved in a communication. An obvious advantage of such a scheme is the increased security resulting from the requirement that IrDA users keep their devices pointing in each other's direction during the whole connection time.*

Linux supports all the mandatory IrDA protocols and many of the optional protocols. Figure 3-2 presents the architecture of Linux's IrDA subsystem.

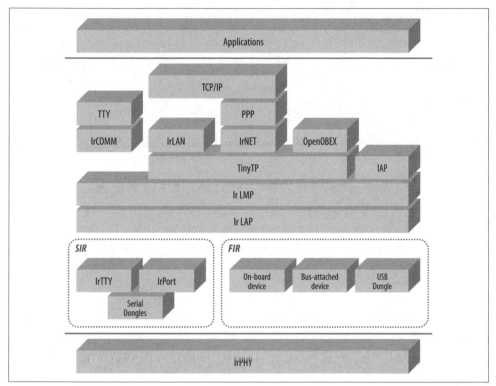

Figure 3-2. Linux IrDA subsystem architecture

IrPHY is the actual physical infrared device through which the data is transferred. It is usually located on the side of the device it is part of. In a PDA, for instance, it is often located on the top side of the device so the user can view the PDA's screen while pointing his IrDA port to that of another user's PDA or any other IrDA-enabled device.

The IrDA standard categorizes IrPHY devices according to their speed. There are currently three speed categories: serial infrared (SIR) at up to 115.2 Kbps, medium speed infrared (MIR) at up to 1.152 Mbps, and fast infrared (FIR) at 4.0 Mbps. In the future, very fast infrared (VFIR) at 16 Mbps should be part of the standard as well.

---

* Any "intruder" would have to be in direct view of the users involved in the communication.

The Linux kernel includes the following drivers for SIR and FIR devices:

IrTTY

IrTTY provides support for 16550-UART-compatible IrDA ports. This driver uses the kernel's serial driver and provides speeds of up to 115200 bps.

IrPORT

IrPORT is a half-duplex serial port driver that is meant to eventually replace IrTTY.

Serial Dongles

To provide IrDA support for a system that doesn't have an IrDA port built into it, an IrDA dongle can be attached to the system's serial port. The kernel build configuration menu contains the complete list of serial dongles supported by Linux.

On-board and bus-attached devices

The kernel supports a number of chips found in on-board and bus-attached IrDA devices. The kernel build configuration menu contains the complete list of chips supported by Linux.

USB dongle

Like serial dongles, USB dongles provide a removable IrDA interface. Instead of SIR throughput rates, however, they provide FIR rates.

The IrDA stack operates on top of the device drivers to provide IrDA functionality in Linux. Most components of this stack are implemented as specified in the IrDA standard, but some components implemented are not part of the standard. These are the stack layers implemented in the kernel:

IrLAP

IrLAP is the link access protocol layer of the IrDA specification. It provides and maintains a reliable link between IrDA devices. In addition to the normal connection-oriented protocol, Linux supports connectionless exchanges using the *Ultra* protocol.

IrLMP

IrLMP is the link management protocol layer of the IrDA specification. It provides for and manages multiple connections over IrLAP.

TinyTP

Tiny Transport Protocol (TinyTP) implements flow control over IrLMP connections.

IAP

The Information Access Protocol (IAP) is Linux's equivalent to the IrDA's Information Access Service (IAS). As with IAS, IAP provides service discovery capabilities.

IrCOMM

IrCOMM is an emulation layer that provides IrDA connection capabilities to legacy applications that usually communicate through common serial and parallel port devices. Since these types of functionalities are accessed through TTYs, applications use the kernel's TTY layer to access IrCOMM. Note that IrCOMM does not rely on TinyTP.

IrLAN

The IrDA specifies IrLAN to enable LAN-like connections between IrDA devices. IrLAN acts as a network device from the point of view of upper layer protocols. It is, for instance, possible to establish a TCP/IP network on top of an IrDA link using IrLAN.

IrNET

IrNET is also meant to enable LAN-like connections between IrDA devices. Instead of implementing a full network device, as with IrLAN, IrNET acts as a very thin layer over which PPP can be used to provide a full network device. Note, however, that IrNET is not part of the official IrDA standard. Microsoft first introduced IrNET as part of their Windows 2000 IrDA stack, replacing IrCOMM and IrLAN. The Linux implementation is based on the same concepts found in Microsoft's IrNET and can interoperate with it.

OpenOBEX

The IrDA standard specifies IrOBEX as an HTTP-like service for the exchange of objects. OpenOBEX is the IrOBEX implementation for Linux. It consists of a user-space library that can be found at: *http://sourceforge.net/projects/openobex/*.

In conjunction with the stack layers, you will need user-space tools to operate Linux's IrDA capabilities. These tools are part of the IrDA Utils package. This package and many other IrDA-related resources are available through the Linux-IrDA Project web site at *http://irda.sourceforge.net/*.

For further information regarding Linux's IrDA stack and related tools and projects, you may want to take a look at the Infrared HOWTO available from the LDP. Also, Jean Tourrilhes, a major contributor to the Linux-IrDA project, maintains a number of very interesting Linux-IrDA pages at *http://www.hpl.hp.com/personal/Jean_Tourrilhes/*. Unlike other such standards, all the IrDA standards are readily available for download directly from the association's web site at *http://www.irda.org/*.

IEEE 802.11 (Wireless)

The 802.11 working group was set up by the IEEE 802 committee in 1990. The first 802.11 standard was published in 1997 and has been maintained and updated since then by the same group. The standard provides for wireless communication between computers using the 2.4 GHz (802.11b) and 5 GHz (802.11a) frequencies. Today, 802.11 is the wireless equivalent of Ethernet in terms of widespread adoption and mainstream support.

Although many traditional embedded devices were equipped with some form or another of wireless technology, recent embedded systems with 802.11 support are mostly user-oriented devices such as PDAs. Connecting such devices to an 802.11 network is akin to connecting a laptop or workstation to this type of network.

Hence, you may use reference material discussing the latter and apply it to your 802.11-enabled embedded device with little effort.

Linux has extensive support for 802.11b hardware. For a complete list of all the supported 802.11 hardware and related drivers and tools, I refer you to Jean Tourrilhes' Linux Wireless LAN HOWTO found at his web site, *http://www.hpl.hp.com/personal/Jean_Tourrilhes/*. Support for on-board or non-PCMCIA bus-attached devices is included with the kernel and can be selected during kernel build configuration. Support for PCMCIA 802.11 cards, on the other hand, is part of David Hinds' PCMCIA package mentioned earlier in "PCMCIA."

Since most 802.11 devices' operation is similar to that of Ethernet devices, the kernel does not need any additional subsystem to support them. Instead, most of the same tools usually used for Ethernet devices can be used for 802.11 devices once the appropriate device driver has been loaded and initialized. Nonetheless, there are tools required to address the particularities of 802.11, such as setting identification and encryption keys, and monitoring signal strength and link quality. These tools are available through the Wireless Tools for Linux section of Jean's web site.

In addition to Jean's web site, the Wireless HOWTO available from the LDP provides some background information on the use of wireless devices with Linux. If you intend to make extensive use of 802.11 devices, you may want to take a look at Matthew Gast's *802.11 Wireless Networks: The Definitive Guide* (O'Reilly). It contains a thorough discussion of the technology and its use with Linux. You can also obtain copies of the actual standard from the IEEE. At the time of this writing, they were freely available for download in PDF from the IEEE's web site. Jean's web site contains the appropriate link, but you should note that the availability of these documents is subject to change, as is stated on the IEEE's web site.

Bluetooth

Bluetooth was developed by Ericsson with help from Intel and was introduced in 1994. A Bluetooth SIG was formed by Ericsson, IBM, Intel, Nokia, and Toshiba. Today, the SIG has more than 1,900 member companies. Today, a wide range of devices such as PDAs and cell phones, are already Bluetooth-enabled with more on the way.

Bluetooth operates on the 2.4 GHz band and uses spread spectrum frequency hopping to provide wireless connectivity to devices within the same *piconet*.* Some have called it a "cable replacement" and others have called it "wireless USB." In essence, it enables seamless wireless communication between devices. Hence, Bluetooth devices do not need any configuration to become part of a piconet. Rather, devices automatically detect each other and advertise their services so that the other devices in the piconet can in turn use these services.

---

* Piconets are wireless networks comprising Bluetooth devices. Since Bluetooth devices can belong to more than one piconet, piconets can overlap.

Linux has a few Bluetooth stacks. The four main ones are: BlueZ, OpenBT, Affix, and BlueDrekar. BlueZ was originally written by Qualcomm and is now an open source project available under the terms of the GPL from the project's web site at *http://bluez.sourceforge.net/*. In the following, I will mainly discuss BlueZ, as it is the Bluetooth stack included in the mainstream kernel tree.

OpenBT was developed and is still maintained by Axis Communications AB. It is available for download from the project's web site at *http://developer.axis.com/software/bluetooth/*. OpenBT has better documentation and source code comments than BlueZ. But OpenBT is structured as a serial abstraction (i.e., it is accessible through */dev/ttyBT0*, */dev/ttyBT1*, etc.) whereas BlueZ is structured as a network protocol—accessible using the AF_BLUETOOTH socket type—which in many regards, is more appropriate for Bluetooth, since it is itself a protocol.

Affix was developed and continues to be maintained by Nokia. It is available from its SourceForge web site at *http://affix.sourceforge.net/*. Both user-space utilities and the kernel patch are available for download under the terms of the GPL. The README available from the project's web site is fairly rich and so is the packages' documentation. Like BlueZ, it is structured as a networking protocol—accessible using the AF_AFFIX socket type.

Finally, the BlueDrekar stack was developed and is distributed by IBM through the project's web site at *http://www.alphaworks.ibm.com/tech/bluedrekar/*. Although Blue-Drekar can be freely downloaded, it is not an open source project, and I will therefore not discuss it further.

Figure 3-3 presents the architecture of the BlueZ stack. If you are familiar with Bluetooth, you will notice that BlueZ does not support Telephony Control protocol Specification Binary (TCS-bin) or OBEX.* Although Linux supports IrDA OBEX, the existing Linux implementation, OpenOBEX, cannot, at the time of this writing, operate with OpenBT and can only function in a preliminary way with BlueZ. This is because OpenBT doesn't implement OBEX and BlueZ's support for OBEX is in its early stages. Nevertheless, OpenOBEX can be used with Affix, since it implements OBEX.

The Host Controller Interface (HCI) is the lowest layer of the Bluetooth stack and is responsible for interfacing with the actual Bluetooth hardware. BlueZ currently supports the following types of HCI adapters:

HCI-USB

These are USB-attached Bluetooth devices. Do not confuse this with the "USB Bluetooth" support found in the USB support submenu of the kernel build configuration menu. The latter requires OpenBT, not BlueZ.

HCI-UART

These are Bluetooth devices attached to the serial interface.

---

* This is the same OBEX found in the IrDA standard. Instead of inventing a new protocol, the Bluetooth standard simply uses the IrDA OBEX specification for the implementation of an HTTP-like binary exchange service.

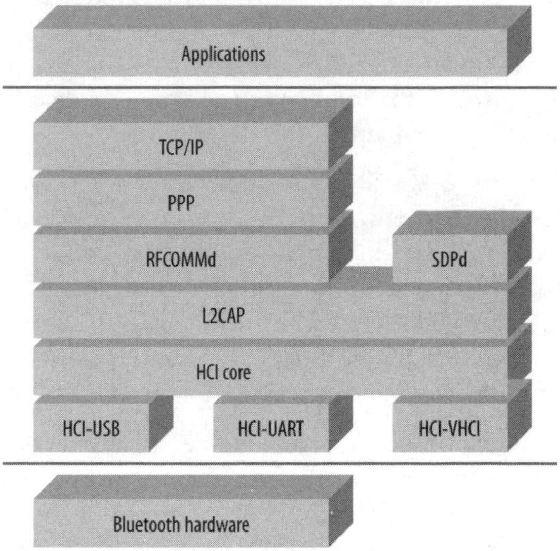

Figure 3-3. Linux BlueZ Bluetooth subsystem architecture

HCI-VHCI

VHCI stands for *Virtual* HCI. Consequently, VHCI acts as a virtual Bluetooth device that can be used for testing and development.

The HCI core is immediately above the HCI hardware device drivers and enables them to interoperate with the higher levels of the protocol stack. BlueZ comprises the following stack layers:

L2CAP

The Logical Link Control and Adaptation Protocol (L2CAP) is responsible for link multiplexing, packet segmentation and reassembly, and quality of service.

RFCOMMd

The Bluetooth standard specifies the RFCOMM protocol to provide serial communication between Bluetooth devices. BlueZ implements RFCOMM as a daemon, RFCOMMd, which uses pseudo-TTYs for communication. PPP can then be used on top of RFCOMMd to enable TCP/IP networking between Bluetooth devices.

SDPd

The Service Discovery Protocol (SDP) lets a device discover services provided by other Bluetooth-enabled devices and the advertisement of the services offered by a device. SDP is implemented as a daemon, SDPd, in BlueZ.

In addition to the protocol stack, you will need the user-space tools available from BlueZ's project web site. In addition to RFCOMMd and SDPd, these tools include *l2ping* for L2CAP pinging and *hcidump* for HCI packet analysis.

Here are some relevant resources:

- Further information on the operation of the BlueZ stack can be found in the BlueZ HOWTO from the project's web site.

- Information on OpenBT and its use is available on the project's SourceForge workspace at *http://sourceforge.net/projects/openbt/*.

- Delbert Matlock maintains a list of Linux Bluetooth resources at *http://delbert. matlock.com/linux-bluetooth.htm*, which you may find useful if you are considering the use of Bluetooth with Linux.

- Prentice Hall publishes two popular Bluetooth books—*Bluetooth Revealed: The Insider's Guide to an Open Specification for Global Wireless Communications* by Brent Miller and Chatschik Bisdikian and *Bluetooth: Connect Without Cables* by Jennifer Bray and Charles Sturman.

You may also be interested in becoming a Bluetooth SIG member. The Bluetooth SIG's web site is located at *http://www.bluetooth.org/*. You can obtain the official Bluetooth standard from the official Bluetooth web site at *http://www.bluetooth.com/*.

Industrial Grade Networking

As with other computerized applications, industrial control and automation rely increasingly on computerized networks. General-purpose networking or connectivity solutions such as plain Ethernet or Token Ring are, however, ill-adapted to the harsh and demanding environment of industrial applications. Common Ethernet, for instance, is too vulnerable to EMI (Electromagnetic Interference) and RFI (Radio Frequency Interference) to be used in most industrial environments.

Therefore, quite a few specialized, industrial-grade networking solutions have been developed over time. In addition to being more adapted to industrial environments, these industrial networks, commonly known as *fieldbuses*, contribute to reducing wiring, increasing modularity, providing diagnostics capabilities, enabling self-configuration, and facilitating the setup of enterprise-wide information systems.

In the following sections, I will cover the industrial networks supported by Linux and briefly discuss the other industrial networks that have little or no Linux support. If you are new to fieldbuses, you may want to take a look at Rob Hulsebos' *Fieldbus Pages* located at *http://ourworld-top.cs.com/rahulsebos/*. The web site includes a large collection of links and references to all sorts of fieldbus systems.

CAN

The *Controller Area Network* (CAN) is not only the most common fieldbus, but probably one of the most pervasive forms of networking ever used. CAN was introduced in 1986 by Robert Bosch Gmbh. as a serial bus system for the automotive industry and has since been put to use in many other industries. CAN's development received early contributions from engineers at Mercedes-Benz and Intel, which provided the first CAN chip, the 82526. Today, more than 100 million new CAN devices are sold every year. Application fields range from upper-class cars, such as Mercedes, to factory automation networks.

CAN specifies a hardware interface and a communication mechanism. It is a multi-master serial networking protocol with error detection capabilities, where message identification is done through content rather than through the receiver node or the transmitter node. CAN is managed and promoted by the *CAN in Automation* (CiA) group and is subject to ISO standard 11898 published in 1993.

Since CAN is a low-level protocol, akin to Ethernet, many higher-level protocols have been put forward to complete it. Four such protocols are J1939, DeviceNet, Smart Distributed System (SDS), and CANopen. J1939 was introduced and continues to be maintained by the Society of Automotive Engineers (SAE), and is very popular in the automotive industry. DeviceNet is another popular CAN-based higher-level protocol and is managed by the Open DeviceNet Vendor Association (ODVA). SDS was put forth by Honeywell and continues to be promoted and managed by the same company. CANopen was introduced and is managed by the same group that maintains CAN, the CiA. SDS has not been as popular as DeviceNet and J1939, because it was never standardized, while J1939, DeviceNet, and CANopen were.

Although there is no formal support for CAN within the kernel, many open source projects provide support for CAN hardware in Linux. The following are the most important ones:

Linux CAN-bus Driver Project
> This is the main open source CAN-support project. The project provides a kernel module that supports many CAN boards based on the Intel 82527 and the Philips sja1000. The project is located at *http://home.wanadoo.nl/arnaud/*. The project's web site provides documentation, a HOWTO, and links to CAN-related sites.

Alessandro Rubini's Ocan driver
> This is a driver for CAN boards based on the Intel 82587. It is maintained by Alessandro Rubini, one of the authors of *Linux Device Drivers* (O'Reilly). The driver is available at *http://www.linux.it/~rubini/software/#ocan* under the terms of the GPL and is remarkably well documented.

can4linux
> can4linux used to be maintained by the Linux Lab Project. It is now available from *http://www.port.de/engl/canprod/sw_linux.html*. The package includes a driver for the Philips 82c200-based boards and application examples.

CanFestival
> CanFestival provides CAN and CANopen capabilities within Linux for the ADLINK PCI 7841 board. The software for the board can be used both in standard Linux mode and in real time using the RTLinux framework. The package

and its documentation are available from *http://perso.wanadoo.fr/edouard. tisserant/CanFestival/*.

ss5136dn Linux Driver

This package provides both CAN and DeviceNet capabilities within Linux for the SST 5136-DN family of CAN bus/DeviceNet interface boards. The package at *http://home.att.net/~marksu/dn5136man.html* includes rich documentation and a user-space library.

For more information on CAN, CAN-related hardware, and CANopen, consult the CiA's web site at *http://www.can-cia.org/*. The CiA provides its specifications online. SAE provides subscription-based access to the J1939 standard through its web site at *http://www.sae.org/products/j1939.htm*. Information on DeviceNet can be found on the ODVA's web site at *http://www.odva.org/*. The DeviceNet specification is available in printed form from the ODVA for a fee that covers reproduction costs and provides a life time unlimited royalty-free license to develop DeviceNet products. If you are interested in SDS, you can find more information about it, including specifications, on Honeywell's web site at *http://content.honeywell.com/sensing/prodinfo/sds/*.

ARCnet

The *Attached Resource Computer NETwork* (ARCnet) was introduced by Datapoint Corporation in 1977 as a general purpose network, much like Ethernet. Today, ARCnet is seldom used in office LANs anymore, but it is still popular as an industrial fieldbus. ARCnet is now an ANSI standard and is managed and promoted by the ARCnet Trade Association (ATA).

ARCnet is a token-based network that can use either a star topology or a bus topology. An ARCnet NIC (Network Interface Card) can be compatible with one of the two topologies, but not both. Apart from its low cost, ARCnet has many advantages compared to standard office networks, including deterministic performance, automatic reconfiguration, multi-master capability, and immunity to noise. Also, ARCnet guarantees the safe arrival of packets and guarantees notification in case of transmission failure.

Support for ARCnet has been part of the Linux kernel for quite some time now. Since ARCnet NICs have almost identical programming interfaces, there is no need for a broad range of device drivers. Instead, the kernel includes drivers for the two standard ARCnet chipsets, COM90xx and COM20020. In addition to the drivers, the kernel includes three different protocols to be used with ARCnet hardware. The first and most common protocol conforms to RFC1201 and enables the transmission of IP traffic over ARCnet networks. When a system is configured with the RFC1201 protocol, for instance, the kernel's own TCP/IP stack can be used to provide TCP/IP networking on ARCnet hardware. The second protocol conforms to RFC1051, which was replaced by RFC1201 already mentioned. This protocol is provided to enable interaction with old networks. Finally, the kernel provides an Ethernet-encapsulation protocol, which enables ARCnet networks to transport Ethernet packets.

Information regarding the Linux ARCnet drivers is available from the ARCnet for Linux project web site at *http://www.worldvisions.ca/~apenwarr/arcnet/*. The site includes the Linux-ARCnet HOWTO, which provides extensive discussion on the use of ARCnet with Linux. The HOWTO includes jumper settings information and card diagrams for many ARCnet NICs. It also includes cabling instructions for ARCnet networks. A text copy of this HOWTO is included in the kernel's sources in the *Documentation* directory.

The ATA's web site, found at *http://www.arcnet.com/* contains more information about ARCnet, including forms for ordering the ANSI standard and other manuals.

Modbus

The Modbus Protocol was introduced by Modicon in 1978 as a simple way to transfer control data between controllers and sensors using RS232 in a master-slave fashion. Modicon was later acquired by Schneider Electric, which owns the Modbus trademark and continues to steer the development of the protocol and its descendants.

Since Modbus specifies a messaging structure, it is independent of the underlying physical layer. There are two formats used to transmit information with Modbus, ASCII, and RTU. The first sends each byte as two ASCII characters, while the second sends each byte as two 4-bit hexadecimal characters. Modbus is usually implemented on top of a serial interface such as RS232, RS422, or RS485. In addition to Modbus, Schneider specifies the Modbus TCP/IP protocol, which uses TCP/IP and Ethernet to transmit Modbus messages.

Two open source projects provide Modbus capabilities to Linux:

jModbus
> This project aims at providing a Java implementation of Modbus RTU, Modbus ASCII, and Modbus TCP/IP. It is housed at *http://jmodbus.sourceforge.net/* and is distributed with documentation and examples under a BSD-style license.

MAT LinuxPLC
> This is the same automation project I mentioned earlier in "Process Control." The MAT project now contains code in its CVS repository implementing Modbus RTU and Modbus TCP/IP. Although the source code is commented, there is little other documentation.

For more information about Modbus, read the Modbus specifications, available at *http://www.modbus.org/*.

A Word on the Other Industrial Networks

There are, of course, many other industrial networks, most of which are not supported by Linux. There is, for instance, currently no support for ControlNet, Seriplex, AS-Interface, or Sercos in Linux. Still other fieldbuses have some form of support in Linux, but will require a certain amount of further work before we can classify them as having Linux support. The following is a list of such fieldbuses:

Interbus
> A driver is available for kernel Versions 2.0 and 2.2 for the Phoenix Contact Interbus board. The driver is available from *http://www.santel.lu/projects/wallace/interbus.html* and comes with documentation and examples.

LonWorks
> A driver is available for kernel Version 2.2 for Easylon interfaces. The driver is released for evaluation purposes and comes with little documentation or examples. It is available from *http://www.gesytec.de/englisch/support/linux_readme.htm*.

In addition, there is a driver for Applicom cards in the Linux kernel. Though the driver was mainly used for Profibus by its author, Applicom cards can handle many protocols. When used, the card is seen as a character device in */dev*.

Also, Hilscher Gmbh. provides a device driver for its CIF boards and a user-level framework that enables the development of fieldbus-independent applications. The framework and device driver is distributed under the terms of the GPL with extensive documentation and is available from Hilscher's web site at *http://www.hilscher.com/device_drivers_linux.htm*. The device driver included in the package can be accessed from user space using the unified framework API. This, in turn, enables control applications to be developed independently from the underlying fieldbus technology. Although only Hilscher's hardware driver is currently part of the package, the approach used by Hilscher and the framework it provides may be useful in helping Linux provide wide and uniform support to industrial network technologies in the future.

System Monitoring

Both hardware and software are prone to failing, sometimes drastically. Although the occurrence of failures can be reduced through careful design and runtime testing, they are sometimes unavoidable. It is the task of the embedded system designer to plan for such a possibility and to provide means of recovery. Often, failure detection and recovery is done by means of system monitoring hardware and software such as watchdogs.

Linux supports two types of system monitoring facilities: watchdog timers and hardware health monitoring. There are both hardware and software implementations of watchdog timers, whereas health monitors always require appropriate hardware. Watchdog timers depend on periodic reinitialization so as not to reboot the system. If the system hangs, the timer eventually expires and causes a reboot. Hardware health monitors provide information regarding the system's physical state. This information can in turn be used to carry out appropriate actions to signal or solve actual physical problems such as overheating or voltage irregularities.

The kernel includes drivers for many watchdog timers. The complete list of supported watchdog devices can be found in the kernel build configuration menu in the Watchdog Cards submenu. The list includes drivers for watchdog timer peripheral cards, a software watchdog, and drivers for watchdog timers found in some CPUs such as the MachZ and the SuperH. Although you may want to use the software watchdog to avoid the cost of a real hardware watchdog, note that the software watchdog may fail to reboot the system in some circumstances. Timer watchdogs are seen as */dev/watchdog* in Linux and have to be written to periodically to avoid system reboot. This updating task is traditionally carried out by the watchdog daemon available from *ftp://metalab.unc.edu/pub/linux/system/daemons/watchdog/*. In an actual embedded system, however, you may want to have the main application carry out the update instead of using the watchdog daemon, since the latter may have no way of knowing whether the main application has stopped functioning properly.

In addition to the software watchdog available in the Linux kernel, RTAI provides an elaborate software watchdog with configurable policies. The main purpose of the RTAI watchdog is to protect the system against programming errors in RTAI applications. Hence, misbehaving tasks cannot hang the system. Upon detecting the offending task, the RTAI watchdog can apply a number of remedies to it including suspending it, killing it, and stretching its period. The RTAI watchdog and appropriate documentation are part of the mainstream RTAI distribution.

Finally, Linux supports quite a few hardware monitoring devices through the "Hardware Monitoring by lm_sensors" project found at *http://www2.lm-sensors.nu/~lm78/*. The project's web site contains a complete list of supported devices along with extensive documentation on the installation and operation of the software. The lm_sensors package available from the project's web site includes both the device drivers and user-level utilities to interface with the drivers. These utilities include *sensord*, a daemon that can log sensor values and alert the system through the ALERT syslog level when an alarm condition occurs. The site also provides links to external projects and resources related to lm_sensors.

## CHAPTER 4

Development Tools

Much like mainstream software developers, embedded system developers need compilers, linkers, interpreters, integrated development environments, and other such development tools. The embedded developer's tools are different, however, in that they typically run on one platform while building applications for another. This is why these tools are often called cross-platform development tools, or cross-development tools, for short.

This chapter discusses the setup, configuration, and use of cross-platform development tools. First, I will discuss how to use a practical project workspace. I will then discuss the GNU cross-platform development toolchain, the C library alternatives, Java, Perl, Python, Ada, other programming languages, integrated development environments, and terminal emulation programs.

Using a Practical Project Workspace

In the course of developing and customizing software for your target, you will need to organize various software packages and project components in a comprehensive and easy-to-use directory structure. Table 4-1 shows a suggested directory layout you may find useful. Feel free to modify this structure to fit your needs and requirements. When deciding where to place components, always try to find the most intuitive layout. Also, try to keep your own code in a directory completely separated from all the packages you will download from the Net. This will minimize any confusion regarding the source's ownership and licensing status.

Table 4-1. Suggested project directory layout

Directory	Content
bootldr	The bootloader or bootloaders for your target
build-tools	The packages and directories needed to build the cross-platform development toolchain
debug	The debugging tools and all related packages

Table 4-1. Suggested project directory layout (continued)

Directory	Content
doc	All the documentation you will need for your project
images	The binary images of the bootloader, the kernel, and the root filesystem ready to be used on the target
kernel	The different kernel versions you are evaluating for your target
project	Your own source code for this project
rootfs	The root filesystem as seen by the target's kernel at runtime
sysapps	The system applications required for your target
tmp	A temporary directory to experiment and store transient files
tools	The complete cross-platform development toolchain and C library

Of course, each of these directories contains many subdirectories. We will populate these directories as we continue through the rest of the book.

The location of your project workspace is up to you, but I strongly encourage you *not* to use a system-wide entry such as */usr* or */usr/local*. Instead, use an entry in your home directory or a directory within the */home* directory shared by all the members of your group. If you really want to have a system-wide entry, you may want to consider using an entry in the */opt* directory. For the example embedded control system, I have the following layout in my home directory:

```
$ ls -l ~/control-project
total 4
drwxr-xr-x    13 karim    karim         1024 Mar 28 22:38 control-module
drwxr-xr-x    13 karim    karim         1024 Mar 28 22:38 daq-module
drwxr-xr-x    13 karim    karim         1024 Mar 28 22:38 sysmgnt-module
drwxr-xr-x    13 karim    karim         1024 Mar 28 22:38 user-interface
```

Since they all run on different targets, each control system component has a separate entry in the *control-project* directory in my home directory. Each entry has its own project workspace as described above. Here is the *daq-module* workspace for example:

```
$ ls -l ~/control-project/daq-module
total 11
drwxr-xr-x     2 karim    karim         1024 Mar 28 22:38 bootldr
drwxr-xr-x     2 karim    karim         1024 Mar 28 22:38 build-tools
drwxr-xr-x     2 karim    karim         1024 Mar 28 22:38 debug
drwxr-xr-x     2 karim    karim         1024 Mar 28 22:38 doc
drwxr-xr-x     2 karim    karim         1024 Mar 28 22:38 images
drwxr-xr-x     2 karim    karim         1024 Mar 28 22:38 kernel
drwxr-xr-x     2 karim    karim         1024 Mar 28 22:38 project
drwxr-xr-x     2 karim    karim         1024 Mar 28 22:38 rootfs
drwxr-xr-x     2 karim    karim         1024 Mar 28 22:38 sysapps
drwxr-xr-x     2 karim    karim         1024 Mar 28 22:38 tmp
drwxr-xr-x     2 karim    karim         1024 Mar 28 22:38 tools
```

Because you may need to provide the paths of these directories to some of the utilities you will build and use, you may find it useful to create a short script that sets appropriate environment variables. Here is such a script called *develdaq* for the DAQ module:

```
export PROJECT=daq-module
export PRJROOT=/home/karim/control-project/${PROJECT}
cd $PRJROOT
```

In addition to setting environment variables, this script moves you to the directory containing the project. You can remove the *cd* command if you would prefer not to be moved to the project directory right away. To execute this script in the current shell so that the environment variables are immediately visible, type:[*]

```
$ . develdaq
```

Future explanations will rely on the existence of the PROJECT and PRJROOT environment variables.

 Since the distribution on your workstation has already installed many of the same packages you will be building for your target, it is very important to clearly separate the two types of software. To ensure such separation, I strongly encourage you not to carry out any of the instructions provided in the rest of this book while being logged in as root, unless I provide explicit instructions otherwise. Among other things, this will avoid any possible destruction of the native GNU toolchain installed on your system and, most importantly, the C library most of your applications rely on. Therefore, instead of logging in as root, log in using a normal user account with no particular privileges.

GNU Cross-Platform Development Toolchain

The toolchain we need to put together to cross-develop applications for any target includes the binary utilities, such as *ld*, *gas*, and *ar*, the C compiler, *gcc*, and the C library, glibc. The rest of the discussion in the later chapters relies on the cross-platform development toolchain we will put together here.

You can download the components of the GNU toolchain from the FSF's FTP site at *ftp://ftp.gnu.org/gnu/* or any of its mirrors. The binutils package is in the *binutils* directory, the gcc package is in the *gcc* directory, and the glibc package is in the *glibc* directory along with glibc-linuxthreads. If you are using a glibc version older than 2.2, you will also need to download the glibc-crypt package, also from the *glibc* directory. This part of the library used to be distributed separately, because U.S. cryptography export laws made it illegal to download this package to a computer outside the U.S. from the FSF's site, or any other U.S. site, for that matter. Since Version 2.2, however, glibc-crypt has been integrated as part of the main glibc package and there is no need to

---

[*] All commands used in this book assume the use of the *sh* or *bash* shell, because these are the shells most commonly used. If you use another shell, such as *csh*, you may need to modify some of the commands accordingly.

download this package separately anymore.* Following the project directory layout suggested earlier, download the packages into the *${PRJROOT}/build-tools* directory.

Note that all the targets discussed in Chapter 3 are supported by the GNU toolchain.

GNU Toolchain Basics

Configuring and building an appropriate GNU toolchain is a complex and delicate operation that requires a good understanding of the dependencies between the different software packages and their respective roles. This knowledge is required, because the GNU toolchain components are developed and released independently from one another.

Component versions

The first step in building the toolchain is selecting the component versions we will use. This involves selecting a binutils version, a gcc version, and a glibc version. Because these packages are maintained and released independently from one another, not all versions of one package will build properly when combined with different versions of the other packages. You can try using the latest versions of each package, but this combination is not guaranteed to work either.

To select the appropriate versions, you have to test a combination tailored to your host and target. Of course, you may find it easier to ask around and see whether someone somewhere tested a certain combination of versions for that setup and reports that her combination works correctly. You may also have to try such combinations for your setup on your own if you do not find a known functional version combination. In that case, start with the most recent stable versions of each package and replace them one by one with older ones if they fail to build.

 In some cases, the version with the highest version number may not have had the time to be tested enough to be considered "stable." At the time glibc 2.3 was released, for example, it may have been a better choice to keep using glibc 2.2.5 until 2.3.1 became available.

At the time of this writing, for instance, the latest version of binutils is 2.13.2.1, the latest version of gcc is 3.2.1, and the latest version of glibc is 2.3.1. Most often, binutils will build successfully and you will not need to change it. Hence, let us assume that gcc 3.2.1 fails to build although all the appropriate configuration flags have been provided. In that case, I would revert to gcc 3.2. If that failed, I would try

---

* The following email from the glibc developer mailing list covers the folding of glibc-crypt into the main glibc package and conformance to U.S. export laws: *http://sources.redhat.com/ml/libc-alpha/2000-02/msg00104. html*. This email, and the ensuing thread, refer to the "BXA" abbreviation. This is the *Bureau of Industry and Security* of the U.S. *Department of Commerce* (*http://www.bxa.doc.gov/*). It is known as the BXA, because it was formerly the *Bureau of Export Administration*.

3.1.1 and so on. It is the same thing with glibc. Version 2.3.1 of glibc may fail to build. In that case, I would revert to 2.3 and later to 2.2.5, if necessary.

You must understand, however, that you cannot go back like this indefinitely, because the most recent package versions expect the other packages to provide certain capabilities. You may, therefore, have to go back to older versions of packages that you successfully built if the other packages down the line fail to build. Using the above versions, for example, if I had to go back to glibc 2.1.3, it might be appropriate to change back to gcc 2.95.3 and binutils 2.10 although the most recent gcc and most recent binutils may have compiled perfectly.

You may also need to apply patches to some versions to get them to properly compile for your target. The web sites and mailing lists provided for each processor architecture in Chapter 3 are the best place to find such patches and package versions suggestions. Another place to look for patches is in the Debian source packages. Each package contains the patches required for all the architectures supported by that package.

Table 4-2 provides a list of known functional version combinations. For each host/target combination, known compatible versions are provided for binutils, gcc, and glibc. The last column indicates whether the tools require patching.

Table 4-2. Known functional package version combinations

Host	Target	Kernel	binutils	gcc	glibc	Patches
i386	PPC		2.10.1	2.95.3	2.2.1	No
PPC	i386		2.10.1	2.95.3	2.2.3	No
PPC	i386		2.13.2.1	3.2.1	2.3.1	No
i386	ARM	2.4.1-rmk1	2.10.1	2.95.3	2.1.3	Yes[a]
PPC	ARM		2.10.1	2.95.3	2.2.3	Yes[a]
i386	MIPS		2.11.2	egcs-1.1.2	2.0.0	Yes[b]
i386	SuperH		2.11.2	3.0.1	2.2.4	Yes[c]
Sparc (Solaris)	PPC	2.4.0	2.10.1	2.95.2	2.1.3	No

[a] See "The -Dinhibit_libc hack" subsection in the "Building the Toolchain" section of "The GNU toolchain" chapter in AlephOne's "Guide to ARMLinux for Developers" (*http://www.aleph1.co.uk/armlinux/book/book1.html*) for further information on the modifications to be made to gcc to make it build successfully.

[b] See Ralf Bächle's MIPS HOWTO (*http://howto.linux-mips.org/*) for further information on the patches to apply.

[c] See Bill Gatliff's "Running Linux on the Sega Dreamcast" (*http://www.linuxdevices.com/articles/AT7466555948.html*) for further information on the patches to apply.

Some of the combinations presented were on the Net as part of cross-platform development toolchain setups. I have kept the kernel version when the original explanation provided one. The kernel version, however, does not really matter for the build of the toolchain. Any recent kernel—Version 2.2.x or 2.4.x—known to work for your target can be used for the toolchain build. I strongly recommend using the actual kernel you will be using in your target, however, to avoid any future conflicts. I will discuss kernel selection in Chapter 5.

Although it is not specifically mentioned in the table, there is one glibc add-on that we will need for the toolchain: glibc-linuxthreads. The package's versions closely follow glibc's numbering scheme. Hence, the linuxthreads version matching glibc 2.2.3 is linuxthreads Version 2.2.3. Although I recommend getting the linuxthreads package, you should be able to build glibc without it. Note that glibc 2.1.x, for instance, does not build properly without linuxthreads. If you are using glibc 2.1.x, remember that you will also need to download the glibc-crypt add-on if you intend to use DES encryption.

By no means is Table 4-2 complete. There are many other combinations that will work just as well. Feel free to try newer versions than the ones presented. Use the same technique discussed earlier by starting with the latest versions and decrementing versions as needed. At worst, you will have to revert to setups presented above.

Whenever you discover a new version combination that compiles successfully, make sure you test the resulting toolchain to ensure that it is indeed functional. Some version combinations may compile successfully and still fail when used. Version 2.2.3 of glibc, for example, builds successfully for a PPC target on an x86 host using gcc 2.95.3. The resulting library is, nevertheless, broken and will cause a core dump when used on the target. In that particular setup, we can obtain a functional C library by reverting to glibc 2.2.1.

There are also cases where a version combination was found to work properly on certain processors within a processor family while failing to work on other processors of the same family. Versions of glibc earlier than 2.2, for example, worked fine for most PPC processors except those that were part of the MPC8xx series. The problem was that glibc assumed 32-byte cache lines for all PPC processors, while the processors in the MPC8xx series have 16-byte cache lines. Version 2.2 fixed this problem by assuming 16-byte cache lines for all PPC processors.

The following sections describe the building of the GNU toolchain for a PPC host and an i386 target using binutils 2.10.1, gcc 2.95.3, and glibc 2.2.3. This was the second entry in Table 4-2.

Build requirements

To build a cross-platform development toolchain, you will need a functional native toolchain. Most mainstream distributions provide this toolchain as part of their packages. If it was not installed on your workstation or if you chose not to install it to save space, you will need to install it at this point using the procedure appropriate to your distribution. With a Red Hat distribution, for instance, you will need to install the appropriate RPM packages.

You will also need a valid set of kernel headers for your host. These headers must usually be located in the */usr/include/linux*, */usr/include/asm*, and */usr/include/asm-generic* directories, and should be the headers used to compile the native glibc installed on your system. In older distributions, and in some installations still, these directories are actually symbolic links to directories within the */usr/src/linux* directory. In turn, this directory is itself a symbolic link to the actual kernel installed by your distribution. If your distribution uses the older setup, and you have updated your kernel or modified the content of the */usr/src/linux* directory, you will need to make sure the */usr/src/linux* symbolic link is set appropriately so that the symbolic links in */usr/include* point to the kernel that was used to build your native glibc, and that was installed by your distribution. In recent distributions, however, the content of */usr/include/linux*, */usr/include/asm*, and */usr/include/asm-generic* is independent of the content of */usr/src/linux*, and no kernel update should result in such problems.

Build overview

With the appropriate tools in place, let us take a look at the procedure used to build the toolchain. These are the five main steps:

1. Kernel headers setup
2. Binary utilities setup
3. Bootstrap compiler setup
4. C library setup
5. Full compiler setup

The first thing that you probably noticed, looking at these steps, is that the compiler seems to be built twice. This is normal and required, because some languages supported by gcc, such as C++, require glibc support. Hence, a first compiler is built with support for C only, and a full compiler is built once the C library is available.

Although I placed the kernel headers setup as the first step, the headers will not be used until the C library setup. Hence, you could alter the steps and set up the kernel headers right before the C library setup. Given the workspace directory layout we are using, however, you will find the original ordering of the steps given above to be more appropriate.

Obviously, each step involves many iterations of its own. Nonetheless, the steps remain similar in many ways. Most toolchain build steps involve carrying out the following actions:

1. Unpack the package.
2. Configure the package for cross-platform development.
3. Build the package.
4. Install the package.

Some toolchain builds differ slightly from this sequence. The kernel headers setup, for instance, does not require that we build the kernel or install it. Actually, we will save much of the discussions about configuring, building, and installing the kernel for Chapter 5. Also, since the compiler will have already been unpacked for the bootstrap compiler's setup, the full compiler setup does not require unpacking the gcc package again.

Workspace setup

According to the workspace directory layout I suggested earlier, the toolchain will be built in the *${PRJROOT}/build-tools* directory, while the components built will be installed in the *${PRJROOT}/tools* directory. To this end, we need to define some additional environment variables. They ease the build process and are based on the environment variables already defined. Using the same example project as before, here is the new *develdaq* script with the new variables:

```
export PROJECT=daq-module
export PRJROOT=/home/karim/control-project/${PROJECT}
export TARGET=i386-linux
export PREFIX=${PRJROOT}/tools
export TARGET_PREFIX=${PREFIX}/${TARGET}
export PATH=${PREFIX}/bin:${PATH}
cd $PRJROOT
```

The TARGET variable defines the type of target for which your toolchain will be built. Table 4-3 provides some of the other possible values for TARGET. Notice that the target definition does not depend on the type of host. A target is defined by its own hardware and the operating system used on it, which is Linux in this case. Also, note that only TARGET needs to be modified in case we change targets. Of course, if we had already compiled the complete GNU toolchain for a different target, we would need to rebuild it after changing the value of TARGET. For a more complete list of TARGET values, look at the manual included in the glibc sources.

Table 4-3. Example values for TARGET

Actual target	Value of TARGET
PowerPC	powerpc-linux
ARM	arm-linux
MIPS (big endian)	mips-linux
MIPS (little endian)	mipsel-linux
SuperH 4	sh4-linux

The PREFIX variable provides the component configuration scripts with a pointer to the directory where we would like the target utilities to be installed. Conversely, TARGET_PREFIX is used for the installation of target-dependent header files and libraries. To have access to the newly installed utilities, we also need to modify the PATH variable to point to the directory where the binaries will be installed.

Some people prefer to set PREFIX to */usr/local*. This results in the tools and libraries being installed within the */usr/local* directory where they can be accessed by any user. I find this approach not to be useful for most situations, however, because even projects using the same target architecture may require different toolchain configurations.

If you need to set up a toolchain for an entire development team, instead of sharing tools and libraries via the */usr/local* directory, I suggest that a developer build the toolchain within an entry shared by all project members in the */home* directory, as I said earlier. In a case in which no entry in the */home* directory is shared among group members, a developer may build the toolchain within an entry in her workstation's */opt* directory and then share her resulting *${PRJROOT}/tools* directory with her colleagues. This may be done using any of the traditional sharing mechanisms available, such as NFS, or using a tar-gzipped archive available on an FTP server. Each developer using the package will have to place it in a filesystem hierarchy identical to the one used to build the toolchain for the tools to operate adequately. In a case in which the toolchain was built within the */opt* directory, this means placing the toolchain in the */opt* directory.

If you choose to set PREFIX to */usr/local*, you will also have to issue the commands shown below while being logged-in as root, with all the risks this entails. You could also set the permission bits of the */usr/local* directory to allow yourself or your user group to issue the commands without requiring root privileges.

Notice that TARGET_PREFIX is set to *${PREFIX}/${TARGET}*, which is a target-dependent directory. If you set PREFIX to */usr/local*, successive installations of development toolchains for different targets will result in the libraries and header files of the latest installation being placed in different directories from the libraries and header files of previous toolchain installations.

Regardless of the value you give to PREFIX, setting TARGET_PREFIX to *${PREFIX}/ ${TARGET}* is the configuration the GNU toolchain utilities expect to find during their configuration and installation. Hence, I strongly suggest that you use this value for TARGET_PREFIX. The following explanations may require changes if you modify TARGET_PREFIX's value.

Again, you can remove the *cd* command from the script if you would prefer not to move directly to the project directory.

Preparing the build-tools directory

At this point, you should have the different packages required for building the toolchain in the *build-tools* directory. As with other packages, a new directory will be created when you extract the files from the package archive. This new directory will contain the complete source code necessary to build the packages and all appropriate Makefiles. Although it is possible to build the package within this source directory, I highly recommend that you build each package in a directory separate from its source directory, as is suggested in the FSF's installation manuals.

Building a package in a directory different from the one holding its source may seem awkward if you are used to simply typing *configure; make; make install*, but I will shortly explain how this is done. First, though, we need to create the directories that will hold the packages being built. Create one directory for each toolchain component. Four directories are therefore needed: one for the binutils, one for the bootstrap C compiler, one for the C library, and one for the complete compiler. We can use the following commands to create the necessary entries:

```
$ cd ${PRJROOT}/build-tools
$ mkdir build-binutils build-boot-gcc build-glibc build-gcc
```

We can now look at the content of the build-tools directory with the packages and the build directories (the last line in this example is truncated to fit the page):

```
$ ls -l
total 35151
-rw-r--r--    1 karim    karim     7284401 Apr  4 17:33 binutils-2.10.1.tar.gz
drwxrwxr-x    2 karim    karim        1024 Apr  4 17:33 build-binutils
drwxrwxr-x    2 karim    karim        1024 Apr  4 17:33 build-boot-gcc
drwxrwxr-x    2 karim    karim        1024 Apr  4 17:33 build-gcc
drwxrwxr-x    2 karim    karim        1024 Apr  4 17:33 build-glibc
-rw-r--r--    1 karim    karim    12911721 Apr  4 17:33 gcc-2.95.3.tar.gz
-rw-r--r--    1 karim    karim    15431745 Apr  4 17:33 glibc-2.2.3.tar.gz
-rw-r--r--    1 karim    karim      215313 Apr  4 17:33 glibc-linuxthreads-2.2.3.t
```

Everything is now almost ready for building the actual toolchain.

Resources

Before proceeding to the actual building of the toolchain, let us look at some resources you may find useful in case you run into problems during the build process.

First and foremost, each package comes with its own documentation. Although you will find the binutils package to be the leanest in terms of installation documentation, it is also the least likely to cause any problems. The gcc and glibc packages, however, are amply documented. Within the gcc package, you will find an FAQ file and an *install* directory containing instructions on how to configure and install gcc. This includes an extensive explanation of the build configuration options. Similarly, the glibc package contains an *FAQ* and *INSTALL* files. The *INSTALL* file covers the build configuration options and the installation process, and provides recommendations for compilation tool versions.

In addition, you may want to try using a general search engine such as Google to look for reports by other developers who may have already encountered and solved problems similar to yours. Often, using a general search engine will be the most effective way to solve a GNU toolchain build problem.

On the matter of cross-compiling, there are two CrossGCC FAQs available: the Scott Howard FAQ and the Bill Gatliff FAQ. The Scott Howard CrossGCC FAQ is available at *http://www.sthoward.com/CrossGCC/*. This FAQ is rather outdated, however. The Bill Gatliff CrossGCC FAQ is available at *http://crossgcc.billgatliff.com/*.

Though the Scott Howard FAQ is outdated, and though it isn't limited to Linux and attempts to provide general explanations for all the platforms the GNU toolchain can be built for, it does provide pieces of information that can be hard to find otherwise. It covers, for instance, what is known as *Canadian Crosses*,* a technique for building cross-platform development tools for development on another platform. An example of this would be building cross-platform development tools for an ARM target and an i386 host on a PPC workstation.

As with the Scott Howard FAQ, the Bill Gatliff FAQ is not limited to Linux. In addition to the FAQ, Bill Gatliff actively maintains a CrossGCC Wiki site, which provides information on a variety of cross-platform development issues, including tutorials, links to relevant articles, and explanations about GNU toolchain internals. Since this is a Wiki site, you can register to modify and contribute to the site yourself. The Wiki site is accessed through the same URL as the Bill Gatliff FAQ.

Both FAQs provide scripts to automate the building of the toolchain. Similar scripts are also available from many other sites. You may be interested in taking a look at these scripts, but I will not rely on any scripts for my future explanations as I would rather you fully understand all the steps involved.

Finally, there is a crosgcc mailing list hosted by Red Hat at *http://sources.redhat.com/ml/crossgcc/*. You will find this mailing list quite useful if you ever get stuck, because many on this list have a great deal of experience with the process of building cross-platform development toolchains. Often, just searching or browsing the archive will help you locate immediate answers to your questions.

A word on prebuilt cross-platform toolchains

A lot of prebuilt cross-platform toolchains are available either online or commercially. Since I do not know the actual process by which each was built, I cannot offer any advice regarding those packages. You may still choose to use such packages out of convenience instead of carrying out the procedure explained here. In that case, make sure you have documentation as to how these packages were configured and built. Most importantly, make sure you know what package versions were used, what patches were applied, if any, and where to get the patches that were applied in case you need them.

Kernel Headers Setup

As I said earlier, the setup of the kernel headers is the first step in building the toolchain. In this case, we are using kernel Version 2.4.18, but we could have used any other version appropriate for our target. We will discuss kernel selection further in Chapter 5.

Having selected a kernel, the first thing you need to do is download a copy of that kernel into the directory in which you have chosen to store kernels. In the case of the

---

* In reference to the fact that Canada had three national parties at the time a name was needed for this procedure.

workspace hierarchy I suggested earlier, this would be in *${PRJROOT}/kernel*. You can obtain all the Linux kernels from the main kernel repository at *http://www.kernel. org/* or any other mirror site, such as the national mirrors.* There are other sites that provide kernels more adapted to certain targets, and I will cover these in Chapter 5.

For some time now, each version of the kernel has been available both as a tar-gzipped file (with the *.tar.gz* extension) and as a tar-bzip2'd file (with the *.tar.bz2* extension). Both contain the same kernel, except that tar-bzip2'd files are smaller and require less download time than tar-gzipped files.

With the kernel now in your kernel directory, you can extract it using the appropriate command. In our case, we use one the following commands, depending on the file we downloaded:

```
$ tar xvzf linux-2.4.18.tar.gz
```

or:

```
$ tar xvjf linux-2.4.18.tar.bz2
```

Some older versions of *tar* do not support the *j* option and you may need to use *bzip2 -d* or *bunzip2* to decompress the archive before using *tar*.

For all kernels up to 2.4.18, the *tar* command creates a directory called *linux* that contains the extracted files from the archive. Starting with 2.4.19, however, the kernel extracts immediately into a directory that has the version number appended to its name. Hence, Linux 2.4.19 extracts directly into the *linux-2.4.19* directory. This avoids accidently overwriting an older kernel with a new one. If you are using a kernel that is older than 2.4.19, I recommend that you rename the directory right away to avoid any accidental overwriting:

```
$ mv linux linux-2.4.18
```

Overwriting a kernel version with another because the directory of the previous version wasn't renamed is a common and often costly mistake, so it is really important that you rename the directory as soon as you extract the kernel from the archive, if need be.

With the kernel now extracted, we proceed to configuring it:

```
$ cd linux-2.4.18
$ make ARCH=i386 CROSS_COMPILE=i386-linux- menuconfig
```

This will display a menu in your console where you will be able to select your kernel's configuration. Instead of *menuconfig*, you can specify *config* or *xconfig*. The former requires that you provide an answer for every possible configuration option one by one at the command line. The latter provides an X Window dialog, which is often considered the most intuitive way to configure the kernel. Beware of *xconfig*,

---

* In some countries, there are local national mirrors, which may be preferable for you to use instead of the main U.S. site. These mirrors' URLs are usually in the *http://www.COUNTRY.kernel.org/* form. *http://www.it. kernel.org/* and *http://www.cz.kernel.org/* are two such mirrors.

however, as it may fail to set some configuration options and forget to generate some headers required by the procedure I am describing. The use of *config* may also result in some headers not being created. You can check whether the kernel configuration has successfully created the appropriate headers by verifying whether the *include/linux/version.h* file exists in the kernel sources after you finish the configuration process. If it is absent, the instructions outlined below will fail at the first instance where kernel headers are required; usually during the compilation of glibc.

As you probably noticed, the values of ARCH and CROSS_COMPILE depend on your target's architecture type. Had this been a PPC target and an i386 host, we would have used ARCH=ppc and CROSS_COMPILE=powerpc-linux-. (The trailing hyphen in the CROSS_COMPILE=powerpc-linux- variable is not an accident.) Strictly speaking, it is not necessary to set CROSS_COMPILE for all kernel *make* targets. The various configuration targets I just covered don't usually need it, for example. In fact, it is only necessary when code is actually being cross-compiled as a result of the kernel Makefile rules. Nevertheless, I will continue to specify it for all kernel *make* targets throughout this book, even when it isn't essential, to highlight its importance. You are free to set it only when needed in your actual day-to-day work.

I will cover the intricacies of kernel configuration in Chapter 5. If you are not familiar with kernel configuration, you may want to have a peek at that chapter first. The most important configuration options we need to set at this time are the processor and system type. Although it is preferable to fully configure the kernel before proceeding, just setting the processor and system type is usually enough to generate the appropriate headers for the toolchain build.

With the kernel now configured, exit the menu by selecting the Exit item with your right arrow. The configuration utility then asks you if you want to save the configuration and, upon confirmation, proceeds to write the kernel configuration and creates the appropriate files and links.

We can now create the *include* directory required for the toolchain and copy the kernel headers to it:

```
$ mkdir -p ${TARGET_PREFIX}/include
$ cp -r include/linux/ ${TARGET_PREFIX}/include
$ cp -r include/asm-i386/ ${TARGET_PREFIX}/include/asm
$ cp -r include/asm-generic/ ${TARGET_PREFIX}/include
```

Keep in mind that we are using a PPC host and an i386 target. Hence, the *asm-i386* directory in the path above is the directory containing the target-specific headers, not the host-specific ones. If this were a PPC target, for example, we would have to replace *asm-i386* with *asm-ppc*.

Note that you will *not* need to rebuild the toolchain every time you reconfigure the kernel. The toolchain needs one valid set of headers for your target, which is provided by the procedure given earlier. You may later choose to reconfigure your kernel or use another one entirely without impacting your toolchain, unless you change the processor or system type.

Binutils Setup

The binutils package includes the utilities most often used to manipulate binary object files. The two most important utilities within the package are the GNU assembler, *as*, and the linker, *ld*. Table 4-4 contains the complete list of utilities found in the binutils package.

Table 4-4. Utilities found in the binutils package

Utility	Use
as	The GNU assembler
ld	The GNU linker
gasp	The GNU assembler pre-processor
ar	Creates and manipulates archive content
nm	Lists the symbols in an object file
objcopy	Copies and translates object files
objdump	Displays information about the content of object files
ranlib	Generates an index to the content of an archive
readelf	Displays information about an ELF format object file
size	Lists the sizes of sections within an object file
strings	Prints the strings of printable characters in object files
strip	Strips symbols from object files
c++filt	Converts low-level mangled assembly labels resulting from over-loaded c++ functions into their user-level names
addr2line	Converts addresses into line numbers within original source files

Note that although *as* supports many processor architectures, it does not necessarily recognize the same syntax as the other assemblers available for a given architecture. The syntax recognized by *as* is actually a machine-independent syntax inspired by BSD 4.2 assembly language.

The first step in setting up the binutils package is to extract its source code from the archive we downloaded earlier:

```
$ cd ${PRJROOT}/build-tools
$ tar xvzf binutils-2.10.1.tar.gz
```

This will create a directory called *binutils-2.10.1* with the package's content. We can now move to the build directory for the second part of the build process, the configuration of the package for cross-platform development:

```
$ cd build-binutils
$ ../binutils-2.10.1/configure --target=$TARGET --prefix=${PREFIX}
Configuring for a powerpc-unknown-linux-gnu host.
Created "Makefile" in /home/karim/control-project/daq-module/build-...
Configuring intl...
creating cache ../config.cache
checking for a BSD compatible install... /usr/bin/install -c
```

```
checking how to run the C preprocessor... gcc -E
checking whether make sets ${MAKE}... yes
checking for gcc... gcc
checking whether the C compiler (gcc -g -O2 -W -Wall ) works... yes
checking whether the C compiler (gcc -g -O2 -W -Wall ) is a cross-c...
checking whether we are using GNU C... yes
checking whether gcc accepts -g... yes
checking for ranlib... ranlib
checking for POSIXized ISC... no
checking for ANSI C header files... yes
    ...
```

What I've shown is only part of the output from the *configure* script. It will actually continue printing similar messages on the console until it has prepared each utility in the package for compilation. This may take a minute or two to complete, but it is a relatively short operation.

During its run, *configure* checks for the availability of certain resources on the host and creates appropriate Makefiles for each tool in the package. Since the command is not being issued in the directory containing the binutils source code, the result of the *configure* command will be found in the directory where it was issued, the *build-binutils* directory.

We control the creation of the Makefiles by passing the appropriate options to *configure*. The *--target* option enables us to specify the target for which the binutils are being built. Since we had already specified the name of the target in the TARGET environment variable, we provide this variable as is. The *--prefix* option enables us to provide the configuration script with the directory within which it should install files and directories. The directory for *--prefix* is the same as the one we specified earlier in the PREFIX environment variables.

With the Makefiles now ready, we can build the actual utilities:

```
$ make
```

The actual build of the binutils may take anywhere between 10 and 30 minutes, depending on your hardware. Using a 400 MHz PowerBook host, it takes at most 15 minutes to build the binutils for the i386 target used here. You may see some warnings during the build but they can be ignored, unless you're one of the binutils developers.

With the package now built, we can install the binutils:

```
$ make install
```

The binutils have now been installed inside the directory pointed to by PREFIX. You can check to see that they have been installed properly by listing the appropriate directory:

```
$ ls ${PREFIX}/bin
i386-linux-addr2line   i386-linux-ld        i386-linux-readelf
i386-linux-ar          i386-linux-nm        i386-linux-size
i386-linux-as          i386-linux-objcopy   i386-linux-strings
i386-linux-c++filt     i386-linux-objdump   i386-linux-strip
i386-linux-gasp        i386-linux-ranlib
```

Notice that the name of each utility is prepended by the value of TARGET we set earlier. Had the target been a powerpc-linux, for instance, the names of the utilities would have been prepended with *powerpc-linux-*. When building an application for a target, we can therefore use the appropriate tools by prepending the name of the target type.

A copy of some of the utilities without the prepended target name will also be installed in the *${PREFIX}/${TARGET}/bin* directory. Since this directory will later be used to install target binaries by the C library build process, we will need to move the host binaries to a more appropriate directory. For now, we will leave them as is and address this issue later.

Bootstrap Compiler Setup

In contrast to the binutils package, the gcc package contains only one utility, the GNU compiler, along with support components such as runtime libraries. At this stage, we will build the bootstrap compiler, which will support only the C language. Later, once the C library has been compiled, we will recompile gcc with full C++ support.

Again, we start by extracting the gcc package from the archive we downloaded earlier:

```
$ cd ${PRJROOT}/build-tools
$ tar xvzf gcc-2.95.3.tar.gz
```

This will create a directory called *gcc-2.95.3* with the package's content. We can now proceed to the configuration of the build in the directory we had prepared for the bootstrap compiler:

```
$ cd build-boot-gcc
$ ../gcc-2.95.3/configure --target=$TARGET --prefix=${PREFIX} \
> --without-headers --with-newlib --enable-languages=c
```

This will print output similar to that printed by the binutils configuration utility we discussed earlier. Here too, *configure* checks for the availability of resources and builds appropriate Makefiles.

The *--target* and *--prefix* options given to *configure* have the same purpose as with binutils, to specify the target and the installation directory, respectively. In addition, we use options that are required for building a bootstrap compiler.

Since this is a cross-compiler and there are no system header files for the target yet—they will be available once glibc is built—we need to use the *--without-headers* option. We also need to use the *--with-newlib* option to tell the configuration utility not to use glibc, since it has not yet been compiled for the target. This option, however, does not force us to use newlib as the C library for the target. It is just there to enable gcc to properly compile, and we will be free to choose any C library at a later time.

The *--enable-languages* option tells the configuration script which programming languages we expect the resulting compiler to support. Since this is a bootstrap compiler, we need only include support for C.

Depending on your particular setup, you may want to use additional options for your target. For a complete list of the options recognized by *configure*, see the installation documentation provided with the gcc package.

With the Makefiles ready, we can now build the compiler:

```
$ make all-gcc
```

The compile time for the bootstrap compiler is comparable to that of the binutils. Here, too, you may see warnings during the compilation, and you can safely ignore them.

With the compilation complete, we can now install gcc:

```
$ make install-gcc
```

The bootstrap compiler is now installed alongside the binutils, and you can see it by relisting the content of *${PREFIX}/bin*. The name of the compiler, like the utilities, is prepended with the name of the target and is called *i386-linux-gcc* in our example.

C Library Setup

The glibc package is made up of a number of libraries and is the most delicate and lengthy package build in our cross-platform development toolchain. It is an extremely important software component on which most, if not all, applications available or being developed for your target will rely. Note that although the glibc package is often called the C library—a confusion maintained within GNU's own documentation—glibc actually generates many libraries, one of which is the actual C library, libc. We will discuss the complete list of libraries generated by glibc in Chapter 6. Until then, I will continue to use "C library" and "glibc" interchangeably.

As with the previous packages, we start by extracting the C library from the archive we downloaded earlier:

```
$ cd ${PRJROOT}/build-tools
$ tar xvzf glibc-2.2.3.tar.gz
```

This will create a directory called *glibc-2.2.3* with the package's content. In addition to extracting the C library, we extract the linuxthreads package in the glibc directory for the reasons stated earlier in the chapter:

```
$ tar -xvzf glibc-linuxthreads-2.2.3.tar.gz --directory=glibc-2.2.3
```

We can now proceed to preparing the build of the C library in the *build-glibc* directory:

```
$ cd build-glibc
$ CC=i386-linux-gcc ../glibc-2.2.3/configure --host=$TARGET \
> --prefix="/usr" --enable-add-ons \
> --with-headers=${TARGET_PREFIX}/include
```

Notice that this configuration command is somewhat different from the previous ones. First, we precede the call to *configure* with *CC=i386-linux-gcc*. The effect of this command is to set the CC environment variable to i386-linux-gcc. Therefore, the compiler used to build the C library will be the bootstrap cross-compiler we have just built.

Using gcc 3.2 and Above

The instructions provided in the previous section will fail to work with gcc 3.2 and the subsequent 3.2.1 release existing at the time of this writing, because the *--without-headers* configuration option is broken and has not yet been fixed. To solve the problem, we must install appropriate glibc headers before attempting to compile the bootstrap compiler. This sidebar provides the commands used to install the headers, but does not explain the various command options in detail, since they are already covered by the previous and next sections. Here, we are using binutils 2.13.2.1, gcc 3.2.1, and glibc 2.3.1. Note that a native gcc 3.2 must be available on the host for the following procedure to work.

First, we must extract the glibc package and its add-ons, as we would do when setting up the C library:

```
$ cd ${PRJROOT}/build-tools
$ tar xvzf glibc-2.3.1.tar.gz
$ tar -xvzf glibc-linuxthreads-2.3.1.tar.gz --directory=glibc-2.3.1
```

Next, we must configure glibc and install its headers:

```
$ mkdir build-glibc-headers
$ cd build-glibc-headers
$ ../glibc-2.3.1/configure --host=$TARGET --prefix="/usr" \
> --enable-add-ons --with-headers=${TARGET_PREFIX}/include
$ make cross-compiling=yes install_root=${TARGET_PREFIX} \
> prefix="" install-headers
```

Because we are not setting CC to point to an existing cross-compiler, we must set the cross-compiling variable to yes so that the glibc build scripts do not attempt to build parts of the library natively. Installing the headers is achieved by using the install-headers Makefile target.

Next, we create a dummy *stubs.h* file required for gcc to build (a version of this file will be generated properly during the installation of the cross-compiled glibc):

```
$ mkdir -p ${TARGET_PREFIX}/include/gnu
$ touch ${TARGET_PREFIX}/include/gnu/stubs.h
```

Finally, we can build the bootstrap gcc compiler:

```
$ cd ${PRJROOT}/build-tools/build-boot-gcc
$ ../gcc-3.2.1/configure --target=$TARGET --prefix=${PREFIX} \
> --disable-shared --with-headers=${TARGET_PREFIX}/include \
> --with-newlib --enable-languages=c
$ make all-gcc
```

In addition to the options we used in the previous section, we are also using the *--disable-shared* configuration option to avoid the build scripts from trying to create the shared gcc library. If this option is not used, gcc 3.2 fails to build.

Once the bootstrap compiler is installed, the steps for building and installing the rest of the GNU toolchain are the same as those described in this chapter.

Also, we now use the --*host* option instead of the --*target* option, since the library runs on our target and not on our build system.* In other words, the host from the point of view of the library is our target, contrary to the tools we built earlier, which all run on our build system.

Although we still use the --*prefix* option, its purpose here is to indicate to the configuration script the location of the library components once on the target's root filesystem. This location is then hardcoded into the glibc components during their compilation and used at runtime. As is explained in the *INSTALL* file in the glibc source directory, Linux systems expect to have some glibc components installed in */lib* and others in */usr/lib*. By setting --*prefix* to */usr*, the configuration script recognizes this setup and the relevant directory paths are properly hardcoded in the glibc components. As a result, the dynamic linker, for example, will expect to find shared libraries in */lib*, which is the appropriate location for these libraries in any Linux system, as we shall see in Chapter 6. We will not, however, let the build script install the libraries into the build system's */usr* directory. Rather, as we shall see later in this section, we will override the install directory when issuing the *make install* command.

We also instruct the configuration script to use the add-on we downloaded with the --*enable-add-ons* option. Since we are using linuxthreads only, we could have given the exact list of add-ons we want to be configured by using the --*enable-add-ons=linuxthreads* option. If you are using glibc 2.1.x and had applied the glibc-crypt add-on, you would need to use the --*enable-add-ons=linuxthreads,crypt* option instead. The full command I provided earlier, which doesn't include the full list of add-ons, will work fine nonetheless with most glibc versions.

Finally, we tell the configuration script where to find the kernel headers we set up earlier using the --*with-headers* option. If this option was omitted, the headers found through */usr/include* would be used to build glibc and these would be inappropriate, since they are the build system's headers, not the target's.

During the actual build of the library, three sets of libraries are built: a shared set, a static set, and a static set with profiling information. If you do not intend to use the profiling version of the library, you may instruct the configuration script not to include it as part of the build process by using the --*disable-profile* option. The same applies to the shared set, which can be disabled using the --*disable-shared* option. If you do not intend to have many applications on your target and plan to link all your applications statically, you may want to use this option. Be careful, however, as your target may eventually need the shared library. You can safely leave its build enabled and still link your applications statically. At least then you will be able to change your mind about how to link your application without having to rebuild the C library.

Another option that has an effect on static versus dynamic linking is --*enable-static-nss*. This option generates libraries which enable the static linking of the *Name Service*

---

* Practically speaking, the build system is our development host.

Switch (NSS) components. In brief, the NSS part of glibc allows some of the library components to be customizable to the local configuration. This involves the use of the */etc/nsswitch.conf* file to specify which */lib/libnss_NSS_SERVICE* library is loaded at runtime. Because this service is specifically designed to load libraries dynamically, it doesn't allow true static linking unless it is forced to. Hence, if you plan to statically link applications that use NSS, add the *--enable-static-nss* option to the configuration script's command line. The web servers discussed in Chapter 10, for example, use NSS and will either not function properly on the target or will simply fail to build if you instruct the linker to statically link them against a glibc that doesn't allow static NSS linking. Look at the glibc manual for a complete discussion of NSS.

If you are compiling glibc for a target that lacks an FPU, you may also want to use the *--without-fp* option to build FPU emulation into the C library. In some cases, you may also need to add the *-msoft-float* option to the C flags used to build the library. In the case of the PPC, at least, the C flags are appropriately set (since glibc 2.3) whenever *--without-fp* is used to configure glibc.

If you have chosen not to download the linuxthreads package, or the crypt package if you were using glibc 2.1.x, you may try to compile the C library by removing the *--enable-add-ons* option and adding the *--disable-sanity-checks* option. Otherwise, the configuration script will complain about the missing linuxthreads. Note, however, that although glibc may build successfully without linuxthreads, it is possible that the full compiler's build will fail when including C++ support later.

With the configuration script done, we can now compile glibc:

```
$ make
```

The C library is a very large package and its compilation may take several hours, depending on your hardware. On the PowerBook system mentioned earlier, the build takes approximately an hour. Regardless of your platform, this is a good time to relax, grab a snack, or get some fresh air. One thing you may want to avoid is compiling the C library in the background while trying to use your computer for other purposes in the meantime. As I said earlier, the compilation of some of the C library's components uses up a lot of memory, and if the compiler fails because of the lack of available memory, you may have to restart the build of the library from scratch using *make clean* followed by *make*. Some parts of the build may not be restarted gracefully if you just retype *make*.

Once the C library is built, we can now install it:

```
$ make install_root=${TARGET_PREFIX} prefix="" install
```

In contrast to the installation of the other packages, the installation of the C library will take some time. It won't take as much time as the compilation, but it may take between 5 and 10 minutes, again depending on your hardware.

Notice that the installation command differs from the conventional *make install*. We set the install_root variable to specify the directory where we want the library's components to be installed. This ensures that the library and its headers are installed in the target-dependent directory we had assigned to `TARGET_PREFIX` earlier, not in the build system's */usr* directory. Also, since the use of the `--prefix` option sets the `prefix` variable's value and since the value of `prefix` is appended to `install_root`'s value to provide the final installation directory of the library's components, we reset the value of `prefix` so that all glibc components are installed directly in the *${TARGET_PREFIX}* directory. Hence, the glibc components that would have been installed in *${TARGET_PREFIX}/usr/lib* are installed in *${TARGET_PREFIX}/lib* instead.

If you are building tools for a target that is of the same architecture as your host (compiling for a PPC target on a PPC host, for instance), you may want to set the cross-compiling variable to yes as part of the *make install* command. Because the library's *configure* script will have detected that the architectures are identical during the build configuration, the Makefile assumes that you are not cross-compiling and the installation of the C library fails as a result of the Makefile using a different set of rules.

There is one last step we must carry out to finalize glibc's installation: the configuration of the *libc.so* file. This file is used during the linking of applications to the C library and is actually a link script. It contains references to the various libraries needed for the real linking. The installation carried out by our *make install* above assumes that the library is being installed on a root filesystem and hence uses absolute pathnames in the *libc.so* link script to reference the libraries. Since we have installed the C library in a nonstandard directory, we must modify the link script so that the linker will use the appropriate libraries. Along with the other components of the C library, the link script has been installed in the *${TARGET_PREFIX}/lib* directory.

In its original form, *libc.so* looks like this:

```
/* GNU ld script
   Use the shared library, but some functions are only in
   the static library, so try that secondarily.  */
GROUP ( /lib/libc.so.6 /lib/libc_nonshared.a )
```

This is actually quite similar, if not identical, to the *libc.so* that has already been installed by your distribution for your native C library in */usr/lib/*. Since you may need your target's default script sometime, I suggest you make a copy before modifying it:

```
$ cd ${TARGET_PREFIX}/lib
$ cp ./libc.so ./libc.so.orig
```

You can now edit the file and remove all absolute path references. In essence, you will need to remove */lib/* from all the library filenames. The new *libc.so* now looks like this:

```
/* GNU ld script
   Use the shared library, but some functions are only in
   the static library, so try that secondarily.  */
GROUP ( libc.so.6 libc_nonshared.a )
```

By removing the references to an absolute path, we are now forcing the linker to use the libraries found within the same directory as the *libc.so* script, which are the appropriate ones for your target, instead of the native ones found on your host.

Full Compiler Setup

We are now ready to install the full compiler for your target with both C and C++ support. Since we had already extracted the compiler from its archive in "Bootstrap Compiler Setup," we will not need to repeat this step. Overall, the build of the full compiler is much simpler than the build of the bootstrap compiler.

From the *build-tools/build-gcc* directory enter:

```
$ cd ${PRJROOT}/build-tools/build-gcc
$ ../gcc-2.95.3/configure --target=$TARGET --prefix=${PREFIX} \
> --enable-languages=c,c++
```

The options we use here have the same meaning as when building the bootstrap compiler. Notice, however, that there are fewer options and that we now add support for C++ in addition to C. If you had set `TARGET_PREFIX` to something other than *${PREFIX}/${TARGET}* as we did earlier, you will need to use the *--with-headers* and *--with-libs* options to tell the configuration script where to find the headers and libraries installed by glibc.

With the full compiler properly configured, we can now build it:

```
$ make all
```

This build will take slightly longer than the build of the bootstrap compiler. Again, you may see warnings that you can ignore. Notice that we didn't use `all-gcc` as with the bootstrap compiler, but rather `all`. This will result in the build of all the rest of the components included with the gcc package, including the C++ runtime libraries.

If you didn't properly configure the *libc.so* link script file as previously explained, the build will fail during the compilation of the runtime libraries. Also, if you didn't install the linuxthreads package during the C library setup, the compilation may fail under some versions of gcc. Version 2.95.3 of gcc, for instance, will fail to build without linuxthreads.

With the full compiler now built, we can install it:

```
$ make install
```

This will install the full compiler over the bootstrap compiler we had previously installed. Notice that we didn't use `install-gcc` as we had done earlier for the bootstrap compiler, but rather `install`. Again, this is because we are now installing both gcc and its support components.

Finalizing the Toolchain Setup

The full cross-platform development toolchain is now set up and almost ready to be used. I have only a couple of final observations left.

First, let's take a look at what has been installed in the tools directory and how we will be using it in the future. Table 4-5 provides the list of first-level subdirectories found in the tools directory.

Table 4-5. Contents of the ${PRJROOT}/tools directory

Directory	Content
bin	The cross-development utilities.
i386-linux	Target-specific files.
include	Headers for cross-development tools.
info	The gcc info files.
lib	Libraries for cross-development tools.
man	The manual pages for cross-development tools.
share	The files shared among cross-development tools and libraries. This directory is empty.

The two most important directories are *bin* and *i386-linux*. The first contains all the tools within the cross-development toolchain that we will use on the host to develop applications for the target. The second contains all the software components to be used on the target. Mainly, it contains the header files and runtime libraries for the target. Table 4-6 provides a list of the first-level subdirectories found in *i386-linux*.

Table 4-6. Contents of the ${PRJROOT}/tools/i386-linux directory

Directory	Content
bin	glibc-related target binaries and scripts.
etc	Files that should be placed in the target's */etc* directory. Only contains the *rpc* file.
include	The headers used to build applications for the target.
info	The glibc info files.
lib	The target's */lib* directory.
libexec	Binary helpers. This directory only contains *pt_chown*, which you will not need for most targets.
sbin	The target's */sbin* directory.
share	Subdirectories and files related to internationalization.
sys-include	Would have been used by the gcc configuration script to copy the target's headers had glibc not installed the main target headers in the *include* directory.

Within the *i386-linux* directory, the two most important directories are *include* and *lib*. The first contains the header files that will be used to build any application for the target. The second contains the runtime libraries for the target.

Notice that this last directory contains a lot of large libraries. By itself, the directory weighs in at around 80 MB. Most embedded systems do not have this quantity of storage available. As we will see in "C Library Alternatives," there are other libraries that can be used instead of glibc. Also, we will see in Chapter 6 ways to minimize the number and size of the libraries you choose to use.

As I said earlier, a copy of some of the host utilities without the prepended target name have been installed in the *${PREFIX}/${TARGET}/bin* directory. Since this directory now contains target binaries installed by the C library build process, I highly suggest that you move the host binaries out of this directory and into another directory more appropriate for host binaries. The utilities affected by this are *as*, *ar*, *gcc*, *ld*, *nm*, *ranlib*, and *strip*. You can verify that these are indeed host binaries using the *file* command:

```
$ cd ${PREFIX}/${TARGET}/bin
$ file as ar gcc ld nm ranlib strip
as:     ELF 32-bit MSB executable, PowerPC or cisco 4500, version 1...
ar:     ELF 32-bit MSB executable, PowerPC or cisco 4500, version 1...
gcc:    ELF 32-bit MSB executable, PowerPC or cisco 4500, version 1...
ld:     ELF 32-bit MSB executable, PowerPC or cisco 4500, version 1...
nm:     ELF 32-bit MSB executable, PowerPC or cisco 4500, version 1...
ranlib: ELF 32-bit MSB executable, PowerPC or cisco 4500, version 1...
strip:  ELF 32-bit MSB executable, PowerPC or cisco 4500, version 1...
```

We must choose an appropriate directory in which to put these binaries and create symbolic links to the relocated binaries, because some GNU utilities, including *gcc*, expect to find some of the other GNU utilities in *${PREFIX}/${TARGET}/bin* and will use the host's utilities if they can't find the target's binaries there. Naturally, this will result in failed compilations, since the wrong system's tools are used. The compiler has a default search path it uses to look for binaries. We can view this path using one of the compiler's own options (some lines wrap; your shell will take care of line wrapping):

```
$ i386-linux-gcc -print-search-dirs
install: /home/karim/control-project/daq-module/tools/lib/gcc-lib/i386-linux/2.95.3/
programs: /home/karim/control-project/daq-module/tools/lib/gcc-lib/i386-linux/2.95.3/
:/home/karim/control-project/daq-module/tools/lib/gcc-lib/i386-linux/:/usr/lib/gcc/
i386-linux/2.95.3/:/usr/lib/gcc/i386-linux/:/home/karim/control-project/daq-module/
tools/i386-linux/bin/i386-linux/2.95.3/:/home/karim/control-project/daq-module/tools/
i386-linux/bin/
libraries: /home/karim/control-project/daq-module/tools/lib/gcc-lib/i386-linux/2.95.
3/:/usr/lib/gcc/i386-linux/2.95.3/:/home/karim/control-project/daq-module/tools/i386-
linux/lib/i386-linux/2.95.3/:/home/karim/control-project/daq-module/tools/i386-linux/
lib/
```

The first entry on the programs line, *${PREFIX}/lib/gcc-lib/i386-linux/2.95.3*, is a directory containing gcc libraries and utilities. By placing the binaries in this directory, you can make the cross-compiler use them instead of the native tools:

```
$ mv as ar gcc ld nm ranlib strip \
> ${PREFIX}/lib/gcc-lib/i386-linux/2.95.3
```

Meanwhile, the native toolchain will continue to operate normally. We can also create symbolic links to the relocated binaries just in case an application still looks for the utilities only in *${PREFIX}/${TARGET}/bin*. Most applications will not look exclusively in this directory, however, and you can almost always skip this step. One case requiring these symbolic links is when you need to recompile components of the GNU cross-platform development toolchain for your target. Nonetheless, because these are symbolic links to host binaries instead of the host binaries themselves, it is easier to tell them apart from the target binaries in case you need to copy the content of the *${PREFIX}/${TARGET}/bin* directory to your target's root filesystem. The following script makes the links:

```
$ for file in as ar gcc ld nm ranlib strip
> do
> ln -s ${PREFIX}/lib/gcc-lib/i386-linux/2.95.3/$file .
> done
```

Regardless of the type of host or the gcc version you use, a directory similar to *${PREFIX}/lib/gcc-lib/i386-linux/2.95.3* will be created during the building of the cross-platform development toolchain. As you can see, the directory path is made up of the target type and the gcc version. Your particular directory should be located in *${PREFIX}/lib/gcc-lib/${TARGET}/GCC_VERSION*, where *GCC_VERSION* is the version of gcc you are using in your cross-platform development toolchain.

Finally, to save disk space, you may choose to get rid of the content of the *${PRJROOT}/build-tools* directory once you have completed the installation of the toolchain components. This may be very tempting, as the build directory now occupies around 600 MB of disk space. I advise you to think this through carefully, nonetheless, and not rush to use the *rm -rf* command. An unforeseen problem may require that you delve into this directory again at a future time. If you insist upon reclaiming the space occupied by the build directory, a compromise may be to wait a month or two and see if you ever need to come back to it.

Using the Toolchain

You now have a fully functional cross-development toolchain, which you can use very much as you would a native GNU toolchain, save for the additional target name prepended to every command you are used to. Instead of invoking *gcc* and *objdump* for your target, you will need to invoke *i386-linux-gcc* and *i386-linux-objdump*.

The following is a Makefile for the control daemon on the DAQ module that provides a good example of the cross-development toolchain's use:

```
# Tool names
CROSS_COMPILE = ${TARGET}-
AS             = $(CROSS_COMPILE)as
AR             = $(CROSS_COMPILE)ar
CC             = $(CROSS_COMPILE)gcc
CPP            = $(CC) -E
LD             = $(CROSS_COMPILE)ld
NM             = $(CROSS_COMPILE)nm
OBJCOPY        = $(CROSS_COMPILE)objcopy
OBJDUMP        = $(CROSS_COMPILE)objdump
RANLIB         = $(CROSS_COMPILE)ranlib
READELF        = $(CROSS_COMPILE)readelf
SIZE           = $(CROSS_COMPILE)size
STRINGS        = $(CROSS_COMPILE)strings
STRIP          = $(CROSS_COMPILE)strip

export AS AR CC CPP LD NM OBJCOPY OBJDUMP RANLIB READELF SIZE STRINGS \
       STRIP
```

```
# Build settings
CFLAGS          = -O2 -Wall
HEADER_OPS      =
LDFLAGS         =

# Installation variables
EXEC_NAME       = command-daemon
INSTALL         = install
INSTALL_DIR     = ${PRJROOT}/rootfs/bin

# Files needed for the build
OBJS            = daemon.o

# Make rules
all: daemon

.c.o:
        $(CC) $(CFLAGS) $(HEADER_OPS) -c $<

daemon: ${OBJS}
        $(CC) -o $(EXEC_NAME) ${OBJS} $(LDFLAGS)

install: daemon
        test -d $(INSTALL_DIR) || $(INSTALL) -d -m 755 $(INSTALL_DIR)
        $(INSTALL) -m 755 $(EXEC_NAME) $(INSTALL_DIR)

clean:
        rm -f *.o $(EXEC_NAME) core

distclean:
        rm -f *~
        rm -f *.o $(EXEC_NAME) core
```

The first part of the Makefile specifies the names of the toolchain utilities we are using to build the program. The name of every utility is prepended with the target's name. Hence, the value of CC will be *i386-linux-gcc*, the cross-compiler we built earlier. In addition to defining the name of the utilities, we also export these values so that subsequent Makefiles called by this Makefile will use the same names. Such a build architecture is quite common in large projects with one main directory containing many subdirectories.

The second part of the Makefile defines the build settings. CFLAGS provides the flags to be used during the build of any C file.

As we saw in the previous section, the compiler is already using the correct path to the target's libraries. The linker flags variable, LDFLAGS, is therefore empty. If the compiler wasn't pointing to the correct libraries or was using the host's libraries (which shouldn't happen if you followed the instructions I provided above), we would have to tell the compiler which libraries to use by setting the link flags as follows:

```
LDFLAGS         = -nostdlib -L${TARGET_PREFIX}/lib
```

If you wish to link your application statically, you need to add the *-static* option to LDFLAGS. This generates an executable that does not rely on any shared library. But given that the standard GNU C library is rather large, this will result in a very large binary. A simple program that uses printf( ) to print "Hello World!", for example, is less than 12 KB in size when linked dynamically and around 350 KB when linked statically and stripped.

The variables in the installation section indicate what, where, and how to install the resulting binary. In this case, the binary is being installed in the */bin* directory of the target's root filesystem.

In the case of the control daemon, we currently only have one file to build. Hence, the program's compilation only requires this single file. If, however, you had used the *-nostdlib* option in LDFLAGS, which you should not normally need to do, you would also need to change the section describing the files required for the build and the rule for generating the binary:

```
STARTUP_FILES = ${TARGET_PREFIX}/lib/crt1.o \
                ${TARGET_PREFIX}/lib/crti.o \
                ${PREFIX}/lib/gcc-lib/${TARGET}/2.95.3/crtbegin.o
END_FILES     = ${PREFIX}/lib/gcc-lib/${TARGET}/2.95.3/crtend.o \
                ${TARGET_PREFIX}/lib/crtn.o
LIBS          = -lc
OBJS          = daemon.o
LINKED_FILES  = ${STARTUP_FILES} ${OBJS} ${LIBS} ${END_FILES}
...
daemon: ${OBJS}
        $(CC) -o $(EXEC_NAME) ${LINKED_FILES} $(LDFLAGS)
```

Here, we add five object files to the one we are generating from our own C file, *crt1.o*, *crti.o*, *crtbegin.o*, *crtend.o*, and *crtn.o*. These are special startup, initialization, constructor, destructor, and finalization files, respectively, which are usually automatically linked to your applications. It is through these files that your application's main( ) function is called, for example. Since we told the compiler not to use standard linking in this case, we need to explicitly mention the files. If you do not explicitly mention them while having disabled standard linking, the linker will complain about the missing _start symbol and fail. The order in which the object files are provided to the compiler is important because the GNU linker, which is automatically invoked by the compiler to link the object files, is a one-pass linker.

The make rules themselves are very much the same ones you would find in a standard, native Makefile. I added the install rule to automate the install process. You may choose not to have such a rule, but to copy the executable manually to the proper directory.

With the Makefile and the source file in your local directory, all you need to do is type *make* to build your program for your target. If you want to build your program for native execution on your host to test your application, for example, you could use the following command line:

```
$ make CROSS_COMPILE=""
```

C Library Alternatives

Given the constraints and limitations of embedded systems, the size of the standard GNU C library makes it an unlikely candidate for use on our target. Instead, we need to look for a C library that will have sufficient functionality while being relatively small.

Over time, a number of libraries have been implemented with these priorities in mind. In the following, we will discuss the two most important C library alternatives, uClibc and diet libc. For each library, I will provide background information, instructions on how to build the library for your target, and instructions on how to build your applications using the library.

uClibc

The uClibc library originates from the uClinux project, which provides a Linux that runs on MMU-less processors. The library, however, has since become a project of its own and supports a number of processors that may or may not have an MMU or an FPU. At the time of this writing, uClibc supports all the processor architectures discussed in depth in Chapter 3. uClibc can be used as a shared library on all these architectures, because it includes a native shared library loader for each architecture. If a shared library loader were not implemented in uClibc for a certain architecture, glibc's shared library loader would have to be used instead for uClibc to be used as a shared library.

Although it does not rely on the GNU C library, uClibc provides most of the same functionality. It is, of course, not as complete as the GNU library and does not attempt to comply with all the standards with which the GNU library complies. Functions and function features that are seldom used, for instance, are omitted from uClibc. Nevertheless, most applications that can be compiled against the GNU C library will also compile and run using uClibc. To this end, uClibc developers focus on maintaining compatibility with C89, C99, and SUSv3.[*] They regularly use extensive test suites to ensure that uClibc conforms to these standards.

uClibc is available for download as a tar-gzipped or tar-bzip2'd archive or by using CVS from the project's web site at *http://uclibc.org/*. It is distributed under the terms of the LGPL. An FAQ is available on the project's web site, and you can subscribe to the uClibc mailing list or browse the mailing list archive if you need help. In the

[*] *Single UNIX Specification* Version 3.

---

following description, we will be using Version 0.9.16 of uClibc, but the explanation should apply to subsequent versions as well. Versions earlier than 0.9.16 depended on a different configuration system and are not covered by the following discussion.

Library setup

The first step in the setup is to download uClibc and extract it in our *${PRJROOT}/ build-tools* directory. In contrast to the GNU toolchain components, we will be using the package's own directory for the build instead of a separate directory. This is mainly because uClibc does not support building in a directory other than its own. The rest of the build process, however, is similar to that of the other tools, with the main steps being configuration, building, and installation.

After extracting the package, we move into the uClibc directory for the setup:

```
$ cd ${PRJROOT}/build-tools/uClibc-0.9.16
```

For its configuration, uClibc relies on a file named *.config* that should be located in the package's root directory. To facilitate configuration, uClibc includes a configuration system that automatically generates a *.config* file based on the settings we choose, much like the kernel configuration utility we will discuss in Chapter 5.* The configuration system can be operated in various ways, as can be seen by looking at the *INSTALL* file included in the package's directory. The simplest way to configure uClibc is to use the curses-based terminal configuration menu:

```
$ make CROSS=i386-linux- menuconfig
```

This command displays a menu that can be navigated using the arrow, Enter, and Esc keys. The main menu includes a set of submenus, which allow us to configure different aspects of uClibc. At the main menu level, the configuration system enables us to load and save configuration files. If we press Esc at this level, we are prompted to choose between saving the configuration to the *.config* file or discarding it.

In the command above, we set CROSS to *i386-linux* , since our cross-platform tools are prepended by this string, as I explained earlier. We could also edit the *Rules.mak* file and set CROSS to ${TARGET}- instead of specifying CROSS= for each uClibc Makefile target.

The main configuration menu includes the following submenus:

- Target Architecture Features and Options
- General Library Settings
- Networking Support
- String and Stdio Support

---

* The uClibc configuration system is actually based on Roman Zippel's kernel configuration system, which was included in the 2.5 development series.

- Library Installation Options
- uClibc hacking options

Through its submenus, the configuration system allows us to configure many options. Fortunately, we can obtain information regarding each option using the "?" key. When this key is pressed, the configuration system displays a paragraph explaining how this option is used and provides its default values. There are two types of options: paths for tools and directories needed for building, installing, and operating uClibc, and options for selecting the functionality to be included in uClibc.

We begin by setting the tool and directory paths in the "Target Architecture Features and Options" and "Library Installation Options" submenus. Table 4-7 lists the values we must set in those submenus to have uClibc compile and install in accordance with our workspace. For each option, the name of the variable used internally by uClibc's configuration system is given in parentheses. Knowing this name is important for understanding the content of the *.config* file, for example.

Table 4-7. uClibc tool and directory path settings

Option	Setting
Linux kernel header location (KERNEL_SOURCE)	*${PRJROOT}/kernel/linux-2.4.18*
Shared library loader path (SHARED_LIB_LOADER_PATH)	*/lib*
uClibc development environment directory (DEVEL_PREFIX)	*${PRJROOT}/tools/uclibc*
uClibc development environment system directory (SYSTEM_DEVEL_PREFIX)	*$(DEVEL_PREFIX)*
uClibc development environment tool directory (DEVEL_TOOL_PREFIX)	*$(DEVEL_PREFIX)/usr*

Notice that we use *${PRJROOT}/tools* instead of *${PREFIX}*, although the former is the value we gave to the PREFIX environment variable in our script. This is because uClibc's use of the PREFIX variable in its build Makefiles and related scripts differs from our use. Mainly, it uses this variable to install everything in an alternate location, whereas we use it to point to the main install location.

KERNEL_SOURCE should point to the sources of the kernel you will be using on your target. If you don't set this properly, your applications may not work at all, because uClibc doesn't attempt to provide binary compatibility across kernel versions.

SHARED_LIB_LOADER_PATH is the directory where shared libraries will be located on your target. All the binaries you link with uClibc will have this value hardcoded. If you later change the location of your shared libraries, you will need to rebuild uClibc. We have set the directory to */lib*, since this is the traditional location of shared libraries.

DEVEL_PREFIX is the directory where uClibc will be installed. As with the other tools, we want it to be under *${PRJROOT}/tools*. SYSTEM_DEVEL_PREFIX and DEVEL_TOOL_PREFIX are other installation variables that are used to control the installation of some of the uClibc binaries and are mostly useful for users who want to build RPM or dpkg packages. For our setup, we can set SYSTEM_DEVEL_PREFIX to the same value as DEVEL_PREFIX, and DEVEL_TOOL_PREFIX to *$(DEVEL_PREFIX)/usr*. This results in all uClibc binaries prepended with the target name, such as *i386-uclibc-gcc*, to be installed in *${PRJROOT}/tools/uclibc/bin*, and all uClibc binaries not prepended with the target name, such as *gcc*, to be installed in *${PRJROOT}/tools/uclibc/usr/bin*. As we shall see later, we only need to add *${PRJROOT}/tools/uclibc/bin* to our path to use uClibc.

Let us now take a look at the options found in each configuration submenu. As I said earlier, you can use the "?" key to obtain more information about each option from the configuration system. Because some options depend on the settings of other options, some of the options listed below may not be displayed in your configuration. While most options are either enabled or disabled, some are string fields, such as the paths we discussed earlier, which must be filled.

The "Target Architecture Features and Options" submenu includes the following options:

- Target Processor Type.
- Target CPU has a memory management unit (MMU) (UCLIBC_HAS_MMU).
- Enable floating (UCLIBC_HAS_FLOATS).
- Target CPU has a floating point unit (FPU) (HAS_FPU).
- Enable full C99 math library support (DO_C99_MATH).
- Compiler Warnings (WARNINGS). This is a string field that allows you to set the compiler flags used for reporting warnings.
- Linux kernel header location (KERNEL_SOURCE). This is the kernel path we discussed earlier.

The "General Library Settings" submenu includes the following options:

- Generate Position Independent Code (PIC) (DOPIC).
- Enable support for shared libraries (HAVE_SHARED).
- Compile native shared library loader (BUILD_UCLIBC_LDSO).
- Native shared library loader 'ldd' support (LDSO_LDD_SUPPORT).
- POSIX Threading Support (UCLIBC_HAS_THREADS).
- Large File Support (UCLIBC_HAS_LFS).
- Malloc Implementation. This is a submenu that allows us to choose between two malloc implementations, malloc and malloc-930716.
- Shadow Password Support (HAS_SHADOW).
- Regular Expression Support (UCLIBC_HAS_REGEX).
- Supports only Unix 98 PTYs (UNIXPTY_ONLY).
- Assume that */dev/pts* is a devpts or devfs filesystem (ASSUME_DEVPTS).

The "Networking Support" submenu includes the following options:

- IP Version 6 Support (`UCLIBC_HAS_IPV6`).
- Remote Procedure Call (RPC) support (`UCLIBC_HAS_RPC`).
- Full RPC support (`UCLIBC_HAS_FULL_RPC`).

The "String and Stdio support" submenu includes the following options:

- Wide Character Support (`UCLIBC_HAS_WCHAR`).
- Locale Support (`UCLIBC_HAS_LOCALE`).
- Use the old vfprintf implementation (`USE_OLD_VFPRINTF`).

We already covered all the options in the "Library Installation Options" submenu earlier in this section. Here they are nevertheless for completeness:

- Shared library loader path (`SHARED_LIB_LOADER_PATH`).
- uClibc development environment directory (`DEVEL_PREFIX`).
- uClibc development environment system directory (`SYSTEM_DEVEL_PREFIX`).
- uClibc development environment tool directory (`DEVEL_TOOL_PREFIX`).

Though you should not normally need to enter the "uClibc hacking options" submenu, here are the options it includes:

- Build uClibc with debugging symbols (`DODEBUG`).
- Build uClibc with runtime assertion testing (`DOASSERTS`).
- Build the shared library loader with debugging support (`SUPPORT_LD_DEBUG`).
- Build the shared library loader with early debugging support (`SUPPORT_LD_DEBUG_EARLY`).

For our DAQ module, we left the options to their default values. For most targets, you should not need to change the options either. Remember that you can always revert to the defaults by removing the *.config* file from the uClibc's directory.

With uClibc now configured, we can compile it:

```
$ make CROSS=i386-linux-
```

The compilation takes approximately 10 minutes in our setup. As with the GNU toolchain, you may see warnings during the build that you can safely ignore.

With the build complete, we can install uClibc:

```
$ make CROSS=i386-linux- PREFIX="" install
```

Given the values we set above, this will install all the uClibc components in the *${PRJROOT}/tools/uclibc* directory. If we had already installed uClibc, the installation procedure will fail while trying to copy files to the *${PRJROOT}/tools/uclibc* directory. In such a case, we should erase the content of that directory before issuing the *make install* command.

Usage

We are now ready to link our applications with uClibc instead of the GNU C library. To facilitate this linking, a couple of utilities have been installed by uClibc in ${PRJROOT}/tools/uclibc/bin. Mainly, uClibc installed an alternate compiler and alternate linker, *i386-uclibc-gcc* and *i386-uclibc-ld*. Instead of using the *i386-linux-* prefix, the utilities and symbolic links installed by uClibc have the *i386-uclibc-* prefix. Actually, the uClibc compiler and linker are wrappers that end up calling the GNU utilities we built earlier while ensuring that your application is properly built and linked with uClibc.

The first step in using these utilities is to amend our path:

```
$ export PATH=${PREFIX}/uclibc/bin:${PATH}
```

You will also want to modify your development environment script to automate this path change. In the case of *develdaq*, here is the new line for the path:

```
export PATH=${PREFIX}/bin:${PREFIX}/uclibc/bin:${PATH}
```

Using the same Makefile as earlier, we can compile the control daemon as follows:

```
$ make CROSS_COMPILE=i386-uclibc-
```

Since uClibc is a shared library by default on the x86, this will result in a dynamically linked binary. We could still compile our application statically, however:

```
$ make CROSS_COMPILE=i386-uclibc- LDFLAGS="-static"
```

The same "Hello World!" program we used earlier is only 2 KB in size when linked with the shared uClibc and 18 KB when linked statically with it. This is a big difference with the figures I gave above for the same program when it was linked with glibc.

Diet libc

The diet libc project was started and is still maintained by Felix von Leitner with aims similar to uClibc. In contrast with uClibc, however, diet libc did not grow from previous work on libraries but was written from scratch with an emphasis on minimizing size and optimizing performance. Hence, diet libc compares quite favorably to glibc in terms of footprint and in terms of code speed. In comparison to uClibc, though, I have not noticed any substantial difference.

Diet libc does not support all the processor architectures discussed in Chapter 3. It supports the ARM, the MIPS, the x86, and the PPC. Also, the authors of diet libc favor static linking over dynamic linking. So, although diet libc can be used as a shared library on some platforms, it is mostly intended to be used as a static library.

One of the most important issues to keep in mind while evaluating diet libc is its licensing. In contrast to most other libraries, including uClibc, which are usually licensed under the LGPL, diet libc is licensed under the terms of the GPL. As I explained in Chapter 1, this means that by linking your code to diet libc, the resulting binary becomes a derived work and you can distribute it only under the terms of the GPL. A commercial license is available from the package's main author if you wish to distribute non-GPL code linked with diet libc.* If, however, you would prefer not to have to deal with such licensing issues, you may want to use uClibc instead.

Diet libc is available for download both as a tar-bzip2'd archive or using CVS from the project's web site at *http://www.fefe.de/dietlibc/*.† The package comes with an FAQ and installation instructions. In the following, we will be using Version 0.21 of diet libc, but my explanations should also apply to previous and subsequent versions.

Library setup

As with uClibc, the first step to setting up diet libc is to download it into our *${PRJROOT}/build-tools* directory. Here too, we will build the library within the package's source directory and not in another directory as was the case for the GNU toolchain. Also, there is no configuration required for diet libc. Instead, we can proceed with the build stage immediately.

Once the package is extracted, we move into the diet libc directory for the setup:

```
$ cd ${PRJROOT}/build-tools/dietlibc-0.21
```

Before building the package for our target, we will build it for our host. This is necessary to create the *diet* utility, which is required to build diet libc for the target and later to build applications against diet libc:

```
$ make
```

In our setup, this creates a *bin-ppc* directory containing a PPC diet libc. We can now compile diet libc for our target:

```
$ make ARCH=i386 CROSS=i386-linux-
```

'You will see even more warnings than with the other packages, but you can ignore them. Here, we must tell the Makefile both the architecture for which diet libc is built and the prefix of the cross-platform development tools.

With the package now built, we can install it:

```
$ make ARCH=i386 DESTDIR=${PREFIX}/dietlibc prefix="" install
```

This installs diet libc components in *${PREFIX}/dietlibc*. Again, as when building the package for our target, we provide the Makefile with the architecture. We also specify the install destination using the DESTDIR variable and reset the Makefile's internal prefix variable, which is different from the capital PREFIX environment variable.

Diet libc has now been installed in the proper directory. There is, however, one correction we need to make to diet libc's installation. By installing the x86 version of

---

* It is not clear whether this license covers the contributions made to diet libc by developers other than the main author.

† Notice the final "/". If you omit this slash, the web server will be unable to locate the web page.

diet libc, we installed the x86 version of the *diet* utility in *${PREFIX}/dietlibc/bin*. Since we intend to compile our applications on the host, we need to overwrite this with the native *diet* utility we built earlier:

```
$ cp bin-ppc/diet ${PREFIX}/dietlibc/bin
```

Usage

As with uClibc, using diet libc involves modifying the path and using the wrapper provided by diet libc to link our applications. In contrast to uClibc, however, instead of substituting the cross-development tools with tools specific to the library, we only need to prepend the calls we make to the tools with the diet libc wrapper.

First, we must change our path to include the directory containing the diet libc binary:

```
$ export PATH=${PREFIX}/dietlibc/bin:${PATH}
```

Again, you will also want to change your development environment script. For example, the path line in our *develdaq* script becomes:

```
export PATH=${PREFIX}/bin:${PREFIX}/dietlibc/bin:${PATH}
```

Notice that I assume that you won't be using both uClibc and diet libc at the same time. Hence, the path line has only diet libc added to it. If you would like to have both diet libc and uClibc on your system during development, you need to add both paths.

To compile the control daemon with diet libc, we use the following command line:

```
$ make CROSS_COMPILE="diet i386-linux-"
```

Since diet libc is mainly a static library, this will result in a statically linked binary by default and you don't need to add LDFLAGS="-static" to the command line. Using the same "Hello World!" program as earlier, I obtain a 24 KB binary when linked with diet libc.

Java

Since its introduction by Sun in 1995, Java™ has become one of the most important programming languages around. Today, it is found in every category of computerized systems, including embedded systems. Although still not as popular as C in the embedded programming world, it is nonetheless being used in an ever-increasing number of designs.

I will not attempt to introduce you to Java or any of the technology surrounding it. Instead, I refer you to the plethora of books on the matter, including many by O'Reilly. There is, nonetheless, one basic issue we need to review before continuing. Essentially, any discussion on Java involves a discussion of three different items: the Java programming language, the Java Virtual Machine (JVM), and the Java Runtime Environment (JRE), which is made up of the various Java classes.

There are many packages, both free and proprietary, that provide Java functionality in Linux. In our discussion, we will concentrate on the freely available packages. Specifically, we will discuss the Blackdown project, the open source virtual machines, and the GNU Compiler for the Java programming language. I will not cover the installation or the use of these tools as there is little difference between installing and using them on a Linux workstation and in an embedded Linux system. I will, nonetheless, refer you to the appropriate documentation for such instructions.

The Blackdown Project

The Blackdown project (*http://www.blackdown.org/*) is the group that ports Sun's Java tools to Linux. This effort is entirely based on Sun's own Java source code and provides Linux ports of Sun's tools, including the Java Development Kit (JDK) and the JRE. This is the JDK and JRE most often used in Linux workstations and servers.

This project has enjoyed a privileged, and sometimes troubled, relationship with Sun. Since this project is entirely based on Sun source code and this code is not available as open source,[*] it is entirely dependent on Sun's goodwill to help the Linux community.

Actually, the Blackdown project does not distribute any source code. Instead, it distributes prebuilt binaries for the various processor architectures to which its developers have ported Sun's Java tools. As the project's FAQ points out, you need to contact Sun to get access to the source code.

According to the licensing agreements between Sun and Blackdown, you are allowed to download the JDK for your own use, but you cannot distribute it without entering into an agreement with Sun. You can, however, download the JRE and distribute it as-is with few limitations.

Before releasing new versions of their work, the Blackdown team must meet the requirements of Sun's compatibility tests. Hence, consecutive Blackdown releases do not necessarily support all the architectures of the previous releases. Release 1.3.0-FCS, for instance, supports the PPC and the x86, while 1.3.1-rc1 supports only the ARM. The complete list of Blackdown releases and supported platforms is available from the project's status page at *http://www.blackdown.org/java-linux/ports.html*.

To run the JDK or the JRE, you will need glibc, at the very least, and the X Window System with its libraries if you wish to use the AWT classes. Given the constraints of most embedded systems, only those with very large amounts of storage and processing power will be able to accommodate this type of application.

---

[*] The source code for Sun's Java tools is available under the terms of the Sun Community Source License (SCSL). The SCSL is not one of the licenses approved by the *Open Source Initiative* (OSI). See *http://opensource.org/licenses/* for the complete list of approved licenses.

For more information regarding the Blackdown project, the tools it provides, how to install them, how to operate them, and the licensing involved, see the Blackdown FAQ at *http://www.blackdown.org/java-linux/docs/support/faq-release/*.

Open Source Virtual Machines

Given Blackdown's hurdles and its dependence on Sun, a number of projects have been started to provide open source, fully functional JVMs, without using any of Sun's source code. The most noteworthy one is Kaffe.

Since there isn't any consensus on the feasibility of using any of the various open source VMs as the main JVM in an embedded Linux project, I will only mention the VMs briefly and will not provide any information regarding their use. You are invited to look at each VM and follow the efforts of the individual teams.

The Kaffe Java Virtual Machine (*http://www.kaffe.org/*) is based on a product sold commercially by Transvirtual Inc., KaffePro VM, and is a clean-room implementation of the JVM.* Although no new releases of the project have been made since July 2000 and although this VM is not 100% compatible with Sun's VM, according to the project's web site, it is still the main open source alternative to Sun's VM.

There are other projects that may eventually become more important, such as Japhar (*http://www.japhar.org/*), Kissme (*http://kissme.sourceforge.net/*), Aegis (*http://aegisvm.sourceforge.net/*), and Sable VM (*http://www.sablevm.org/*). For a complete list of open source VM projects, see the list provided by yet another open source VM project, the joeq VM (*http://joeq.sourceforge.net/*), at *http://joeq.sourceforge.net/other_os_java.htm*. See each project's respective web site and documentation for information on how to install and operate the VM.

The GNU Java Compiler

As part of the GNU project, the *GNU Compiler for the Java programming language* (gcj) is an extension to gcc that can handle both Java source code and Java bytecode. In particular, gcj can compile either Java source code or Java bytecode into native machine code. In addition, it can also compile Java source into Java bytecode. It is often referred to as an ahead-of-time (AOT) compiler, because it can compile Java source code directly into native code, in contrast with popular just-in-time (JIT) compilers that convert Java bytecode into native code at runtime. gcj does, nevertheless, include a Java interpreter equivalent to the JDK's *java* command.

GNU gcj is a fairly active project, and most core Java class libraries are already available as part of the gcj runtime libraries. Although most windowing components, such as AWT, are still under development, the compiler and its runtime environment can already be used to compile and run most command-line applications.

---

* That is, it was written from scratch without using any of Sun's Java source code.

As with other GNU projects, gcj is fairly well documented. A good starting place is the project's web site at *http://gcc.gnu.org/java/*. In the documentation section of the web site, you will find a compile HOWTO, a general FAQ, and instructions on how to debug Java applications with *gdb*. You should be able to use the compile HOWTO in conjunction with my earlier instructions regarding the GNU toolchain to build gcj for your target.

Perl

Perl was introduced by Larry Wall in 1987. This programming language has since become a world of its own. If you are interested in Perl, have a look at Wall, Christiansen, and Orwant's *Programming Perl* or Schwartz's *Learning Perl* (both published by O'Reilly). Briefly, Perl is an interpreted language whose compiler, tools, and libraries are all available as open source under the terms of the Perl Artistic License and the GNU GPL from the *Comprehensive Perl Archive Network* (CPAN) at *http://www.cpan.org/*. Since there is only one Perl toolset, you will not need to evaluate different toolsets to figure out which one best suits your needs.

The main component you will need to run Perl programs on your target is a properly compiled Perl interpreter for your target. Unfortunately, at the time of this writing, Perl is not well adapted to cross-compilation. Efforts are, however, underway to solve the underlying issues. According to Jarkko Hietaniemi, the 5.8 release manager, Perl 5.8.0, should be able to cross-compile itself. For the time being, the 5.7 development branch includes two build options for cross-compiling small versions of the full Perl package: microperl and miniperl. Note that both options are part of the same package and you do not need to download any other package than the one provided by CPAN.

Microperl

The microperl build option was implemented by Simon Cozens based on an idea by Ilya Zakhareivh. It is the absolute bare minimum build of Perl with no outside dependencies other than ANSI C and the *make* utility. Unlike the other builds, microperl does not require that you run the *Configure* script, which performs a great deal of tests on the installation machine before generating the appropriate files for the package's build. Instead, default configuration files are provided with the bare minimum settings that allow the core Perl interpreter to build properly. None of the language's core features are missing from this interpreter. Of course it does not support all the features of the full interpreter, but it is sufficient to run basic Perl applications. Since this code is considered "experimental," for the moment, you will need to evaluate most of microperl's capabilities on your own.

I have successfully built a microperl for my DAQ module using the toolchain set up earlier, uClibc, and Perl 5.7.3. The resulting interpreter was able to adequately

---

execute all Perl programs that did not have any outside references. It failed, however, to run programs that used any of the standard Perl modules.

To build microperl for your target, you must first download a Perl version from CPAN and extract it into the ${PRJROOT}/sysapps directory. Place the package in the sysapps directory, because it will run only on the target and will not be used to build any of the other software packages for your target. With the package extracted, we move into its directory for the build. Here, we cannot use a different build directory, as we did for the GNU toolchain, because Perl does not support this build method.

```
$ cd ${PRJROOT}/sysapps/perl-5.7.3
```

Since microperl is a minimal build of Perl, we do not need to configure anything. We can build the package by using the appropriate Makefile and instructing it to use the uClibc compiler wrapper instead of the standard gcc compiler:

```
$ make -f Makefile.micro CC=i386-uclibc-gcc
```

This will generate a *microperl* binary in the package's root directory. This binary does not require any other Perl components and can be copied directly to the /bin directory of your target's root filesystem, ${PRJROOT}/rootfs.

When dynamically linked with either glibc or uClibc and stripped, the *microperl* binary is around 900 KB in size. When statically linked and stripped, the binary is 1.2 MB in size with glibc, and 930 KB with uClibc. As you can see, uClibc is the better choice in this case for size reasons.

For more information on how microperl is built, have a look at the *Makefile.micro* Makefile and the *uconfig.sh* script. As work continues on microperl, it is expected that more documentation will become available.

Miniperl

Miniperl is less minimalistic than microperl and provides most of what you would expect from the standard Perl interpreter. The main component it lacks is the DynaLoader XS module, which allows Perl subroutines to call C functions. It is therefore incapable of loading XS modules dynamically. This is a minor issue, however, given the type of system miniperl will be running on.

As with the main Perl build, miniperl requires that you run the *Configure* script to determine the system's capabilities. Since the system for which Perl must be built is your target, the script requires you to provide it with information regarding the means it should use to communicate with that target. This includes a hostname, a remote username, and a target-mapped directory. It will then use this information to run its tests on your target to generate the proper build files.

The main caveat concerning this method is its reliance on the existence of a direct network link between the host and the target. In essence, if your target does not have some form of networking, you will be unable to build miniperl for it.

I will not provide the details of the build and installation methodology for miniperl, as it is already very well explained in the *INSTALL* file provided with the 5.7.3 Perl package under the "Cross-compilation" heading.

Cross-Compiling the Impossible

As we've just seen with Perl, not all packages cross-compile easily. As a matter of fact, there is a great number of packages that have not been designed to allow cross-compilation. This book mentions a few of these, but certainly can't list them all.

Beside trying to modify build scripts and using compilation tricks to force packages to compile for another architecture, sometimes the only realistic solution is to actually build the package on the target where it is supposed to run. At first, this may seem unfeasible for most embedded systems because of these systems' typically limited storage space. As we shall in Chapter 9, however, it is possible to mount a system's root filesystem on an server using NFS. By using an NFS-mounted root filesystem, the target can access as much storage space as the server allows it to.

In such a setup, it is therefore possible to cross-compile the gcc compiler itself for the target, and then use this compiler to natively compile any package directly on the target in exactly the same way the package's build scripts expect to operate. Once the package has been compiled, the resulting binaries and libraries can thereafter be copied to a small root filesystem tailored for the target's internal storage device, and used in the field like any other target application. Obviously, there is no need to package the cross-compiled gcc with the rest of the system in the field.

Python

Python was introduced to the public by Guido van Rossum in 1991. It has since gathered many followers and, as with Perl, is a world of its own. If you are interested in Python, read Mark Lutz's *Programming Python* or Lutz, Ascher, and Willison's *Learning Python* (both published by O'Reilly). Python is routinely compared to Perl, since it often serves the same purposes, but because this is the subject of yet another holy war, I will not go any further. Instead, feel free to browse the main Python web site at *http://www.python.org/* for more information on the world of Python. The Python package, which includes the Python interpreter and the Python libraries, is available from that web site under the terms of a composite license called the Python license, which is an approved open source license.

As with Perl, you will need a properly configured interpreter to run Python code on your target. Although the main Python distribution does not support cross-compiling, a patch has been developed to this effect by Klaus Reimer and is available from *http://www.ailis.de/~k/patches/python-cross-compile.diff*. Klaus also provides a very

well written Python cross-compiling HOWTO at *http://www.ailis.de/~k/knowledge/
crosscompiling/python.php*.

You can follow Klaus' instructions to build Python for your target while using the
appropriate names for your target instead of the arm-linux used in the instructions.
To follow the same project workspace organization that we established earlier,
download and extract the Python package in the *${PRJROOT}/sysapps* directory.
Also, instead of building Python directly in its source directory, you can use a *build-
python* directory, as we did with the GNU tools, since Python supports this build
method. In addition, use the *--prefix=${PREFIX}/${TARGET}/usr* option instead of
the values provided by the HOWTO. All the Python material will thereby be
installed in the *${PREFIX}/${TARGET}/usr* directory. This directory can then be customized and copied onto the target's root filesystem.

There are a couple of observations to be made about the resulting package. First, you
will not be able to build Python with diet libc. You will need to build Python against
glibc or uClibc. This means that glibc or uClibc will have to be on your target's root
filesystem. When storage space on your target is limited, I suggest you use uClibc
instead of glibc. Also, if you want to build Python against uClibc, you need to patch
Python using the patch posted by Manuel Novoa on August 27, 2002 on the uClibc
mailing list following the announcement of uClibc 0.9.15.

Second, Python has installed many libraries in the *${PREFIX}/${TARGET}/usr/lib/
python2.2* directory, and many of those are large. You may want to trim down the
content of this directory by deleting the components you are unlikely to use. By
itself, the dynamically linked and stripped Python interpreter is 725 KB in size.

Nevertheless, Python's size and dependencies have not stopped developers from
using it. The team developing the iPAQ's Familiar distribution, for instance, includes
it as part of their standard packages.

Finally, as Klaus explains, you may see some warnings and failures during the build.
This is because some libraries and applications are missing on your target. The
Tkinter interface to *libtk.a* and *libtcl.a* will fail to build, for instance, unless you had
cross-compiled and installed Tcl/Tk for your target. This doesn't mean the Python
build has failed. Rather, it is an indication that one of the Python components has
not built successfully. You will still be able to install and use the Python interpreter
and the modules that built properly on your target.

Ada

Ada was sponsored by the U.S. Department of Defense (DoD). During the 1970s, the
DoD realized that it had a huge software maintenance problem on its hands. Thus, it
started work on a new programming language that met its stringent requirements of
code maintainability and reliability. Ada was first standardized by ANSI in 1983 and
was later updated in 1995 with the release of the Ada95 standard.

Work on a gcc-based Ada compiler was started at New York University and resulted in gnat, the GNU Ada compiler.[*] Work on gnat continued at Ada Core Technologies Inc. (ACT), which maintained it for some time before it was eventually integrated into the main gcc source tree. Every so often, ACT used to release a GPL copy of its most recent work and made it available, along with some prebuilt binaries, at *ftp://cs. nyu.edu/pub/gnat/*. Their latest release, gnat 3.14p, required gcc 2.8.1 to build. To be precise, gnat's source was provided with a patch that had to be applied to the gcc sources, and an *ada* directory that had to be copied into gcc's source directory.

Unfortunately, this led to all sorts of problems. For instance, gcc 2.8.1 was fairly outdated and most gcc versions found in recent distributions failed to build it properly. Hence, if you wanted to use the 3.14p release, you first had to install an old compiler on your system and use it to build gnat. Obviously, this wasn't an endearing prospect.

More recently, ACT's work on gnat has been integrated into the gcc CVS and is now part of gcc 3.2. Though you still need a gnat binary to build the Ada compiler, the integration of gnat into mainstream gcc is likely to simplify the use of Ada in embedded Linux systems in the future.

Apart from the ongoing effort to integrate gnat into mainstream gcc, there are two online projects you may find helpful if you are interested in Ada programming in Linux. First, *The Big Online Book of Linux Ada Programming* is a collective work started by Ken Burtch with the main goal of providing a complete online reference manual for Ada programming in Linux. The manual is available at *http://www. pegasoft.ca/homes/book.html* and has a couple of mirrors.

Second, the *Ada for GNU/Linux Team* (ALT) provides a number of ACT-independent binary packages, RPMs, and patches at *http://www.gnuada.org/alt.html*. The group also provides a number of links to packages providing Ada interfaces and bindings to popular libraries, such as GTK, XML, and X11.

Other Programming Languages

There are, of course, many more programming languages supported in Linux. Whether you are looking for programming in Forth, Lisp, or FORTRAN, a short search on the Net with your favorite search engine should yield rapid results. A good starting point is the "*Other Languages*" section in Chapter 13 of *Running Linux* (O'Reilly).

The cross-compiling and cross-development capabilities of the various language tools will need to be evaluated on a tool-to-tool basis, since few compilers and interpreters lend themselves well to cross-platform development.

---

[*] Remarkably, gnat is entirely written in Ada.

Integrated Development Environments

Many *integrated development environments* (IDEs) are available for Linux. Most of these IDEs are usually used to develop native applications. Nevertheless, they can be customized for cross-development by setting the appropriate compiler names in the IDE's configuration. Table 4-8 provides a list of open source IDEs, their locations, and the list of embedded Linux–relevant programming languages they support.

Table 4-8. Open source IDEs

IDE	Location	Supported languages
Anjuta	*http://anjuta.sourceforge.net/*	Ada, bash, C, C++, Java, make, Perl, Python
Eclipse	*http://www.eclipse.org/*	C, C++, Java
Glimmer	*http://glimmer.sourceforge.net/*	Ada, bash, C, C++, Java, make, Perl, Python, x86 assembly
KDevelop	*http://www.kdevelop.org/*	C, C++, Java
SourceNavigator	*http://sources.redhat.com/sourcenav/*	C, C++, Java, Python

I am reluctant to recommend any particular IDE, because the choice is very much a personal one. I personally prefer *XEmacs* and the command line to any IDE. Others, still, prefer plain-old *vi*. You may want to look at the screenshots sections of each project to get an initial appreciation for it. Ultimately, however, you may wish to download the IDEs and try them to make up your mind.

In terms of popularity, KDevelop is probably the most popular IDE of the list. Although it is very much oriented towards native development of user applications, it can be customized for cross-development. Anjuta is a very active project, and its interface resembles that of many popular Windows IDEs. SourceNavigator is an IDE made available by Red Hat under the terms of the GPL, and is part of Red Hat's *GNUPro* product. Glimmer is a Gnome-based IDE with capabilities similar to the other IDEs. Eclipse is an ambitious project to create an IDE framework that can easily be extended using plug-ins. It was initiated and is still backed by many companies, including IBM, HP, Red Hat, and SuSE.

For more information regarding these projects, visit their web sites and have a look at their documentation.

Terminal Emulators

The most common way to communicate with an embedded system is to use a terminal emulation program on the host to communicate through an RS232 serial port with the target. Although there are a few terminal emulation programs available for Linux, not all are fit for all uses. There are known problems between minicom and U-Boot, for instance, during file transfers over the serial port. Hence, I recommend that you try more than one terminal application to communicate with your target. If nothing else, you are likely to discover one that best fits your personal preferences. Also, see your bootloader's documentation for any warnings regarding any terminal emulator.

Three main terminal emulators are available in Linux: *minicom*, *cu*, and *kermit*. The following sections cover the setup and configuration of these tools, but not their use. Refer to each package's documentation for the latter.

Accessing the Serial Port

Before you can use any terminal emulator, you must ensure that you have the appropriate access rights to use the serial port on your host. In particular, you need read and write access to the serial port device, which is */dev/ttyS0* in most cases, and read and write access to the */var/lock* directory. Access to */dev/ttyS0* is required to be able to talk to the serial port. Access to */var/lock* is required to be able to lock access to the serial port. If you do not have these rights, any terminal emulator you use will complain at startup.[*]

The default permission bits and group settings for */dev/ttyS0* vary between distributions, and sometimes between releases of the same distribution. On Red Hat 6.2, for example, it used to be accessible in read and write mode to the root user only:

```
$ ls -al /dev/ttyS0
crw-------   1 root    tty      4, 64 May  5  1998 /dev/ttyS0
```

As with */dev/ttyS0*, the permission bits and group settings for */var/lock* largely depend on the distribution. For the same Red Hat 6.2, */var/lock* was accessible to the root user and any member of the uucp group:

```
$ ls -ld /var/lock
drwxrwxr-x   5 root    uucp       1024 Oct  2 17:14 /var/lock
```

---

[*] The actual changes required for your distribution may differ from those discussed in this section. Refer to your distribution's documentation in case of doubt.

Though Red Hat 6.2 is outdated, and your distribution is likely to have different values, this setup is a perfect example to illustrate the modifications required to allow proper access to the serial port. In this case, to use a terminal emulator on the serial port as a normal user, you must be part of both the tty and uucp groups, and access rights to /dev/ttyS0 must be changed to allow read and write access to members of the owning group. In some distributions, the access rights to /dev/ttyS0 will be set properly, but /var/lock will belong to the root group. In that case, you may want to change the group setting, unless you want to allow normal users in the root group, which I do not recommend.

Going back to Red Hat 6.2, use *chmod* to change the rights on /dev/ttyS0:

```
$ su
Password:
# chmod 660 /dev/ttyS0
# ls -al /dev/ttyS0
crw-rw----    1 root      tty         4,  64 May  5  1998 /dev/ttyS0
```

Then, edit the /etc/group file using *vigr** and add your username to the uucp and tty lines:

```
...
tty:x:5:karim
...
uucp:x:14:uucp,karim
...
```

Finally, log out from root user mode, log out from your own account, and log back in to your account:

```
# exit
$ id
uid=501(karim) gid=501(karim) groups=501(karim)
$ exit

Teotihuacan login: karim
Password:
$ id
uid=501(karim) gid=501(karim) groups=501(karim),5(tty),14(uucp)
```

As you can see, you need to first log out and then log back in for the changes to take effect. Opening a new terminal window in your GUI may have similar effects, depending on the GUI your are using and the way it starts new terminal windows. Even if it works, however, only the new terminal window will be part of the appropriate groups, but any other window opened before the changes will still be excluded. For this reason, it is preferable to exit your GUI, completely log out, and then log back in.

---

* This command is tailored for the editing of the /etc/group file. It sets the appropriate locks to ensure that only one user is accessing the file at any time. See the manpage for more information.

For more information on the setup of the serial interface, have a look at the Serial HOWTO available from the LDP and Chapter 4 of the *Linux Network Administrator's Guide* (O'Reilly).

Minicom

Minicom is the most commonly used terminal emulator for Linux. Most documentation online or in print about embedded Linux assumes that you are using minicom. However, as I said above, there are known file transfer problems between minicom and at least one bootloader. Minicom is a GPL clone of the *Telix* DOS program and provides ANSI and VT102 terminals. Its project web site is currently located at *http://www.netsonic.fi/~walker/minicom.html*. Minicom is likely to have been installed by your distribution. You can verify this by using *rpm -q minicom* if you are using a Red Hat–based distribution.

Minicom is started by using the *minicom* command:

```
$ minicom
```

The utility starts in full-screen mode and displays the following on the top of the screen:

```
Welcome to minicom 1.83.0

OPTIONS: History Buffer, F-key Macros, Search History Buffer, I18n
Compiled on Mar  7 2000, 06:12:31.

Press CTRL-A Z for help on special keys
```

To enter commands to minicom, press Ctrl-A and then the letter of the desired function. As stated by minicom's welcome message, use Ctrl-A Z to get help from minicom. Refer to the package's manpage for more details about its use.

UUCP cu

Unix to Unix CoPy (UUCP) used to be one of the most popular ways to link Unix systems. Though UUCP is rarely used today, the *cu* command part of the UUCP package can be used to *call up* other systems. The connection used to communicate to the other system can take many forms. In our case, we are mostly interested in establishing a terminal connection over a serial line to our target.

To this end, we must add the appropriate entries to the configuration files used by UUCP. In particular, this means adding a port entry in */etc/uucp/port* and a remote system definition to */etc/uucp/sys*. As the UUCP info page states, "a port is a particular hardware connection on your computer," whereas a system definition describes the system to connect to and the port used to connect to it.

Though UUCP is available from the GNU FTP site under the terms of the GPL, it is usually already installed on your system. On a Red Hat–based system, use *rpm -q uucp* to verify that it is installed.

Here is an example */etc/uucp/port*:

```
# /etc/uucp/port - UUCP ports
# /dev/ttyS0
port      ttyS0       # Port name
type      direct      # Direct connection to other system
device    /dev/ttyS0  # Port device node
hardflow  false       # No hardware flow control
speed     115200      # Line speed
```

This entry states that there is a port called ttyS0 that uses direct 115200 bps connections without hardware flow control to connect to remote systems through */dev/ttyS0*. The name of the port in this case, ttyS0, is used only to identify this port definition for the rest of UUCP utilities and configuration files. If you've used UUCP before to connect using a traditional modem, you will notice that this entry resembles modem definitions. Unlike modem definitions, however, there is no need to provide a carrier field to specify whether a carrier should be expected. Setting the connection type to direct makes carrier default to false.

Here is an example */etc/uucp/sys* file that complements the */etc/uucp/port* file listed earlier:

```
# /etc/uucp/sys - name UUCP neighbors
# system: target
system  target    # Remote system name
port    ttyS0     # Port name
time    any       # Access is possible at any time
```

Basically, this definition states that the system called target can be called up at any time using port ttyS0.

We can now use cu to connect to the target:

```
$ cu target
Connected.
```

Once in a *cu* session, you can issue instructions using the ~ character followed by another character specifying the actual command. For a complete list of commands, use ~?.

For more information on how to configure and customize UUCP for your system, have a look at Chapter 16 in the *Linux Network Administrator's Guide* (O'Reilly), the UUCP HOWTO available from the LDP, and the UUCP info page.

C-Kermit

C-Kermit is one of the packages maintained as part of Columbia University's Kermit project (*http://www.columbia.edu/kermit/*). C-Kermit provides a unified interface for network operations across a wide range of platforms. Although it features many capabilities, terminal emulation is the package's capability we are most interested in.

Though you are free to download C-Kermit for personal and internal use, C-Kermit is not open source software and its licensing makes it difficult for commercial distributions to include it.* C-Kermit is available for download from *http://www. columbia.edu/kermit/ckermit.html*. Follow the documentation in the *ckuins.txt* file included with the package to compile and install C-Kermit. In contrast with most other tools we discuss in this book, C-Kermit should be installed system wide, not locally to your project workspace. Once installed, C-Kermit is started using the *kermit* command.

In terms of usability, *kermit* compares quite favorably to both *minicom* and *cu*. Despite its lack of user menus, as provided by *minicom*, *kermit*'s interactive command language provides a very intuitive and powerful way of interacting with the terminal emulator. When you initiate a file transfer from the target's bootloader, for example, the bootloader starts waiting for the file. You can then switch to *kermit*'s interactive command line on the host using Ctrl-\ C and send the actual file using the *send* command. Among other things, the interactive command line provides Tab filename completion similar to that provided by most shells in Linux. Also, the interactive command line is capable of recognizing commands using the shortest unique character string part of a command name. The *set receive* command, for example, can be shortened to *set rec*.

To use the *kermit* command, you must have a *.kermrc* configuration file in your home directory. This file is run by *kermit* at startup. Here is an example *.kermrc* file that I use on my workstation:

```
; Line properties
set modem type              none ; Direct connection
set line              /dev/ttyS0 ; Device file
set speed                 115200 ; Line speed
set carrier-watch            off ; No carrier expected
set handshake               none ; No handshaking
set flow-control            none ; No flow control

; Communication properties
robust                           ; Most robust transfer settings macro
set receive packet-length   1000 ; Max pack len remote system should use
set send packet-length      1000 ; Max pack len local system should use
set window                    10 ; Nbr of packets to send until ack

; File transfer properties
set file type             binary ; All files transferred are binary
set file names           literal ; Don't modify filenames during xfers
```

---

* Although the license was changed lately to simplify inclusion in commercial distributions such as Red Hat, C-Kermit has yet to be included in most mainstream distributions.

For more information about each of the settings above, try the *help* command provided by *kermit*'s interactive command line. For more information regarding the *robust* macro, for example, use *help robust*. In this case, *robust* must be used before *set receive*, since *robust* sets the maximum packet length to be used by the remote system to 90 bytes, while we want it set to 1000 bytes.

Once the configuration file is created, you can start *kermit*:

```
$ kermit -c
Connecting to /dev/ttyS0, speed 115200
 Escape character: Ctrl-\ (ASCII 28, FS): enabled
Type the escape character followed by C to get back,
or followed by ? to see other options.
------------------------------------------------------
```

If you are looking for more information about the use of C-Kermit and intend to use it more extensively, think about purchasing the *Using C-Kermit* book by Frank Da Cruz and Christine Gianone (Digital Press). Apart from providing information regarding the use of C-Kermit, sales of the book help fund the project. Though the book covers Version 6.0, supplements for Versions 7.0 and 8.0 are freely available from the project's web site.

CHAPTER 5

Kernel Considerations

The kernel is the central software component of all Linux systems. Its capabilities very much dictate the capabilities of the entire system. If the kernel you use fails to support one of your target's hardware components, for instance, this component will be useless as long as this specific kernel runs on your target.

Many books and online documentation already discuss the kernel's internals, its programming, its setup, and its use in user systems at length. I will not, therefore, cover these issues here. If you are interested in such issues, have a look at *Running Linux*, *Linux Device Drivers*, and *Understanding the Linux Kernel* by O'Reilly. These books cover the kernel's setup and use, its programming, and its internals, respectively. You may also want to take a look at the Linux Kernel HOWTO available from the LDP.

Our discussion will be limited to issues about the preparation of a Linux kernel for use in an embedded system. Specifically, we will discuss kernel selection, configuration, compilation, and installation. Each step will get us closer to the goal of obtaining a functional kernel with its related modules for our target system. Our discussion will end with coverage of the aspects of the kernel's operation that are specific to embedded systems.

Selecting a Kernel

Though there is only one main repository for the kernel, *http://www.kernel.org/*, the versions available from that site aren't always appropriate for all the architectures supported by Linux. In fact, these versions will often not even build for, much less run on, some of the most popular architectures in embedded Linux systems. This is primarily because the development of Linux for these architectures isn't synchronized with the main kernel releases.

To have a working kernel for your target, you need to obtain one of the versions made available by the development team in charge of your target's underlying processor architecture. Since each architecture is maintained by a different team, the site of choice for a kernel varies accordingly. Table 5-1 provides a list of locations where you will find the most appropriate kernel for your architecture, along with the means of download available from that site.

Table 5-1. Most appropriate kernel location for each processor architecture

Processor architecture	Most appropriate kernel location	Available download means
x86	*http://www.kernel.org/*	ftp, http, rsync
ARM	*http://www.arm.linux.org.uk/developer/*	ftp, rsync
PowerPC	*http://penguinppc.org/*	ftp, http, rsync, bitkeeper
MIPS	*http://www.linux-mips.org/*	cvs
SuperH	*http://linuxsh.sourceforge.net/*	cvs
M68k	*http://www.linux-m68k.org/*	ftp, http

As you can see, most of these sites are the same ones I recommended for each architecture in Chapter 3. That said, these are not the only kernel locations for each target. Other locations may also provide versions for your target. To begin with, some of these sites have mirrors that provide the same content. Then there are the kernels provided by various individuals, companies, and organizations. Exercise caution if you intend to use the latter type of kernel, as these kernels may not be supported by the community* and you may be forced to rely on the provider's support, if available, in case of problems.

Once you have found the download site that is most appropriate for you, you will need to select a kernel version from that site. This is a difficult decision, as some versions have broken features, even if the same features were fully functional in older versions. The best way to find this sort of information is to stay in touch with the community maintaining the kernel for your architecture. This doesn't mean sending any emails or contacting anyone, but it involves subscribing to the appropriate mailing lists and keeping watch of the important moves on that list and on the port's main web site.

Some of these sites, such as the ARM site, don't necessarily distribute full kernels. Rather, they distribute patches to the official kernel. To obtain the appropriate kernel for your architecture, you must then download the kernel from the main repository and apply to it the appropriate patch provided by your port's site.

For our ARM-based user interfaces, we download plain 2.4.18 from *http://www.kernel. org/* and the 2.4.18-rmk5 patch from the official ARM Linux site, *http://www.arm.*

---

* This lack of support from the community won't necessarily be due to lack of code availability (which shouldn't happen since Linux is distributed under the terms of the GPL), but most likely because the modifications to the kernel's functionality made by that provider are understood only by her. It may also be that the kernel modifications are not considered mature enough, or even desirable, by the community to warrant inclusion in the main kernel tree.

linux.org.uk/. By applying the rmk5 patch to the vanilla 2.4.18, we obtain the 2.4.18-rmk5 kernel, which contains all the features required for ARM-based systems.

Most of the time, the latest known-to-be-functional version is the best one to use. So if 2.4.17 and 2.4.18 are known to work on your target, 2.4.18 should be the preferable one. There are cases, however, in which this doesn't hold true. Most folks who follow the kernel's development are aware, for example, that Versions 2.4.10 to 2.4.15, inclusive, are to be avoided, because they were part of a period during which a lot of changes were being integrated into the kernel and are therefore sometimes unstable. Again, this is the sort of information you can obtain by keeping in touch with the appropriate mailing lists and web sites.

If you find it too time consuming to subscribe to your port's mailing list or to the main kernel mailing list, you owe it to yourself to at least visit your port's web site once a week and read the *Kernel Traffic* (*http://kt.zork.net/kernel-traffic/*) weekly newsletter. *Kernel Traffic* provides a summary of the most important discussions that occurred on the main kernel mailing list during the past week.

Once you have found the appropriate kernel version for your target, download it into the *${PRJROOT}/kernel* directory, extract it, and rename it if necessary, as we have done in the previous chapter in "Kernel Headers Setup." Renaming the kernel directory will avoid the mistake of overwriting it while extracting another kernel you might download in the future.

Whichever version you choose, do not refrain from trying a couple of different kernel versions for your target. In addition to the recommendations and bug reports seen on the Net, your evaluation of different versions will provide you with insight on your hardware's interaction with the kernel.

You may also want to try some of the various patches made available by some developers. Extra kernel functionality is often available as an independent patch before it is integrated into the mainstream kernel. Robert Love's kernel preemption patch, for instance, was maintained as a separate patch before it was integrated by Linus into the 2.5 development series. We will discuss a few kernel patches in Chapter 11. Have a look at *Running Linux* (O'Reilly) if you are not familiar with patches.

Configuring the Kernel

Configuration is the initial step in the build of a kernel for your target. There are many ways to configure the kernel, and there are many options from which to choose .

Regardless of the configuration method you use or the actual configuration options you choose, the kernel will generate a *.config* file at the end of the configuration and will generate a number of symbolic links and file headers that will be used by the rest of the build.

We will limit our discussion to the aspects of kernel configuration that differ in embedded systems. You can consult the various references I mentioned earlier if you are not familiar with kernel configuration.

Configuration Options

It is during configuration that you will be able to select the options you want to see included in the kernel. Depending on your target, the option menus available will change, as will their content. Some options, however, will be available no matter which embedded architecture you choose. The following is the list of main menu options available to all embedded Linux architectures:

- Code maturity level options
- Loadable module support
- General setup
- Memory technology devices
- Block devices
- Networking options
- ATA/IDE/MFM/RLL support
- SCSI support
- Network device support
- Input core support
- Character devices
- Filesystems
- Console drivers
- Sound
- Kernel hacking

I will not give the details of each option, since the kernel configuration menu provides help capabilities you can refer to as you perform the configuration. Notice, however, that we discussed many of these options in Chapter 3.

One of the most important option menus is the one in which you choose the exact instance of the processor architecture that best fits your target. The name of this menu, however, varies according to your architecture. Table 5-2 provides the system and processor selection option menu name, along with the correct kernel architecture name for each. When issuing *make* commands, we need to set the ARCH variable to the architecture name recognized by the kernel Makefiles.

Table 5-2. System and processor selection option and kernel architecture name according to processor architecture

Processor architecture	System and processor selection option	Kernel architecture name
x86	Processor type and features	i386
ARM	System type	arm
PPC	Platform support	ppc
MIPS	Machine selection/CPU selection	mips or mips64[a]
SH	Processor type and features	sh
M68k	Platform-dependent support	m68k

[a] Depending on the CPU.

Some options are available only for certain architectures. Table 5-3 lists these options and indicates their availability for each architecture, as displayed by the kernel's configuration menus.

Table 5-3. Hardware support options for each architecture

Option	x86	ARM	PPC	MIPS	SH	M68k
Parallel port support	X	X		X		
IEEE 1394 support	X	X	X		X	
IrDA support	X	X	X	X		
USB support	X	X	X	X		
Bluetooth support	X	X	X			

Some architectures have their own specific configuration option menus. The following is a list of such menus for the ARM architecture:

- Acorn-specific block devices
- Synchronous serial interfaces
- Multimedia capabilities port drivers

Here is the list of menus specific to the PPC:

- MPC8xx CPM options
- MPC8260 communication options

The fact that an option is available in your architecture's configuration menu does not automatically mean that this feature is supported for your target. Indeed, the configuration menus may allow you to enable many kernel features that have never been tested for your target. There is no VGA console, for instance, on ARM systems. The configuration menu of the kernel, however, will allow you to enable support for the VGA console. In this case, the actual kernel build will fail if you enable support for this option. In other cases, the selected feature, or even the entire kernel, will not be functional. To avoid these types of problems, make sure the options you choose are supported for your target. Most of the time, as in the case of the VGA console, it is a matter of common sense. When the choice doesn't seem as evident, visiting the appropriate project web site, such as the ones provided in Chapter 3, will help you determine whether the feature is supported for your target.

In some cases, the fact that an option is not displayed in your architecture's configuration menu doesn't mean that this feature can't actually be used on your target. Many of the features listed in Table 5-3, such as Bluetooth, are mostly architecture independent, and should run on any architecture without a problem. They aren't listed in the configuration menus of certain architectures, because they've either not been tested on those architectures, or the maintainers of those ports or the maintainers of the feature haven't been asked to add the feature in the architecture's main *config.in* file.* Again, the resources listed in Chapter 3 are a good start for finding out about which unlisted features are possibly supported on your target.

Configuration Methods

The kernel supports **four main** configuration methods.

make config
> Provides a command-line interface where you are asked about each option one by one. If a *.config* configuration file is already present, it uses that file to set the default values of the options it asks you to set.

make oldconfig
> Feeds *config* with a an existing *.config* configuration file, and prompts you to configure only those options you had not previously configured. This contrasts with *make config*, which asks you about all options, even those you may have previously configured.

---

* *config.in* files control the options displayed in the configuration menus.

make menuconfig

Displays a curses-based terminal configuration menu. If a *.config* file is present, it uses it to set default values, as with *make config*.

make xconfig

Displays a Tk-based X Window configuration menu. If a *.config* file is present, it uses it to set default values, as with *make config* and *make menuconfig*.

Any of these can be used to configure the kernel. They all generate a *.config* file in the root directory of the kernel sources. (This is the file that contains the full detail of the options you choose.)

Few developers actually use the *make config* command to configure the kernel. Instead, most use *make menuconfig*. You can also use *make xconfig*. Keep in mind, however, that *make xconfig* may have some broken menus in some architectures; as is the case for the PowerPC, for instance.

To view the kernel configuration menu, type the appropriate command at the command line with the proper parameters. For our ARM-based user interface modules, we use the following command line:

```
$ make ARCH=arm CROSS_COMPILE=arm-linux- menuconfig
```

We then proceed to choose the configuration options appropriate to our target. Many features and drivers are available as modules and we can choose here whether to have them built in the kernel or whether to build them as modules. Once we are done configuring the kernel, we use the Escape key or select the Exit item to quit the configuration menu. We are then prompted by the configuration utility to confirm that we want to save the configuration. By choosing Yes, we save the kernel's configuration and create a *.config* file. In addition to creating the *.config* file, a few header files and symbolic links are created. If we choose No, the configuration is not saved and any existing configuration is left unmodified.

Apart from the main configuration options, some architectures, such as the PPC and the ARM, can be configured using custom tailored configurations for the various boards implemented using the architecture. In those cases, the defaults provided with the kernel will be used to generate the *.config* file. For example, here is how I configure the kernel for the TQM860L PowerPC board I have:

```
$ make ARCH=ppc CROSS_COMPILE=powerpc-linux- TQM860L_config
$ make ARCH=ppc CROSS_COMPILE=powerpc-linux- oldconfig
```

Managing Multiple Configurations

It is often desirable to test different configurations using the same kernel sources. By changing the kernel's configuration, however, we destroy the previous configuration, because all the configuration files are overwritten by the kernel's configuration utilities. To save a configuration for future use, we need to save the *.config* files created by the kernel's configuration. These files can later be reused to restore a previous kernel configuration.

The easiest way to back up and retrieve configurations is to use the kernel's own configuration procedures. The menus displayed by both the menuconfig and xconfig Makefile targets allow you to save and restore configurations. In each case, you need to provide an appropriate filename.

You can also save the *.config* files by hand. In that case, you need to copy the configuration file created by the kernel configuration utilities to an alternative location for future use. To use a saved configuration, you will need to copy the previously saved *.config* file back into the kernel's root directory and then use the *make* command with the oldconfig Makefile target to configure the kernel using the newly copied .config. As with the menuconfig Makefile target, the oldconfig Makefile target creates a few headers files and symbolic links.

Whether you copy the files manually or use the menus provided by the various utilities, store the configurations in an intuitive location and use a meaningful naming scheme for saving your configurations. Using our project layout, I suggest that you store all your configurations in the *${PRJROOT}/kernel* directory so that the configuration files may live independently from the actual kernel sources while still remaining with the other kernel-related material. To identify each configuration file, prepend each filename with the kernel version it relates to and a small descriptive comment or a date or both. Leave the *.config* extension as-is, nevertheless, to identify the file as a kernel configuration file.

In the case of the 2.4.18 kernel we are using, for instance, I tried a configuration where I disabled serial port support. I called the corresponding configuration file *2.4. 18-no-serial.config*. I also maintain the latest known "best" configuration as *2.4.18. config*. Feel free to adopt the naming convention that is most intuitive for you, but you may want to avoid generic names such as *2.4.18-test1.config*.

Using the EXTRAVERSION Variable

If you are using multiple variants of the same kernel version, you will find the EXTRAVERSION variable to be quite useful in identifying each instance. The EXTRAVERSION variable is appended to the kernel's version number to provide the kernel being built with its final name. The rmk5 patch we applied on our plain 2.4.18, for example, sets EXTRAVERSION to -rmk5 and the resulting version for that kernel is 2.4.18-rmk5.

The final version number is also used to name the directory where the modules built for the kernel are stored. Hence, modules built for two kernels based on the same initial version but with different EXTRAVERSIONs will be stored in two different directories, whereas modules built for two kernels based on the same initial version but that have no EXTRAVERSION will be stored in the same directory.

You can also use this variable to identify variants based on the same kernel version. To do so, edit the Makefile in the main kernel directory and set EXTRAVERSION to your desired value. You will find it useful to rename the directory containing this modified source code using this same value. If, for example, the EXTRAVERSION of a 2.4.18

kernel is set to -motor-diff, the parent directory should be named *2.4.18-motor-diff*. The naming of the backup *.config* files should also reflect the use of EXTRAVERSION. The configuration file for the kernel with disabled serial support should therefore be called *2.4.18-motor-diff-no-serial.config* in this case.

Compiling the Kernel

Compiling the kernel involves a number of steps: building the kernel dependencies, building the kernel image, and building the kernel modules. Each step uses a separate *make* command and is described separately in this section. However, you could also carry out all these steps using a single command line.

Building Dependencies

Most files in the kernel's sources depend on a number of header files. To build the kernel adequately, the kernel's Makefiles need to know about these dependencies. For each subdirectory in the kernel tree, a hidden *.depend* file is created during the dependencies build. This contains the list of header files that each file in the directory depends on. As with other software that relies on *make*, only the files that depend on a header that changed since the last build will need to be recompiled when a kernel is rebuilt.

From the kernel source's root directory, the following command builds the kernel's dependencies:

```
$ make ARCH=arm CROSS_COMPILE=arm-linux- clean dep
```

As in the configuration of the kernel earlier, we set the ARCH and CROSS_COMPILE variables. As I explained in Chapter 4, CROSS_COMPILE is only required when source code is actually compiled, and could be omitted here. On the other hand, we will need to set at least the ARCH variable for every *make* command we issue because we are cross-compiling the kernel. Even when issuing *make clean* or *make distclean*, we will need to set this variable. Otherwise, the kernel's Makefiles assume that the operations are to be carried out for the kernel code related to the host's architecture.

The ARCH variable indicates the architecture for which this kernel is built. This variable is used by the kernel Makefiles to choose which architecture-dependent directory is going to be used. When compiling the kernel for your target, you must set this variable to your target's architecture.

The CROSS_COMPILE variable is used by the kernel's Makefiles to construct the names of the tools used in the kernel's build. The name of the C compiler, for instance, is the result of the concatenation of the value of CROSS_COMPILE and the letters "gcc". In the case of our ARM target, the C compiler's final name is *arm-linux-gcc*, which is the actual name of the compiler we built for this target using the instructions in Chapter 4. This also explains why the trailing hyphen on the previous command line is important. Without this hyphen, the Makefile would try to use the *arm-linuxgcc* compiler, which doesn't exist.

The building of the dependencies is relatively short. On my PowerBook, this takes two minutes. There are usually no errors possible at this stage. If you do see errors, the kernel you have probably suffers from fundamental problems.

Building the Kernel

With the dependencies built, we can now compile the kernel image:

```
$ make ARCH=arm CROSS_COMPILE=arm-linux- zImage
```

The zImage target instructs the Makefile to build a kernel image that is compressed using the gzip algorithm.* There are, nevertheless, other ways to build a kernel image. The vmlinux target instructs the Makefile to build only the uncompressed image. Note that this image is generated even when a compressed image is requested.

On the x86, there is also the bzImage target. The "bzImage" name stands for "big zImage," and has nothing to do with the *bzip2* compression utility. In fact, both the bzImage and zImage Makefile targets rely on the gzip algorithm. The difference between the two Makefile targets is that the compressed kernel images generated using zImage cannot be larger than 512 KB, while those generated using bzImage are not bound by this limit. If you want more information regarding the differences between zImage and bzImage, have a look at the *Documentation/i386/boot.txt* file included in the kernel sources.

If you chose any options not supported by your architecture during the kernel configuration or if some kernel option is broken, your build will fail at this stage. If all goes well, this should take a few minutes longer than the dependency build. On my hardware configuration, it takes five minutes.

Verifying the Cross-Development Toolchain

Notice that the kernel build is the first real test for the cross-development tools we built in the previous chapter. If the tools you built earlier compile a functional kernel successfully, all the other software should build perfectly. Of course, you will need to download the kernel you built to your target to verify its functionality, but the fact that it builds properly is already a positive sign.

---

* Though zImage is a valid Makefile target for all the architectures we discussed in depth in Chapter 3, there are other Linux architectures for which it isn't valid.

Building the Modules

With the kernel image properly built, we can now build the kernel modules:

```
$ make ARCH=arm CROSS_COMPILE=arm-linux- modules
```

The duration of this stage depends largely on the number of kernel options you chose to build as modules instead of having linked as part of the main kernel image. This stage is seldom longer than the build of the kernel image. As with the kernel image, if your configuration is inadequate for your target or if a feature is broken, this stage of the build may fail.

With both the kernel image and the kernel modules now built, we are ready to install them for our target. Before we do so, note that if you needed to clean up the kernel's sources and return them to their initial state prior to any configuration, dependency building, or compilation, you could use the following command:

```
$ make ARCH=arm CROSS_COMPILE=arm-linux- distclean
```

Be sure to backup your kernel configuration file prior to using this command, since *make distclean* erases all the files generated during the previous stages, including the *.config* file, all object files, and the kernel images.

Installing the Kernel

Ultimately, the kernel we generated and its modules will have to be copied to your target to be used. I will cover the actual copying of the kernel and its modules in Chapters 6 and 9. Meanwhile, we will discuss how to manage multiple kernel images and their corresponding module installations. The configuration of the target's boot layout and its root filesystem depend on the techniques we discuss below.

Managing Multiple Kernel Images

In addition to using separate directories for different kernel versions, you will find it useful to have access to multiple kernel images to test on your target. Since these images may be built using the same sources, we need to copy them out of the kernel source and into a directory where they can be properly identified. In our setup, the repository for these images is the *${PRJROOT}/images* directory.

For each kernel configuration, we will need to copy four files: the compressed kernel image, the uncompressed kernel image, the kernel symbol map, and the configuration file. The last three are found within the kernel sources' root directory and are called *vmlinux*, *System.map*, and *.config*, respectively. The compressed kernel image file is found in the *arch/YOUR_ARCH/boot* directory, where *YOUR_ARCH* is the name of your target's architecture, and is called *zImage* or *bzImage*, depending on the Makefile target you used earlier. For our ARM-based target, the compressed kernel image is *arch/arm/boot/zImage*.

Some architectures, such as the PPC, have many boot directories. In those cases, the kernel image to use is not necessarily the one located at *arch/YOUR_ARCH/boot/zImage*. In the case of the TQM board mentioned above, for example, the compressed kernel image that should be used is *arch/ppc/images/vmlinux.gz*. Have a look at the *arch/YOUR_ARCH/Makefile* for a full description of all the Makefile boot image targets for your architecture. In the case of the PPC, the type of boot image generated depends on the processor model for which the kernel is compiled.

To identify the four files needed, we use a naming scheme similar to that of the kernel's version. In the case of the kernel generated using *2.4.18-rmk5* sources, for instance, we copy the files as follows:

```
$ cp arch/arm/boot/zImage ${PRJROOT}/images/zImage-2.4.18-rmk5
$ cp System.map ${PRJROOT}/images/System.map-2.4.18-rmk5
$ cp vmlinux ${PRJROOT}/images/vmlinux-2.4.18-rmk5
$ cp .config ${PRJROOT}/images/2.4.18-rmk5.config
```

You could also include the configuration name in the filenames. So in the case of the kernel without serial support, for instance, we could name the four kernel files *zImage-2.4.18-rmk5-no-serial*, *System.map-2.4.18-rmk5-no-serial*, *vmlinux-2.4.18-rmk5-no-serial*, and *2.4.18-rmk5-no-serial.config*.

Installing Kernel Modules

The kernel Makefile includes the `modules_install` target for installing the kernel modules. By default, the modules are installed in the */lib/modules* directory. Since we are in a cross-development environment, however, we need to instruct the Makefile to install the modules in another directory.

As the kernel modules need to be used with the corresponding kernel image, we will install the modules in a directory with a name similar to that of the kernel image. So in the case of the 2.4.18-rmk5 kernel we are using, we install the modules in the *${PRJROOT}/images/modules-2.4.18-rmk5* directory. The content of this directory will later be copied to the target's root filesystem for use with the corresponding kernel on the target. To install the modules in that directory, we use:

```
$ make ARCH=arm CROSS_COMPILE=arm-linux- \
> INSTALL_MOD_PATH=${PRJROOT}/images/modules-2.4.18-rmk5 \
> modules_install
```

The `INSTALL_MOD_PATH` variable is prepended to the */lib/modules* path, so the modules are therefore installed in the *${PRJROOT}/images/modules-2.4.18-rmk5/lib/modules* directory.

Once it is done copying the modules, the kernel tries to build the module dependencies needed for the module utilities during runtime. Since *depmod*, the utility that builds the module dependencies, is not designed to deal with cross-compiled modules, it will fail.

To build the module dependencies for your modules, you will need to use another module dependency builder provided with the BusyBox package. We will discuss BusyBox at length in Chapter 6. For now, download a copy of the BusyBox archive from *http://www.busybox.net/* into your *${PRJROOT}/sysapps* directory and extract it there.* From the BusyBox directory, copy the *scripts/depmod.pl* Perl script into the *${PREFIX}/bin* directory.

We can now build the module dependencies for the target:

```
$ depmod.pl \
> -k ./vmlinux -F ./System.map \
> -b ${PRJROOT}/images/modules-2.4.18-rmk5/lib/modules > \
> ${PRJROOT}/images/modules-2.4.18-rmk5/lib/modules/2.4.18-rmk5/modules.dep
```

The *-k* option is used to specify the uncompressed kernel image, the *-F* option is used to specify the system map, and the *-b* option is used to specify the base directory containing the modules for which we need to build dependencies. Because the tool's output goes to the standard output, we redirect it to the actual dependency file, which is always called *modules.dep*.

In the Field

Let's take a look at the kernel's operation once it's installed on your target and ready to run. Because the algorithms and underlying source code is the same for embedded and regular systems, the kernel will behave almost exactly the same as it would on a workstation or a server. For this reason, the other books and online material on the subject, such as *Linux Device Drivers* and *Understanding the Linux Kernel* from O'Reilly, are much more appropriate for finding in-depth explanations of the kernel. There are, nevertheless, aspects particular to embedded Linux systems or that warrant particular emphasis.

Dealing with Kernel Failure

The Linux kernel is a very stable and mature piece of software. This, however, does not mean that it or the hardware it relies on never fail. *Linux Device Drivers* covers issues such as oops messages and system hangs. In addition to keeping these issues in mind during your design, you should think about the most common form of kernel failure: kernel panic.

When a fatal error occurs and is caught by the kernel, it will stop all processing and emit a kernel panic message. There are many reasons a kernel panic can occur. One of the most frequent is when you forget to specify to the kernel the location of its root filesystem. In that case, the kernel will boot normally and will panic upon trying to mount its root filesystem.

---

* Download BusyBox Version 0.60.5 or later.

The only means of recovery in case of a kernel panic is a complete system reboot. For this reason, the kernel accepts a boot parameter that indicates the number of seconds it should wait after a kernel panic to reboot. If you would like the kernel to reboot one second after a kernel panic, for instance, you would pass the following sequence as part of the kernel's boot parameters: panic=1.

Depending on your setup, however, a simple reboot may not be sufficient. In the case of our control module, for instance, a simple reboot may even be dangerous, since the chemical or mechanical process being controlled may get out of hand. For this reason, we need to change the kernel's panic function to notify a human operator who could then use emergency manual procedures to control the process. Of course, the actual panic behavior of your system depends on the type of application your system is used for.

The code for the kernel's panic function, panic(), is in the *kernel/panic.c* file in the kernel's sources. The first observation to be made is that the panic function's default output goes to the console.* Since your system may not even have a terminal, you may want to modify this function according to your particular hardware. An alternative to the terminal, for example, would be to write the actual error string in a special section of flash memory that is specifically set aside for this purpose. At the next reboot, you would be able to retrieve the text information from that flash section and attempt to solve the problem.

Whether you are interested in the actual text message or not, you can register your own panic function with the kernel. This function will be called by the kernel's panic function in the event of a kernel panic and can be used to carry out such things as signaling an emergency.

The list that holds the functions called by the kernel's own panic function is panic_notifier_list. The notifier_chain_register function is used to add an item to this list. Conversely, notifier_chain_unregister is used to remove an item from this list.

The location of your own panic function has little importance, but the registration of this function must be done during system initialization. In our case, we add a *mypanic.c* file in the *kernel/* directory of the kernel sources and modify that directory's Makefile accordingly. Here is the *mypanic.c* for our control module:

```
#include <linux/kernel.h>
#include <linux/init.h>
#include <linux/notifier.h>

static int my_panic_event(struct notifier_block *,
                          unsigned long,
                          void *);

static struct notifier_block my_panic_block = {
        notifier_call:   my_panic_event,
```

---

* The console is the main terminal to which all system messages are sent.

```
        next:           NULL,
        priority:       INT_MAX
};

int __init register_my_panic(void)
{
        printk("Registering buzzer notifier \n");

        notifier_chain_register(&panic_notifier_list,
                            &my_panic_block);

        return 0;
}

void ring_big_buzzer(void)
{
        ...
}

static int my_panic_event(struct notifier_block *this,
                        unsigned long event,
                        void *ptr)
{
        ring_big_buzzer();

        return NOTIFY_DONE;
}

module_init(register_my_panic);
```

The module_init(register_my_panic); statement ensures that the register_my_panic function is called during the kernel's initialization without requiring any modification of the kernel's startup functions. The registration function adds my_panic_block to the list of other blocks in the panic notifier list. The notifier_block structure has three fields. The first field is the function to be called, the second is a pointer to the next notifier block, and the third is the priority of this block. In our case, we want to have the highest possible priority. Hence the use of INT_MAX.

In case of kernel panic, my_panic_event is called as part of the kernel's notification of all panic functions. In turn, this function calls on ring_big_buzzer, which contains code to start a loud alarm to attract the human operator's attention to the imminent problem.

Root Filesystem Content

One of the last operations conducted by the Linux kernel during system startup is mounting the root filesystem. The root filesystem has been an essential component of all Unix systems from the start. The root filesystem's current organization is a bit idiosyncratic and contains some redundancy because of how it grew over time and was influenced by Unix developments. I will not attempt to cover the reasons for the current structure and underlying conventions. Instead, I will explain how to organize the various components to adhere to the accepted standards and, thereby, obtain a functional root filesystem. In the process, we will use many of the components we built earlier, such as the kernel modules and the C library.

First, we will discuss the basic root filesystem structure. Then, we will discuss how and where to install the system libraries, the kernel modules, kernel images, device nodes, main system applications, and custom applications. Finally, we will discuss how to configure the system initialization scripts. At the end of this chapter, you will have a fully functional root filesystem for your target. In the next chapters, we will discuss how you can place this root filesystem on an actual filesystem type on a storage device for use in your target.

Basic Root Filesystem Structure

The top-level directories in the root filesystem each have a specific use and purpose. Many of these are meaningful only in multiuser systems in which a system administrator is in charge of many servers and/or workstations used by different users. In most embedded Linux systems, where there are no users and no administrators, the rules to build a root filesystem can be loosely interpreted. This doesn't mean that all rules can be violated, but it does mean that breaking some rules will have little to no effect on the system's proper operation. Interestingly, even mainstream commercial distributions for workstations and servers do not always adhere to the established rules for root filesystems.

The "official" rules to build a root filesystem are contained in the Filesystem Hierarchy Standard (FHS) introduced in Chapter 1. The document is less than 30 pages long and is fairly easy to read. If you are looking for answers or clarifications regarding the root filesystem, the FHS is probably the best place to start. Table 6-1 provides the complete list of root filesystem top-level directories and their content as specified by the FHS.

Table 6-1. Root filesystem top-level directories

Directory	Content
bin	Essential user command binaries
boot	Static files used by the bootloader
dev	Devices and other special files
etc	System configuration files, including startup files
home	User home directories, including entries for services such as FTP
lib	Essential libraries, such as the C library, and kernel modules
mnt	Mount point for temporarily mounted filesystems
opt	Add-on software packages
proc	Virtual filesystem for kernel and process information
root	Root user's home directory
sbin	Essential system administration binaries
tmp	Temporary files
usr	Secondary hierarchy containing most applications and documents useful to most users, including the X server
var	Variable data stored by daemons and utilities

If you are using Linux for your day-to-day work, you are already familiar with some of these directories. Nevertheless, let's take a closer look at the content of a typical root filesystem for use in an embedded Linux system.

First, all the directories that pertain to providing a multiuser extensible environment, such as */home*, */mnt*, */opt*, and */root*, can be omitted. We could trim the root filesystem even further by removing */tmp* and */var*, but these omissions may jeopardize the operation of certain programs. I do not encourage such a minimalistic approach.

> This discussion does not revolve around size issues, but rather functionality. In fact, omitting a directory entry changes little to the resulting root filesystem's size. The reason I state that */home* can be omitted, for example, is that even if it were present in an embedded Linux system, it would be empty, because its content, as prescribed by the FHS, is useful only in workstation and server setups.

Depending on your bootloader and its configuration, you may not need to have a */boot* directory. This will depend on whether your bootloader can retrieve kernel images from your root filesystem before your kernel is booted. You will be able to decide whether you should use a */boot* directory and how to use it for your target after you read Chapter 9. Of course, you can redesign the root filesystem at any later time if need be.

The remaining directories, */bin*, */dev*, */etc*, */lib*, */proc*, */sbin*, and */usr*, are essential.

At the extreme, you could omit */proc*, which is useful only for mounting the virtual filesystem that has the same name. However, it would then become very hard to understand what is happening on your target if you needed to analyze it in the field. If you are very tight for space, you can configure your kernel without */proc* support, but I encourage you to enable it whenever possible.

Two of the root directories, */usr* and */var*, have a predefined hierarchy of their own, much like that of the root directory. We will briefly discuss these hierarchies as we populate both directories in the steps below.

Confusing Similarities

One of the most confusing aspects of the root filesystem is the apparent similarity in purpose of some directories. In particular, newcomers often ask what difference there is between the various directories containing binaries and the various directories containing libraries.

There are four main directories for binaries on the root filesystem: */bin*, */sbin*, */usr/bin*, and */usr/sbin*. The directory in which a binary is placed largely depends on its role in the system. Binaries that are *essential* to both users and system administrators are in */bin*. Binaries that are essential to system administration, but will never be used by ordinary users, are located in */sbin*. In contrast, most nonessential user binaries are located in */usr/bin* and most nonessential system administration tools are in */usr/sbin*.

As for the location of libraries, the rationale is similar. The libraries required to boot the system and run the most essential commands are located in */lib*, while */usr/lib* contains all the other libraries. Often, packages will create subdirectories in */usr/lib* to contain their own libraries. The Perl 5.x packages, for instance, have a */usr/lib/perl5* directory that contains all the Perl-related libraries and modules.

A look on your Linux workstation's own root filesystem in these directories will show you actual examples of the application of these criteria by your distribution's designers.

To work on the root filesystem, let's move into the directory we created for this purpose:

```
$ cd ${PRJROOT}/rootfs
```

We now create the core root filesystem directories required for our system:

```
$ mkdir bin dev etc lib proc sbin tmp usr var
$ chmod 1777 tmp
```

Notice that we did not create */boot*. We will come back to it later and create it if it becomes necessary. Also, note that we changed the permissions for the */tmp* directory to turn the "sticky bit" on. This bit in the directory permissions field will ensure that files created in the */tmp* directory can be deleted only by the user that created them. Though most embedded Linux systems are single-user systems, as I said above, there are cases in which embedded applications must not run with root privileges, hence the need to follow some basic rules about root filesystem permission bits. The OpenSSH package we discuss in Chapter 10, for example, is such an application.

We can proceed with the creation of the */usr* hierarchy:

```
$ mkdir usr/bin usr/lib usr/sbin
```

On a fully featured root filesystem, the */usr* directory usually contains many more entries. A simple demonstration of this is easily conducted by typing *ls -al /usr* on your workstation. You will find directories such as *man*, *src*, and *local*. The FHS contains a section addressing the layout of this directory in detail. For the purposes of most embedded Linux systems, nonetheless, the three directories we created will suffice.

The last entries to create are in the */var* directory:

```
$ mkdir var/lib var/lock var/log var/run var/tmp
$ chmod 1777 var/tmp
```

Here, too, this directory usually contains many more entries. Directories such as *cache*, *mail*, and *spool* are useful for a workstation or a server, but few embedded systems need those directories. The directories we created are the bare minimum required for the normal operation of most applications found in an embedded Linux system. Of course, if you need functionality such as web page serving or printing, then you may want to add some of the additional directories required by the applications providing this functionality. See the FHS and the documentation provided with your application to find out your actual requirements.

With the root filesystem skeleton now ready, let's place the various software components in their appropriate locations.

Libraries

In Chapter 4 we discussed how to build, install, and use the GNU C library and its alternatives for application development. Here, we will discuss how to install those same libraries on the target's root filesystem so that they can be used at runtime by the applications we develop. We will not discuss diet libc, because it is mainly used as a static library.

glibc

As I said earlier, the glibc package contains a number of libraries. You can see the entire list of libraries installed during the package's build process by looking at your *${TARGET_PREFIX}/lib* directory. This directory contains mainly four types of files:

Actual shared libraries
> These files' names are formatted as `libLIBRARY_NAME-GLIBC_VERSION.so`, where `LIBRARY_NAME` is the name of the library and `GLIBC_VERSION` is the version of the glibc package you are using. The name of the math library for glibc 2.2.3 is *libm-2.2.3.so*.

Major revision version symbolic links
> Major revision versions do not follow the same numbering as the actual glibc version. The major revision version for the actual shared C library in glibc 2.2.3, *libc-2.2.3.so*, is 6. In contrast, the major revision version for *libdl-2.2.3.so* is 2. The names of the symbolic links for the major revision version are formatted as `libLIBRARY_NAME.so.MAJOR_REVISION_VERSION`, where `MAJOR_REVISION_VERSION` is the major revision version of the library. For the actual C library, for instance, the symbolic link is *libc.so.6*. For libdl, it is *libdl.so.2*. Once a program has been linked to a library, it will refer to this symbolic link. At startup, the loader will therefore look for this file before loading the program.

Version-independent symbolic links to the major revision version symbolic links
> The role of these links is to provide a universal entry for all the programs that need to link with a particular library, regardless of the actual major revision or the version of glibc involved. These symbolic links are typically formatted as `libLIBRARY_NAME.so`. For example, *libm.so* points to *libm.so.6*, which itself points to the actual shared library, *libm-2.2.3.so*. The only exception to this is *libc.so*,

which, as I said in Chapter 4, is a link script. The version-independent symbolic link is the one used when linking programs.

Static library archives

These archives are used by applications that choose to link statically with a library. The names of these archives are formatted as *libLIBRARY_NAME.a*. The static archive for libdl, for instance, is *libdl.a*.

You will also find some other types of files in *${TARGET_PREFIX}/lib*, such as *crti.o* and *crt1.o*, but you will not need to copy these to your target's root filesystem.

Out of the four types of files described above, we will need only two for each library: the actual shared libraries and the major revision version symbolic links. The two other file types are needed only when linking executables and are not required for the runtime operation of our applications.

In addition to the library files, we will need to copy the dynamic linker and its symbolic link. The dynamic linker itself follows the naming convention of the various glibc libraries, and is usually called *ld-GLIBC_VERSION.so*. In what is probably one of the most bizarre aspects of the GNU toolchain, however, the name of the symbolic link to the dynamic linker depends on the architecture for which the toolchain has been built. If the toolchain is built for the i386, the ARM, the SuperH, or the m68k, the symbolic link to the dynamic linker is usually called *ld-linux.so.MAJOR_REVISION_VERSION*. If the toolchain is built for the MIPS or the PowerPC, the symbolic link to the dynamic linker is usually called *ld.so.MAJOR_REVISION_VERSION*.

Before we actually copy any glibc component to the target's root filesystem, however, we need to select the glibc components required for our applications. Table 6-2 provides the description of all the components in glibc[*] and provides inclusion guidelines for each component. In addition to my guidelines, you will need to evaluate which components your programs need, depending on their linking.

Table 6-2. Library components in glibc and root filesystem inclusion guidelines

Library component	Content	Inclusion guidelines
ld	Dynamic linker.[a]	Compulsory.
libBrokenLocale	Fixup routines to get applications with broken locale features to run. Overrides application defaults through preloading. (Need to use LD_PRELOAD).	Rarely used.
libSegFault	Routines for catching segmentation faults and doing backtraces.	Rarely used.
libanl	Asynchronous name lookup routines.	Rarely used.
libc	Main C library routines.	Compulsory.

[*] See the glibc manual for a complete description of the facilities provided.

Table 6-2. Library components in glibc and root filesystem inclusion guidelines (continued)

Library component	Content	Inclusion guidelines
libcrypt	Cryptography routines.	Required for most applications involved in authentication.
libdl	Routines for loading shared objects dynamically.	Required for applications that use functions such as dlopen( ).
libm	Math routines.	Required for math functions.
libmemusage	Routines for heap and stack memory profiling.	Rarely used.
libnsl	NIS network services library routines.	Rarely used.
libnss_compat	Name Switch Service (NSS) compatibility routines for NIS.	Loaded automatically by the glibc NSS.[b]
libnss_dns	NSS routines for DNS.	Loaded automatically by the glibc NSS.
libnss_files	NSS routines for file lookups.	Loaded automatically by the glibc NSS.
libnss_hesiod	NSS routines for Hesiod name service.	Loaded automatically by the glibc NSS.
libnss_nis	NSS routines for NIS.	Loaded automatically by the glibc NSS.
libnss_nisplus	NSS routines for NIS plus.	Loaded automatically by the glibc NSS.
libpcprofile	Program counter profiling routines.	Rarely used.
libpthread	Posix 1003.1c threads routines for Linux.	Required for threads programming
libresolv	Name resolver routines.	Required for name resolution.
librt	Asynchronous I/O routines.	Rarely used.
libthread_db	Thread debugging routines.	Loaded automatically by *gdb* when debugging threaded applications. Never actually linked to by any application.
libutil	Login routines, part of user accounting database.	Required for terminal connection management.

[a] This library component is actually not a library itself. Instead, *ld.so* is an executable invoked by the ELF binary format loader to load the dynamically linked libraries into an application's memory space.
[b] See Chapter 4 for details.

Apart from keeping track of which libraries you link your applications with, you can usually use the *ldd* command to find out the list of dynamic libraries that an application depends on. In a cross-platform development environment, however, your host's *ldd* command will fail when provided with target binaries. You could still use the cross-platform *readelf* command we installed in Chapter 4 to identify the dynamic libraries that your application depends on. Here is an example showing how the BusyBox utility's dependencies can be retrieved using *readelf*:

```
$ powerpc-linux-readelf -a ${PRJROOT}/rootfs/bin/busybox | \
> grep "Shared library"
 0x00000001 (NEEDED)                     Shared library: [libc.so.0]
```

Ideally, however, if you installed uClibc, you should use the cross-platform capable *ldd*-like command installed by uClibc. For our control module target, which is based on a PowerPC board, the command's name is *powerpc-uclibc-ldd*. This way, you can build the list of libraries your target binaries depend on. Here are the dependencies of the BusyBox utility, for example (one line has been wrapped to fit the page):

```
$ powerpc-uclibc-ldd ${PRJROOT}/rootfs/bin/busybox
        libc.so.0 => /home/karim/control-project/control-module/tools/uclibc/lib/
            libc.so.0
/lib/ld-uClibc.so.0 => /lib/ld-uClibc.so.0
```

Having determined the library components we need, we can copy them and the relevant symbolic links to the /lib directory of the target's root filesystem. Here is a set of commands that copy the essential glibc components:

```
$ cd ${TARGET_PREFIX}/lib
$ for file in libc libcrypt libdl libm \
> libpthread libresolv libutil
> do
> cp $file-*.so ${PRJROOT}/rootfs/lib
> cp -d $file.so.[*0-9] ${PRJROOT}/rootfs/lib
> done
$ cp -d ld*.so* ${PRJROOT}/rootfs/lib
```

The first *cp* command copies the actual shared libraries, the second one copies the major revision version symbolic links, and the third one copies the dynamic linker and its symbolic link. All three commands are based on the rules outlined earlier in this section regarding the naming conventions of the different files in *${TARGET_PREFIX}/lib*. The -d option is used with the second and third *cp* commands to preserve the symbolic links as-is. Otherwise, the files pointed to by the symbolic links are copied in their entirety.

Of course, you can remove the libraries that are not used by your applications from the list in the set of commands above. If you would rather have the complete set of libraries included in glibc on your root filesystem, use the following commands:

```
$ cd ${TARGET_PREFIX}/lib
$ cp *-*.so ${PRJROOT}/rootfs/lib
$ cp -d *.so.[*0-9] ${PRJROOT}/rootfs/lib
$ cp libSegFault.so libmemusage.so libpcprofile.so \
> ${PRJROOT}/rootfs/lib
```

If you have applications that use the glibc NSS, don't forget to copy the *libnss_SERVICE* libraries you need to your target's root filesystem. *libnss_files* and *libnss_dns* are the ones most often used. You will also need to copy the sample *nsswitch.conf* provided with glibc to your target's /etc directory and customize it to your setup:[*]

```
$ cp ${PRJROOT}/build-tools/glibc-2.2.1/nss/nsswitch.conf \
> ${PRJROOT}/rootfs/etc
```

Whether you copy all or part of the glibc libraries, you will notice that some of these libraries are large. To reduce the size of the libraries installed, we can use the

---

[*] Have a look at *Linux Network Administrator's Guide* (O'Reilly) for details about the customization of the *nsswitch.conf* file.

cross-platform *strip* utility we built earlier. Be careful not to strip the original libraries, since you would have to install them all over again. Strip the libraries only after you copy them to the root filesystem:

```
$ powerpc-linux-strip ${PRJROOT}/rootfs/lib/*.so
```

On my control module, the *${PRJROOT}/rootfs/lib* directory with all the glibc libraries weighs around 10 MB before stripping. By stripping all the libraries, the directory is reduced to 2.5 MB.

The glibc components have now been installed on the target's root filesystem and are ready to be used at runtime by our applications.

uClibc

As with glibc, uClibc contains a number of libraries. You can see the entire list by looking at your *${PREFIX}/uclibc/lib* directory. This directory contains the same four different types of files as the glibc directory.

Because uClibc is meant to be a glibc replacement, the names of the uClibc components and their use is identical to the glibc components. Hence, you can use Table 6-2 for uClibc components. Note, however, that not all glibc components are implemented by uClibc. uClibc implements only *ld*, *libc*, *libcrypt*, *libdl*, *libm*, *libpthread*, *libresolv*, and *libutil*. Use the same method as described for glibc to identify the uClibc components you will need on your target.

Having determined the list of components we need, we can now copy them and their relevant symbolic links to the */lib* directory of our target's root filesystem. The following set of commands copies the essential uClibc components:

```
$ cd ${PREFIX}/uclibc/lib
$ for file in libuClibc ld-uClibc libc libdl \
> libcrypt libm libresolv libutil
> do
> cp $file-*.so ${PRJROOT}/rootfs/lib
> cp -d $file.so.[*0-9] ${PRJROOT}/rootfs/lib
> done
```

The commands are likely to report that two files haven't been found:

```
cp: libuClibc.so.[*0-9]: No such file or directory
cp: libc-*.so: No such file or directory
```

This is not a problem, since these files don't exist. The set of commands above is meant to be easy to type in, but you could add conditional statements around the *cp* commands if you prefer not to see any errors.

As with glibc, you can modify the list of libraries you copy according to your requirements. Note that, in contrast to glibc, you will not save much space by copying only a select few uClibc components. For my control module, for instance, the root filesystem's */lib* directory weighs around 300 KB when *all* the uClibc components are copied. The following commands copy all uClibc's components to your target's root filesystem:

```
$ cd ${PREFIX}/uclibc/lib
$ cp *-*.so ${PRJROOT}/rootfs/lib
$ cp -d *.so.[*0-9] ${PRJROOT}/rootfs/lib
```

There is no need to strip uClibc components, since they were already stripped by uClibc's own build scripts. You can verify this using the *file* command.

Kernel Modules

In Chapter 5, we built the kernel modules and installed them in a temporary directory, *${PRJROOT}/images*. We are now ready to copy these modules to their final destination in the target's */lib* directory.

Since you may have compiled many kernels to test for your target, you will need to select which set of kernel modules to copy to the root filesystem. In the case of my control module, for example, I chose a 2.4.18 kernel for my target. The following command copies that kernel's entire *modules* directory to the root filesystem:

```
$ cp -a ${PRJROOT}/images/modules-2.4.18/* ${PRJROOT}/rootfs
```

We the use *cp*'s *-a* option here to copy the files and directories in archive mode. This has the effect of preserving file attributes and links, and copying directories recursively. Note that there is no need to explicitly append the */lib/modules* path to *${PRJROOT}/rootfs* in the above command because of the way we installed the modules in the *${PRJROOT}/images/modules-2.4.18* directory in Chapter 5.

That's it; the kernel modules are now ready for use on your target. You may also want to add a */etc/modules.conf* file to automate the loading of the modules during system operation. See Chapter 11 in *Linux Device Drivers* for more details regarding module management and the use of the */etc/modules.conf* file.

Kernel Images

As I said earlier, the presence of the actual kernel image on your root filesystem largely depends on your bootloader's capabilities. If you anticipate that your bootloader's setup will provide for booting a kernel from the root filesystem, you may copy the kernel image to your target's root filesystem at this time:

```
$ mkdir ${PRJROOT}/rootfs/boot
$ cd ${PRJROOT}/images
$ cp zImage-2.4.18 ${PRJROOT}/rootfs/boot
```

In addition to the kernel image, you may want to make it a standard practice to copy the configuration file used to create the kernel so that you may be able to service units for which the original project workspace may be lost:

```
$ cp 2.4.18.config ${PRJROOT}/rootfs/boot
```

Because we are discussing the actual bootloader setup in Chapter 9, there is nothing more to be done here about the kernel's setup for now. We will continue the kernel image's setup later.

Device Files

Following Unix tradition, every object in a Linux system is visible as a file, including devices.[*] All the device files (a.k.a. device "nodes") in a Linux root filesystem are located in the */dev* directory. Most workstation and server distributions come packaged with a */dev* directory containing more than 2,000 entries to account for all the possible system variations. Because embedded Linux systems are custom built, there is no need to fill the target's */dev* directory with as many entries as a Linux workstation or server. Only the entries required for the system's proper operation should be created.

Identifying which entries you need can be difficult if you don't have the required information. If you choose to use devfs instead of creating fixed static device entries, you will avoid having to look for the device information. Devfs has not been widely adopted, however, and static device entries are still the norm.

The official source of information for static device major and minor numbers is the *Documentation/devices.txt* file in the kernel sources. You can consult this file whenever you are uncertain about the name or numbering of a certain device.

Table 6-3 lists the most basic entries you will need in your */dev* directory. Depending on your particular setup, you will probably need to add a few extra entries. In some cases, you may even need to use entries other than the ones listed below. On some systems, for example, the first serial port is not *ttyS0*. Such is the case of SuperH-based systems, for instance, where the first serial port is *ttySC0* (major number: 204, minor number: 8), and StrongARM-based systems where the first serial port is *ttySA0* (major number: 204, minor number: 5).

Table 6-3. Basic /dev entries

Filename	Description	Type	Major number	Minor number	Permission bits
mem	Physical memory access	char	1	1	600
null	Null device	char	1	3	666
zero	Null byte source	char	1	5	666
random	Nondeterministic random number generator	char	1	8	644
tty0	Current virtual console	char	4	0	600
tty1	First virtual console	char	4	1	600

---

[*] The notable exception to this is networking interfaces, such as Ethernet cards, for which there are no device files.

Table 6-3. Basic /dev entries (continued)

Filename	Description	Type	Major number	Minor number	Permission bits
ttyS0	First UART serial port	char	4	64	600
tty	Current TTY device	char	5	0	666
console	System console	char	5	1	600

Chapter 6 of *Running Linux* explains how to create device files. Essentially, you will need to use the *mknod* command for each entry to be created. In contrast to most other commands we have used up until now, you will need to be logged in as root to use this command. Remember to log out from the root user mode once you are done creating the device files.

Here is a simple example showing the creation of the first few entries in Table 6-3:

```
$ cd ${PRJROOT}/rootfs/dev
$ su -m
Password:
# mknod -m 600 mem c 1 1
# mknod -m 666 null c 1 3
# mknod -m 666 zero c 1 5
# mknod -m 644 random c 1 8
...
# exit
```

In addition to the basic device files, there are a few compulsory symbolic links that have to be part of your */dev* directory. Table 6-4 provides a description of these symbolic links. As with other symbolic links, you can use the *ln -s* command to create these links.

Table 6-4. Compulsory /dev symbolic links

Link name	Target
fd	/proc/self/fd
stdin	fd/0
stdout	fd/1
stderr	fd/2

We have now prepared a basic */dev* directory for our target. We will come back to this directory later to create some additional entries for some types of storage devices. You can consult *Linux Device Drivers* for a more complete discussion about device files and device drivers in general.

Main System Applications

Beyond the kernel's functionality and the root filesystem's structure, Linux inherits Unix's very rich command set. The problem is that a standard workstation or server

Automated Creation of /dev Entries

The creation tools of some filesystems, such as JFFS2 and CRAMFS, have been extended by Erik Andersen to allow the creation of */dev* entries on the fly using a device table file. With such a file, it is no longer necessary to log in as root and use the *mknod* command to create entries in your target's root filesystem. Instead, the file creation tool parses the device table file and creates the entries while it builds the rest of the file-system without requiring root login. Support for JFFS2 device table files is already part of the MTD tools package, which includes the *mkfs.jffs2* command. Support for CRAMFS device table files is available in the form of a patch to be applied to the CRAMFS source package. The patch and the latest CRAMFS filesystem creation code are available at *http://sourceforge.net/projects/cramfs/*. I will not detail the use of device table files, since they can only be used with a very limited number of Linux filesystems at the time of this writing. Their format and their use are, however, fairly well explained in the *device_table.txt* file provided in both the MTD tools package and the CRAMFS patch. We will, nevertheless, discuss the MTD tools in Chapter 7 and the JFFS2 and CRAMFS filesystems in Chapter 8.

distribution comes equipped with thousands of command binaries, each providing its own set of capabilities. Obviously, developers cannot be expected to cross-compile such a large amount of binaries one by one, nor do most embedded systems require such a large body of binaries.

There are, therefore, two possibilities: either we choose a few select standard commands, or we try to group as many commands as possible into a very few trimmed-down applications that implement the essential overall functionality. In the following, we will start by discussing the first approach. I do not favor this approach, however, because it is tedious at best. Instead, I will mostly focus on the second approach and the various projects that implement it. In particular, we will discuss BusyBox, TinyLogin, and Embutils, which are the main packages used for this purpose.

Complete Standard Applications

If you would like to selectively include some of the standard applications found in mainstream distributions, your best bet is to start with the Linux From Scratch project located at *http://www.linuxfromscratch.org/*. This project aims at providing explanations and links to packages to help you build your own custom distributions. The *Linux From Scratch* book available through the project's web site is its main documentation. It includes instructions and links to build each application one by one. For each package, the instructions provide build-time and disk-space estimates.

Alternatively, you can download applications off the Net one by one and follow the instructions of each package for compiling and cross-compiling. Because few packages include full cross-compilation instructions, you may need to look in the packages' Makefiles to determine the appropriate build flags or make the proper modifications for the packages to cross-compile adequately.

BusyBox

The BusyBox project was initiated by Bruce Perens in 1996 to help build install disks for the Debian distribution. Since 1999, the project has been maintained by Erik Andersen, the maintainer of uClibc, first as part of Lineo's open source efforts and currently as a vendor-independent project. During this time, the BusyBox project has grown extensively and is now one of the corner stones of many embedded Linux systems. It is included in most embedded Linux distributions and has a very active user community. The project's current location is *http://www.busybox.net/*. The project's web site includes documentation, links, and a mailing list archive. The BusyBox package is available under the terms of the GNU GPL from this same web site.

Enthusiasm for BusyBox stems from the functionality it provides while still remaining a very small-sized application. BusyBox implements many commands. Here are a few: *ar, cat, chgrp, chmod, chown, chroot, cp, cpio, date, dd, df, dmesg, dos2unix, du, echo, env, expr, find, grep, gunzip, gzip, halt, id, ifconfig, init, insmod, kill, killall, ln, ls, lsmod, md5sum, mkdir, mknod, modprobe, more, mount, mv, ping, ps, pwd, reboot, renice, rm, rmdir, rmmod, route, rpm2cpio, sed, stty, swapon, sync, syslogd, tail, tar, telnet, tftp, touch, traceroute, umount, uname, uuencode, vi, wc, which,* and *whoami.*

Although BusyBox does not support all the options provided by the commands it replaces, the subset it provides is sufficient for most typical uses. See the *docs* directory of the BusyBox distribution for the documentation in a number of different formats.

BusyBox supports all the architectures covered in Chapter 3. It can be linked both statically and dynamically to either glibc or uClibc. You can also modify the BusyBox default build configuration to remove support for the commands you are unlikely to use.

Setup

First, you need to download a copy of the BusyBox package from the project's web site and into your *${PRJROOT}/sysapps* directory. For my control module, I will be using BusyBox 0.60.5.

Once the package is extracted, we can move into its directory for the rest of the setup:

```
$ cd ${PRJROOT}/sysapps/busybox-0.60.5
```

Although the CVS version includes a terminal-based menu utility for configuring options, such as the one I described for uClibc in Chapter 4, the main stable version, such as the one I'm using, has to be configured by editing the appropriate file. The main file for configuring options is *Config.h*. This file contains C-language #define

---

statements for each option. By commenting out an option's #define using // (slash slash) you effectively disable this option.

There are two types of options that can be configured: command support options and feature support options. Disabling or enabling a command support option removes or adds the corresponding command. Changing the #define BB_MKNOD line to //#define BB_MKNOD disables support for the *mknod* command in BusyBox. Feature support options have a similar behavior. Features, however, are not necessarily related to a particular command. Consequently, every #define BB_FEATURE_ ... line is preceded with a comment line describing the feature.

Make sure you verify the command support options selected by default. Some important commands, such as *ifconfig*, *insmod*, and *ping*, are disabled by default.

In addition to the configuration file, the main Makefile contains a few flags to control the way BusyBox is built. Most of these flags are used during the development of BusyBox for debugging purposes and are disabled in the standard distribution. The only flag you may be interested in modifying is the DOSTATIC flag. When set to true, the resulting BusyBox binary is statically linked with the C library. The default value of DOSTATIC is false, causing the binary to be dynamically linked. You can change this either by modifying the Makefile or by adding DOSTATIC=true as part of the *make* command.

Once BusyBox is configured, we can compile and install it. When linking with glibc, use the following command:

```
$ make TARGET_ARCH=ppc CROSS=powerpc-linux- \
> PREFIX=${PRJROOT}/rootfs all install
```

The TARGET_ARCH variable is used by the Makefile to determine whether some architecture-dependent optimizations can be carried out. CROSS is used, as in other circumstances, to specify the prefix of the cross-platform development tools. Finally, PREFIX is set to the root filesystem base directory. The Makefile will install all BusyBox's components within this directory.

To build BusyBox with uClibc instead of the GNU C library, use the following command:

```
$ make TARGET_ARCH=ppc CROSS=powerpc-uclibc- \
> PREFIX=${PRJROOT}/rootfs all install
```

BusyBox has now been installed on your target's root filesystem and is ready to be used.

Usage

To understand how best to use BusyBox, let's first take a look at the components installed on the target's root filesystem by BusyBox's build process. As expected, only one executable was installed, */bin/busybox*. This is the single binary with support for all the commands configured using *Config.h*. This binary is never called directly, however. Instead, symbolic links bearing the original commands' names have been created to */bin/busybox*. Such symbolic links have been created in all the directories in which the original commands would be found, including */bin*, */sbin*, */usr/bin*, and */usr/sbin*.

When you type a command during the system's normal operation, the *busybox* command is invoked via the symbolic link. In turn, *busybox* determines the actual command you were invoking using the name being used to run it. */bin/ls*, for instance, points to */bin/busybox*. When you type *ls*, the *busybox* command is called and it determines that you were trying to use the *ls* command, because *ls* is the first argument on the command line.[*]

Although this scheme is simple and effective, it means you can't use arbitrary names for symbolic links. Creating a symbolic link called */bin/dir* to either */bin/ls* or */bin/busybox* will not work, since *busybox* does not recognize the *dir* command.

Note that, though symbolic links are the usual way of linking commands to */bin/busybox*, BusyBox can also be instructed to create hard links instead of symbolic ones during its installation. Its behavior at runtime is the same, however, regardless of the type of links being used.

The documentation on the project's web site, which is also provided with the package, describes all the options available for each command supported. In most cases, the options supported by BusyBox have the same function as the options provided by the original commands. For instance, Using the *-al* options to BusyBox's *ls* will have the same effect as using the same options with the original *ls*.

When using one of the shells provided in BusyBox, such as *ash*, *lash*, or *msh*, you will find it convenient to use a */etc/profile* file to define a few global variables for all shell users. Here is a sample */etc/profile* file for a single-user target:

```
# Set path
PATH=/bin:/sbin:/usr/bin:/usr/sbin
export PATH
```

In addition to setting the path, you could set the LD_LIBRARY_PATH environment variable, which is used during the startup of each application to locate the libraries it depends on. Though the default location for libraries is */lib*, your system may have libraries located in other directories. If that is the case, you can force the dynamic linker to look for the other libraries by adding the appropriate directory paths to LD_LIBRARY_PATH. As with the PATH environment variable, you can add more directories to the library path by separating each directory path with a colon.

Note that on a workstation or a server LD_LIBRARY_PATH would actually be used only as a temporary holding place for new library paths. Instead, the */etc/ld.so.conf* is the file to edit to permanently add another library path. This file is then used by the *ldconfig* command to generate */etc/ld.so.cache*, which is itself read by the dynamic linker to find libraries for dynamically linked applications. Though *ldconfig* was

---

[*] As any other application, *busybox*'s main( ) function is passed the command line used to invoke it.

generated when we compiled glibc in Chapter 4, it is a target binary and cannot be run on the host to generate a target *ld.so.cache*.

TinyLogin

Much like BusyBox, TinyLogin is a collection of many login utilities into a single binary. TinyLogin is often used in conjunction with BusyBox, although it can be used alone. Both packages are maintained by the same developers and are therefore easy to use together. Because of their common use together, the project developers have integrated all of TinyLogin's functionality into the BusyBox CVS, and once the CVS development version is released as a stable version, it will be possible to rely on a single package instead of two. There are, however, advantages to continue using the TinyLogin functionality separately from BusyBox. Mainly, many of the commands implemented in TinyLogin must run with root privileges, which in turn requires that the TinyLogin binary file belong to the root user and have its "set user" permission bit enabled—a configuration commonly known as "setuid root." Since TinyLogin uses symbolic links in the same way BusyBox does, a single binary containing the functionality of both packages would also result in having commands such as *ls* and *cat* run as root, which increases the likeliness that a programming error in one command could be exploited to gain root privileges. Though BusyBox drops its root privileges when unnecessary, and though it can be configured to check a configuration file for those commands requiring root privileges, it remains that using separate packages is the safest setup.

The TinyLogin project's web site is located at *http://tinylogin.busybox.net/*. It contains documentation, a mailing list archive, links to other sites, and pointers to download the TinyLogin package both using FTP or CVS. For my control module, I will be using TinyLogin 1.2.

As with BusyBox, TinyLogin supports all the architectures we discussed in depth in Chapter 3 and can be linked either statically or dynamically with glibc or uClibc. TinyLogin can effectively replace the following commands: *addgroup*, *adduser*, *delgroup*, *deluser*, *getty*, *login*, *passwd*, *su*, *sulogin*, and *vlock*.

Setup

The first step in installing TinyLogin is to download the package and extract it into your *${PRJROOT}/sysapps* directory. Once this is done, we can move into the package's directory for the rest of the setup:

```
$ cd ${PRJROOT}/sysapps/tinylogin-1.2
```

The configuration of TinyLogin is done much the same as with BusyBox, by editing the *Config.h* configuration file and commenting out the unwanted command support options and feature options. TinyLogin also has a Makefile with similar options to BusyBox. The same rules explained above for BusyBox's *Config.h* file and Makefile also apply to TinyLogin.

Apart from the other options you need to configure, pay special attention to the USE_ SYSTEM_PWD_GRP and USE_SYSTEM_SHADOW options in the Makefile. The explanations above the statements in the Makefile provide a good idea about the effect of these options. Mainly, USE_SYSTEM_PWD_GRP should be set to false unless you plan to use glibc's NSS libraries with a properly configured *etc/nsswitch.conf* file. If you set this option to false, TinyLogin will directly use the *etc/passwd* and *etc/group* files instead of using the password and group functions provided by glibc.

Similarly, if you set USE_SYSTEM_SHADOW to false, TinyLogin will use its own shadow functions for accessing shadow passwords. Traditionally, *etc/passwd* could be read by anyone in the system and this in turn became a security risk as more and more programs for cracking passwords were available. Hence, the use of so-called shadow passwords became the norm. When in use, the password fields in *etc/passwd* only contain filler characters and the real encrypted passwords are stored in *etc/shadow*, which can be read only by a process running with root privileges. Note that if you had configured uClibc without shadow password support, setting USE_SYSTEM_SHADOW to true and linking with uClibc will result in a failed build.

As with BusyBox, you can set DOSTATIC to true if you would like TinyLogin to be built statically.

Once you have completed TinyLogin's configuration, you are ready to build the package. (Instead of compiling and installing the package in the same step, as we did for BusyBox, you will first compile and then install for the reasons explained below.)

To compile TinyLogin with glibc, use the following command:

```
$ make CROSS=powerpc-linux- \
> PREFIX=${PRJROOT}/rootfs all
```

To compile TinyLogin with uClibc, use the following command:

```
$ make CROSS=powerpc-uclibc- \
> PREFIX=${PRJROOT}/rootfs all
```

Once the package has been built, you can now install the package. Because the installation process must setuid the TinyLogin binary, the installation command must be done while logged in as root:

```
$ su -m
Password:
# make PREFIX=${PRJROOT}/rootfs install
# exit
```

TinyLogin has now been installed in the target's root filesystem and is ready to be used.

Usage

The TinyLogin installation copied only one binary to the root filesystem, */bin/ tinylogin*. As with BusyBox, symbolic links were created with the original commands' names in the appropriate binary directories.

You will need to create appropriate group, password, and shadow password files (*/etc/group*, */etc/passwd*, and */etc/shadow*, respectively) for use by the various TinyLogin commands. Unfortunately, the TinyLogin package does not provide a means to create these files prior to having TinyLogin running on the target. Hence, you will have to copy existing files and edit them manually for use on your target's root filesystem. A simple alternative is to use those files that are part of your workstation setup and keep only those entries for users who will exist on your target as well. Usually, this ends up being only the root user.

The group and password files on your workstation can be copied as-is to your target's */etc* directory. You can then edit your target's copies by hand and remove the entries that will not be used on your target. The shadow password file requires a little more care, however, since you may not want to reveal your own workstation's passwords to the users of your embedded system. To create valid entries in your target's shadow file, the simplest method is to create phony users on your workstation, set those users' passwords, and then copy the resulting entries. Here's the entry for a phony "tmp" user I added to my workstation:

```
tmp:$1$3cdOSELf$XWRLoKIL7vMSfLYbRCWaf/:11880:0:99999:7:-1:-1:0
```

I set this user's password to "root" for convenience. I then copied this entry as-is to my target's shadow file and edited the username appropriately:

```
root:$1$3cdOSELf$XWRLoKIL7vMSfLYbRCWaf/:11880:0:99999:7:-1:-1:0
```

There is now a user known as "root" with the password "root" on my target.

Remember that the password file contains the name of the shell used for each user. Since the command name for the shell provided by BusyBox is *sh*, and since the default on most workstations is *bash*, you need to change this to the shell on your target. Here is the password file entry for the root user for the same system:

```
root:x:0:0:root:/root:/bin/sh
```

By default, TinyLogin will set the path of each user as follows:

```
PATH=/bin:/usr/bin
```

If you would like to change this, you can either create a global */etc/profile* file, as I explained earlier, or a *.profile* file in each user's home directory. You will find the following *.profile* file useful for the root user:

```
PATH=/bin:/sbin:/usr/bin:/usr/sbin
export PATH
```

For more information on the creation and manipulation of group, password, or shadow password files, and system administration in general, see the Linux System Administrator's Guide from the LDP, *Running Linux* from O'Reilly, and the *Linux From Scratch* book I mentioned earlier.

embutils

embutils is a set of miniaturized and optimized replacements for mainstream Unix commands. embutils was written and is maintained by Felix von Leitner, the author of diet libc, with goals very similar to those of diet libc. Currently, embutils supports four of the architectures discussed in Chapter 3, the ARM, the i386, the PPC, and the MIPS. embutils is available from *http://www.fefe.de/embutils/.*[*]

Although embutils groups some of the commands in a single binary, its main approach is to provide one small binary for each command. embutils provides the following commands: *arch, basename, cat, chmgrp, chmod, chown, chroot, chvt, clear, cp, dd, df, dirname, dmesg, domainname, du, echo, env, false, head, hostname, id, install, kill, ln, ls, md5sum, mesg, mkdir, mkfifo, mknod, mv, pwd, rm, rmdir, sleep, sleep2, soscp, sosln, soslns, sosmv, sosrm, sync, tail, tar, tee, touch, tr, true, tty, uname, uniq, wc, which, whoami, write,* and *yes.*

As with BusyBox, not all the options provided by the full commands are supported, but the subset provided is sufficient for most system operations. In contrast to BusyBox, however, embutils can only be statically linked with diet libc. It can't be linked to any other library. Because diet libc is already very small, the resulting command binaries are reasonably small. In terms of overall size, nevertheless, BusyBox and embutils are fairly similar.

Setup

Before we start the setup, you will need to have diet libc installed on your host system as I described in Chapter 4. Now download embutils and extract it in your *${PRJROOT}/sysapps* directory. For my control module, for example, I use embutils 0.15. You can then move into the package's directory for the rest of the setup:

```
$ cd ${PRJROOT}/sysapps/embutils-0.15
```

There is no configuration capability for embutils. You can, therefore, build the package right away:

```
$ make ARCH=ppc CROSS=powerpc-linux- all
```

You can then install embutils:

```
$ make ARCH=ppc DESTDIR=${PRJROOT}/rootfs prefix="" install
```

The options and variables used in the build and installation of embutils have the same meaning as those used for diet libc.

---

[*] As with diet libc, the last slash ("/") is important.

Usage

The embutils installation procedure has copied quite a few statically linked binaries to your target root filesystem's */bin* directory. In contrast to BusyBox, this is the only directory where binaries have been installed.

A BusyBox-like all-in-one binary has also been installed, *allinone*. This binary reacts the same way as BusyBox when proper symbolic links are created to it. Note that unlike BusyBox, you need to create these symbolic links manually, since they are not created automatically by the installation scripts. *allinone* provides the following commands: *arch*, *basename*, *chvt*, *clear*, *dmesg*, *dirname*, *domainname*, *echo*, *env*, *false*, *hostname*, *pwd*, *sleep*, *sync*, *tee*, *true*, *tty*, *uname*, *which*, *whoami*, and *yes*.

Custom Applications

There are many places in the root filesystem where you can put your own application, depending on the number and types of components it has. Usually, it is preferable to follow the FHS's guidelines to place your software.

If your application consists of a relatively small number of binaries, placing them in */bin* is probably the best choice. This is the actual installation path used for the control daemon in Chapter 4.

If your application consists of a complex set of binaries, and possibly datafiles, consider adding an entry in the root filesystem for your project. You may either call this new directory *project* or name it after your own project. In the case of my control module, this directory could be *control-module*.

The custom directory can contain a hierarchy of its own that you can customize to best suit your needs. You may have to set the PATH environment variable on your target to include the custom directory if your binaries are placed there.

Note that the addition of a custom entry in the root filesystem is contrary to the FHS. This is a minor violation to the standard, however, since your filesystem is custom built for your target and is unlikely to become a distribution of its own.

System Initialization

System initialization is yet another particularity of Unix systems. As explained in Chapter 2, the kernel's last initialization action is to start the *init* program. This program is in charge of finalizing system startup by spawning various applications and starting some key software components. In most Linux systems, *init* mimics System V *init* and is configured much the same way. In embedded Linux systems, the flexibility of System V *init* is overkill since such systems are rarely run as multiuser systems.

There is no actual requirement for you to have a standard *init* program, such as System V *init*, on your root filesystem. The kernel itself doesn't really care. All it needs is an application it can start once it's done initializing the system. For instance, you can add an `init=PATH_TO_YOUR_INIT` boot parameter to tell the kernel to use your *init*, which could be your main application. There are, however, drawbacks to this approach, since your application will be the one and only application the kernel ever starts. Your application would then be responsible for starting other applications on the system. Furthermore, if your application unexpectedly dies, its exit will cause a kernel panic followed by a system reboot; as would an unexpected exit of System V *init*. Though this may be the desired behavior in some cases, in most cases, the system is most likely rendered useless. For these reasons, it is usually much safer and useful to actually have a real *init* on your root filesystem.

In the following subsections, I will cover the standard *init* package found in most Linux distributions, the BusyBox *init*, and Minit, a miniature *init* provided by the author of embutils and diet libc.

As with other issues in Unix, *init* is a broad subject. There are quite a few documents that discuss Linux *init* at length. Chapter 5 of *Running Linux* describes the mainstream workstation and server *init* setups. Alessandro Rubini wrote a very interesting piece about *init* that goes into the nuances of the various initialization schemes. His article is available at *http://www.linux.it/kerneldocs/init/*.

Standard System V init

The standard *init* package found in most Linux distributions is written by Miquel van Soorenburg and is available at *ftp://ftp.cistron.nl/pub/people/miquels/sysvinit/*. By using this package, you get the same flexibility to configure your target's startup as you would in configuring the startup of a workstation or a server. However, the extra functionality and flexibility requires additional space. Also, it requires that you keep track of the development of yet another software package. The package includes the following commands: *halt*, *init*, *killall5*, *last*, *mesg*, *runlevel*, *shutdown*, *sulogin*, *utmpdump*, and *wall*.

The package can be cross-compiled easily. First, download the package and uncompress it into your *${PRJROOT}/sysapps* directory. For my control module, I used sysvinit Version 2.84. Then, move into the package's source directory and build it:

```
$ cd ${PRJROOT}/sysapps/sysvinit-2.84/src
$ make CC=powerpc-linux-gcc
```

Replace the value of CC to match the cross-compiler for your target. With the package now built, we can install it on the target's root filesystem:

```
$ make BIN_OWNER="$(id -un)" BIN_GROUP="$(id -gn)" \
> ROOT=${PRJROOT}/rootfs install
```

This command will install all the binaries in the target's root filesystem but will fail afterward, since the Makefile tries to install the manpages on the root filesystem as well. You can modify the Makefile to avoid this, but you can also ignore the failure.

The command just shown set the BIN_OWNER and BIN_GROUP variables to be that of your own current user. By default, the Makefile attempts to install the various components and set their ownership to the root user. Since you aren't logged in as root, the Makefile would fail. The ownership of the binaries matters little on the target, since it isn't a multiuser system. If it were, however, you need to log in as root and then run the install command. Be very careful, in any case, to appropriately set the value of ROOT to point to your target's root filesystem. Otherwise, you may end up overwriting your workstation's *init* with a target binary. Alternatively, to avoid having to log in as root, you could still run the install command using your normal user privileges and then use the *chown* command as root to change the privileges on each file installed. This, however, involves going through the Makefile to find each file installed and its destination.

With *init* installed on your target's root filesystem, you will need to add the appropriate */etc/inittab* file and fill the */etc/rc.d* directory with the appropriate files. In essence, */etc/inittab* will define the runlevels for your system, and the files in */etc/rc.d* will define which services run on each runlevel. Table 6-5 lists *init*'s seven runlevels and their typical use in a workstation and server distribution.

Table 6-5. System V init runlevels

Runlevel	Description
0	System is halted
1	Only one user on system, no need for *login*
2	Multiuser mode without NFS, command-line *login*
3	Full multiuser mode, command-line *login*
4	Unused
5	X11, graphical user interface *login*
6	Reboot the system

Each runlevel corresponds to a certain set of applications. When entering runlevel 5 on a workstation, for example, *init* starts X11 and the user is prompted to enter his username and password using a graphical *login*. When switching between runlevels, the services started in the previous runlevel are shut down and the services of the new runlevel are started. In this scheme, runlevels 0 and 6 have a special meaning. Particularly, they are used for stopping the system safely. This may involve, for example, unmounting all the filesystems except the root filesystem and remounting the root filesystem read-only so that no filesystem corruption occurs.

On most workstations, the default runlevel at system startup is 5. For an embedded system, it can be set to 1, if no access control is necessary. The system's runlevel can be changed after system startup either using *init* or *telinit*, which is a symbolic link to *init*. In both cases, the newly issued *init* command communicates with the original *init* through the */dev/initctl* fifo. To this end, we need to create a corresponding entry in our target's root filesystem:

```
$ mknod -m 600 ${PRJROOT}/rootfs/dev/initctl p
```

For more information on the format of */etc/inittab* and the files found in */etc/rc.d*, refer to the resources provided above.

BusyBox init

Among the commands it supports by default, BusyBox provides *init*-like capabilities. As with the original mainstream *init*, BusyBox can handle the system's startup. BusyBox *init* is particularly well adapted to embedded systems, because it provides most of the *init* functionality an embedded system typically needs without dragging the weight of the extra features found in System V *init*. Also, because BusyBox is a single package, there is no need to keep track of an additional software package when developing or maintaining your system. There are cases, however, where BusyBox *init* may not be sufficient for your system. BusyBox *init*, for example, does not provide runlevel support.

Since I already described how to obtain, configure, and build BusyBox, I will limit this discussion to the setup of the *init* configuration files.

Because */sbin/init* is a symbolic link to */bin/busybox*, BusyBox is the first application to run on the target system. BusyBox identifies that the command being invoked is *init* and immediately jumps to the *init* routine.

The *init* routine of BusyBox carries out the following main tasks in order:

1. Sets up signal handlers for *init*.
2. Initializes the console(s).
3. Parses the inittab file, */etc/inittab*.
4. Runs the system initialization script. */etc/init.d/rcS* is the default for BusyBox.
5. Runs all the inittab commands that block (action type: `wait`).
6. Runs all the inittab commands that run only once (action type: `once`).

Once it has done this, the *init* routine loops forever carrying out the following tasks:

1. Runs all the inittab commands that have to be respawned (action type: `respawn`).
2. Runs all the inittab commands that have to be asked for first (action type: `askfirst`).

During console initialization, BusyBox determines whether the system was configured to run the console on a serial port (by passing `console=ttyS0` as a kernel boot parameter, for instance). If so, BusyBox versions prior to 0.60.4 used to disable all virtual terminals. Since 0.60.4, however, BusyBox continues through its initialization without disabling virtual terminals. If in fact there are no virtual terminals, its attempts to start shells on some virtual terminals later will fail anyway, so there is no need to disable virtual terminals outright.

After having initialized the console, BusyBox checks for the existence of an */etc/inittab* file. If no such file exists, BusyBox uses a default inittab configuration. Mainly, it sets up default actions for system reboot, system halt, and *init* restart. Also, it sets up actions to start shells on the first four virtual consoles, */dev/tty1* through */dev/tty4*. BusyBox will complain if you haven't created these device entries.

If an */etc/inittab* file is found, it is parsed and the commands it contains are recorded inside internal structures to be carried out at the appropriate time. The format of the inittab file as recognized by BusyBox is well explained in the documentation included in the BusyBox package. The documentation provided in the BusyBox package includes an elaborate example inittab file.

Each line in the inittab file follows this format:

```
id:runlevel:action:process
```

Although this format resembles that of traditional System V *init*, take note that the meaning of *id* is different in BusyBox *init*. Mainly, the *id* is used to specify the controlling tty for the process to be started. You can safely leave this entry empty if the process to be started isn't an interactive shell. Interactive shells, such as BusyBox's *sh*, should always have a controlling tty. BusyBox's *sh* will actually complain if it has no controlling tty. BusyBox completely ignores the *runlevel* field, so you can leave it blank. The *process* field specifies the path of the program to run, along with its command-line options. The *action* field is one of eight recognized actions to be applied to *process* as described in Table 6-6.

Table 6-6. Types of inittab actions recognized by BusyBox init

Action	Effect
sysinit	Provide *init* with the path to the initialization script.
respawn	Restart the process every time it terminates.
askfirst	Similar to respawn, but is mainly useful for reducing the number of terminal applications running on the system. It prompts *init* to display "Please press Enter to activate this console." at the console and wait for the user to press Enter before restarting the process.
wait	Tell *init* that it has to wait for the process to complete before continuing.
once	Run process only once without waiting for them.
ctrlaltdel	Run process when the Ctrl-Alt-Delete key combination is pressed.
shutdown	Run process when the system is shutting down.
restart	Run process when *init* restarts. Usually, the process to be run here is *init* itself.

The following is a simple inittab file for my control module:

```
::sysinit:/etc/init.d/rcS
::respawn:/sbin/getty 115200 ttyS0
```

```
::respawn:/control-module/bin/init
::restart:/sbin/init
::shutdown:/bin/umount -a -r
```

This inittab file does the following:

1. Sets */etc/init.d/rcS* as the system initialization file.
2. Starts a login session on the serial port at 115200 bps.
3. Starts the control module's custom software initialization script.
4. Sets */sbin/init* as the program to execute if *init* restarts.
5. Tells *init* to run the *umount* command to unmount all filesystems it can at system shutdown and set the others as read-only to preserve the filesystems.

The *id* is left blank in this case, because it doesn't matter to the normal operation of the commands. *runlevel* is also left blank, since it's completely ignored by BusyBox.

As shown earlier, however, none of these actions will take place until *init* runs the system initialization script. This script can be quite elaborate and can actually call other scripts. Use this script to set all the basic settings and initialize the various components of the system that need special handling. Particularly, this is a good place to:

- Remount the root filesystem in read-write mode.
- Mount additional filesystems.
- Initialize and start networking interfaces.
- Start system daemons.

Here is the initialization script for my control module:

```
#!/bin/sh

# Remount the root filesystem in read-write (requires /etc/fstab)
mount -n -o remount,rw /

# Mount /proc filesystem
mount /proc

# Start the network interface
/sbin/ifconfig eth0 192.168.172.10
```

The above initialization script depends on the existence of an */etc/fstab* file in the target's root filesystem. I will not discuss the content and use of this file as it is already discussed in depth in *Running Linux*. Nevertheless, here's the */etc/fstab* file I use for my control module during development:

```
# /etc/fstab
# device       directory    type    options
#
/dev/nfs       /            nfs     defaults
none           /proc        proc    defaults
```

In this case, I mount the target's root filesystem on NFS to simplify development. We will discuss filesystem types in Chapter 8 and NFS mounting in Chapter 9.

Minit

Minit is part of the miniaturized tools developed by Felix von Leitner, such as diet libc and embutils. Minit is available from *http://www.fefe.de/minit/*.* As with the other tools distributed by Felix, Minit requires a properly configured diet libc.

Minit's initialization procedure is a complete departure from the traditional System V *init*. Instead of using a */etc/inittab*, for instance, Minit relies on the existence of a properly built */etc/minit* directory. Firdtjof Busse wrote a description of how Minit operates at *http://www.fbunet.de/minit.shtml*. Firdtjof also provides pointers to example */etc/minit* directories.

Unfortunately, as of Version 0.8, Minit is not yet as mature as the other tools provided by Felix. Its Makefile, for instance, is unable to deal with installing the various components in a root filesystem other than the host's own. For the time being, Minit is not appropriate for an embedded system, but it may be worth considering sometime in the near future.

* As with the other tools available from *fefe.de*, the last slash ("/") is important.

CHAPTER 7
Storage Device Manipulation

The storage devices used in embedded systems are often quite different from those used in workstations and servers. Embedded systems tend to use solid-state storage devices such as flash chips and flash disks. As with any other Linux system, these devices must be properly set up and configured to be used by the kernel. Because these storage devices differ greatly from typical workstation and server disks, the tools to manipulate them (for partitioning, copying files, and erasing, for instance) are also different. These tools are the subject of this chapter.

In this chapter, we will discuss the manipulation of embedded storage devices for use with Linux. We will start with our primary topic: the manipulation of devices supported by the MTD subsystem. I will also briefly cover the manipulation of disk devices. If you intend to use a conventional disk device as part of your system, however, I recommend that you look at one of the books that discusses Linux system maintenance, such as O'Reilly's *Running Linux*, for more extensive coverage. The last section of this chapter will cover the use of swap in embedded systems.

MTD-Supported Devices

As we saw earlier in "Memory Technology Devices" in Chapter 3, the MTD subsystem is rich and elaborate. To use it on your target, you will need a properly configured kernel and the MTD tools available from the project's web site. We will discuss both of the issues below.

As with other kernel subsystems, the development of the MTD subsystem and the MTD tools is independent of the mainline kernel. Hence, the latest kernel often does not include the latest code in the MTD CVS repository. You can, nevertheless, retrieve the latest code and use it instead of the MTD code already included in the kernel you have selected.

Because the MTD code in the kernel releases is not in sync with the MTD development, however, you can sometimes encounter problems. I was unable, for instance, to get vanilla Linux 2.4.18 to boot from a DiskOnChip (DOC) 2000, because there is a bug in the default MTD code in that kernel. To fix the problem, I had to manually modify the MTD code according to instructions found in the MTD mailing list archive. For this reason, you will find the MTD mailing list and its archive helpful.

In the following sections, we will start by discussing the usage basics of the MTD subsystem. This will cover issues such as configuring the kernel, installing the required utilities, and creating appropriate entries in *dev*. The discussion will then focus on the use of the MTD subsystem with the two solid state storage devices most commonly used in embedded Linux systems: native CFI-compliant flash and DOC devices.

MTD Usage Basics

Having already covered the detailed architecture of the MTD subsystem, we can now concentrate on the actual practical use of its components. First, we will discuss the *dev* entries required for MTD abstractions. Second, we will discuss the basic MTD kernel configuration options. Third, we will discuss the tools available to manipulate MTD storage devices in Linux. Finally, we will describe how to install these tools both on the host and on the target.

MTD /dev entries

There are five types of MTD */dev* entries and seven corresponding MTD user modules.[*] In practice, many MTD user modules share the same */dev* entries and each */dev* entry can serve as an interface to many MTD user modules. Table 7-1 describes each type of MTD */dev* entry and the corresponding MTD user modules, and Table 7-2 provides the minor number ranges and describes the naming scheme used for each device type.

Table 7-1. MTD /dev entries, corresponding MTD user modules, and relevant device major numbers

/dev entry	Accessible MTD user module	Device type	Major number
mtdN	char device	char	90
mtdrN	char device (read-only)	char	90
mtdblockN	block device, read-only block device, JFFS, and JFFS2	block	31
nftlLN	NFTL	block	93
ftlLN	FTL	block	44

Table 7-2. MTD /dev entries, minor numbers, and naming schemes

/dev entry	Minor number range	Naming scheme
mtdN	0 to 32 per increments of 2	$N = minor / 2$
mtdrN	1 to 33 per increments of 2	$N = (minor - 1) / 2$
mtdblockN	0 to 16 per increments of 1	$N = minor$

[*] See "Memory Technology Devices" in Chapter 3 for the definition of MTD "user modules."

Table 7-2. MTD /dev entries, minor numbers, and naming schemes (continued)

/dev entry	Minor number range	Naming scheme
nftlLN	0 to 255 per sets of 16	L = set;[a] N = minor - (set - 1) × 16; N is not appended to entry name if its value is zero.
ftlLN	0 to 255 per sets of 16	`Same as NFTL.`

[a] As with other partitionable block device entries in */dev*, device sets are identified by letters. The first set is "a," the second set is "b," the third set is "c," and so on.

The use of each type of MTD */dev* entry is as follows:

mtdN
> Each entry is a separate MTD device or partition. Remember that each MTD partition acts as a separate MTD device.

mtdrN
> Each entry is the read-only equivalent of the matching */dev/mtdN* entry.

mtdblockN
> Each entry is the block device equivalent of the matching */dev/mtdN* entry.

nftlLN
> Each set is a separate NFTL device, and each entry in a set is a partition on that device. The first entry in a set is the entire device. */dev/nftlb*, for instance, is the second NFTL device in its entirety, while */dev/nftlb3* is the third partition on the second NFTL device.

ftlLN
> Same as NFTL.

As we'll see later, you don't need to create all these entries manually on your host. You will, however, need to create some of these entries manually on your target's root filesystem to use the corresponding MTD user module. Also, note that the naming scheme described above differs slightly from the one described in the *devices.txt* file mentioned earlier. The naming scheme presented here is the one used in practice.

Configuring the kernel

As I mentioned in Chapter 5, the configuration of the MTD subsystem is part of the main menu of the kernel configuration options. Whether you are configuring the kernel using the curses-based terminal configuration menu or through the Tk-based X Window configuration menu, you will need to enter the "Memory Technology Devices (MTD)" submenu to configure the MTD subsystem for your kernel.

The MTD submenu contains a list of configuration options that you can choose to build as part of the kernel, build as separate modules, or disable completely. Here are the main options you can configure in the MTD submenu:

Memory Technology Device (MTD) support, `CONFIG_MTD`
> Enable this option if you want to include core MTD subsystem support. If you disable this option, this kernel will not have any MTD support. When this

option is set to be built as a module, the resulting functionality is found in the module called *mtdcore.o*.

MTD partitioning support, CONFIG_MTD_PARTITIONS

Enable this option if you want to be able to divide your MTD devices into separate partitions. If you compile this as a module, the module's filename is *mtdpart.o*. Note that MTD partitioning does not apply to DOC devices. These devices are partitioned using conventional disk partitioning tools.

Direct char device access to MTD devices, CONFIG_MTD_CHAR

This is the configuration option for the char device MTD user module that is visible as */dev/mtdN* and */dev/mtdrN*. If you configure this as a module, the module's filename is *mtdchar.o*.

Caching block device access to MTD devices, CONFIG_MTD_BLOCK

This is the configuration option for the read-write block device MTD user module that is visible as */dev/mtdblockN*. If you configure this as a module, the module's filename is *mtdblock.o*.

Read-only block device access to MTD devices, CONFIG_MTD_BLOCK_RO

This is the configuration option for the read-only block device MTD user module that is visible using the same */dev* entries as the read-write block device. If you configure the read-only block device user module as a module, the module's filename is *mtdblock_ro.o*.

FTL (Flash Translation Layer) support, CONFIG_FTL

Set this option if you would like to include the FTL user module in your kernel. When configured as a module, the module's filename is *ftl.o*. The FTL user module is accessible through the */dev/ftlLN* device entries.

NFTL (NAND Flash Translation Layer) support, CONFIG_NFTL

Set this option if you would like to include the NFTL user module in your kernel. When configured as a module, the module's filename is *nftl.o*. The NFTL user module is accessible through the */dev/nftlLN* device entries.

Write support for NFTL (BETA), CONFIG_NFTL_RW

You must enable this option if you want to be able to write to your NFTL-formatted devices. This will only influence the way the NFTL user module is built and is not a separate user module in itself.

 Notice that only one of the two block device MTD user modules can be built in the kernel, although both can be configured as modules (*mtdblock.o* and *mtdblock_ro.o*). In other words, if you set the read-write block device user module to be built into the kernel—not as a module—you will not be able to configure the read-only block device user module, either built-in or as a module. As we saw earlier, both block device MTD user modules use the same */dev* entry, and cannot therefore be active simultaneously.

The preceding list is primarily made up of the user modules I described earlier. The remaining MTD user modules, JFFS and JFFS2, are not configured as part of the MTD subsystem configuration. Rather, they are configured within the "File systems" submenu. Nevertheless, you will need to enable MTD support to enable support for either JFFS or JFFS2.

The MTD submenu also contains four submenus to configure support for the actual MTD hardware device drivers. Here are the submenus found in the MTD submenu and their descriptions:

RAM/ROM/Flash chip drivers
> Contains configuration options for CFI-Compliant flash, JEDEC-compliant flash, old non-CFI flash, RAM, ROM, and absent chips.

Mapping drivers for chip access
> Contains configuration options for mapping drivers. Includes one generic mapping driver that can be configured by providing the physical start address of the device and its size in hexadecimal notation, and its bus width in octets. This submenu also contains one entry for each board for which there is an existing mapping driver included in the kernel.

Self-contained MTD device drivers
> Contains configuration options for uncached system RAM, virtual memory test driver, block device emulation driver, and DOC devices.

NAND Flash Device Drivers
> Contains configuration options for non-DOC NAND flash devices.

Before configuring your kernel's MTD subsystem, make sure you have read the MTD subsystem discussion in Chapter 3, since many of the options described here were amply covered in my earlier discussion.

When configuring the kernel for your host, you will find it useful to configure all the MTD subsystem options as modules, since you will be able to test different device setup combinations. For your target, however, you will need to compile all the options required to support your solid state storage device as part of your kernel rather than as modules. Otherwise, your target will not be able to mount its root filesystem from its solid state storage device. If you forget to configure your target's kernel so that it can mount its root filesystem from the MTD device, your kernel will panic during startup and complain about its inability to mount its root filesystem with a message similar to the following:

```
Kernel panic: VFS: unable to mount root fs on ...
```

The MTD utilities

Because the MTD subsystem's functionality is different from that of other kernel subsystems, a special set of utilities is required to interact with it. We will see in the next sections how to obtain and install these utilities. For now, let's take a look at the available tools and their purposes.

The MTD utilities are powerful tools. Make sure you understand exactly the operations being performed by a tool before using it. Also, make sure you understand the particularities of the device on which you are using the tools. DOC devices, for example, require careful manipulation. You can easily damage your DOC device if you do not use the MTD tools appropriately.

Within the MTD tool set, there are different categories of tools, each serving a different MTD subsystem component. Here are the different tool categories and the tools they contain:

Generic tools
> These are the tools that can be used with all types of MTD devices:

> *einfo device*
>> Provides information regarding a device's erase regions.

> *erase device start_address number_of_blocks*
>> Erases a certain number of blocks from a device starting at a given address.

> *eraseall [options] device*
>> Erases the entire device.

> *unlock device*
>> Unlocks* all the sectors of a device.

> *lock device offset number_of_blocks*
>> Locks a certain number of blocks on a device.

> *fcp [options] filename flash_device*
>> Copies a file to a flash_device.

> *doc_loadbios device firmware_file*
>> Writes a bootloader to the device's boot region. Though this command is usually used with DOC devices only, it is not DOC specific.

> *mtd_debug operation [operation_parameters]*
>> Provides useful MTD debugging operations.

Filesystem creation tools
> These tools create the filesystems that are later used by the corresponding MTD user modules:

> *mkfs.jffs2 [options] -r directory -o output_file*
>> Builds a JFFS2 filesystem image from a directory.

> *mkfs.jffs [options] -d directory -o output_file*
>> Builds a JFFS filesystem image from a directory.

> *jffs2reader image [options] path*
>> Lists the content of a path in the JFFS2 filesystem image.

---

* Some devices can be protected from accidental writes using write "locks." Once a device, or some portion of it, is locked, it cannot be written to until it is unlocked.

NFTL tools
> These tools interact with NFTL partitions:
>
> *nftl_format device [start_address [size]]*
>> Formats a device for use with the NFTL user module.
>
> *nftldump device [output_file]*
>> Dumps the content of an NFTL partition to a file.

FTL tools
> These tools interact with FTL partitions:
>
> *ftl_format [options] device*
>> Formats an FTL device.
>
> *ftl_check [options] device*
>> Checks and provides information regarding an FTL device.

NAND chip tools
> These tools are provided for manipulating NAND chips:
>
> *nandwrite device input_file start_address*
>> Writes the content of a file to a NAND chip.
>
> *nandtest device*
>> Tests NAND chips, including those in DOC devices.
>
> *nanddump device output_file [offset] [number_of_bytes]*
>> Dumps the content of a NAND chip to a file.

Most of these tools are used on */dev/mtdN* devices, which are the char device interfaces to the various MTD devices. I will describe the typical uses of the most important MTD tools over the next few chapters, covering the actual MTD hardware in this chapter, preparation of the root filesystem in Chapter 8, and the boot setup in Chapter 9.

Installing the MTD utilities for the host

The MTD utilities are maintained as part of the MTD development CVS. You can retrieve the latest tool versions using CVS. You can also download a CVS snapshot from *ftp://ftp.uk.linux.org/pub/people/dwmw2/mtd/cvs/*. For my DAQ module, I am using the snapshot dated 2002-07-31.

Download the snapshot of your choice to your *${PRJROOT}/build-tools* directory and extract it. You can then move to this directory and prepare to compile the tools:

```
$ cd ${PRJROOT}/build-tools/mtd/util
$ automake --foreign; autoconf
$ ./configure --with-kernel=/usr/src/linux
```

When issuing the *configure* command, you must provide the path to the kernel that will be used to compile the tools. Since you are building the tools for your host, you need to provide the path to your host's kernel sources. By default, these should be located at */usr/src/linux*.

As in other build scenarios, *configure* builds the Makefile required to compile the tools. You can now compile the tools:

```
$ make clean
$ make
```

Make sure you issue the *make clean* command, as there are files in the utilities source code that need to be deleted to allow symbolic links with the same names to be created to files in the kernel sources.

If the build process fails while compiling *compr.c* because of an undefined KERN_ WARNING symbol, you will need to edit the *Makefile.am* file and replace the following lines:

```
compr.o: compr.c
        $(COMPILE) $(CFLAGS) $(INCLUDES) -Dprintk=printf \
        -DKERN_NOTICE= -c -o $@ $<
```

with:

```
compr.o: compr.c
        $(COMPILE) $(CFLAGS) $(INCLUDES) -Dprintk=printf \
        -DKERN_WARNING= -DKERN_NOTICE= -c -o $@ $<
```

Once you have completed the modification, you will need to restart the build from the start, as already described, after having issued a *make distclean* command.

With the utilities built, you can now install them in your *tools* directory:

```
$ make prefix=${PREFIX} install
```

This will install the utilities in *${PREFIX}/sbin*. You will need to add this directory to your path, if it's not already part of it. See my earlier explanation in Chapter 4 about installing uClibc's utilities for a complete description on how to add a new directory to your development path.

Now that the utilities have been installed, you need to create the MTD device entries in your host's */dev* directory. The *MAKEDEV* script found in the *util* directory takes care of the device creation. Have a look inside this file if you are interested in the devices being created. *MAKEDEV* mainly creates the */dev* entries I covered earlier in "MTD /dev entries." Because *MAKEDEV* uses the *mknod* command, you will need to run it as root:

```
# ./MAKEDEV
```

Although you may later want to update your MTD tool set, you should not need to use *MAKEDEV* again. If your MTD devices are accessible on the host because you are using the removable storage setup or the standalone setup we discussed in Chapter 2, you are ready to manipulate your MTD devices immediately. If you are using the linked setup or want to use the MTD utilities on your target in a removable storage setup, read the next section for instructions on how to build the MTD utilities for your target.

Installing the MTD utilities for the target

To install the MTD utilities for your target, you need to first download and install zlib. Earlier, when you installed the MTD utilities on your host, you didn't need to install zlib, because zlib is part of most mainstream distributions. Zlib is available at *http://www.gzip.org/zlib/*. For my DAQ module, I used zlib 1.1.4.

Download zlib and extract it in your *${PRJROOT}/build-tools* directory. You can then move to the library's directory to prepare its compilation:

```
$ cd ${PRJROOT}/build-tools/zlib-1.1.4
$ CC=i386-linux-gcc LDSHARED="i386-linux-ld -shared" \
> ./configure --shared
```

By default, the zlib build process generates a static library. To build zlib as a shared library, you must set the LDSHARED variable and provide the *--shared* option when invoking *configure*. With the Makefile created, you can compile and install the library:

```
$ make
$ make prefix=${TARGET_PREFIX} install
```

As with the other target libraries we installed earlier, we install zlib in *${TARGET_ PREFIX}/lib*. Once the library is installed, you can install it on your target's root filesystem:

```
$ cd ${TARGET_PREFIX}/lib
$ cp -d libz.so* ${PRJROOT}/rootfs/lib
```

You are now ready to build the MTD utilities. Download the MTD snapshot into your *${PRJROOT}/sysapps* and extract it. Now move into the utilities directory and build the tools:

```
$ cd ${PRJROOT}/sysapps/mtd/util
$ automake --foreign; autoconf
$ CC=i386-linux-gcc ./configure \
> --with-kernel=${PRJROOT}/kernel/linux-2.4.18
$ make clean
$ make
```

In this case, the kernel path points to your target's kernel. As in the previous section, if the build process fails while compiling *compr.c* because of an undefined KERN_ WARNING symbol, you will need to edit the *Makefile.am* file, make the appropriate changes, and restart the build from the beginning after issuing *make distclean*.

With the utilities built, you can now install them in your target's root filesystem:

```
$ make prefix=${PRJROOT}/rootfs install
```

This will install the utilities in *${PRJROOT}/rootfs/sbin*. We will not run the *MAKEDEV* script here, because it is not well adapted to creating device entries other than on the root filesystem of the system on which it runs. If you want to use the script as is, you would have to copy it to your target's root filesystem and then run it once you have the target running. This, however, would waste filesystem resources on the target, since the script creates entries for all the MTD devices you can possibly have in a system. We will see in the following sections how to create just the devices needed on the target's root filesystem.

How NOR and NAND Flash Work

Flash devices, including NOR flash devices such as CFI flash chips and NAND flash devices such as the DOC, are not like disk storage devices. They cannot be written to and read from arbitrarily. To understand how to operate flash chips properly, we must first look at how they operate internally. Flash devices are generally divided into *erase blocks*. Initially, an empty block will have all its bits set to 1. Writing to this block amounts to clearing bits to 0. Once all the bits in a block are cleared (set to 0), the only possible way to erase this block is to set *all* of its bits to 1 simultaneously. With NOR flash devices, bits can be set to 0 individually in an erase block until the entire block is full of 0s. NAND flash devices, on the other hand, have their erase blocks divided further into pages, of 512 bytes typically, which can only be written to a certain number of times—typically less than 10 times—before their content becomes undefined. Pages can then only be reused once the blocks they are part of are erased in their entirety.

Native CFI Flash

Most recent small-to-medium–sized non-x86 embedded Linux systems are equipped with some form of CFI flash. Setting up CFI flash to be used with Linux is relatively easy. In this section, we will discuss the set up and manipulation of CFI devices in Linux. We will not discuss the use of filesystems on such devices, however, since these will be covered in the next chapter. The order to the subsections below tries to follow the actual steps involved in using CFI flash devices with Linux as much as possible. You can, nevertheless, use these instructions selectively according to your current manipulation.

Kernel configuration

You will need to enable kernel support for the following options to use your CFI flash device:

- Memory Technology Device (MTD) support
- MTD partitioning support, if you would like to partition your flash device
- Direct char device access to MTD devices
- Caching block device access to MTD devices
- In the "RAM/ROM/Flash chip drivers" submenu, Detect flash chips by Common Flash Interface (CFI) probe
- In the "Mapping drivers for chip access" submenu, the CFI flash device mapping driver for your particular board

You may also choose to enable other options, but these are the bare minimum. Also, remember to set the options to "y" instead of "m" if you intend to have the kernel mount its root filesystem from the CFI device.

Partitioning

Unlike disk or DOC devices, CFI flash cannot generally be partitioned using tools such as *fdisk* or *pdisk*, because partition information is not usually stored on CFI flash devices. Instead, the device's partitions are hardcoded in the mapping driver and are registered with the MTD subsystem during the driver's initialization. The actual device does not contain any partition information whatsoever. You will, therefore, have to edit the mapping driver's C source code to modify the partitions.

Take TQM8xxL PPC boards, for instance, which are good candidates for my control module. Such boards can contain up to two 4 MB flash banks. Each 32 bit–wide memory addressable flash bank is made of two 16 bit–wide flash chips. To define the partitions on these boards, the boards' mapping driver contains the following structure initializations:

```
static struct mtd_partition tqm8xxl_partitions[ ] = {
    {
        name:   "ppcboot",                      /* PPCBoot Firmware */
        offset: 0x00000000,
        size:   0x00040000,                     /* 256 KB */
    },
    {
        name:   "kernel",                       /* default kernel image */
        offset: 0x00040000,
        size:   0x000C0000,
    },
    {
        name:   "user",
        offset: 0x00100000,
        size:   0x00100000,
    },
    {
        name:   "initrd",
        offset: 0x00200000,
        size:   0x00200000,
    }
};

static struct mtd_partition tqm8xxl_fs_partitions[ ] = {
    {
        name:   "cramfs",
        offset: 0x00000000,
        size:   0x00200000,
    },
```

```
    {
        name:   "jffs2",
        offset: 0x00200000,
        size:   0x00200000,
    }
};
```

In this case, `tqm8xxl_partitions` defines four partitions for the first 4 MB flash bank, and `tqm8xxl_fs_partitions` defines two partitions for the second 4 MB flash bank. Three attributes are defined for each partition: `name`, `offset`, and `size`.

A partition's `name` is an arbitrary string meant only to facilitate human usability. This name is not used by either the MTD subsystem or the MTD utilities to enforce any sort of structure on said partition. The `offset` is used to provide the MTD subsystem with the start address of the partition, while the `size` is self-explanatory. Notice that each partition on a device starts where the previous one ended; no padding is necessary. Table 7-3 presents the actual physical memory address ranges for these partitions on a TQM860L board where the two 4 MB banks are mapped consecutively starting at address 0x40000000.

Table 7-3. Flash device partition physical memory mapping for TQM860L board

Device	Start address	End address	Partition name
0	0x40000000	0x40040000	ppcboot
0	0x40040000	0x40100000	kernel
0	0x40100000	0x40200000	user
0	0x40200000	0x40400000	initrd
1	0x40400000	0x40600000	cramfs
1	0x40600000	0x40800000	jffs2

During the registration of this device's mapping, the kernel displays the following message:

```
TQM flash bank 0: Using static image partition definition
Creating 4 MTD partitions on "TQM8xxL Bank 0":
0x00000000-0x00040000 : "ppcboot"
0x00040000-0x00100000 : "kernel"
0x00100000-0x00200000 : "user"
0x00200000-0x00400000 : "initrd"
TQM flash bank 1: Using static file system partition definition
Creating 2 MTD partitions on "TQM8xxL Bank 1":
0x00000000-0x00200000 : "cramfs"
0x00200000-0x00400000 : "jffs2"
```

You can also see the partitions by looking at */proc/mtd*. Here is its content for my control module:

```
# cat /proc/mtd
dev:    size    erasesize   name
mtd0: 00040000 00020000 "ppcboot"
```

```
mtd1: 000c0000 00020000 "kernel"
mtd2: 00100000 00020000 "user"
mtd3: 00200000 00020000 "initrd"
mtd4: 00200000 00020000 "cramfs"
mtd5: 00200000 00020000 "jffs2"
```

Notice that the partitions are on erase size boundaries. Because flash chips are erased by block, not by byte, the size of the erase blocks must be taken in account when creating partitions. In this case, erase blocks are 128 KB in size, and all partitions are aligned on 128 KB (0x20000) boundaries.

Another Way to Provide MTD Partition Information

For some time now, the MTD subsystem has been able to accept partition information as part of the kernel boot options for the ARM architecture. This capability is used by the iPAQ Familiar distribution to provide the iPAQ's kernel with the partition information for the device's CFI flash chips.

Lately, a generalized form of this capability for all the architectures has been integrated into the main MTD source code CVS repository. Though these changes had not yet made their way into the main kernel tree at the time of this writing, they will eventually be integrated and, therefore, enable the passing of the partition information at the kernel boot options on all architectures supported by Linux.

Here is an example boot option line used to provide the kernel with the same partition information provided in the previous section for the TQM8xxL board (the line appears wrapped on the page, but must be written as a single line):

```
mtdparts=0:256k(ppcboot)ro,768k(kernel),1m(user),-(initrd);1:2m(cramfs),-
    (jffs2)
```

Required /dev entries

You need to create /dev entries for the char device and block device MTD user modules to access your CFI flash device. Create as many entries for each type of user module as you have partitions on your device. For example, the following commands create root filesystem entries for the six partitions of my TQM860L board:

```
$ cd ${PRJROOT}/rootfs/dev
$ su -m
Password:
# for i in $(seq 0 5)
> do
> mknod mtd$i c 90 $(expr $i + $i)
> mknod mtdblock$i b 31 $i
> done
# exit
```

Here are the resulting entries:

```
$ ls -al mtd*
crw-rw-r--  1 root      root      90,  0 Aug 23 17:19 mtd0
crw-rw-r--  1 root      root      90,  2 Aug 23 17:20 mtd1
crw-rw-r--  1 root      root      90,  4 Aug 23 17:20 mtd2
crw-rw-r--  1 root      root      90,  6 Aug 23 17:20 mtd3
crw-rw-r--  1 root      root      90,  8 Aug 23 17:20 mtd4
crw-rw-r--  1 root      root      90, 10 Aug 23 17:20 mtd5
brw-rw-r--  1 root      root      31,  0 Aug 23 17:17 mtdblock0
brw-rw-r--  1 root      root      31,  1 Aug 23 17:17 mtdblock1
brw-rw-r--  1 root      root      31,  2 Aug 23 17:17 mtdblock2
brw-rw-r--  1 root      root      31,  3 Aug 23 17:17 mtdblock3
brw-rw-r--  1 root      root      31,  4 Aug 23 17:17 mtdblock4
brw-rw-r--  1 root      root      31,  5 Aug 23 17:17 mtdblock5
```

Erasing

Before you can write to a CFI flash device, you need to erase its content. This can be done using one of the two erase commands available as part of the MTD utilities, *erase* and *eraseall*.

Before updating the initial RAM disk on my control module, for example, I need to erase the "initrd" partition:

```
# eraseall /dev/mtd3
Erased 2048 Kibyte @ 0 -- 100% complete.
```

Writing and reading

Whereas flash filesystems such as JFFS2 take advantage of the capability of continuing to set bits to 0 in an erase block to allow transparent read and write access, you cannot usually use user-level tools to write to an MTD device more than once. If you want to update the content of an MTD device or partition using its raw char */dev* entry, for example, you must usually erase this device or partition before you can write new data to it.

Writing to a raw flash device can be done using traditional filesystem commands such as *cat* and *dd*. After erasing the "initrd" partition on my control module, for example, I use the following command to write a new initial RAM disk image to the designated partition:

```
# cat /tmp/initrd.bin > /dev/mtd3
```

In this case, my target's root filesystem is mounted via NFS, and I am running the MTD commands on my target. I could have also used the *dd* command instead of *cat*. Nevertheless, the end result is the same in this case.

Reading from a CFI MTD partition is no different from reading from any other device. The following command on my control module, for instance, will copy the binary image of the bootloader partition to a file:

```
# dd if=/dev/mtd0 of=/tmp/ppcboot.img
```

Since the bootloader image itself may not fill the entire partition, the *ppcboot.img* file may contain some extra unrelated data in addition to the bootloader image.

DiskOnChip

DOC devices are quite popular in x86-based embedded Linux systems, and the MTD subsystem goes a long way in providing support for them. I use it, for example, in my DAQ module. It remains that the DOC is a peculiar beast that requires an attentive master. The reasons for such a statement will become evident shortly.

Preliminary manipulations

Unlike most other devices found in embedded Linux systems, you will need to equip yourself with, at the very least, a bootable DOS diskette loaded with M-Systems' DOS DOC tools to make proper use of any DOC device. There are two basic reasons for this:

- Like all NAND flash devices, DOC devices can contain a certain number of manufacturing defects that result in bad blocks. Before a DOC device is shipped from the factory, a *Bad Block Table* (BBT) is written on it. Although this table is not write-protected, it is essential to the operation of all software that reads and writes to a DOC. As such, M-Systems' DOC software is capable of reading this table and storing it to a file. Linux, however, does not currently have any utility to retrieve this table.

- The NFTL driver included in most 2.4.x kernels (up to 2.4.19 at least) is unable to deal with some versions of the M-Systems' DOC firmware. Versions 5.0 and later are the most likely to cause problems. Hence, you may need to replace your DOC's current firmware with an older version, using M-Systems' tools, for Linux to operate with your device properly. Currently, the firmware provided with Version 4.2 of M-Systems' TrueFFS tools works fine with all kernels.

In addition, there are two ways to install a bootloader on the DOC and format it for NFTL. The first, which is most recommended by the MTD maintainer, is to use M-Systems' *dformat* DOS utility. The second, which gives you the greatest degree of control over your DOC device from within Linux, is to use the *doc_loadbios* and *nftl_format* MTD utilities. We will discuss both methods in the following sections.

M-Systems' DOS DOC tools and related documentation are available from the company's web site at *http://www.m-sys.com/*. If you plan to use the Linux method to install a bootloader on the DOC and format it, you need both Version 4.2 and Version 5.0 or later of M-Systems' tools. If you plan to use the DOS method, you only need Version 5.0 or later of the M-Systems tools. At the time of this writing, the latest version is 5.1.2. The example below is based on a 32 MB DOC 2000 device. The output of the various tools will depend on the actual device you are using, but should closely resemble the output presented here.

Start by preparing a DOS diskette with the latest tools. Once you have prepared the DOS diskette, boot the system containing your DOC device with that diskette. Now, use the tools as follows:[*]

1. Using Version 5.0 or later of the DOC tools, make a copy of the BBT:

```
A:\>dformat /win:d000 /noformat /log:docbbt.txt
DFORMAT Version 5.1.0.25 for DOS
Copyright (C) M-Systems, 1992-2002

DiskOnChip 2000 found in 0xd0000.
32M media, 16K unit

OK
```

The *dformat* command is usually used to format the DOC for use with DOS. In this case, we instruct *dformat* not to format the device by using the */noformat* option. In addition, we instruct it to record the BBT of the device starting at segment 0xD000[†] to the *docbbt.txt* file. Once *dformat* finishes retrieving the BBT, store a copy of *docbbt.txt* in a safe repository, since you may have to restore it if you erase the entire DOC device in Linux. Have a look at M-Systems' *dformat* documentation for information on how to restore a lost BBT.

Note that your DOC device may be free of bad blocks. In that case, the *docbbt. txt* will be empty and you will not need to worry about restoring the BBT if you erase the device completely.

If you are using the DOS method to install a bootloader and format the DOC, you are done with the preliminary manipulations and should proceed immediately to the next section, "Kernel configuration."

2. Using Version 5.0 or later of the DOC tools, check the firmware version:

```
A:\>dinfo /exb

                    D I N F O - utility
          Version 5.1.1.0, Last Update: 17 Jun 2002
               Copyright (C) M-Systems, 1992 - 2001
          ----------------------------------------
    GENERAL INFO.
    ■■■■■■■■■■■■■■■
         Physical Address:  0xD0000
         DiskOnChip Type :  DiskOnChip 2000
         Flash Type      :  Toshiba TC58128
         FormatType      :  NFTL
         TrueFFS version :  5.1
         Driver Version  :  DOS
         Sectors         :  4
         Heads           :  16
```

---

[*] See M-Systems' manuals for a full explanation of the tools' semantics and usage.

[†] "Real-mode" addresses on the PC are represented using a segment and offset couple in the following way: *segment:offset*. It's usually shorter to provide just the segment whenever the offset is null. In this case, for example, segment 0xD000 starts at address 0xD0000, as is displayed by *dformat* in its output.

```
Cylinders        :  1001
Boot Area Size   :  49152 Bytes
Logical Sectors  :  64064
Phy. UnitSize    :  16384 Bytes
Physical Size    :  33554432 (32 MB)
Unit Size        :  16384 Bytes
Media Size       :  33554432 Bytes (32 MB)
Chip Size        :  16777216 Bytes (16 MB)
No Of Chips      :  2
Interleaving     :  1

EXB INFO.
■■■■■■■■■■■
     Version     :  4.2
     Copyright   :  SPL_DiskOnChip (c) M-Systems
     RunTime ID  :  0xC3
     Exb Flags   :  No Flags Found
```

The *dinfo* command displays a lot of information. You can identify the version of the firmware by looking at the Version line in the EXB INFO section. In this case, the firmware version is 4.2. Do not be confused by the TrueFFS version line in the GENERAL INFO section. This is not the firmware version.

3. If your firmware is Version 5.0 or later, update the firmware version using Version 4.2 of the DOC tools:

```
A:\>dformat /win:d000 /s:doc42.exb
DFORMAT Version 3.3.9 for DiskOnChip 2000 (V4.2)
Copyright (C) M-Systems, 1992-2000

Driver not loaded - using direct access
WARNING: All data on DiskOnChip 2000(R) will be destroyed. Continue ? (Y/N)y

Medium physical size is 32768 KBytes
Boot-image size is 48 KBytes


Finished 32768 KBytes
Writing Boot-Image
Format complete. Formatted size is 32032 KBytes.
Please reboot to let DiskOnChip 2000(R) install itself.
```

Once you have formatted the chip with Version 4.2 of the firmware, I recommend that you power-cycle your system. Shut the system off and then put it back on. A simple reboot may work to get the firmware installed properly, but a full power-cycle is necessary on some systems.

You are now ready to use your DOC device with Linux.

Kernel configuration

At the time of this writing, if you are using the DOS method to install a bootloader and format the DOC, you need to patch your kernel with the latest MTD code from the MTD CVS repository to proceed. See the MTD project's web site (*http://www.*

---

linux-mtd.infradead.org/) for information on how to retrieve the code from the CVS repository.

You will need to enable kernel support for the following options to use your DOC device:

- Memory Technology Device (MTD) support
- MTD partitioning support, if you would like to partition your flash device
- Direct char device access to MTD devices
- NFTL (NAND Flash Translation Layer) support
- Write support for NFTL (BETA)
- In the "Self-contained MTD device drivers" submenu, M-Systems Disk-On-Chip 2000 and Millennium

As with CFI flash, you may choose to select other options. If you compile the options just listed as modules, the DOC support will be separated in three files, *docecc.o*, *doc2000.o*, and *docprobe.o*. Issuing a *modprobe docprobe* command should load all three modules automatically. Whether it is part of the kernel or loaded as a module, the DOC probe driver will analyze potential memory addresses for DOC devices. For each memory address it analyzes, the probe driver outputs a message regarding its findings. Here is an example of output from the probe driver on my DAQ module:

```
Possible DiskOnChip with unknown ChipID FF found at 0xc8000
...
Possible DiskOnChip with unknown ChipID FF found at 0xce000
DiskOnChip 2000 found at address 0xD0000
Flash chip found: Manufacturer ID: 98, Chip ID: 73 (Toshiba TH58V128DC)
2 flash chips found. Total DiskOnChip size: 32 MiB
Possible DiskOnChip with unknown ChipID FF found at 0xd2000
Possible DiskOnChip with unknown ChipID FF found at 0xd4000
...
```

M-Systems' DOC Driver

M-Systems provides a DOC driver for Linux as part of their Linux tools packages. This driver, however, is not under the GPL and you can use it only as a loadable kernel module. Distributing a kernel with this driver built in is a violation of the GPL. Hence, if you want to boot from a DOC with a kernel that uses M-Systems' driver, you need to use an init RAM disk to load the binary driver. Also, postings on the MTD mailing list suggest that the driver uses a lot of system resources and can sometimes cause data loss on the serial port. For these reasons, I recommend that you avoid using M-Systems' Linux DOC driver. Instead, use the GPL MTD drivers, as I describe here.

Required /dev entries

You need to create */dev* entries for the char device and the NFTL MTD user modules in order to access your DOC device. Create as many char device entries and sets of NFTL entries as you have DOC devices in your system. For each NFTL set, create as many entries as you will create partitions on your device. For my DAQ module, for instance, I have one DOC device with only one main partition. I use the following commands to create the relevant entries:

```
$ cd ${PRJROOT}/rootfs/dev
$ su -m
Password:
# mknod mtd0 c 90 0
# mknod nftla b 93 0
# mknod nftla1 b 93 1
# exit
```

Here are the resulting entries:

```
$ ls -al mtd* nftl*
crw-rw-r--  1 root    root    90,  0 Aug 29 12:48 mtd0
brw-rw-r--  1 root    root    93,  0 Aug 29 12:48 nftla
brw-rw-r--  1 root    root    93,  1 Aug 29 12:48 nftla1
```

Erasing

Erasing a DOC device is done in very much the same way as other MTD devices, using the *erase* and *eraseall* commands. Before using any such command on a DOC device, make sure you have a copy of the BBT, because an erase of the device will wipe out the BBT it contains.

To erase the entire DOC device in my DAQ modules, for instance, I use the following command on my DAQ module:

```
# eraseall /dev/mtd0
Erased 32768 Kibyte @ 0 -- 100% complete.
```

Typically, you will need to erase a DOC device only if you want to erase the boot-loader and the current format on the device. If you installed a Linux bootloader, for example, and would like to revert back to M-Systems' SPL, you will need to use the *eraseall* command before you can install M-Systems' SPL with M-Systems' tools. Whenever you erase the entire device, however, you need to use M-Systems' tools to restore the BBT.

Installing bootloader image

If your target does not boot from its DOC device, you can skip this step. Otherwise, you need to build the bootloader, as I describe in Chapter 9, before going any further. First, nonetheless, let's see how a system boots from the DOC.

During system startup on x86 systems, the BIOS scans the memory for BIOS extensions. When such an extension is found, it is executed by the BIOS. DOC devices contain a ROM program called the *Initial Program Loader* (IPL) that takes advantage of this characteristic to install another program called the *Secondary Program Loader* (SPL) that acts as a bootloader during system startup. By default, the SPL is provided by M-Systems' own firmware. To boot Linux from a DOC device, however, the SPL must be replaced with a bootloader able to recognize the format used by Linux on a DOC. We will discuss the various DOC-capable Linux bootloaders in Chapter 9. For now, let us take a look at how we can install our own SPL on a DOC.

Here is the command I use to install the GRUB bootloader image, *grub_firmware*, on the DOC in Linux:

```
# doc_loadbios /dev/mtd0 grub_firmware
Performing Flash Erase of length 16384 at offset 0
Performing Flash Erase of length 16384 at offset 16384
Performing Flash Erase of length 16384 at offset 32768
Performing Flash Erase of length 16384 at offset 49152
Performing Flash Erase of length 16384 at offset 65536
Performing Flash Erase of length 16384 at offset 81920
Writing the firmware of length 92752 at 0... Done.
```

Here is the command I use to install the GRUB bootloader image on the DOC in DOS:

```
A:\>dformat /win:d000 /bdkf0:grub_firmware
DFORMAT Version 5.1.0.25 for DOS
Copyright (C) M-Systems, 1992-2002
WARNING: All data on DiskOnChip will be destroyed. Continue ? (Y/N)y

DiskOnChip 2000 found in 0xd0000.
32M media, 16K unit

Formatting            2042
Writing file to BDK 0   92752
OK
Please reboot to let DiskOnChip install itself.
```

As with updating the firmware version earlier, you need to power-cycle your system after using *doc_loadbios* or *dformat* for the firmware to be installed properly. That said, do not use *doc_loadbios* or *dformat* before reading the explanations pertaining to its use with a bootloader in Chapter 9.

NFTL formatting

Currently, the only way to use DOC devices in Linux is to format them for NFTL. Once we format a DOC device for NFTL, we can use conventional block device tools and filesystems in conjunction with the device.

If you would like to boot from the DOC, read the sections in Chapter 9 regarding x86 bootloaders before carrying out any further operations on your DOC.

If you used the *dformat* utility earlier to install GRUB on the DOC, your DOC is already formatted for NFTL. If you used *doc_loadbios* in Linux, you must use the *nftl_format* command to format the device for NFTL.

The following MTD command formats the entire DOC device for NFTL:

```
# nftl_format /dev/mtd0
$Id: ch07,v 1.10 2003/04/01 17:10:50 free2 Exp ldolby $
Phase 1. Checking and erasing Erase Zones from 0x00000000 to 0x02000000
        Checking Zone #2047 @ 0x1ffc000
Phase 2.a Writing NFTL Media Header and Bad Unit Table
Phase 2.b Writing Spare NFTL Media Header and Spare Bad Unit Table
Phase 3. Writing Unit Control Information to each Erase Unit
```

This command takes some time to go through the various zones on the DOC. Should *nftl_format* encounter bad blocks on the DOC, it outputs the following message:

```
Skipping bad zone (factory marked) #BLOCK_NUM @ 0xADDRESS
```

The *BLOCK_NUM* and *ADDR* values output by *nftl_format* should match the values found in the *docbbt.txt* file generated earlier.

 For the *nftl_format* command to operate properly, it needs to have total control and exclusive access over the raw DOC device it is formatting. Total control is guaranteed by the fact that the commands provided earlier use the */dev/mtdX* device entries. Because these entries are handled by the char device MTD user module, there is no conversion layer between the operations conducted on these devices and the actual hardware. Hence, any operation carried out by *nftl_format* has a direct effect on the hardware.

Exclusive access to the raw DOC device is a little trickier, however, because of the NFTL driver. Basically, once the NFTL driver recognizes a DOC device, it assumes that it has total control over the device. Hence, no other software, including *nftl_format*, should attempt to manipulate a DOC device while the NFTL driver controls it. There are a few ways to avoid this type of conflict, depending on the configuration of the kernel you are using.

If the NFTL driver was configured as a module, unload the module before running *nftl_format*. You can reload it once *nftl_format* is done formatting the device. If the NFTL driver was built in, you can either use another kernel or build one, if need be, that doesn't have the NFTL driver built in. If you want to continue to use the same kernel that has the NFTL driver built in, you can use the *eraseall* command to erase the device entirely. The next time your restart your system after the erase, the built-in NFTL driver will not recognize the DOC and will, therefore, not interfere with *nftl_format*'s operations. Finally, if you are carrying out these instructions for the first time, the NFTL driver should not be able to recognize any format on the DOC device at this stage and should, therefore, not cause any problems.

If you have installed a Linux bootloader on the DOC using *doc_loadbios*, you need to skip the region where the bootloader was written and start formatting at its end. To do so, you need to provide an offset to *nftl_format*. Here is the command I use to format my DOC for NFTL in the case where I had already installed GRUB as the SPL:

```
# nftl_format /dev/mtd0 98304
$Id: ch07,v 1.10 2003/04/01 17:10:50 free2 Exp ldolby $
Phase 1. Checking and erasing Erase Zones from 0x00018000 to 0x02000000
        Checking Zone #2047 @ 0x1ffc000
Phase 2.a Writing NFTL Media Header and Bad Unit Table
Phase 2.b Writing Spare NFTL Media Header and Spare Bad Unit Table
Phase 3. Writing Unit Control Information to each Erase Unit
```

The 98304 offset is determined by the output of the *doc_loadbios* command shown earlier. The last erase message output by the command reported erasing 16384 bytes at offset 81920. 98304 is therefore the first address following the last region erased for the bootloader.

With the DOC device formatted for NFTL, reboot the system as a precautionary step. When the NFTL driver is activated, either at kernel startup or when loading the *nftl.o* module, it should output a message similar to the following:

```
NFTL driver: nftlcore.c $Revision: 1.10 $, nftlmount.c $Revision:…
Cannot calculate an NFTL geometry to match size of 0xfea0.
Using C:1018 H:16 S:4 (== 0xfe80 sects)
```

If the NFTL driver can see a DOC device but is unable to recognize its format, it will output this message instead:

```
Could not find valid boot record
Could not mount NFTL device
```

Although this message is normal if you have not yet used *nftl_format* on the DOC device, it is a sign that an error occurred if you already used *nftl_format* on the DOC.

The error message may be followed by a message similar to:

```
Sorry, we don't support UnitSizeFactor 0x06
```

or:

```
Sorry, we don't support UnitSizeFactor of != 1 yet.
```

There are many reasons why you may encounter these messages. None of them are your fault if you have followed the instructions above, as well as those in Chapter 9. As a first resort, you can try using different MTD and GRUB versions. For example, I had such messages when I tried using a November 2002 CVS version of GRUB with the DOC on my DAQ module. For some reason, the firmware image generated by that version of GRUB confused the NFTL driver in 2.4.18. To solve the problem and have the NFTL driver recognize my NFTL-formatted device, I used GRUB 0.92 instead of the latest CVS version. You may encounter a similar error if you used *dformat* to install GRUB on the DOC but forgot to patch your kernel to use the latest MTD code from the CVS.

Whenever you encounter such a message, review your manipulations and make sure you have faithfully followed the steps we discussed. If it is not a manipulation error, you can choose to dig deeper and use your hacking skills to figure out the problem on your own. It is often a good idea, nevertheless, to search the MTD mailing list archive and to consult with the MTD mailing list, because others may have encountered a similar problem and may have already solved it. When sending a message to the MTD mailing list, or any other mailing list for that matter, try to be as verbose as possible. It is very frustrating for mailing list subscribers to receive pleas for help that have little or no detail. Specifically, provide the versions of all the software components involved, explain the exact steps you followed, and provide the output of all the tools you used.

Partitioning

With the DOC device formatted for NFTL, you can now partition the device using *fdisk*. Here is the transcript of an *fdisk* session in which I create one partition on my NFTL device:

```
# fdisk /dev/nftla
Device contains neither a valid DOS partition table, nor Sun or S...
Building a new DOS disklabel. Changes will remain in memory only,
until you decide to write them. After that, of course, the previous
content won't be recoverable.


Command (m for help): p

Disk /dev/nftla: 16 heads, 4 sectors, 1018 cylinders
Units = cylinders of 64 * 512 bytes

        Device Boot    Start       End    Blocks   Id  System

Command (m for help): d
Partition number (1-4): 1

Command (m for help): n
   e   extended
   p   primary partition (1-4)
p
Partition number (1-4): 1
First cylinder (1-1018, default 1):
Using default value 1
Last cylinder or +size or +sizeM or +sizeK (1-1018, default 1018):
Using default value 1018

Command (m for help): p

Disk /dev/nftla: 16 heads, 4 sectors, 1018 cylinders
Units = cylinders of 64 * 512 bytes
```

```
       Device Boot    Start      End    Blocks   Id  System
/dev/nftla1                 1     1018    32574   83  Linux

Command (m for help): w
The partition table has been altered!

Calling ioctl( ) to re-read partition table.

WARNING: If you have created or modified any DOS 6.x
partitions, please see the fdisk manual page for additional
information.
Syncing disks.
```

Note that we delete the first partition before creating it again. This is because the use of *dformat* to install the bootloader and format the DOC also results in the creation of a single FAT partition spanning the entire device. If you had used the Linux *doc_ loadbios*, *fdisk* will display the following error message regarding the partition deletion, which you can ignore:

```
Warning: partition 1 has empty type
```

Also, note that instead of using a single partition on the DOC, or any other storage device for that matter, you could delete all partitions and store your filesystem on the entire device.

See Chapter 3 in *Running Linux* for a full description of how to use *fdisk*. With the DOC partitioning done, you can manipulate the newly created partitions like any conventional disk partition. Among other things, you can format and mount the NFTL partitions. We will discuss these issues in detail in Chapter 8.

Disk Devices

Manipulating disk devices* for use in embedded Linux devices is similar to what you do in Linux workstations or servers. In the following, we will concentrate on only those aspects that differ from conventional disk manipulations. I encourage you to consult other documents discussing Linux system maintenance in general, such as *Running Linux*, to get the rest of the details.

CompactFlash

A CompactFlash (CF) card is accessible in Linux in two ways: either as an IDE disk, when plugged in a CF-to-IDE or a CF-to-PCMCIA adapter, or as a SCSI disk, when accessed through a USB CF reader. In practice, it is often convenient to use a USB

---

* I use the term "disk devices" here to designate all devices that, in one way or another, appear as magnetic disk devices to the Linux kernel. Hence, this includes CompactFlash devices, which appear as ATA (IDE) disks.

reader to program the CF card on the host while using a CF-to-IDE or a CF-to-PCM-CIA adapter in the target to access the device. Hence, the CF card is visible as a SCSI disk on the host, while being seen by the target as an IDE disk. The fact that the same CF card can be accessed through two very different kernel disk subsystems can be problematic, however, as we'll see during the configuration of LILO for a CF card in Chapter 9. Of course, there would be no problem if a CF device would always be accessed through the same disk subsystem.

To access the CF card through a USB CF reader on the host, you must have kernel support for USB storage devices. Most distributions are shipped with USB device support built as modules. Therefore, all you have to do is load the appropriate USB modules and SCSI disk drivers on your host:

```
# modprobe usb-storage
# modprobe uhci
# modprobe sd_mod
```

Though the *uhci* module is used in this example, some systems, such as Apple's systems, require *usb-ohci* instead. Once the modules are loaded, you can now look at the appropriate entries in */proc* to see your CF reader. For example, this is how the SanDisk SDDR-31 reader I have on my PC host is seen by the SCSI subsystem:

```
# cat /proc/scsi/scsi
Attached devices:
Host: scsi0 Channel: 00 Id: 00 Lun: 00
  Vendor: SanDisk  Model: ImageMate II     Rev: 1.30
  Type:   Direct-Access                    ANSI SCSI revision: 02
# cat /proc/scsi/usb-storage-0/0
   Host scsi0: usb-storage
       Vendor: SanDisk Corporation
      Product: ImageMate CompactFlash USB
Serial Number: None
     Protocol: Transparent SCSI
    Transport: Bulk
         GUID: 078100020000000000000000
     Attached: Yes
```

In this case, because the reader is the first device on the SCSI bus, it can be accessed as */dev/sda*. Therefore, I can partition, format, and mount the CF card the same way I would partition, format, and mount a conventional SCSI disk:

```
# fdisk /dev/sda
...
# mkdir /mnt/cf
# mke2fs /dev/sda1
# mount -t ext2 /dev/sda1 /mnt/cf
```

The partitions you put on the CF card and the use of the various partitions depends largely on your target. If your target is an x86 PC derivative, you can use a single partition. If your target is PPC using the U-Boot bootloader, you need to have a few small partitions to hold kernel images and one large partition to hold your root filesystem. This is because U-Boot can read CF device partitions and the data on those partitions, but it does not recognize any filesystem organization. Hence, kernel images must be written to raw partitions to be loadable by U-Boot. We will discuss example uses of CF cards as boot devices in Chapter 9.

Floppy Disk

If you intend to use a floppy disk as your main storage device for your embedded Linux project, have a look at the "Putting them together: Making the diskette(s)" section of Tom Fawcett's Linux Bootdisk HOWTO, available from the LDP. Tom explains in detail how to create a bootable floppy using either LILO or the kernel alone. Although you do not need to read other sections of the HOWTO, the instructions assume that you have created a RAM disk image containing your root filesystem. See Chapter 8 for an explanation of how to create this RAM disk image.

We will not discuss the use of floppy disks in embedded Linux systems any further, because they are very seldom used in production systems and because the Linux Bootdisk HOWTO already covers the issues involved quite well.

Hard Disk

When configuring a hard disk for use in an embedded Linux system, the most convenient setup to bootstrap the target is to attach the hard disk destined for the target to the host's own disk interface. In this way, the target's hard disk can be manipulated directly on the host.

If the host already has one IDE disk that is seen as hda, for example, the target's IDE disk may be seen as hdb or hdc, depending on the host's setup. We can then format and mount this drive as we would any other hard disk. The only difference, however, is that the target's disk, seen on the host as a secondary disk such as hdb or hdc, will very likely be seen as hda on the target. This poses certain problems when configuring bootloaders. We will discuss these issues further in Chapter 9.

To Swap or Not to Swap

Swapping is an essential component of most Linux workstation and server installations. It enables the system to address more memory than is physically available by emulating the additional memory on a storage device. Most embedded storage devices, such as flash and DOC devices, however, are ill-adapted to this use, because they have limited erase and write cycles. Since your application has little control over the kernel's use of swapping, it is therefore possible to accelerate the wear on the storage device used for swapping. Hence, I encourage you to find alternatives to swapping. Try reducing your applications' memory usage and having only the minimal set of binaries required for your system's proper behavior loaded at any time.

Of course, if your storage device is a real hard disk—not a CF card—then swapping is a viable option. The use of swap may, however, result in slower response times.

CHAPTER 8
Root Filesystem Setup

Having built the root filesystem and prepared the target's storage device, we are now ready to set up the root filesystem as it will be used on the target. First, we need to select a filesystem type for the root filesystem. Then, we need to convert the root filesystem's content to the selected filesystem format or install the root filesystem on a device formatted for the selected filesystem type.

This chapter begins by discussing the basic filesystem selection criteria. This is followed by a section describing how to use NFS to transfer filesystem images to the target's flash, a technique we use often in this chapter. We then concentrate on the setup of root filesystems for use on CRAMFS, JFFS2, NFTL, and RAM disks, respectively. Finally, we discuss the use of TMPFS for mounting certain directories, and how to update an embedded system's root filesystem dynamically. At the end of this chapter, the only issue remaining to getting a fully functional embedded system will be the setup and configuration of the bootloader. I will cover these issues in the next chapter.

Selecting a Filesystem

Selecting a filesystem type for your root filesystem is a delicate process. The final decision is often a compromise between the filesystem's capabilities and the target's purpose. It is, for example, useless to choose a filesystem that provides persistent write storage, such as JFFS2, if the target never needs to permanently store any data. For such a target, a filesystem with no persistent storage, such as CRAMFS, is a much better choice.

Furthermore, you may want to consider using many filesystems for the same system. A system that needs read and write access to temporary files only, for instance, could have most of its root filesystem mounted on CRAMFS while having its */var/tmp* directory mounted on TMPFS or a RAM disk, and its */tmp* being a symbolic link to */var/tmp*.

Characterizing Filesystems

To select the best filesystem or best combination of filesystems for a certain application, we need to have a minimum set of characteristics that can be used to compare filesystems. Table 8-1 summarizes the characteristics of the filesystems typically used in embedded Linux systems. For each filesystem type, these are the questions used to characterize it:

Write
> Can the filesystem be written to?

Persistent
> Does the filesystem preserve modifications across reboots?

Power down reliability
> Can a modified filesystem recover from a power failure?

Compression
> Is the content of the mounted filesystem compressed?

Lives in RAM
> Is the filesystem's content first extracted from the storage device into RAM before being mounted?

Table 8-1. Filesystem characteristics

Filesystem	Write	Persistent	Power down reliability	Compression	Lives in RAM
CRAMFS	No	N/A	N/A	Yes	No
JFFS2	Yes	Yes	Yes	Yes	No
JFFS	Yes	Yes	Yes[a]	No	No
Ext2 over NFTL	Yes	Yes	No	No	No
Ext3 over NFTL	Yes	Yes	Yes	No	No
Ext2 over RAM disk	Yes	No	No	No	Yes

[a] Extensive testing conducted by Vipin Malik shows that JFFS's power down reliability can fail. Such problems do not exist with JFFS2, however. See his article on JFFS and JFFS2 for the complete details: *http://www.embeddedlinuxworks.com/articles/jffs_guide.html*.

As I said above, a system needs a write-capable filesystem only if it needs to update data found on that filesystem. Similarly, a system requires persistent writes only if the updated data needs to be preserved upon reboots. A system that does not provide write capability does not require persistent storage or power down reliability, since none of the data it stores is ever modified.

Compression, on the other hand, is a desired characteristic of most filesystems, because it can lower the cost or increase the yield of storage in embedded systems. In some embedded systems, however, the increased cost, in CPU cycles, of compression and decompression may be undesirable.

While most filesystems are mounted directly from their storage device, filesystems mounted on RAM disks must first be extracted from their storage device into RAM before they can be mounted. Because the original filesystem image on the storage device is never accessed directly, most filesystem images created for use with RAM disks are usually compressed before being placed on a storage device. We will discuss the creation of such compressed filesystem images for use with RAM disks in "Disk Filesystem over RAM Disk."

Finally, no filesystem can be replaced while it is currently mounted. If a system's root filesystem is mounted from a JFFS2-formatted MTD partition, for example, the content of the MTD partition holding this filesystem cannot be overwritten with a new root filesystem. The only case where such a replacement is possible is when a filesystem is first copied into RAM before being mounted, as is the case of RAM disks. In that case, the actual media where the filesystem is stored is not accessed once the filesystem is mounted and can, therefore, be written over safely. As we shall see in "Live Updates," filesystems that are mounted in read and write mode from their original storage device can still be updated in various ways.

As you will have noticed, Linux supports a great deal many more filesystems than I cover in Table 8-1. But most of these filesystems are not well adapted for embedded Linux systems. In addition, although I mention JFFS in the table above, we will not discuss it below, since it has been largely superseded by JFFS2.

Guidelines for Filesystem Selection

Now that we have established a basic set of features for characterizing filesystems, let's review some general guidelines for selecting a filesystem configuration for your MTD-compatible storage device.

ROMFS...Not for ROMs

You will notice a "ROM file system support" item in the "File systems" submenu of the kernel configuration menu. This filesystem is actually not intended for use with any form of physical ROM. Instead, it is mainly intended for use on disks for installation and troubleshooting purposes. ROMFS operates on block devices only, and does not interface with Linux's MTD subsystem in any way. As the project's web site states, if you want to use ROMFS with a real ROM, you must first write a device driver for this ROM that makes it appear as a block device. See *http://romfs.sourceforge.net/* for further information on ROMFS.

If your system has a very small amount of flash but a relatively generous amount of RAM, a RAM disk is probably your best choice, because the filesystem living on a RAM disk is compressed in its entirety on the storage device. The compression ratio on the storage device obtained by using a filesystem on a RAM disk is actually much higher than what can be achieved with a natively compressed filesystem, such as CRAMFS or JFFS2, because such filesystems must still keep their metadata,[*] among other things, uncompressed. The RAM disk's edge in regards to on-storage-device compression are, however, offset by a higher RAM usage, since the entire filesystem lives uncompressed in RAM. Also, a RAM disk isn't appropriate if you need persistent data storage. Nevertheless, if your persistent data storage needs are limited, you can use a RAM disk for most of your root filesystem and mount only the data directories from a persistent filesystem such as JFFS2, as hinted to earlier. Also, using a RAM disk is often the easiest way to obtain a self-hosting target (which is a target that doesn't require a host to obtain its kernel or mount its root filesystem). x86 systems such as my DAQ module, for example, are the most likely to be shipped with RAM disks, since the prices for the components of such systems, including RAM, are low compared to other architectures. Note that although RAM can be cheap, it does consume more power than flash. Using large amounts of RAM for a RAM disk may, therefore, not be a viable option on some systems.

If your system has slightly more flash, or if you would rather save as much RAM as possible for the actual application running on your target and can spare a few extra CPU cycles for runtime decompression, CRAMFS is a very good candidate, granted the filesystem's limitations we discuss in "CRAMFS" aren't a show stopper. Though CRAMFS's compression ratio is lower than a RAM disk, because of the reasons I outlined earlier, its capabilities are usually quite sufficient for most embedded applications that do not require persistent storage. As with RAM disks, nevertheless, you can mount the portion of the root filesystem that doesn't change at runtime on CRAMFS and the rest on a persistent filesystem such as JFFS2.

CRAMFS will not be a viable option, however, if your target must be able to be upgraded in the field. For example, the iPAQ Familiar distribution project switched from CRAMFS to JFFS2 precisely because users were unable to update their iPAQs without reprogramming their devices' flash. On the other hand, as another example, CRAMFS is a good candidate for my control module, because actual control procedures don't change very often in most industrial control applications.

If you need to be able to change any portion of your filesystem at any time, JFFS2 is the best candidate. Though JFFS2 doesn't achieve compression ratios as high as CRAMFS, since JFFS2 has to maintain space for garbage collection and metadata structures that allow filesystem writing, JFFS2 does provide power-down reliability and wear-leveling, which are very important characteristics for devices that rely on flash storage, as we discussed in Chapter 3. My user interface modules, for example, would be completely based on JFFS2 to ease updating and extend the lifetime of the devices' flash. At the

---

[*] This is the data stored by the filesystem to locate files and directories and maintain the filesystem structure in general.

time of this writing, however, JFFS2 is not a viable option if you are using a NAND flash device such as the DiskOnChip (DOC), as I explained in Chapter 3.

If you are using a DOC device and need to be able to change any portion of your filesystem at any time, using a disk filesystem over NFTL is your only available option at the time of this writing. Most embedded x86 devices that are equipped with DOC devices have to use this configuration. My DAQ module, for instance, can be configured to store some of its samples locally from time to time to a disk filesystem mounted over NFTL.

Strictly speaking, there is no such thing as a "disk filesystem." I use this term here and in the rest of the book, however, to contrast filesystems typically used on block devices, such as ext2 and reiserfs, from filesystems typically used on MTD devices, such as JFFS2.

Whether you are using CRAMFS, JFFS2, or a disk filesystem over NFTL, you may want to consider mounting some directories on TMPFS. Though the content of this filesystem is not saved to persistent storage, it does allow you to use part of the RAM to store temporary files such as those typically found in your root filesystem's */tmp* directory. If you are using a CRAMFS-based root filesystem, this allows you to have a directory, or a couple of directories, where you can both read and write files. If you are using either JFFS2 or a disk filesystem over NFTL, this allows you to avoid wearing out the storage device by manipulating data from RAM.

Obviously, these are guidelines only, and each system likely imposes additional limitations that you have to take into account. Nonetheless, these guidelines represent the typical design trade-offs when building embedded Linux systems and they should give you a basic idea of how to choose your final setup. In the rest of this chapter, I will discuss the actual setup of the filesystems we discussed earlier and further detail their use.

Filesystems for Disk Devices

If you are using a conventional disk as your main storage device for your system, such as one that connects to the system using an IDE or SCSI interface, I suggest you take a closer look at the various filesystems currently used in desktop and server Linux installations. In particular, you will find journalling filesystems such as ext3 and reiserfs to be quite well adapted to environments that need power down reliability such as embedded systems. Because the use of these filesystems is already amply covered elsewhere and embedded systems use them no differently from their workstation or server counterparts,[*] I will not discuss their use any further. I refer you to classic texts on the use of Linux on servers and workstations for further details on such filesystems. IBM developerWorks' long series of articles by Daniel Robbins about Linux filesystems is

---

[*] As we discussed in Chapter 1, embedded Linux systems large enough to house actual physical hard disks have the equivalent processing power and RAM resources to deal with such storage.

of special interest here. In his series, Daniel provides in-depth discussion of the main journalling filesystems for Linux, including ext3, reiserfs, JFS, and XFS. See IBM's developerWorks site for Daniel's articles: *http://www.ibm.com/developerworks/linux/*. You may also be interested by Derek Vadala's *Managing RAID on Linux* (O'Reilly).

For a workstation- and server-oriented discussion of filesystems, see Chapter 6 of *Running Linux*.

Using an NFS-Mounted Root Filesystem to Write a Filesystem Image to Flash

Though we will discuss the setup and configuration of the NFS server on the host for providing a root filesystem to a target in detail in Chapter 9, let's take a look at how this configuration can be useful at this stage.

The use of an NFS-mounted root filesystem during early development stages simplifies the development process by allowing quick modification of the files used by the target. Later, the target needs to have a filesystem stored in its flash in order to be self-hosting. Though some bootloaders can be used to copy images to flash, it is also possible to use the MTD utilities running on the target to copy files available on the NFS-mounted root filesystem to flash. To do so, copy the designated filesystem image to the directory containing the NFS-mounted target root filesystem, boot the target, and use MTD commands on the target to copy the filesystem image to flash.

To copy an initial RAM disk image to your target's flash, for example, first configure your target to mount its root filesystem from a directory exported by your host using NFS. On your host, copy the filesystem image to the directory exported to your target. Though the filesystem image is not physically on your target, it will be visible on its root filesystem once the kernel mounts it using NFS at startup. Now, boot your target and use the MTD utilities on your target to copy the filesystem image from the NFS-mounted root filesystem to the appropriate flash device entry in your target's */dev* directory.

CRAMFS

CRAMFS was written by Linus Torvalds as a filesystem with a bare minimum feature set. It is a very simple, and sometimes simplistic, compressed and read-only filesystem aimed at embedded systems. Apart from the characteristics summarized in Table 8-1, CRAMFS has the following limitations:

- The maximum size a file can have is 16 MB.
- There are no current (.) or parent (..) directory entries.

- The UID field for files is 16 bits wide and the GID field is 8 bits wide. Normal filesystems usually support either 16- or 32-bit UIDs and GIDs. On CRAMFS, GIDs are truncated to the lower 8 bits. In other words, the maximum GID usable in a root filesystem built on CRAMFS is 255.[*]

- All file timestamps are set to epoch (00:00:00 GMT, January 1, 1970). The timestamps may be updated at runtime, but the updated values will last only as long as the inode is cached in memory. Once the file is reloaded, its timestamp will revert to epoch.

- CRAMFS images can be read only by kernels using 4096-byte page sizes (The value of PAGE_CACHE_SIZE must be 4096).

- All files, whether they are linked or not, have a link count[†] of 1. Even when multiple filesystem entries point to the same file, that file has a link count of only 1. This is fine for most operations, however, since no files can actually be deleted from CRAMFS.

The truncated GIDs are not problematic if your target's root filesystem does not contain a group with a GID above 255. If your target is a single-user system, you don't need to worry about this limitation. If your system must support a multiuser environment, make sure the GIDs of all files and directories are below 255. Otherwise, any GID above 255 will wrap around to a number below 255 and, possibly, create a security risk. If you absolutely need a filesystem that can support at least 16-bit GIDs, you may want to consider using a disk filesystem over a RAM disk. It provides compression on the storage media, like CRAMFS, and also allows read and write access, instead of read-only access in the case of CRAMFS.

In addition to CRAMFS's limitations, the tools provided for creating CRAMFS filesystem images used to be subject to the host's byte ordering. Hence, you needed to use a host that had the same byte ordering as your target to create a CRAMFS image. The only way to bypass this limitation was to follow the technique I describe in "Using an NFS-Mounted Root Filesystem to Write a Filesystem Image to Flash." In essence, you had to mount the target's root filesystem on NFS, create the CRAMFS image for the target on the NFS-mounted filesystem, and write the created CRAMFS image to flash. Though, at the time of this writing, this limitation still applies to the CRAMFS creation tools found in the kernel sources, there is a patch that can be applied to the latest version of the CRAMFS tools to obtain filesystem creation tools that are independent of the host's byte ordering. The latest CRAMFS tools package is found at *http://sourceforge.net/projects/cramfs/*, and the byte swapping patch is in the "Patches" section of the site.

---

[*] See Chapter 5 in *Running Linux* for a discussion about UIDs and GIDs.

[†] As in other Unix systems, named links can be created toward files with most Linux filesystems. Typically, filesystems maintain a count of the number of links toward a file, and when this count reaches 0 the file is deleted.

If your system can function with CRAMFS's limitations, it is probably a serious candidate for your project. If you are interested in CRAMFS but chaff at its limitations, you may want to ask around for modified versions of CRAMFS. As the host byte ordering problem mentioned above shows, there are people who have modified CRAMFS to bypass some of its limitations. Some reports on the linuxppc-embedded mailing list mentioned in Chapter 3, for example, suggest that some people have modified CRAMFS to avoid the page size issues. Although such modifications are not part of the CRAMFS code found from the mainstream kernel sources, you may find them useful. Have a look at the "Patches" section of the site provided above for a list of commonly available CRAMFS patches.

To create a CRAMFS image of your root filesystem, you first need to create and install the CRAMFS tools, *cramfsck* and *mkcramfs*. Both of these utilities are part of the package distributed by the project site and are found in the kernel's sources in the *scripts/cramfs* directory. To build the utilities from the kernel's sources, move to the *scripts/cramfs* directory and issue the *make* command:

```
$ cd ${PRJROOT}/kernel/linux-2.4.18/scripts/cramfs
$ make
```

Now, copy the tools to an appropriate directory:

```
$ cp cramfsck mkcramfs ${PREFIX}/bin/
```

You can now create a CRAMFS image of your target's root filesystem:

```
$ cd ${PRJROOT}
$ mkcramfs rootfs/ images/cramfs.img
  bin
  boot
  dev
  etc
  lib
  linuxrc
  proc
  sbin
  tmp
  usr
'bin':
  addgroup
...
'boot':
  boot.b
...
'sbin':
  chroot
Directory data: 6484 bytes
166.67% (+15 bytes)      addgroup
-31.46% (-2196 bytes)    allinone
-40.27% (-240 bytes)     arch
185.71% (+13 bytes)      ash
...
```

```
-49.60% (-3700 bytes)   wall
-49.54% (-695 bytes)     include
Everything: 3560 kilobytes
Super block: 76 bytes
CRC: f18594b6
warning: gids truncated to 8 bits.  (This may be a security concern.)
```

In this case, *rootfs/* contains 7840 KB while the CRAMFS image's size is 3560 KB, a compression ratio of approximately 50%. This ratio is consistent with CRAMFS's typical yields.

With the filesystem image ready, we can now write it to our storage device:

```
$ su -m
Password:
# cat rootfs/cramfs.img > /dev/mtd4
# exit
```

Of course the commands above assume that the storage device is accessible on the host. If that is not the case, use an NFS-mounted root filesystem first, as I describe in "Using an NFS-Mounted Root Filesystem to Write a Filesystem Image to Flash." To verify the content of a CRAMFS filesystem, use the *cramfsck* utility built earlier.

JFFS2

I have already described JFFS2's features in Chapter 3. One caveat I have not covered yet is JFFS2's behavior when full. Because of its architecture, JFFS2 implements garbage collection on MTD blocks. This scheme works fine in most cases. When the filesystem approaches its limits, however, JFFS2 spends an increasing amount of time garbage collecting. Furthermore, as the filesystem reaches its limits, the system is unable to truncate or move files and the access to files is slowed down. If you are using JFFS2, make sure your application's data does not grow to fill the entire filesystem. In other words, make sure your applications check for available filesystem space before writing to it in order to avoid severe slowdown and system crashes. Also, try running benchmarks on your target to determine the threshold at which JFFS2 starts misbehaving.

With that in mind, let us now concentrate on the creation and installation of a JFFS2 filesystem image. Mainly, we will use the *mkfs.jffs2* utility installed in the previous chapter as part of the MTD utilities installation.

The creation of a JFFS2 image is fairly simple:

```
$ cd ${PRJROOT}
$ mkfs.jffs2 -r rootfs/ -o images/rootfs-jffs2.img
```

We use the *-r* option to specify the location of the directory containing the root filesystem, and the *-o* option to specify the name of the output file where the filesystem image should be stored. In addition to these options, we could use *-l* or *-b* to create little endian or big endian images, respectively. The JFFS2 compression ratio is much smaller than CRAMFS. For a root filesystem containing 7840 KB, for example, the resulting JFFS2 image is 6850 KB in size. The compression ratio is a little above 10%.

Once you create the JFFS2 image, you can write it to its designated MTD device. If this device is accessible on the host, you can carry out the appropriate commands directly on the host. Otherwise, follow the instructions in "Using an NFS-Mounted Root Filesystem to Write a Filesystem Image to Flash": boot your target with an NFS-mounted root filesystem, place the JFFS2 image on that filesystem, and issue the commands on the target to write the image to the designated MTD device. Regardless of your setup, you first need to erase the MTD device where the image will be placed:

```
# eraseall /dev/mtd5
Erased 8192 Kibyte @ 0 -- 100% complete.
```

Obviously, the space available on the MTD storage device must be equal to or larger than the JFFS2 image you are placing on it. With the MTD device erased, copy the JFFS2 image to the MTD partition:

```
# cat images/rootfs-jffs2.img > /dev/mtd5
```

Now, mount the copied filesystem to take a look at it:

```
# mount -t jffs2 /dev/mtdblock5 /mnt
# mount
...
/dev/mtdblock5 on /mnt type jffs2 (rw)
# ls mnt
bin     etc     linuxrc sbin    usr
dev     lib     proc    tmp     var
# umount mnt
```

Unlike disk filesystems, JFFS2 cannot be mounted on loopback using a *mount -o loop* ... command to view its content. Instead, it must be mounted from a real MTD device as done above. If you have no real MTD device on your host, such as CFI flash, you could use the virtual memory MTD device presented in Chapter 3. You could also use the *jffs2reader* command introduced in the previous chapter to view the image's content.

If your target had previously been using an NFS-mounted root filesystem, you are now ready to boot it using the JFFS2 filesystem as its root filesystem.

Disk Filesystem over NFTL

We have already discussed the installation and use of NFTL with DOC devices in the previous chapter. We are now ready to discuss the use of a disk filesystem over the block device emulated by NFTL. The most widely used disk filesystem with NFTL is ext2. We will, therefore, concentrate on discussing that particular case. Note, however, that ext2 over NFTL does not provide power down reliability. For that, you should use a journalling filesystem, such as ext3, XFS, JFS, or reiserfs, with NFTL.

The instructions that follow can be easily modified for any of the existing disk filesystems, including journalling filesystems.

First, create a filesystem on the designated NFTL partition for the selected filesystem type:

```
# mke2fs /dev/nftla1
mke2fs 1.18, 11-Nov-1999 for EXT2 FS 0.5b, 95/08/09
Filesystem label=
OS type: Linux
Block size=1024 (log=0)
Fragment size=1024 (log=0)
8160 inodes, 32574 blocks
1628 blocks (5.00%) reserved for the super user
First data block=1
4 block groups
8192 blocks per group, 8192 fragments per group
2040 inodes per group
Superblock backups stored on blocks:
        8193, 24577

Writing inode tables: done
Writing superblocks and filesystem accounting information: done
```

Now, mount the partition and copy the root filesystem to it:

```
# mkdir /mnt/doc
# mount -t ext2 /dev/nftla1 /mnt/doc
# cp -a rootfs/* /mnt/doc
```

Here, I assume you are issuing these commands from your project's *${PRJROOT}* directory. I also assume that the DOC device is accessible on your host as */dev/nftla*, and that you want to create an ext2 filesystem on the first partition of that device. If the DOC device is not accessible on your host, use an NFS-mounted root filesystem as I describe in "Using an NFS-Mounted Root Filesystem to Write a Filesystem Image to Flash" to copy the content of the root filesystem onto your DOC device.

Disk Filesystem over RAM Disk

RAM disks, as their name indicates, live in RAM and act like block devices. The kernel supports having many RAM disks active in the same time. Because they act like block devices, any disk filesystem can be used with them. Since their content lasts only as long as the system isn't rebooted, RAM disks are usually populated using compressed images of disk filesystems, such as ext2, known as compressed RAM disk images. One instance where the use of such compressed RAM disk images is particularly attractive for embedded Linux systems is during system initialization. Mainly, the kernel is capable of extracting an *initial RAM disk* (initrd) image from a storage device for use as its root filesystem. At startup, the kernel verifies whether its boot options indicate the presence of an initrd. If so, it extracts the filesystem image, whether it be compressed or not, from the designated storage media into a RAM disk, and mounts it as its root filesystem. The initrd mechanism is, in fact, the simplest method to provide a kernel with its root filesystem. In this section, we will discuss the creation of a compressed RAM disk image for use as an initrd. I will explain how this image can actually be used as an initrd in Chapter 9.

For our purposes, we will create an ext2-based RAM disk image for use in our target. Although ext2 is the filesystem most commonly used with RAM disks, other disk filesystems can also be used, as I hinted to above. Some developers, for instance, report using CRAMFS instead.

Note that although we are creating a filesystem image for use on a RAM disk in the following procedures, all the operations are carried out on your host's disk. Hence, none of the following steps involve using an actual RAM disk on the host.

First, create a blank filesystem image for the root filesystem:

```
$ cd ${PRJROOT}
$ mkdir tmp/initrd
$ dd if=/dev/zero of=images/initrd.img bs=1k count=8192
8192+0 records in
8192+0 records out
```

The *dd* command creates a 8192 KB filesystem image and initializes it using */dev/zero*. By initializing the filesystem in this way, we will achieve a maximum compression ratio for the unused portions of the filesystem later when we use *gzip* to compress the entire image. In comparison, if we were to reuse an existing image of the same size as the one we need, such as an image created previously following this section's instructions, instead of using the *dd* command as shown above, the image's compression would yield a lower compression ratio given that it already contains non-uniform data. Practically, this means that you should never try updating an existing filesystem image. Instead, always create a fresh filesystem image using your target's updated root filesystem directory, *${PRJROOT}/rootfs*.

With the filesystem image initialized, create a filesystem on it and mount it:

```
$ su -m
Password:
# /sbin/mke2fs -F -v -m0 images/initrd.img
mke2fs 1.18, 11-Nov-1999 for EXT2 FS 0.5b, 95/08/09
Filesystem label=
OS type: Linux
Block size=1024 (log=0)
Fragment size=1024 (log=0)
2048 inodes, 8192 blocks
0 blocks (0.00%) reserved for the super user
First data block=1
1 block group
8192 blocks per group, 8192 fragments per group
2048 inodes per group
```

```
Writing inode tables: done
Writing superblocks and filesystem accounting information: done
# mount -o loop images/initrd.img tmp/initrd
```

We use the *-F* option with *mke2fs* to force it to run on a file. Otherwise, *mke2fs* complains that *images/initrd.img* is not a block device. The *-v* option specifies that the command should be verbose, and the *-m0* option specifies that no blocks should be reserved for the super user on the filesystem. Whereas reserving blocks for the super user makes sense for a filesystem created for use in a workstation or server, it isn't very useful in embedded systems, since they are usually built as single-user systems.

Now, copy the root filesystem to the RAM disk and unmount it:

```
# cp -av rootfs/* tmp/initrd
rootfs/bin -> tmp/initrd/bin
rootfs/bin/busybox -> tmp/initrd/bin/busybox
rootfs/bin/ash -> tmp/initrd/bin/ash
rootfs/bin/cat -> tmp/initrd/bin/cat
rootfs/bin/chgrp -> tmp/initrd/bin/chgrp
rootfs/bin/chmod -> tmp/initrd/bin/chmod
...
# umount tmp/initrd
# exit
```

After issuing the first command, you will see the complete list of all the files in your root filesystem with their complete path as shown in the example. The *images/initrd. img* file now contains the complete root filesystem for your target. The final step is to compress this filesystem to obtain a compressed RAM disk:

```
$ gzip -9 < images/initrd.img > images/initrd.bin
$ ls -al images/initrd*
-rw-rw-r--  1 karim    karim    3101646 Aug 16 14:47 images/initrd.bin
-rw-rw-r--  1 karim    karim    8388608 Aug 16 14:46 images/initrd.1mg
```

The filesystem is compressed using the *gzip* command. The *-9* option tells the command to use the highest compression algorithm available. In this case, the compression ratio is above 60%, which is superior to both CRAMFS and JFFS2. This gain is, however, subject to the caveat I mentioned earlier in "Selecting a Filesystem" regarding the fact that RAM disks live in RAM.

You can place the RAM disk image created here, *images/initrd.bin*, on the appropriate device on your target and configure your bootloader accordingly. As I said earlier, we will discuss the use of RAM disks as initrds in Chapter 9.

Mounting Directories on TMPFS

TMPFS is a virtual memory–based filesystem that can grow and shrink according to its content. Although its content is not saved across reboots, it is quite useful for storing temporary files. Hence, instead of mounting all the directories from a single

Init RAMFS

At the time of this writing, though initrds are still commonly used, the initrd mechanism is increasingly showing its age, and kernel developers intend to replace it in the 2.5 series with *init RAMFS* (initramfs). In the future, each kernel is likely to have an initramfs image that would contain much of the initialization code currently hard-coded in the kernel. In that case, the definitive root filesystem would be mounted by the last procedure running on the initramfs using the pivot_root( ) system call once initialization is complete. Until initramfs becomes ready for mainstream use, initrds remain the standard way for providing a kernel with a root filesystem at boot time.

filesystem, you can choose to mount directories that do not require permanent storage, such as */tmp*, on TMPFS. Because content stored on TMPFS is not saved across reboots, however, essential directories such as */usr*, */etc*, or */bin* cannot be stored on TMPFS. To use TMPFS, enable the "Virtual memory file system support (former shm fs)" item in the "File systems" submenu in the kernel configuration menu.

With kernel support for TMPFS enabled, you can mount a 4 MB TMPFS filesystem on */tmp*, for example:

```
# mount -t tmpfs none /tmp -o size=4m
```

Alternatively, you can add a line in your */etc/fstab* file and modify your */etc/init.d/rcS* file to mount TMPFS at boot time. If you do not provide a size limit, the filesystem will grow according to its content.

In contrast with most other *mount* commands, TMPFS does not require a device or file to be mounted, hence the use of none as the device. The name of the device for TMPFS is actually ignored by *mount*, and replacing none by any other name would have no effect on the command.

If you would like more information regarding TMPFS, take a look at part three of the IBM developerWorks filesystem series mentioned earlier, *Using the virtual memory (VM) filesystem and bind mounts*.

Live Updates

As we saw earlier in this chapter, no filesystem can be replaced in its entirety while being mounted from the storage media where it is being stored. Hence, we need to look for ways to update a filesystem's content while it is mounted. There are quite a few ways to do this, each with their own advantages and disadvantages. In this section we will discuss three such methods, the *rsync* utility, package management tools, and ad-hoc scripts.

The rsync Utility

rsync is a remote updating utility that allows you to synchronize a local directory tree with a remote server. It relies on the rsync algorithm to transfer only the differences between the local and remote files. It can preserve file permissions, file ownership, symbolic links, access times, and device entries. *rsync* can use either *rsh* or *ssh* to communicate with the remote server. Given its features, *rsync* is a good candidate for updating network-enabled embedded systems. *rsync* is available from its project web site, along with documentation and a mailing list, at *http://samba.anu.edu.au/rsync/*. In addition to the documentation available from the project's site, there is a very good introductory tutorial by Michael Holve available at *http://everythinglinux.org/rsync/*.

To use *rsync*, you must have the rsync daemon running on a server and an rsync client running in the embedded system. I will not cover the installation of an rsync server nor the detailed use of the rsync client, since they are already well covered by the tutorial mentioned earlier and the rest of the *rsync* documentation. I will, nevertheless, explain how to cross-compile, and install *rsync* for use on your target.

To begin, download and extract a copy of the *rsync* package to your *${PRJROOT}/ sysapps* directory. For my UI module, for example, I used *rsync* 2.5.6. With the package extracted, move to its directory for the rest of the manipulations:

```
$ cd ${PRJROOT}/sysapps/rsync-2.5.6/
```

Now, configure and compile the package:

```
$ CC=arm-linux-gcc CPPFLAGS="-DHAVE_GETTIMEOFDAY_TZ=1" ./configure \
> --host=$TARGET --prefix=${TARGET_PREFIX}
$ make
```

Replace *arm-linux-gcc* with *arm-uclibc-gcc* to compile against uClibc instead of glibc. Here we must set CPPFLAGS to define HAVE_GETTIMEOFDAY_TZ to 1, otherwise, the compilation fails because the *configure* script is unable to correctly determine the number of arguments used for gettimeofday( ) on the target.

With the compilation complete, install the *rsync* binary on your target's root filesystem and strip it:

```
$ cp rsync ${PRJROOT}/rootfs/bin
$ arm-linux-strip ${PRJROOT}/rootfs/bin/rsync
```

The stripped binary is 185 KB in size when dynamically linked with either uClibc or glibc, 270 KB when statically linked with uClibc, and 655 KB when statically linked with glibc.

The same binary can be used both on the command line and as a daemon. The *--daemon* option instructs *rsync* to run as a daemon. In our case, we will be using *rsync* on the command line only. To use *rsync*, you need to have either *rsh* or *ssh* installed on your target. *rsh* is available as part of the netkit-rsh package from *ftp://ftp.uk.linux.*

org/pub/linux/Networking/netkit/. *ssh* is available as part of the OpenSSH package, which we will discuss in depth in Chapter 10. Though that discussion concentrates on the use of the SSH daemon generated by OpenSSH (*sshd*), the SSH client (*ssh*) is also generated during the compilation of the OpenSSH package. In the following, I will assume that you are using *ssh*, not *rsh*, since it provides a secure transfer channel. The downside to using *ssh*, however, is that the dynamically linked and stripped SSH client is above 1.1 MB in size, and is even larger when linked statically. *rsh*, on the other hand, is only 8 KB when dynamically linked and stripped.

Once *rsync* is installed on your target, you can use a command such as the following on your target to update its root filesystem:

```
# rsync -e "ssh -l root" -r -l -p -t -D -v --progress \
> 192.168.172.50:/home/karim/control-project/user-interface/rootfs/* /
root@192.168.172.50's password:
receiving file list ... done
bin/
dev/
etc/
lib/
sbin/
tmp/
usr/bin/
usr/sbin/
bin/busybox
750756 (100%)
bin/tinylogin
39528 (100%)
etc/inittab
377 (100%)
etc/profile
58 (100%)
lib/ld-2.2.1.so
111160 (100%)
lib/libc-2.2.1.so
1242208 (100%)
...
sbin/nftl_format
8288 (100%)
sbin/nftldump
7308 (100%)
sbin/unlock
3648 (100%)
bin/
dev/
etc/
lib/
sbin/
wrote 32540 bytes  read 2144597 bytes  150147.38 bytes/sec
total size is 3478029  speedup is 1.60
```

This command copies the content of my UI module project workspace *rootfs* directory from my host, whose IP address is 192.168.172.50, to my target's root directory. For this command to run successfully, my host must be running both *sshd* and the *rsync* daemon.

The options you need are:

-e Passes to *rsync* the name of the application to use to connect to the remote server. (In this case, we use *ssh -l root* to connect as root to the server. You could replace root with whichever username is most appropriate. If no username is provided, *ssh* tries to connect using the same username as the session's owner.)

-r Recursively copies directories.

-l Preserves symbolic links.

-p Preserves file permissions.

-t Preserves timestamps.

-D Preserves device nodes.

-v Provides verbose output.

--progress
      Reports transfer progress.

While running, *rsync* provides a list of each file or directory copied, and maintains a counter displaying the percentage of the transfer already completed. When done, *rsync* will have replicated the remote directory locally, and the target's root filesystem will be synchronized with the up-to-date directory on the server.

If you would like to check which files would be updated, without carrying out the actual update, you can use the *-n* option to do a "dry run" of *rsync*:

```
# rsync -e "ssh -l root" -r -l -p -t -D -v --progress -n \
> 192.168.172.50:/home/karim/control-project/user-interface/rootfs/* /
root@192.168.172.50's password:
receiving file list ... done
bin/busybox
bin/tinylogin
etc/inittab
etc/profile
lib/ld-2.2.1.so
lib/libc-2.2.1.so
...
sbin/nftl_format
sbin/nftldump
sbin/unlock
wrote 176 bytes  read 5198 bytes  716.53 bytes/sec
total size is 3478029  speedup is 647.20
```

For more information on the use of *rsync*, both as a client and a server, have a look at the command's manpage and the documentation available from the project's web site.

Package Management Tools

Updating simultaneously all the software packages that make up a root filesystem, as we have done in the previous section using *rsync*, is not always possible or desirable. Sometimes, the best approach is to upgrade each package separately using a package management system such as those commonly used in workstation and server distributions. If you are using Linux on your workstation, for example, you are probably already familiar with one of the two main package management systems used with Linux, the *RPM Package Manager* (RPM) or the *Debian package* (dpkg), whichever your distribution is based on. Because of these systems' good track records at helping users and system administrators keep their systems up to date and in perfect working condition, it may be tempting to try to cross-compile the tools that power these systems for use in an embedded system. Both systems are, however, demanding in terms of system resources, and are not well adapted for direct use in embedded systems.

Fortunately, there are tools aimed at embedded systems that can deal with packages in a way that enables us to obtain much of the functionality provided by more powerful packaging tools without requiring as much system resources. Two such tools are BusyBox's *dpkg* command and the *Itsy Package Management System* (iPKG). The *dpkg* BusyBox command allows us to install dpkg packages in an embedded system. Much like other BusyBox commands, it can be optionally configured as part of the *busybox* binary. iPKG is the package management system used by the Familiar distribution I mentioned earlier in this book. It is available from its project web site at *http://www.handhelds.org/z/wiki/iPKG*, along with usage documentation. iPKG relies on its own package format, but can also handle dpkg packages.

Instructions on how to build iPKG packages are available at *http://www.handhelds. org/z/wiki/BuildingIpkgs*. For instructions on how to build dpkg packages, have a look at the *Debian New Maintainers' Guide* and the *Dpkg Internals Manual* both available from *http://www.debian.org/doc/devel-manuals*. The use of the BusyBox *dpkg* command is explained in the BusyBox documentation, and the use of the *ipkg* tool part of the iPKG package management system is explained on the project's web site.

Ad Hoc Scripts

If, for some reason, the tools discussed earlier are not adapted to the task of updating an embedded system's root filesystem, we can still update it using more basic file-handling utilities. In essence, we can either copy each file using the *cp* command or patch sets of files using the *patch* command, or use a combination of both. Either way, we need to have a method to package the modifications on the host, and a method to apply the modification packages on the target. The simplest way to create and apply modification packages is to use shell scripts.

> # diff and patch
>
> Although the *diff* and *patch* pair can be used to patch entire directory hierarchies, these tools deal with symbolic links as if they were ordinary files and end up copying the content of the linked file instead of creating a symbolic link. Hence, the patch created by *diff -aurN oldrootfs/ rootfs/* is useless. Plans for modifying the utilities to deal appropriately with symbolic links are part of both packages' future projects.

In creating such scripts, we need to make sure that the dependencies between files are respected. If, for example, we are updating a library, we must make sure that the binaries on the filesystem that depend on that library will still be functional with the new library version. For example, the binary format used by uClibc has changed between Versions 0.9.14 and 0.9.15. Hence, any application linked with uClibc Version 0.9.14 and earlier must be updated if uClibc is updated to 0.9.15 or later. Although such changes are infrequent, they must be carefully considered. In general, any update involving libraries must be carefully carried out to avoid rendering the system unusable. For further information on the correct way to update libraries, see the "Upgrading Libraries" subsection of Chapter 7 in *Running Linux*.

Installing the patch utility

The first step in creating update scripts is having the appropriate tools available both on the host and the target. Since *diff* and *patch* are most likely already installed on your host, let's see how *patch* can be installed for the target.

To install *patch* on your target's root filesystem, start by downloading the GNU patch utility from the GNU project's FTP site at *ftp://ftp.gnu.org/gnu/patch/*. For my UI module, for example, I used *patch* 2.5.4. With the package downloaded, extract it in your *${PRJROOT}/sysapps* directory.

Now, create a build directory for the utility:

```
$ cd ${PRJROOT}/sysapps
$ mkdir build-patch
$ cd build-patch
```

Configure, build, and install the package:

```
$ CC=arm-uclibc-gcc ../patch-2.5.4/configure --host=$TARGET \
> --prefix=${TARGET_PREFIX}
$ make LDFLAGS="-static"
$ make install
```

Notice that we are using uClibc and are linking the command statically. We could have also used glibc or diet libc. Regardless of the library being used, linking *patch* statically ensures that it will not fail to run on your target during an update because of a missing or an incomplete library installation.

The *patch* utility has been installed in *${TARGET_PREFIX}/bin*. You can copy it from that directory to your root filesystem's */bin* directory for use on your target. Once in your target's root filesystem, use the appropriate *strip* command to reduce the size of the utility. For example, here is how I install *patch* for my UI module:

```
$ cp ${TARGET_PREFIX}/bin/patch ${PRJROOT}/rootfs/bin
$ cd ${PRJROOT}/rootfs/bin
$ ls -al patch
-rwxrwxr-x   1 karim     karim       252094 Sep  5 16:23 patch
$ arm-linux-strip patch
$ ls -al patch
-rwxrwxr-x   1 karim     karim       113916 Sep  5 16:23 patch
```

Scripts for performing updates

Using the target update guidelines discussed earlier, here is a basic shell script that can be used on the host to create a package for updating the target's root filesystem:

```
#!/bin/sh

# File: createupdate
# Parameter $1: directory containing original root filesystem
# Parameter $2: directory containing updated root filesystem
# Parameter $3: directory where patches and updates are to be stored
# Parameter $4: updated uClibc library version

# Diff the /etc directories
diff -urN $1/etc $2/etc > $3/etc.diff

# Copy BusyBox and TinyLogin
cp $2/bin/busybox $2/bin/tinylogin $3/

# Copy uClibc components
cp $2/lib/*$4* $3
```

The script makes a few assumptions. First, it assumes that neither */etc* nor any of its subdirectories contain symbolic links. Though this is true in most cases, we can still exclude any such symbolic links explicitly using the *-x* or *-X* options. Also, the script updates BusyBox, TinyLogin, and uClibc. You need to add the appropriate *cp* and *diff* commands for your setup.

The script can be used as follows:

```
$ cd ${PRJROOT}
$ mkdir tmp/rootfsupdate
$ createupdate oldrootfs/ rootfs/ tmp/rootfsupdate/ 0.9.14
```

In this case, *oldrootfs* contains the root filesystem as found on the target, *rootfs* contains the latest version of the root filesystem, *tmp/rootfsupdate* contains the files and patches used to update the target, and the new uClibc version is 0.9.14.

The following script updates the target using the update directory created above:

```
#!/bin/sh

# File: applyupdate
# Parameter $1: absolute path of dir containing patches and updates
# Parameter $2: old uClibc version
# Parameter $3: new uClibc version

# Patch /etc
patch -p1 < $1/etc.diff

# Copy BusyBox and TinyLogin
cp $1/busybox $1/tinylogin /bin/

# Copy updated uClibc components
cp $1/*$3* /lib

# Update uClibc symbolic links
ln -sf libuClibc-$3.so /lib/libc.so.0
for file in ld-uClibc libcrypt libdl libm libpthread libresolv libutil
do
ln -sf $file-$3.so /lib/$file.so.0
done

# Remove old uClibc components
rm -rf /lib/*$2*
```

This script is a little longer than the script used to create the update. The added complexity is due to the care taken in replacing the C library components. Notice that we use *ln -sf* instead of deleting the links and then using *ln -s*. This is very important because deleting the links outright would render the system unusable. You would then have to shut down the target and reprogram its storage device using the appropriate means.

To run the script, copy the *rootfsupdate* directory to your target's */tmp* directory and run the script:

```
# applyupdate /tmp/rootfsupdate 0.9.13 0.9.14
```

You can run the update script on your host to test it before using it on your actual target. Here are the steps involved:

1. From the *${PRJROOT}* directory, copy the old root filesystem (possibly *oldrootfs*) to *tmp*.

2. Modify the script to remove absolute references to /. Replace, for example, references to */etc* with references to *etc*.

3. Run the script on the copied filesystem.

4. Verify manually that everything has been updated adequately.

Copying an Entire Directory Tree Without GNU cp

When building an embedded Linux system, you will often need to copy entire directories from one location to another as efficiently as possible while keeping files, directories, and symbolic links intact. I have already done this a few times in the course of my earlier explanations and have repeatedly used the *cp -a* command to accomplish this. Although the *-a* option has been part of GNU *cp* for some time, it may not be installed on your system *if* you are not using Linux. If, for some reason, GNU *cp* is not available on your system, you can still obtain the same result as *cp -a* using a command that is a combination of *cd* and *tar*. Let's take a closer look at this command and how it works. This is how the command looks in its generalized form:

```
$ (cd SRC_DIR && tar cf - .) | (cd DEST_DIR && tar xvf -)
```

This command has two parts. The one on the left of the | character changes directories to *SRC_DIR* and initiates a *tar* in that directory. Specifically, *tar* is told to create a tar archive of the content of the directory from which it runs and to dump the resulting archive to the standard output. In simple uses of *tar* for archiving, the command is followed by a greater-than sign (>) and the name of either a tape device or a disk file. Here we aren't actually saving the output; we're just using *tar* as a convenient way to put the files into a stream and put it elsewhere.

On Unix command shells, the | is used to create a pipe between the output of the command on the left and the input of the command on the right. Hence, the archive dumped on the standard output by the command on the left is fed as the standard input for the command on the right. In turn, the command on the right of | changes to the *DEST_DIR* and initiates a *tar* in that directory. Contrary to the first *tar*, this one extracts the content found on its standard input into the directory from which it is executed.

The net effect of this command is that the files and directories found in the *SRC_DIR* directory are copied as-is to the *DEST_DIR* directory. The content of *DEST_DIR* is thereafter identical to that of *SRC_DIR*.

Though this command is of little use if your system already has GNU *cp*, you may find it helpful on systems that don't have GNU *cp*. If you are using a standard Linux workstation or server distribution, *cp -a* remains the better option for copying entire directory trees.

CHAPTER 9
Setting Up the Bootloader

Though the bootloader runs for a very short time during the system's startup and is mainly responsible for loading the kernel, it is a very important system component. Setting up a bootloader is, to some extent, a task common to all Linux systems. It is a special task, nevertheless, for embedded Linux systems, because the bootloaders used in such systems are either completely different from those used in common systems or, even when they are the same, are configured and operated in very different ways.

Chapter 7 discussed the manipulation of embedded storage devices, and Chapter 8 explained how to set up a root filesystem for use in an embedded target. We are now ready to set up the bootloader along with the other components created earlier so we may obtain a bootable and functional embedded system. Because hardware architectures differ greatly among each other and because boards based on the same architecture differ greatly among themselves, the selection, set up, and configuration of a bootloader depend largely on the hardware you are using.

There is a slew of bootloaders available for Linux, thousands upon thousands of embedded boards, and many possible boot configurations for a same board. It is, therefore, inconceivable to cover all the possible combinations within a single chapter. Nor is it possible to give an in-depth discussion of the use of each of the bootloaders covered. Many existing bootloaders for Linux either already have an entire book describing their use or need one to be written for them.

Also, the number and quality of bootloaders vary greatly between architectures. Some architectures, such as the PPC and the x86, have well known, established bootloaders providing support for a range of hardware. Other architectures have few or no standard bootloaders and mainly rely on the use of bootloaders provided by the hardware manufacturer. If you are using a bootloader provided by the manufacturer, make sure you have all the binaries and documentation. If possible, obtain the source code too so you can reprogram your target freely.

This chapter will concentrate on the bootloader/boot setup combinations most commonly used in embedded systems to load Linux. Although GRUB can be installed and used on hard disks, for example, its most common use in embedded Linux systems is to load Linux from DOC devices. Hence, the GRUB section will cover only GRUB's use to load Linux from DOC devices.

First, we start by looking at the plethora of embedded bootloaders available for use with Linux. We then discuss how to set up and configure a server to provide BOOTP/DHCP and NFS services for targets that use these services to obtain a kernel image and mount their root filesystem, respectively. This is followed by in-depth discussions of the use of LILO with disk devices, the use of GRUB with DOC devices, and the use of U-Boot.

At the end of this chapter, you will either have installed all the components we created earlier, configured your target with the appropriate bootloader, and be ready to boot your system, or you will know where to get the rest of the information you need to achieve this.

Bootloaders Galore

As I said above, many bootloaders can be used with Linux on various hardware. In this section, I will introduce the most popular and most versatile open source bootloaders for each architecture. Some architectures, such as the MIPS and the m68k, have no standard bootloaders at all. If your target is based on an MIPS or m68k processor, refer to the documentation provided by the manufacturer for instructions on how to set up and boot your hardware.

Also, some publications make a distinction between "bootloader" and "monitor." In those cases, the bootloader is just the component that boots a device and launches the main software, whereas a monitor provides, in addition to booting capabilities, a command-line interface that can be used for debugging, reading/writing memory, flash reprogramming, configuring, etc. In this chapter, I will refer to both types of software as "bootloaders," while explicitly mentioning a bootloader's monitor capabilities when available.

In comparing bootloaders, keep in mind that the availability and extent of monitor capabilities are important during development. Once development is over, however, these capabilities may become a liability, because the priority is to ensure that the user cannot inadvertently enter the monitor mode. Some bootloaders, such as U-Boot for example, can be reconfigured to allow or disallow access to monitor features. Your production hardware may also be built to prevent physical access to the serial port.

Table 9-1 presents the open source bootloaders that can be used with Linux and the architectures they support. For each bootloader, the table also indicates whether the bootloader provides monitor capabilities, and provides a short description of the bootloader. Use this table as a starting point for identifying which bootloader is best for your embedded system.

Table 9-1. Linux-capable open source bootloaders and the architectures they support

Bootloader	Monitor	Description	x86	ARM	PowerPC	MIPS	SuperH	m68k
			Architectures					
LILO	No	The main disk bootloader for Linux	X					
GRUB	No	GNU's successor to LILO	X					
ROLO	No	Loads Linux from ROM without a BIOS	X					
Loadlin	No	Loads Linux from DOS	X					
Etherboot	No	ROMable loader for booting systems through Ethernet cards	X					
LinuxBIOS	No	Linux-based BIOS replacement	X					
Compaq's bootldr	Yes	Versatile loader mainly intended for Compaq iPAQ		X				
blob	No	Loader from the LART hardware project		X				
PMON	Yes	Loader used in Agenda VR3				X		
sh-boot	No	Main loader of the LinuxSH project					X	
U-Boot	Yes	Universal loader based on PPCBoot and ARMBoot	X	X	X			
RedBoot	Yes	eCos-based loader	X	X	X	X	X	X

In addition to the above table, there are a few observations to be made regarding the various bootloaders available for each architecture:

x86

There are two main bootloaders used for the x86: LILO and GRUB. LILO is the mainstream bootloader for most x86 workstation and server distributions. On Red Hat's distribution, however, GRUB has replaced LILO. There are other, less known bootloaders, such as Rolo and EtherBoot, which you may be interested in using under certain circumstances.

As you can see, few x86 bootloaders currently provide monitor capabilities. The most glaring limitation of x86 bootloaders is that most require an x86-based host for your development. The Makefiles of LILO and GRUB, for example, are not built to allow cross-compilation. Moreover, it is difficult to install either LILO or GRUB from a non-x86 host on storage media designated for an x86 target. Hence, even if you carry out all your development on a non-x86 host, you may need to use an x86 host to compile and install the x86 bootloader you select.

ARM

Though U-Boot aims at becoming the standard ARM bootloader, there is no standard bootloader for ARM-based systems at the time of this writing. There are, nevertheless, a couple of ARM bootloaders as shown in Table 9-1, each supporting a different set of hardware. There are also many other bootloaders that can be used to boot Linux on an ARM system. Some of these bootloaders are outdated or haven't been updated for a long time, others are particular to one type of board or are not available under an open source license.

PowerPC

The main bootloader found in most PPC systems is U-Boot (formerly known as PPCBoot.)

MIPS

There is no standard bootloader for MIPS-based embedded Linux systems. Though PMON may be useful as an initial codebase, you will most probably need to port it to your target before using it. At the time of this writing, efforts are underway to add MIPS support to U-Boot.

SuperH

Though sh-boot is the main bootloader for SH-based embedded Linux systems, you may find other bootloaders, such as RedBoot, better adapted to your system.

M68k

Though RedBoot supports some m68k-based systems, there is no standard bootloader for m68k-based embedded Linux systems.

Now that I've introduced the various bootloaders and outlined the bootloader support for each architecture, let's take a closer look at each bootloader.

LILO

The *LInux LOader* (LILO) was introduced by Werner Almesberger very early in Linux's history. Now, LILO is maintained by John Coffman and the latest releases are available from *http://brun.dyndns.org/pub/linux/lilo/*. LILO is a very well documented bootloader. The LILO package, for instance, includes a user manual and an internals manual. The LILO mini-HOWTO available from the LDP completes this documentation by answering some of the most common questions about LILO's use. In addition, *Running Linux* contains a "*Using LILO*" section in Chapter 5.

GRUB

The *GRand Unified Bootloader* (GRUB) is the main bootloader for the GNU project. GRUB was originally written by Erich Boleyn in the course of finding an appropriate bootloader for what would later be known as GNU Mach. Eric's work was later picked up by Gordon Matzigkeit and Okuji Yoshinori, who currently continue to maintain and develop GRUB. The GRUB project's web site is located at *http://www.*

gnu.org/software/grub/. There, you will find the GRUB manual, which discusses the package's use extensively. One aspect of GRUB's capabilities you may find helpful during development is its ability to boot over the network using TFTP, and BOOTP or DHCP. Though GRUB's code can be retrieved using CVS, the latest stable releases are tar-gzipped and made available for download through the project's web site.

ROLO

The *ROmable LOader* (ROLO) was written and is being maintained by Robert Kaiser from Sysgo Gmbh. as part of Sysgo's ELinos distribution. ROLO can boot Linux directly from ROM without requiring any BIOS. ROLO is available from *ftp://ftp.elinos.com/pub/elinos/rolo/*. Though the package contains little documentation, Vipin Malik has written a thorough article on the use of ROLO in an embedded system at *http://www.embeddedlinuxworks.com/articles/rolo_guide.html*.

loadlin

loadlin is a DOS utility to load Linux maintained by Hans Lermen at *http://elserv.ffm.fgan.de/~lermen/*. Though you should avoid building your system in a way that requires DOS to be loaded first, there are cases where such a utility can be very handy. One case where it can be useful, for example, is if you want to use M-Systems's DOS tools to boot from a DOC device. In that case, you can write an *autoexec.bat* file that uses the *loadlin* utility to load Linux. As we will see below, however, you can boot Linux directly from a DOC device using GRUB.

EtherBoot

Many NICs are shipped with a socket for inserting ROM chips. When present and properly signed, these ROM chips are recognized as BIOS extensions and executed during startup. EtherBoot uses this capability to support the booting of diskless systems through the network. EtherBoot has been used in many environments, including X-terminals, routers, and clusters. It is available with complete documentation from *http://etherboot.sourceforge.net/*. The web site provides links to manufacturers who sell EPROMs preloaded with EtherBoot.

LinuxBIOS

LinuxBIOS is a complete BIOS replacement that boots Linux from ROM at startup. LinuxBIOS was developed as part of clustering research conducted at the Los Alamos National Laboratory and has gathered support from many hardware manufacturers. The LinuxBIOS package and documentation are available at *http://www.linuxbios.org/*.

Compaq's bootldr

Though initially developed for the Compaq iPAQ only, Compaq's bootldr currently supports Intel's Assabet and HP's Jornada 720. Though it is limited in the range of hardware it supports, bootldr provides a very rich command set and is capable of loading kernels directly from JFFS2 MTD partitions. Bootldr is part of the software collection maintained by *http://www.handhelds.org/* and is available for download from *ftp://ftp.handhelds.org/bootldr/*.

blob

blob was introduced as the bootloader for the LART hardware project.[*] Since its introduction, blob has been ported to many other ARM-based systems, including Intel's Assabet and Brutus, Shannon, and Nesa boards. Unlike ARMBoot and Compaq's bootldr, blob does not provide monitor capabilities, though it can be used to reprogram the flash and can load kernels directly from JFFS2 MTD partitions. blob is available from the LART web site along with documentation at *http://www.lart. tudelft.nl/lartware/blob/*.

PMON

The *Prom Monitor* (PMON) was written by Phil Bunce to support LSI LOGIC's MIPS boards. It is distributed under a very simplistic license, which stipulates that PMON comes with no warranty and that you are free to redistribute it without any restriction. Though Phil's PMON has not been updated since 1999, it is still available at *http://www.carmel.com/pmon/*. Others have nevertheless used PMON for more recent projects. It was ported to the now discontinued Agenda VR3 Linux PDA by Bradely LaRonde. That version is available from the AGOS SourceForge workspace at *http://agos.sourceforge.net/* and information on its use is available from the Agenda Wiki site at *http://agendawiki.com/*. It remains that there is no central authority or roadmap for PMON, and few boards are actually supported. As I said earlier, you may find the PMON codebase a good starting point, but you will most probably need to port it to your system to use it.

sh-Boot

sh-boot is developed as part of the Linux SH project on SourceForge. Unfortunately, sh-boot has not been updated for a while, so you may need to evaluate its usability for your system. Also, sh-boot is a simple bootloader and does not provide any monitor capabilities. The bootloader is available using CVS through the Linux SH project site at *http://linuxsh.sourceforge.net/*.

---

[*] See LART description in Appendix B.

U-Boot

Though there are quite a few other bootloaders, "Das U-Boot," the *universal boot-loader*, is arguably the richest, most flexible, and most actively developed open source bootloader available. It is currently maintained by Wolfgang Denk of DENX Software Engineering, and is contributed to by a wide range of developers. U-Boot is based on the PPCBoot and ARMBoot projects. PPCBoot was itself based on 8xxrom sources, and ARMBoot was an ARM port of PPCBoot done by Sysgo Gmbh. At the time of this writing, U-Boot supports around 100 different PPC-based boards, more than a dozen ARM-based boards, and a handful of x86-based boards. U-Boot's success in scaling to a wide range of hardware has prompted developers to continue porting it to even more new boards and architectures.

Among other things, U-Boot is capable of booting a kernel through TFTP, from an IDE or SCSI disk, and from a DOC. Also, it includes read-only support for JFFS2. Besides having an extensive command set and quite a few capabilities, it is also fairly well documented. The *README* included with the package provides an in-depth discussion of the use of U-Boot. The *doc* directory in the package's source includes any extra instructions required for certain boards. In addition to the instructions found in the package, Wolfgang wrote the *DENX PPCBoot and Linux Guide*, available at *http://www.denx.de/re/DPLG.html*, which provides many practical examples of the use of PPCBoot with Linux on a TQM8xxL board. Though the discussion assumes that you are using PPCBoot and DENX's Embedded Linux Development Kit (ELDK) distribution,* the sections relating to the use of PPCBoot apply with little or no changes to U-Boot, and are helpful regardless of whether you use any distribution.

The U-Boot project workspace is located at *http://sourceforge.net/projects/u-boot*. The U-Boot package is available from that site. If you intend to use U-Boot often, you will find it useful to subscribe to the very active U-Boot users mailing list at that site. Though there is no on-site documentation for U-Boot at the time of this writing, you can still rely on the documentation and background provided by the two projects on which U-Boot is based, PPCBoot and ARMBoot. PPCBoot's web site is located at *http://ppcboot.sourceforge.net/*, and ARMBoot's project web site is located at *http://armboot.sourceforge.net/*. We will explore U-Boot's use later in this chapter.

RedBoot

RedBoot is supposed to be a next generation bootloader from Red Hat, replacing CygMon and GDB stubs with a firmware supporting a very wide range of hardware. Although Red Hat has stopped active development of eCos, the OS on which Red-Boot is based, eCos has now been relicensed under the GPL and continues to be maintained by some of the Red Hat core eCos developers. eCos' future, and Red-Boot's as well, is therefore in the hands of those developers.

---

* The ELDK is an open source development and target distribution.

Despite its dependency on eCos,* RedBoot remains a very powerful bootloader. It is, for instance, the only open source bootloader that currently supports all the architectures presented in depth in Chapter 3 and a wide range of boards based on these architectures. Also, the RedBoot package is fairly well documented, including a *RedBoot User's Guide* that provides actual examples of its use on more than a dozen different systems. RedBoot's web site is located at *http://sources.redhat.com/redboot/* and its sources are available with the rest of the eCos sources using CVS. Lately, eCosCentric Ltd., the company formed by the core eCos developers from Red Hat, has been providing CVS snapshots at *http://www.ecoscentric.com/snapshots/*.

Server Setup for Network Boot

As we saw in Chapter 2, setting up a target for network boot is ideal during the early stages of development, because you can gradually modify the kernel and the root filesystem without having to update the target's storage devices every time you make a modification. Though not all bootloaders can use this setup to boot, I recommend that you use such a setup whenever possible.

As I said earlier, the simplest way to boot your target from the network is to use BOOTP/DHCP, TFTP, and NFS. BOOTP/DHCP is the standard way to provide a network host with basic boot information, including the location of other servers such as TFTP and NFS. TFTP is the simplest network protocol for downloading remote files. In the case of an embedded Linux system, it is used by the target to obtain a kernel image from the TFTP server. Finally, NFS is the standard and simplest protocol for sharing entire directory trees between a client and a server. In the case of an embedded Linux system, it is used by the target to mount its root filesystem from the NFS server. NFS cannot be used for any earlier activity, because it requires a booted Linux kernel to operate. Together, these three protocols provide a very efficient host/target development setup.

To enable network booting of the target, you must set up the development host's network services so that the target can access the components it needs. In particular, you need to set up a host to respond to BOOTP/DHCP requests, provide a kernel using a TFTP server, and enable NFS mounts. The subsections below discuss each issue separately.

Setting Up the DHCP Daemon

Unlike other network services, DHCP is not dependent on the internet super-server. Instead, the DHCP daemon is a service of its own, and you need to start it manually. First, you need to make sure that the DHCP server is installed on your system.

---

* RedBoot is part of the eCos source code tree and requires some of the code provided by that OS to provide its own services. Hence, RedBoot's development is tied to, but not entirely dependent on, eCos' development. Some platforms supported by RedBoot, for example, aren't supported by eCos.

Though you can download it from *http://www.isc.org/*, the DHCP server is part of most mainstream distributions.

If you are using an RPM-based distribution, use the following command to check for the presence of the DHCP daemon:

```
$ rpm -q dhcp
dhcp-2.0-5
```

In this case, DHCP 2.0-5 is already installed. If it is not already installed on your system, use the appropriate tools for your distribution to install the DHCP server. Note that most distributions include two DHCP packages, a client and a server. The package containing the client is usually called *dhcpc-VERSION*. There is an additional "c" after "dhcp" to identify the client package.

To operate properly, the kernel on which the DHCP server runs has to be configured with the `CONFIG_PACKET` and `CONFIG_FILTER` options. The kernels shipped by default in most distributions almost always have these enabled. If you are in the habit of building your own kernels for your workstation, as I often do, watch out for those options when configuring the kernel. If the kernel wasn't built properly, the DHCP daemon will output the following message when it tries to start:

```
socket: Protocol not available - make sure CONFIG_PACKET and CONFIG_FILTER are
defined in your kernel configuration!
exiting.
```

With the package installed and the kernel properly configured, create or edit the */etc/dhcpd.conf* file and add an entry for your target. For example, here is the */etc/dhcpd.conf* file for my control module:

```
subnet 192.168.172.0 netmask 255.255.255.0 {
        option routers 192.168.172.50;
        option subnet-mask 255.255.255.0;

        host ctrl-mod {
                hardware ethernet 00:D0:93:00:05:E3;
                fixed-address 192.168.172.10;
                option host-name "ctrl-mod";
                next-server 192.168.172.50;
                filename "/home/karim/vmlinux-2.4.18.img";
                option root-path "/home/karim/ctrl-rootfs";
        }
}
```

Essentially, this entry states that the host and target are on the 192.168.172.0 network, that the TFTP server is located at 192.168.172.50, and that the address allocated to the target when it issues its DHCP or BOOTP request is 192.168.172.10. The `hardware ethernet` field uniquely identifies the target through its MAC address, which is 00:D0:93:00:05:E3 for my control module. The `fixed-address` field tells the DHCP server which IP address should be allocated to the designated MAC address. The `option host-name` field gives the hostname to the target so that it can use it internally.

The next-sever tells the target where the TFTP server is located. The `filename` field is the filename* of the image that has to be loaded by the target. According to RFC 2131, which specifies DHCP, the filename is limited to 128 bytes. Finally, the `option root-path` field provides the path to the target's root filesystem on the NFS server. If your target does not need to load its root filesystem from an NFS server, you can omit this last field. Because the host is the only network link to the target in this case, `option routers` points to the host's address. If the target was linked to an entire network with a real router, `option routers` should point to that network's default router.

The example configuration provided above should be easy to adapt to your own target. If you need more information regarding the configuration of the DHCP server, have a look at the manpage for *dhcpd.conf* and the sample configuration file installed by your distribution, if one is present.

Note that if you are using a version of the DHCP daemon later than 3.0b2pl11, such as the one shipped with Red Hat 8.0, you will need to add the following line to your *dhcpd.conf* file:

```
ddns-update-style ad-hoc;
```

With the DHCP server configured for the target, you are almost ready to start the DHCP server. Before you do so, however, you need to make sure the */var/state/dhcp/dhcpd.leases* file exists. If it doesn't, create it using the *touch* command. If the file isn't created, the DHCP daemon will refuse to start.

Finally, start the DHCP server. On distributions based on Red Hat, enter:

```
# /etc/init.d/dhcpd start
```

Setting Up the TFTP Daemon

The first step in setting up the TFTP daemon is to make sure the TFTP package is installed. Though the latest version of the TFTP daemon is available for download as part of the NetKit package at *ftp://ftp.uk.linux.org/pub/linux/Networking/netkit/*, TFTP was most likely already installed on your system as part of your distribution or is available to be installed from your distribution's CDs.

If you are using an RPM-based distribution, use the following command to check for the presence of the TFTP daemon:

```
$ rpm -q tftp
tftp-0.16-5
```

In this case, TFTP 0.16-5 is already installed. If it is not available on your system, install the TFTP package using the appropriate tool for your distribution. Alternatively, if your system doesn't rely on a package manager or if some components have

---

* For the example to fit in the printed page's width, I avoid using the complete */home/karim/control-project/control-module/...* path. Use the actual complete path for your own development.

been installed without a package manager, you can also check for the presence of the actual TFTP daemon binary using the *whereis* command.

Once the package is installed, enable the TFTP service by modifying the appropriate internet super-server configuration file. In brief, the internet super-server listens on designated ports on behalf of the various network services. When a request for certain service is received, the super-server spawns the appropriate daemon and hands it the request. Hence, only the minimal number of daemons run at all times. TFTP is one of the daemons normally handled by the super-server.

To enable the TFTP service in a system based on the *inetd* super-server, edit */etc/inetd.conf*, uncomment the line for the TFTP service by removing the # character at the beginning, and send a SIGHUP signal to the *inetd* process so that it rereads its configuration file. To enable the TFTP service in a system based on the *xinetd* super-server, edit */etc/xinetd.d/tftp* and comment the line containing disable = yes by adding a # character at the beginning. As with *inetd*, you must send a SIGHUP to *xinetd*.

Finally, you must provide the TFTP server with a list of directories containing files that should be made available to TFTP clients. In a system based on the *inetd* super-server, append the list of directories to the TFTP line in */etc/inetd.conf*. In a system based on the *xinetd* super-server, edit the */etc/xinetd.d/tftp* file and append the list of directories to the server_args = line. The default directory for TFTP is */tftpboot*. You may choose to modify this to match your setup. Whichever directory you choose, make sure its access permissions include read and execute for the "other" permission.

For example, here is a TFTP line in */etc/inetd.conf* for a host using the *inetd* super-server:

```
tftp    dgram  udp    wait   root  /usr/sbin/tcpd  in.tftpd /home/karim/
```

In this case, images are placed in the */home/karim* directory, which has the following permissions:

```
$ ls -ld /home/karim
drwxr-xr-x   4 karim     karim        4096 Aug 29 16:13 karim
```

Here is a modified */etc/xinetd.d/tftp* file from a Red Hat–based installation providing the same functionality for a host using the *xinetd* super-server:

```
service tftp
{
        socket_type           = dgram
        protocol              = udp
        wait                  = yes
        user                  = root
        server                = /usr/sbin/in.tftpd
        server_args           = /home/karim
#        disable               = yes
        per_source            = 11
        cps                   = 100 2
}
```

Regardless of the super-server in use on a host, the TFTP service is usually disabled by default. Hence, even if you use the default */tftpboot*, you will need to modify the super-server's configuration files to enable TFTP.

Mounting a Root Filesystem on an NFS Server

As I explained in Chapter 2, while a bootloader and kernel must be stored locally or retrieved to local storage through one of the methods shown earlier, the target's kernel can mount its root filesystem from a remote NFS server. To this end, the NFS server must be properly installed and configured. Chapter 6 showed how to build your target's root filesystem. Though Chapter 8 showed how to prepare this filesystem for use in the target, the root filesystem we created in Chapter 6 does not need any special preparation for use by the NFS server.

The NFS server daemon is available in two flavors: as a standalone user application or as a part of the kernel. Besides being faster, the latter is also the standard way most distributions are configured. In addition to the NFS server itself, you need to have the NFS utilities installed. Usually, there is an nfs-utils package as part of your distribution. Use the following command to identify whether nfs-utils is installed:

```
$ rpm -q nfs-utils
nfs-utils-0.3.1-13
```

With the nfs-utils installed, you need to make sure that the appropriate configuration files are present and that the corresponding services are started.

The main file we need to configure for the NFS server is */etc/exports*. Entries in this file describe the directories each host or set of hosts can access. As an example, here is the entry in my */etc/exports* for my control module:

```
/home/karim/ctrl-rootfs 192.168.172.10(rw,no_root_squash)
```

This entry states that the machine with address 192.168.172.10 has read and write (rw) access to the */home/karim/ctrl-rootfs* directory, which is the path to the root filesystem we built for the target in Chapter 6. In addition, the no_root_squash argument indicates that the server should allow the remote system to access the directory with its root privileges. These are very powerful rights that we are granting to the target. If we have total control over access to the device, as is the case in most development setups, there is obviously no security risk. If, however, the target's location is less secure or if it is directly connected to the Internet, for example, you may prefer to use the default root_squash instead. In that case, the target will not be able to write to most of its own root filesystem, though it will still be able to read and write to all directories and files that are readable and writable by anybody. In practical terms, however, the target's operation will be very limited.

Because offering the NFS service also involves the risk of network abuse, it is often pertinent to use some minimal protection mechanisms to avoid intrusions. One simple way to do this is to customize the */etc/hosts.deny* and */etc/hosts.allow* files to restrict access to network services. For example, here is the *etc/hosts.deny* file for my Red Hat–based host:

```
#
# hosts.deny
#

portmap: ALL
lockd: ALL
mountd: ALL
rquotad: ALL
statd: ALL
```

and here is my *etc/hosts.allow* file:

```
#
# hosts.allow
#

portmap: 192.168.172.10
lockd: 192.168.172.10
mountd: 192.168.172.10
rquotad: 192.168.172.10
statd: 192.168.172.10
```

The rules specified in these files restrict access to the various file-sharing services. Together, these files indicate that only the machine with address 192.168.172.10 can use the NFS services. This is fine in the case of my setup, since I don't want to share my workstation with anyone else. Even if you do not customize *etc/hosts.deny* and *etc/hosts.allow*, I encourage you to take security issues to heart and use whichever means necessary, such as backups, to protect your work.

Once the configuration files are created, you can start the portmapper service, which is required by the NFS server:

```
# /etc/init.d/portmap start
```

Finally, you can start the NFS server itself:

```
# /etc/init.d/nfs start
```

If you would like more information on the configuration of remote boot using NFS, see the two Diskless root NFS HOWTOs on the issue at the LDP. Also, you may be interested by the NFS HOWTO, also at the LDP.

Using LILO with Disk and CompactFlash Devices

Because there is already ample documentation on the installation, configuration, and use of LILO, I will cover only its specific use in embedded PC-like systems. Specifically, I will provide the instructions to use on the host to install LILO on a storage device meant to be used in the target.

The installation of LILO on a target's storage device requires the use of the removable storage setup as explained in Chapter 2. In this scenario, the target's storage device is removed from the target and connected to the host's own hardware to be programmed. Hence, the target's storage device is controlled by the host's operating system like any other host device. The target's storage device is therefore seen as an extra storage device for the host. It can be seen, for example, as a secondary IDE disk (*/dev/hdb*) or as a primary SCSI disk (*/dev/sda*). Regardless of the way it is seen by the host's kernel, LILO needs to be used in a specific way to install itself on this secondary storage and not on the host's boot media, as is the default.

As we discussed in Chapter 8, CF devices are quite peculiar in this regard, because they can be seen on the host as a SCSI disk (*/dev/sdX*) when accessed through a USB CF reader, while being seen on the target as an IDE disk (*/dev/hdX*) when accessed through a CF-to-IDE or CF-to-PCMCIA adapter. The configuration file example I provide below takes care of this issue by using the appropriate BIOS and kernel flags so that the disk seen as a SCSI disk on the host can boot normally as an IDE disk once put back in the target.

In the following, I assume that the storage device where LILO will be installed is accessible on your host, and that you are using LILO Version 22.3 or later. If you are using an earlier version, an important command will fail, as I will explain shortly. Follow these steps to install LILO on a secondary IDE or SCSI storage device on your host:

1. Create appropriate */dev* entries in your target's root filesystem for the storage device where LILO is to be installed. This is not the storage device as it will be accessed once in your target. Rather, this is the storage device entry used by the host to access the designated storage device. If, for example, you want to install LILO on */dev/sda* (usually the first SCSI hard disk in your system), there must be a */dev/sda* entry on your target's root filesystem. It is very likely that this entry does not correspond to a valid device on your target. Indeed, it is possible that the disk accessed as */dev/sda* on the host may be accessed as */dev/hda* once on the target. Nevertheless, you must create the */dev/sda* entry in your target's root filesystem for LILO to use when running on the host. The reasons for this will soon become evident. For more information on the relationship between */dev* entries and the actual physical storage devices, see Chapter 3 of *Running Linux*.

2. Create a LILO configuration file on your target root filesystem. To avoid damaging your host's configuration when installing LILO on the target's storage device, put your LILO configuration in */etc/target.lilo.conf* on your target's root filesystem instead of the usual */etc/lilo.conf*. Hence, if you accidentally issue a LILO command that modifies your host, the tool will complain about a missing file and no damage will be done to your host.

   Here is a sample */etc/target.lilo.conf* to boot my DAQ module from a CF card:

   ```
   boot = /dev/sda
   disk = /dev/sda
     bios = 0x80
   ```

```
image = /boot/bzImage-2.4.18
  root = /dev/sda1
  append = "root=/dev/hda1"
  label = Linux
  read-only
```

In this case, the CF card is accessed through a USB CF reader and is visible on my host as a SCSI disk through */dev/sda*. On the target, however, it will be accessed through a CF-to-IDE adapter and will be visible as an IDE drive through */dev/hda*. If you use a normal LILO configuration file to configure LILO, it would guess the BIOS ID of the disk it is operating on, and would use that ID at startup to make access requests to the BIOS. Since, in this case, it is operating on a SCSI disk, it would assume a SCSI BIOS ID and would make access requests for such a disk. Since no such disk exists on the target, the BIOS would return an error and LILO would fail to boot. The trick in the configuration file above lies in the bios = 0x80 line. This informs LILO that it is booting from the disk with BIOS ID 0x80, which is the first IDE drive in the system. Because of the confusion between SCSI and IDE, I must also append a root=/dev/hda1 option to the kernel's boot parameters. Otherwise, the kernel would fail to find its root filesystem and crash while trying to mount it.[*]

Alternatively, if you want to install LILO on */dev/hdb*, replace the */dev/sda* entries above with */dev/hdb*. In this case, you won't need to append the *root=/dev/hda1* option to the kernel's boot instructions, because the disk appears as IDE both on the host and the target.

When LILO is run with the configuration file above, it opens the host's */dev/sda* device and installs itself there. Because this configuration file is located in *${PRJROOT}/rootfs/etc/target.lilo.conf* instead of */etc/lilo.conf*, special options must be used with LILO to provide it with the location of this alternative configuration file. I will present the complete LILO command line to use in this configuration shortly.

For a complete discussion of how LILO is installed on an alternative storage device, see the Installing hdc to Boot as hda and Using bios= section in the LILO mini-HOWTO provided by the LDP.

3. If necessary, partition the storage device using *fdisk*.

4. Create filesystems on the storage device for the filesystem types you selected using the appropriate filesystem creation tools. For an ext2 filesystem, for example, use *mke2fs*.

5. Mount the root filesystem partition on an appropriate directory in */mnt*.

---

[*] Normally, you shouldn't need to append a root= option to the kernel's boot parameters if you already have a root line in your image description. In this case, however, the software involved takes for granted that disks cannot change types, and fails to configure the boot process properly without the double declaration.

6. Copy the root filesystem to its designated partition using *cp -a*. The root filesystem must contain the kernel image referenced by the /etc/target.lilo.conf file created earlier, /boot/bzImage-2.4.18 in this case.

7. Install LILO on the storage device. For my DAQ module's storage device, for example, which is mounted as /mnt/cf on my host, I use the following command:

```
# lilo -r /mnt/cf -C etc/target.lilo.conf
Warning: etc/target.lilo.conf should be owned by root
Warning: LBA32 addressing assumed
Added Linux *
```

This command instructs *lilo* to use the chroot( ) system call to change its root directory to /mnt/cf directory and to use the *etc/target.lilo.conf* configuration file found in that directory. The command programs the devices specified in the *target.lilo.conf* configuration file. The /dev entries specified in the configuration file are located starting from the root directory entry, /mnt/cf. If /dev/sda must be programmed, for example, LILO attempts to open and program /mnt/cf/dev/sda.

If you had forgotten to create the /dev entries specified in *target.lilo.conf* on your target's root filesystem, this command will fail. It will also fail if there is no /tmp directory on your target's root filesystem. Furthermore, if you are using a LILO version earlier than 22.3, the command will report the following error and fail:

```
Fatal: open /boot/boot.b: No such file or directory
```

This error message is due to the fact that, prior to Version 22.3, LILO's components were separated across different files, some of which were .b files. Since 22.3, all .b files are part of the *lilo* binary.

8. Unmount the root filesystem partition.

You can now remove the storage device from your host, either by shutting down the host and removing the hard disk or by removing the CF card from the CF reader, instaling it in your target, and booting it.

A Word on Using LILO with DiskOnChip Devices

To boot from a DOC device, LILO must be patched, since it doesn't support the DOC by default. Both the Linux tools package provided by M-Systems and the MTD package provide a patch for LILO. In light of the common experience of many individuals on the MTD mailing list and the fact that GRUB is the bootloader receiving most of the MTD development team's attention, however, I strongly recommend that you use GRUB instead of LILO for booting from a DOC device. If you still would like to use LILO, look at the relevant entries in the MTD mailing list archive or, if you fail to find what you need in the archive, ask the mailing list for guidance.

Using GRUB with DiskOnChip Devices

Since the use of GRUB with conventional disk devices is already amply covered in the GRUB manual, we will mainly concentrate on the installation and use of GRUB with DOC devices. Before I start covering the details of how to compile and use GRUB with a DOC device, I must warn you that an improper configuration of GRUB for your DOC can render your system unbootable. Let's see why this happens and how it can be avoided.

As I explained in Chapter 7 when describing the use of the *doc_loadbios* command, DOC devices contain a ROM program called the IPL that is detected as a BIOS extension at startup and is executed by the BIOS. When it runs, this IPL installs another program, the SPL. To boot from a DOC device using GRUB, the SPL must be replaced by a version of GRUB specifically tailored to boot from a DOC.

Since there may be other BIOS extensions in the system, the SPL loaded by the IPL cannot boot the system right away. Instead, it must install a *Terminate and Stay Resident* (TSR) program that will lay dormant until the BIOS is ready to boot the system. In the case of GRUB, the GRUB SPL replaces the BIOS's bootstrap interrupt, INT 19h, with a custom interrupt handler that will execute the rest of the GRUB code to finish booting from the DOC device. Hence, the other BIOS extensions get to run and GRUB is called only when the system is ready to be booted.

The problem with this scheme, however, is that the default bootstrap handler installed by the BIOS never gets a chance to run, and any boot configuration option you may have selected in your BIOS—such as booting from disk or floppy first—will be completely ignored by GRUB when its handler is invoked. This is fine if the configuration file on the DOC is correct. At worst, you would then boot using the DOC, change the configuration file in Linux, or completely remove GRUB from the DOC to set the system as you desire.

If you make any mistakes in the GRUB configuration file that result in boot failure, however, you will be unable to restart your system normally without finding a way to disable the replacement of the bootstrap interrupt handler at startup. There are four known ways to do this:

- You can physically remove the DOC from the system before starting it. The problem with this choice is that your only way to reprogram the DOC thereafter, if you do not have access to a hardware DOC programer, is to insert the DOC *after* the system has been started. In other words, you would have to connect the DOC to a live electronic circuit. Needless to say, neither the DOC nor the electronic circuits interfacing with it have been designed for this sort of manipulation. Also, I neither encourage you to try this nor take any responsibility if you are crazy enough to do it. However, a few courageous people on the MTD mailing list have reported that they successfully inserted their DOC in a running system in this way to reprogram it.

- If jumpers are available for configuring the address region to which the DOC device is mapped, you can try removing the jumpers completely and starting the system. In some cases, such as when using the ISA DOC evaluation board provided by M-Systems, this will result in the BIOS not recognizing the IPL and, hence, not running it. In other cases, however, this may result in a system hang. If this trick works for you, you will be able to boot the system using the BIOS's configuration. However, to access the DOC again once the system is running, you will have to insert the jumper *while* the system is powered on. Again, though this is reported to work, the hardware was not designed for this, I don't encourage you to do it, and I take no responsibility whatsoever for any possible outcome.

- The configuration of GRUB allows it to use the ROM BASIC interrupt, INT 18h, instead of the bootstrap interrupt. Lately, in addition to being the ROM BASIC interrupt, INT 18h is sometimes used for network boot. When configured to use this interrupt, GRUB would kick in only if the BIOS configuration is set to network boot or if there are no boot devices set in the BIOS. This approach has a few drawbacks. First, it requires changing the BIOS configuration every time you want to switch from booting from the DOC to booting from a hard disk. This can be time-consuming during development. In addition, the use of INT 18h by recent BIOSes is not standardized, as the case of the BIOSes using it to provide network boot demonstrates.

- Having seen the above choices while writing this book, your author decided to find a "cleaner" way of doing things. Hence, I set out digging in some of my old DOS and BIOS hacking books and came up with a solution that's both elegant and simple. Basically, instead of replacing the default bootstrap interrupt handler outright, my modified GRUB SPL makes a copy of the original handler, replaces it with the GRUB bootstrap handler, and lets the BIOS continue looking for other extensions in the system. When GRUB's bootstrap handler is invoked, it then checks whether the user is holding down the Ctrl key. If so, the original bootstrap handler is restored, and the BIOS is left to continue the bootstrap using the boot configuration chosen by the user. If the Ctrl key isn't held down, GRUB continues its normal procedure to load whatever is on the DOC. As you can see, this solution does not involve any dangerous hardware manipulations; save, maybe, for people suffering from carpal tunnel syndrome.

For obvious reasons, I strongly encourage you to use the last solution. This enhancement is, however, fairly recent at the time of this writing and you will only find it starting with GRUB patch *grub-2002-10-08-doc.patch*, which is available in the MTD CVS. I will explain how this option is enabled during GRUB's configuration in the next section.

Having covered the dangers of using GRUB to boot from a DOC, let's discuss the building, installation, and use of GRUB with a DOC.

Configuring and Building GRUB for the DOC

As I said earlier, you will need an x86 host to build GRUB. The following instructions assume that you are using such an x86 host. GRUB will fail to build or will create unusable binaries on any other type of host.

To start, download GRUB into your *${PRJROOT}/bootldr* directory and extract it there. Then copy the GRUB patch from the *${PRJROOT}/sysapps/mtd/patches* directory to the GRUB directory in *${PRJROOT}/bootldr*. In the case of my DAQ module, for example, I used GRUB 0.92 and the *grub-2002-02-19-doc.patch* patch. Now apply the patch to GRUB:

```
$ cd ${PRJROOT}/bootldr/grub-0.92
$ patch -p0 < grub-2002-02-19-doc.patch
```

Because this patch was originally meant for GRUB 0.90, there were some warnings and one failure when applying it to 0.92. The failure in this case was in *ChangeLog* and can therefore be ignored.

If you want to use the Ctrl key method discussed in the previous section to avoid having to hotplug your DOC, use the *grub-2002-10-08-doc.patch* patch or a later version against a GRUB version retrieved from the CVS repository. Because the CVS repository is constantly changing, however, this patch may not apply cleanly to the latest CVS contents. To get the patch to apply as cleanly as possible and have the resulting source tree compile, for example, I had to retrieve the GRUB sources from the CVS repository as they were on October 10, 2002 and then manually edit a couple of files in the source code. To retrieve the code as it was on the date I mentioned, I used the following command:

```
$ cvs -z3 -d:pserver:anoncvs@subversions.gnu.org:/cvsroot/grub \
> co -D"10/10/02" grub
```

With the code patched, you are ready to build GRUB. First, create the Makefile using the automake tools:

```
$ aclocal && automake && autoconf
```

Now, configure GRUB to build for the DOC:

```
$ ./configure --enable-diskonchip-2000 \
> --enable-diskonchip-ctrlbypass \
> --enable-ext2fs \
> --disable-ffs --disable-xfs --disable-jfs --disable-vstafs \
> --disable-reiserfs --disable-minix --disable-fat
```

This command line disables GRUB's support for all filesystems except ext2 and enables support for the DOC 2000 device. It also enables the Ctrl key bypass method I described in the previous section using the *--enable-diskonchip-ctrlbypass* option. There are a few other configuration options relevant to the DOC. If you are using DOC Millennium, for example, you may want to use the *--enable-diskonchip-mil256* or *--enable-diskonchip-mil512* option, depending on whether your DOC Millennium is using 256- or 512-byte page sizes. You can also use the *--enable-diskonchip-bios-netboot* option to boot GRUB on the network boot interrupt instead of the bootstrap interrupt as described earlier. For a complete description of the options available for configuring GRUB for the DOC, have a look at the *README_DiskOnChip* created in the GRUB package directory when the DOC patch was applied earlier.

Once the configuration is done, you can build GRUB:

```
$ make
```

Once the compilation is done, the *stage1/grub_firmware* file will contain the GRUB image to be written to the DOC. Copy this file to *${PRJROOT}/images/grub_firmware-0.92* for future use:

```
$ cp stage1/grub_firmware ${PRJROOT}/images/grub_firmware-0.92
```

Installing GRUB on a DOC

I have already covered the installation of the GRUB bootloader image in "Installing bootloader image" in Chapter 7. Follow the instructions given in that section to install the GRUB image created here on your DOC device.

Configuring GRUB to Boot from a DOC

As with LILO, GRUB uses a configuration file to determine the boot media and kernel it has to boot. Unlike LILO, however, you do not need to run the GRUB binary to parse and update its configuration. Instead, the GRUB configuration file, *menu.lst*, is placed as-is in the */boot/grub* directory of the target's root filesystem and is read by GRUB at startup. To configure GRUB to boot from a DOC, this is the file that we must create.

As an example, here is a simple *menu.lst* file for booting from a DOC device:

```
timeout 5
default 0

title DiskOnChip 2000 Boot
kernel (dc0,0)/boot/bzImage-2.4.18 root=/dev/nftla1

title HD Boot
kernel (hd0,0)/boot/bzImage-2.4.18 root=/dev/hda1
```

This file states that there are two boot possibilities. The first, which is also the default, involves booting kernel */boot/bzImage-2.4.18* from the first partition of the first DOC, dc0. The second involves booting a kernel by the same name as the previous item from the first partition of the first hard disk, hd0. For each configuration, the root= option indicates the device where the booting kernel will find its root filesystem.

This configuration is useful during development, since it allows you to choose between booting from the DOC and from your hard disk. On a production system, you probably want to remove the entry for the hard disk and set the timeout to zero so that booting from the DOC becomes the only possible option.

You can further modify GRUB's configuration and allow for a number of boot options. Look at GRUB's manual for a complete description of the configuration file format.

U-Boot

As I said earlier, U-Boot is a richly documented bootloader. The *README* file included with the package, for example, covers the use of U-Boot extensively. Among other things, it discusses the package's source code layout, the available build options, U-Boot's command set, and the typical environment variables used in U-Boot. In the following, I will cover the essential aspects of U-Boot and provide practical examples of its use. An in-depth discussion of U-Boot would, however, require a book of its own. For this reason, I encourage you to print a copy of the *README* provided with U-Boot and have a look at the other documentation written by the project maintainer.

Compiling and Installing

Start by downloading and extracting the latest version of U-Boot in your *${PRJROOT}/bootldr* directory. As of this writing, the latest U-Boot version is 0.2.0. Once extracted, move to the package's directory:

```
$ cd ${PRJROOT}/bootldr/u-boot-0.2.0
```

Physical RAM and Flash Location

The board used in the following explanations has 16 MB of RAM and 8 MB of flash. The RAM is mapped from address 0x0000000 to address 0x00FFFFFF, and the flash is mapped from address 0x40000000 to address 0x407FFFFF. The documentation provided with U-Boot discusses its use of the physical memory of targets.

Before you can build U-Boot, you need to configure it for your target. The package includes a number of preset configurations for quite a few boards. So, a configuration may very well exist for your target already. Look at the *README* file to see if your board is supported. For each supported board, U-Boot's Makefile includes a *BOARD_NAME*_config target, which is used to configure U-Boot's build for the designated board. The configuration target for the TQM860L board I use for my control module, for example, is `TQM860L_config`. Once you have determined the proper Makefile target to use, configure U-Boot's build process:

```
$ make TQM860L_config
```

Now, build U-Boot:

```
$ make CROSS_COMPILE=powerpc-linux-
```

In addition to generating bootloader images, the build process will compile a few tools to be used on the host for conditioning binary images before downloading them off to the target to a running U-Boot. Table 9-2 lists the files generated during U-Boot's compilation.

Table 9-2. Files generated during U-Boot's compilation

Filename	Description
System.map	The symbol map
u-boot	U-Boot in ELF binary format
u-boot.bin	U-Boot raw binary image that can be written to the boot storage device
u-boot.srec	U-Boot image in Motorola's S-Record format

You can now download the U-Boot image onto your target's boot storage device using the appropriate procedure. If you already have U-Boot, or one its ancestors (PPCBoot or ARMBoot) installed on your target, you can use the installed copy to update U-Boot to a new version, as we shall see in "Updating U-Boot." If you have another bootloader installed, follow the procedures described in that bootloader's documentation for updating bootloaders. Finally, if you have no bootloader whatsoever installed on your target, you need to use a hardware programming device, such as a flash programmer or a BDM debugger, to copy U-Boot to your target.

Whichever method you use to copy the actual bootloader image to your target, make a copy of the relevant bootloader images to your *${PRJROOT}/images* directory. For my control module for example, I copy the images as follows:

```
$ cp System.map ${PRJROOT}/images/u-boot.System.map-0.2.0
$ cp u-boot.bin ${PRJROOT}/images/u-boot.bin-0.2.0
$ cp u-boot.srec ${PRJROOT}/images/u-boot.srec-0.2.0
```

If you intend to debug U-Boot itself, copy the ELF binary also:

```
$ cp u-boot ${PRJROOT}/images/u-boot-0.2.0
```

Finally, install the host tool generated by the U-Boot build:

```
$ cp tools/mkimage ${PREFIX}/bin
```

Booting with U-Boot

Once U-Boot is properly installed on your target, you can boot it while being connected to the target through a serial line and using a terminal emulator to interface with the target. As I said in Chapter 4, not all terminal emulators interact cleanly with all bootloaders. In the case of U-Boot, avoid using *minicom* for file transfers, since problems may occur during such transfers.

Here is a sample boot output for my control module:

```
U-Boot 0.2.0 (Jan 27 2003 - 20:20:21)

CPU:   XPC860xxZPnnD3 at 80 MHz: 4 kB I-Cache 4 kB D-Cache FEC present
Board: TQM860LDB0A3-T80.201
DRAM:  16 MB
FLASH: 8 MB
In:    serial
Out:   serial
Err:   serial
Net:   SCC ETHERNET, FEC ETHERNET
PCMCIA:   No Card found
Hit any key to stop autoboot:  5
```

As you can see, U-Boot prints version information and then provides some detail regarding the hardware it is running on. As soon as it boots, a five second timer starts ticking at the last output line. If you do not press a key during those five seconds, U-Boot boots its default configuration. By pressing a key, you get a prompt:

```
=>
```

One of the first things you probably want to try is obtaining help from U-Boot:

```
=> help
askenv   - get environment variables from stdin
autoscr  - run script from memory
base     - print or set address offset
bdinfo   - print Board Info structure
bootm    - boot application image from memory
bootp    - boot image via network using BootP/TFTP protocol
bootd    - boot default, i.e., run 'bootcmd'
cmp      - memory compare
coninfo  - print console devices and informations
cp       - memory copy
crc32    - checksum calculation
date     - get/set/reset date & time
dhcp     - invoke DHCP client to obtain IP/boot params
diskboot- boot from IDE device
echo     - echo args to console
erase    - erase FLASH memory
flinfo   - print FLASH memory information
go       - start application at address 'addr'
help     - print online help
ide      - IDE sub-system
iminfo   - print header information for application image
loadb    - load binary file over serial line (kermit mode)
loads    - load S-Record file over serial line
loop     - infinite loop on address range
md       - memory display
mm       - memory modify (auto-incrementing)
mtest    - simple RAM test
```

```
mw       - memory write (fill)
nm       - memory modify (constant address)
printenv- print environment variables
protect - enable or disable FLASH write protection
rarpboot- boot image via network using RARP/TFTP protocol
reset    - Perform RESET of the CPU
run      - run commands in an environment variable
saveenv - save environment variables to persistent storage
setenv   - set environment variables
sleep    - delay execution for some time
tftpboot- boot image via network using TFTP protocol
             and env variables ipaddr and serverip
version - print monitor version
?        - alias for 'help'
```

As you can see, U-Boot has a lot of commands. Fortunately, U-Boot also provides per-command help:

```
=> help cp
cp [.b, .w, .l] source target count
   - copy memory
```

When U-Boot appends the [.b, .w, .l] expression to a command, this means that you need to append one of the indicated strings to the command to invoke the desired version of the command. In the case of *cp*, for example, there are three versions, *cp.b*, *cp.w*, and *cp.l*, for copying bytes, words, and longs, respectively.

U-Boot is strict in its argument parsing. It expects most values to be provided in hexadecimal form. In the case of the *cp* command, for example, this means that the source address, the target address, and the byte count must be provided in hexadecimal values. You don't need to prepend or append those values with any sort of special characters, such as "0x" or "h". If your source address is 0x40000000, for example, simply type 40000000.

U-Boot accepts any unique subset of characters that starts a command name. If you want to use the *erase* command, for example, you can type just the first three letters, *era*, since *erase* is the only command to start with those three first letters. On the other hand, you can't type *lo* and expect U-Boot to understand it, since there are three commands that start with those letters: *loadb*, *loads*, and *loop*.

Using U-Boot's Environment Variables

Once U-Boot is up and running, you can configure it by setting the appropriate environment variables. The use of U-Boot environment variables is very similar to the use of environment variables in Unix shells, such as *bash*. To view the current values of the environment variables on your target, use the *printenv* command. Here is a subset of the environment variables found on my control module:

```
=> printenv
bootdelay=5
baudrate=115200
loads_echo=1
```

```
serial#=...
ethaddr=00:D0:93:00:05:E3
netmask=255.255.255.0
ipaddr=192.168.172.10
serverip=192.168.172.50
clocks_in_mhz=1
stdin=serial
stdout=serial
stderr=serial

Environment size: 791/16380 bytes
```

Each environment variable has a different meaning. Some environment variables, such as bootdelay, serial#, or ipaddr, have predetermined uses that are recognized by U-Boot itself. See the *README* file for a complete discussion of U-Boot's environment variables and their meanings.

As with Unix shells, you can add environment variables in U-Boot. To do so, you must use the *setenv* command. Here is an example session where I add a few environment variables to my control module (the third command must be entered as a single line, even though it appears broken on the page):

```
=> setenv rootpath /home/karim/ctrl-rootfs
=> setenv kernel_addr 40100000
=> setenv nfscmd setenv bootargs root=/dev/nfs rw nfsroot=\$(serverip):\$(rootpath)
   ip=\$(ipaddr):\$(serverip):\$(gatewayip):\$(netmask):\$(hostname)::off panic=1\;
   bootm \$(kernel_addr)
=> setenv bootcmd run nfscmd
```

In this case, I set U-Boot to boot from the kernel found at 0x40100000 and to mount its root filesystem using NFS. Notice that I used the \ character to tell U-Boot that the character following \ should not be interpreted as a special character. This is how the nfscmd looks like, for example, after U-Boot has read it:

```
=> printenv nfscmd
nfs2cmd=setenv bootargs root=/dev/nfs rw nfsroot=$(serverip):$(rootpath)
ip=$(ipaddr):$(serverip):$(gatewayip):$(netmask):$(hostname)::off panic=1;bootm
$(kernel_addr)
```

The *setenv* command adds the environment variables to the current session only. Hence, if you reset the system, any environment variable you set only with *setenv* will be lost. For the environment variables to survive reboots, they must be saved to flash. This is done using the *saveenv* command:

```
=> saveenv
Saving Enviroment to Flash...
Un-Protected 1 sectors
Erasing Flash...
. done
Erased 1 sectors
Writing to Flash... done
Protected 1 sectors
```

Be careful when using *saveenv*, since it will save all the environment variables currently defined, even those you may have been using temporarily. Before using *saveenv*, use *printenv* to take a look at the currently defined environment variables to make sure you are saving only the necessary variables. If you want to delete a variable, simply use *setenv* on the variable without providing any values. Here's an example:

```
=> setenv RAMDisk_addr 40500000
=> printenv RAMDisk_addr
RAMDisk_addr=40500000
=> setenv RAMDisk_addr
=> printenv RAMDisk_addr
## Error: "RAMDisk_addr" not defined
```

Note that the = character is not treated as a special character by *setenv*. In fact, it is seen as another character in the string making up the environment variable, as we saw earlier in this section. The following command, for example, is flawed (notice the extra = displayed by *printenv* in comparison to the same *printenv* shown in the previous capture):

```
=> setenv RAMDisk_addr = 40500000
=> printenv RAMDisk_addr
RAMDisk_addr== 40500000
```

Creating Boot Scripts

U-Boot environment variables can be used to create boot scripts. Such boot scripts are actually environment variables containing a set of U-Boot command sequences. By using a combination of the *run* command and the ; (semicolon) operator, you can make U-Boot run boot scripts. The environment variables I set in the previous section, for instance, are actually part of a boot script, nfscmd.

The key to the way the script I provided in the previous section works is the bootcmd environment variable. This variable is recognized by U-Boot as the script to run automatically when the system is booted. I set this variable as run nfscmd. In other words, U-Boot should run the nfscmd script to boot the system. In turn, this environment variable is a set of commands of its own. First, it sets the bootargs environment variable, which U-Boot passes to the kernel as its boot parameters, and then uses the *bootm* command to boot the kernel located at $(kernel_addr). The semicolon separates commands. The use of the $(VAR_NAME) operator tells U-Boot to replace the entire string with the value of the VAR_NAME environment variable. Hence, when nfscmd runs, $(kernel_addr) is replaced by 40100000, which is the value I set earlier. In the same way, $(rootpath) is replaced by /home/karim/ctrl-rootfs, and the rest of the environment variables included in nfscmd are replaced by their respective values.

Though it would have been possible to set bootcmd to contain the entire boot script instead of using run nfscmd, it would have been much harder then to specify alternative boot scripts at the boot command line. By using the *run* command in the bootcmd script, multiple boot scripts can coexist within U-Boot's environment variables. You can then change the system's default boot using:

```
=> setenv bootcmd run OTHER_BOOT_SCRIPT
```

Or you can run boot scripts directly from the command line without changing the value of the bootcmd environment variable:

```
=> run OTHER_BOOT_SCRIPT
```

Scripts are a very useful feature of U-Boot and you should use them whenever you need to automate a certain task in U-Boot.

Preparing Binary Images

Since the raw flash is not structured like a filesystem and does not contain any sort of file headers, binary images downloaded to the target must carry headers for U-Boot to recognize their content and understand how to load them. The *mkimage* utility we installed earlier was packaged with U-Boot for this purpose. It adds the information U-Boot needs to binary images while attaching a checksum for verification purposes.

 While the use of image headers is not a technical requirement for a bootloader, such headers are very convenient both during development and in the field. Hence, their use by U-Boot.

To see the typical use of *mkimage*, type the command without any parameters:

```
$ mkimage
Usage: mkimage -l image
          -l ==> list image header information
       mkimage -A arch -O os -T type -C comp -a addr -e ep -n name
       -d data_file[:data_file...] image
          -A ==> set architecture to 'arch'
          -O ==> set operating system to 'os'
          -T ==> set image type to 'type'
          -C ==> set compression type 'comp'
          -a ==> set load address to 'addr' (hex)
          -e ==> set entry point to 'ep' (hex)
          -n ==> set image name to 'name'
          -d ==> use image data from 'datafile'
          -x ==> set XIP (execute in place)
```

For example here is how I create a U-Boot image of the 2.4.18 kernel I compiled for my control module:

```
$ cd ${PRJROOT}/images
$ mkimage -n '2.4.18 Control Module' \
> -A ppc -O linux -T kernel -C gzip -a 00000000 -e 00000000 \
> -d vmlinux-2.4.18.gz vmlinux-2.4.18.img
Image Name:   2.4.18 Control Module
Created:      Wed Feb  5 14:19:08 2003
Image Type:   PowerPC Linux Kernel Image (gzip compressed)
```

```
Data Size:    530790 Bytes = 518.35 kB = 0.51 MB
Load Address: 0x00000000
Entry Point:  0x00000000
```

The command takes quite a few flags, but their meaning is easily understood by looking at the usage message provided by *mkimage*. Note that the name of the image, provided in the *-n* option, cannot be more than 32 characters. Any excess characters will be ignored by *mkimage*. The rest of the command line tells *mkimage* that this is a gzipped PPC Linux kernel image that should be loaded at address 0x00000000 and started from that same address. The image being provided in input is *vmlinux-2.4.18.gz* and the U-Boot–formatted image will be output to *vmlinux-2.4.18.img*.

RAM disk images can be processed in a similar fashion:

```
$ mkimage -n 'RAM disk' \
> -A ppc -O linux -T ramdisk -C gzip \
> -d initrd.bin initrd.boot
Image Name:   RAM disk
Created:      Wed Feb  5 14:20:35 2003
Image Type:   PowerPC Linux RAMDisk Image (gzip compressed)
Data Size:    470488 Bytes = 459.46 kB = 0.45 MB
Load Address: 0x00000000
Entry Point:  0x00000000
```

In this case, the number of parameters is shorter, since we don't need to specify start and load addresses. Note that the image type has changed to ramdisk.

We can also create a multi-type image that combines both the kernel image and a RAM disk. In that case, the files included are listed sequentially using a colon separator:

```
$ mkimage -n '2.4.18 Ctrl and Initrd' \
> -A ppc -O linux -T multi -C gzip -a 00000000 -e 00000000 \
> -d vmlinux-2.4.18.gz:initrd.bin \
> vmlinux-2.4.18-initrd.img
Image Name:   2.4.18 Ctrl and Initrd
Created:      Wed Feb  5 14:23:29 2003
Image Type:   PowerPC Linux Multi-File Image (gzip compressed)
Data Size:    1001292 Bytes = 977.82 kB = 0.95 MB
Load Address: 0x00000000
Entry Point:  0x00000000
Contents:
   Image 0:    530790 Bytes =  518 kB = 0 MB
   Image 1:    470488 Bytes =  459 kB = 0 MB
```

Once you have prepared an image with *mkimage*, it is ready to be used by U-Boot and can be downloaded to the target. As we'll see below, U-Boot can receive binary images in a number of different ways. One way is to use images formatted in Motorola's S-Record format. If you intend to use this format, you need to further process the images generated by *mkimage* by converting them to the S-Record format. Here is an example conversion of the multi-type image generated above:

```
$ powerpc-linux-objcopy -I binary -O srec \
> vmlinux-2.4.18-initrd.img vmlinux-2.4.18-initrd.srec
```

Booting Using BOOTP/DHCP, TFTP, and NFS

If you have properly configured a server to provide the target with DHCP, TFTP, and NFS services, as I explained earlier, you can boot your target remotely. Back from U-Boot's prompt on my control module, here is how I boot my target remotely, for example:

```
=> bootp
BOOTP broadcast 1
DHCP client bound to address 192.168.172.10
ARP broadcast 1
TFTP from server 192.168.172.50; our IP address is 192.168.172.10
Filename '/home/karim/vmlinux-2.4.18.img'.
Load address: 0x100000
Loading: ################################################ ...
done
Bytes transferred = 530854 (819a6 hex)
```

The *bootp* command issues a request that is answered by the DHCP server. Using the DHCP server's answer, U-Boot contacts the TFTP server and obtains the *vmlinux-2.4.18.img* image file, which it places at address 0x00100000 in RAM. You can verify the image's header information using the *iminfo* command:

```
=> imi 00100000

## Checking Image at 00100000 ...
   Image Name:    2.4.18 Control Module
   Created:       2003-02-05  19:19:08 UTC
   Image Type:    PowerPC Linux Kernel Image (gzip compressed)
   Data Size:     530790 Bytes = 518.3 kB
   Load Address: 00000000
   Entry Point:  00000000
   Verifying Checksum ... OK
```

As you can see, the information printed out by *iminfo* on the target is very similar to that printed out on the host by *mkinfo*. The OK string reported for the checksum means that the image has been downloaded properly and that we can boot it:

```
=> bootm 00100000
## Booting image at 00100000 ...
   Image Name:    2.4.18 Control Module
   Created:       2003-02-05  19:19:08 UTC
   Image Type:    PowerPC Linux Kernel Image (gzip compressed)
   Data Size:     530790 Bytes = 518.3 kB
   Load Address: 00000000
   Entry Point:  00000000
   Verifying Checksum ... OK
   Uncompressing Kernel Image ... OK
Linux version 2.4.18 (karim@Teotihuacan) (gcc version 2.95.3 20010315 ...
On node 0 totalpages: 4096
```

```
zone(0): 4096 pages.
zone(1): 0 pages.
zone(2): 0 pages.
Kernel command line: root=/dev/nfs rw nfsroot= ...
Decrementer Frequency: 5000000
Calibrating delay loop... 79.66 BogoMIPS
...
VFS: Cannot open root device "" or 02:00
Please append a correct "root=" boot option
Kernel panic: VFS: Unable to mount root fs on 02:00
  <0>Rebooting in 180 seconds..
```

In this case, the kernel panics because it is unable to find any root filesystem. To solve this problem, we must use the environment variables to create a boot script for passing appropriate boot options to the kernel. The following commands create a new boot script, bootpnfs, and modify the special bootcmd script, as we did in "Using U-Boot's Environment Variables," in order for the system to boot using BOOTP/ DHCP, TFTP, and NFS:

```
=> setenv bootpnfs bootp\; setenv kernel_addr 00100000\; run nfscmd
=> printenv bootpnfs
bootpnfs=bootp; setenv kernel_addr 00100000; run nfscmd
=> setenv bootcmd run bootpnfs
=> printenv bootcmd
bootcmd=run bootpnfs
```

In this case, the bootpnfs script automatically executes the *bootp* instruction we used earlier in this section to obtain a kernel from the TFTP server. It then uses the nfscmd script we created in "Using U-Boot's Environment Variables" to boot this kernel. The value of kernel_addr is changed so that the nfscmd script would use the kernel loaded using TFTP, not the one located at 40100000.

If you use the *boot* command now, U-Boot will boot entirely from the network. It will download the kernel through TFTP and mount its root filesystem on NFS. If you would like to save the environment variables we just set, use the *saveenv* command before rebooting the system, otherwise, you will have set the same variables again at the next reboot.

Downloading Binary Images to Flash

Booting from the network is fine for early development and testing. For production use, the target must have its kernel stored in flash. As we will see shortly, there are a few ways to copy a kernel from the host to the target and store it to flash. Before you can copy any kernel image, however, you must first choose a flash region to store it and erase the flash region for the incoming kernel. In the case of my control module, I store the default kernel between 0x40100000 and 0x401FFFFF. Hence, from U-Boot's prompt, I erase this region:

```
=> erase 40100000 401FFFFF
Erase Flash from 0x40100000 to 0x401fffff
```

```
........ done
Erased 8 sectors
```

The simplest way to install a kernel in the target's flash is to first download it into RAM and then copy it to the flash. You can use the *tftpboot* command to download a kernel from the host to RAM:

```
=> tftpboot 00100000 /home/karim/vmlinux-2.4.18.img
ARP broadcast 1
TFTP from server 192.168.172.50; our IP address is 192.168.172.10
Filename '/home/karim/vmlinux-2.4.18.img'.
Load address: 0x100000
Loading: ################################################## ...
done
Bytes transferred = 530854 (819a6 hex)
```

When *tftpboot* is run, it adds the `filesize` environment variable to the existing environment variables and sets it to the size of the file downloaded:

```
=> printenv filesize
filesize=819a6
```

You can use this environment variable in subsequent commands to avoid typing in the file size by hand. Don't forget to erase this environment variable before saving the environment variables, or it, too, will be saved.

In addition to *tftpboot*, you can use the *loadb* command to download images to the target:

```
=> loadb 00100000
## Ready for binary (kermit) download ...
```

At this point, U-Boot suspends and you must use the terminal emulator on the host to send the image file to the target. In this case, U-Boot expects to download the data according to the kermit binary protocol, and you must therefore use *kermit* to download a binary image to U-Boot. Once the transfer is done, U-Boot will output:

```
## Total Size      = 0x000819a6 = 530854 Bytes
## Start Addr      = 0x00100000
```

Here, too, U-Boot will set the `filesize` environment variable to the size of the file downloaded. As we did earlier, you may want to use the *iminfo* command to verify that the image has been properly downloaded.

Once the image is in RAM, you can copy it to flash:

```
=> cp.b 00100000 40100000 $(filesize)
Copy to Flash... done
=> imi 40100000

## Checking Image at 40100000 ...
   Image Name:   2.4.18 Control Module
   Created:      2003-02-05  19:19:08 UTC
```

```
Image Type:    PowerPC Linux Kernel Image (gzip compressed)
Data Size:     530790 Bytes = 518.3 kB
Load Address: 00000000
Entry Point:  00000000
Verifying Checksum ... OK
```

Alternatively, instead of downloading the image to RAM first using *tfptboot* or *loadb* and then writing it to flash, you can download the image directly to flash using *loads*. In this case, the host sends the image to the target in S-Record format. In comparison to the two previous methods, however, downloading an S-Record file is extremely slow. In most cases, it is preferable to use *tftpboot* or *loadb* instead.*

To download S-Record files, you will need to use the *cu* terminal emulator to transfer them to the target, because the other terminal emulators don't interact properly with U-Boot when downloading this sort of file. When connected through *cu*, use the following commands:

```
=> loads 40100000
## Ready for S-Record download ...
~>vmlinux-2.4.18.srec
1 2 3 4 5 6 7 8 9 10 11 12 13 14 ...
...
...176 33177 33178 33179 33180 33181
[file transfer complete]
[connected]

## First Load Addr = 0x40100000
## Last  Load Addr = 0x401819A5
## Total Size      = 0x000819A6 = 530854 Bytes
## Start Addr      = 0x00000000
```

The ~> string shown here is actually part of the input you have to type. It is actually the *cu* command used to initiate a file download.

As before, you can verify the image once it's in memory:

```
=> iml 40100000

## Checking Image at 40100000 ...
   Image Name:   2.4.18 Control Module
   Created:      2003-02-05  19:19:08 UTC
   Image Type:   PowerPC Linux Kernel Image (gzip compressed)
   Data Size:    530790 Bytes = 518.3 kB
   Load Address: 00000000
   Entry Point:  00000000
   Verifying Checksum ... OK
```

Every time you want to load a new image to flash, you have to start back at the *erase* command shown in the beginning of this section.

---

*The *loadb* command and, by default, the *tftpboot* command can't be used to download directly to flash. Though U-Boot can be configured at compile time to allow direct flash download using *tftpboot*, direct flash download using *loadb* is not supported.

Booting Using a RAM Disk

The first step in booting from a RAM disk is to download the RAM disk from the host and install it on the target's flash. Many of the commands are the same as those shown and explained in previous sections. Here is how I do this for my control module:

```
=> tftpboot 00100000 /home/karim/initrd.boot
ARP broadcast 1
TFTP from server 192.168.172.50; our IP address is 192.168.172.10
Filename '/home/karim/initrd.boot'.
Load address: 0x100000
Loading: ################################################# ...
done
Bytes transferred = 470552 (72e18 hex)
=> imi 00100000

## Checking Image at 00100000 ...
   Image Name:    RAM disk
   Created:       2003-02-05   19:20:35 UTC
   Image Type:    PowerPC Linux RAMDisk Image (gzip compressed)
   Data Size:     470488 Bytes = 459.5 kB
   Load Address: 00000000
   Entry Point:  00000000
   Verifying Checksum ... OK
=> printenv filesize
filesize=72e18
=> imi 40200000

## Checking Image at 40200000 ...
   Bad Magic Number
=> erase 40200000 402FFFFF
Erase Flash from 0x40200000 to 0x402fffff
........ done
Erased 8 sectors
=> cp.b 00100000 40200000 $(filesize)
Copy to Flash... done
=> imi 40200000

## Checking Image at 40200000 ...
   Image Name:    RAM disk
   Created:       2003-02-05   19:20:35 UTC
   Image Type:    PowerPC Linux RAMDisk Image (gzip compressed)
   Data Size:     470488 Bytes = 459.5 kB
   Load Address: 00000000
   Entry Point:  00000000
   Verifying Checksum ... OK
```

Since I had already installed a kernel, I can boot the kernel available in flash with the RAM disk I just installed:

```
=> bootm 40100000 40200000
## Booting image at 40100000 ...
```

```
   Image Name:    2.4.18 Control Module
   Created:       2003-02-05   19:19:08 UTC
   Image Type:    PowerPC Linux Kernel Image (gzip compressed)
   Data Size:     530790 Bytes = 518.3 kB
   Load Address: 00000000
   Entry Point:  00000000
   Verifying Checksum ... OK
   Uncompressing Kernel Image ... OK
## Loading RAMDisk Image at 40200000 ...
   Image Name:    RAM disk
   Created:       2003-02-05   19:20:35 UTC
   Image Type:    PowerPC Linux RAMDisk Image (gzip compressed)
   Data Size:     470488 Bytes = 459.5 kB
   Load Address: 00000000
   Entry Point:  00000000
   Verifying Checksum ... OK
   Loading Ramdisk to 00f2c000, end 00f9edd8 ... OK
Linux version 2.4.18 (karim@Teotihuacan) (gcc version 2.95.3 20010 ...
On node 0 totalpages: 4096
zone(0): 4096 pages.
zone(1): 0 pages.
zone(2): 0 pages.
Kernel command line:
Decrementer Frequency: 5000000
Calibrating delay loop... 79.66 BogoMIPS
...
RAMDISK driver initialized: 16 RAM disks of 4096K size 1024 blocksize
...
RAMDISK: Compressed image found at block 0
...
VFS: Mounted root (ext2 filesystem).
...
```

Here, too, we can use environment variables to automate the booting process. Also, instead of using separate images for the kernel and the RAM disk, we could use a single image containing both, such as the one we created in the section "Preparing Binary Images." As I said earlier, U-Boot is a very flexible bootloader with many possible configurations. Though we cannot hope to cover all its possibilities here, feel free to experiment with U-Boot to obtain the setup that suits you best.

Booting from CompactFlash Devices

Before booting a kernel from a CF card using U-Boot, you need to properly partition and populate the CF card. Use *pdisk* or *fdisk* to partition the CF device, depending on your host. Since U-Boot does not recognize any disk filesystem, you will need to create a few small partitions to hold raw binary images and one large partition to hold your root filesystem, as I explained in Chapter 7.

For my control module, for example, I used a 32 MB CF card on which I created three partitions using *fdisk*: two 2 MB partitions to hold one stable kernel and one experimental kernel, and one 28 MB partition to hold my root filesystem. To copy the kernels to their respective partitions, I used the *dd* command:

```
# dd if=vmlinux-2.4.18.img of=/dev/sda1
1036+1 records in
1036+1 records out
# dd if=vmlinux-2.4.18-preempt.img of=/dev/sda2
1040+1 records in
1040+1 records out
```

I formatted */dev/sda3* using *mke2fs*, mounted it on */mnt/cf*, and copied the root filesystem to it using the techniques described in the previous chapter.

After I inserted the CF card in the PCMCIA port using a CF-to-PCMCIA adapter, here was the output of U-Boot at startup:

```
U-Boot 0.2.0 (Jan 27 2003 - 20:20:21)

CPU:   XPC860xxZPnnD3 at 80 MHz: 4 kB I-Cache 4 kB D-Cache FEC present
Board: TQM860LDB0A3-T80.201
DRAM:  16 MB
FLASH:  8 MB
In:    serial
Out:   serial
Err:   serial
Net:   SCC ETHERNET, FEC ETHERNET
PCMCIA: 3.3V card found: SunDisk SDP 5/3 0.6
            Fixed Disk Card
            IDE interface
            [silicon] [unique] [single] [sleep] [standby] [idle] [low power]
Bus 0: OK
  Device 0: Model: SanDisk SDCFB-32 Firm: vde 1.10 Ser#: 163194D0310
            Type: Removable Hard Disk
            Capacity: 30.6 MB = 0.0 GB (62720 x 512)
Hit any key to stop autoboot:  5
```

U-Boot identifies the storage device at startup. U-Boot provides a wide range of *ide* commands for manipulating IDE storage devices. You can see these commands by typing the *help* command:

```
=> help ide
ide reset - reset IDE controller
ide info  - show available IDE devices
ide device [dev] - show or set current device
ide part [dev] - print partition table of one or all IDE devices
ide read  addr blk# cnt
ide write addr blk# cnt - read/write `cnt' blocks starting at block `blk#'
    to/from memory address `addr'
```

We can further use U-Boot's command line to get more information regarding the device:

```
=> ide part

Partition Map for IDE device 0  --   Partition Type: DOS
```

```
Partition    Start Sector    Num Sectors    Type
    1                   62           4154      83
    2                 4216           4154      83
    3                 8370          54312      83
```

This command reads the partition table of the CF device and prints it out. In this case, the partition printed out by U-Boot fits the description provided earlier.

Loading a kernel image from one of the partitions on the CF device is done using the *diskboot* command. This command takes two arguments: the address where the kernel is to be loaded and a partition identifier. The latter is a concatenation of the device number and the partition number on that device separated by a colon. This is how I load the kernel image found on partition 1 of device 0 to address 0x00400000:

```
=> diskboot 00400000 0:1

Loading from IDE device 0, partition 1: Name: hda1
  Type: U-Boot
   Image Name:   2.4.18 Control Module
   Created:      2003-02-05  19:19:08 UTC
   Image Type:   PowerPC Linux Kernel Image (gzip compressed)
   Data Size:    530790 Bytes = 518.3 kB
   Load Address: 00000000
   Entry Point:  00000000
=> imi 00400000

## Checking Image at 00400000 ...
   Image Name:   2.4.18 Control Module
   Created:      2003-02-05  19:19:08 UTC
   Image Type:   PowerPC Linux Kernel Image (gzip compressed)
   Data Size:    530790 Bytes = 518.3 kB
   Load Address: 00000000
   Entry Point:  00000000
   Verifying Checksum ... OK
```

Once the kernel is loaded, you can use the *bootm* command to boot that kernel. This can also be automated by setting the autostart environment variable to yes. In that case, *diskboot* will automatically boot the kernel it loads:

```
=> setenv autostart yes
=> disk 00400000 0:1

Loading from IDE device 0, partition 1: Name: hda1
  Type: U-Boot
   Image Name:   2.4.18 Control Module
   Created:      2003-02-05  19:19:08 UTC
   Image Type:   PowerPC Linux Kernel Image (gzip compressed)
   Data Size:    530790 Bytes = 518.3 kB
   Load Address: 00000000
   Entry Point:  00000000
Automatic boot of image at addr 0x00400000 ...
## Booting image at 00400000 ...
   Image Name:   2.4.18 Control Module
   Created:      2003-02-05  19:19:08 UTC
```

```
Image Type:    PowerPC Linux Kernel Image (gzip compressed)
Data Size:     530790 Bytes = 518.3 kB
Load Address: 00000000
Entry Point:  00000000
Verifying Checksum ... OK
Uncompressing Kernel Image ... OK
Linux version 2.4.18 (karim@Teotihuacan) (gcc version 2.95.3 ...
On node 0 totalpages: 4096
...
```

As we did in "Using U-Boot's Environment Variables" and "Booting Using BOOTP/
DHCP, TFTP, and NFS," you can script the bootup from the CF device by setting
the appropriate U-Boot environment variables. Also, if you wish, you can write to the
disk directly from U-Boot using the *ide write* command. Have a look at the *help* output and the documentation for more information regarding the use of U-Boot's IDE
capabilities.

Updating U-Boot

U-Boot is like any other open source project; it continues to evolve over time as contributions are made and bug fixes are integrated to the codebase. Consequently, you
may feel the need to update your target's firmware version. Fortunately, because U-
Boot runs from RAM, it can be used to update itself. Essentially, we have to download a new version to the target, erase the old firmware version, and copy the new
version over it.

 There are obvious dangers to this operation, because a mistake or a
power failure will render the target unbootable. Hence, utmost caution must be used when carrying out the following steps. Make sure
you have a copy of the original bootloader you are about to replace so
that you can at least fall back to a known working version. Also, seriously consider avoiding the replacement of your firmware if you have
no hardware means to reprogram the target's flash if the upgrade fails.
If you do not have access to a BDM debugger or a flash programmer,
for example, there is a great risk that you will be left with a broken system if one of the following steps fails. Dealing with buggy software is
one thing; ending up with unusable hardware is another.

Once you have taken the necessary precautions, download the U-Boot image into
RAM using TFTP:

```
=> tftp 00100000 /home/karim/u-boot.bin-0.2.0
ARP broadcast 1
TFTP from server 192.168.172.50; our IP address is 192.168.172.10
Filename '/home/karim/u-boot.bin-0.2.0'.
Load address: 0x100000
Loading: #################################
done
Bytes transferred = 166532 (28a84 hex)
```

If you do not have a TFTP server set up, you can also use the terminal emulator to send the image:

```
=> loadb 00100000
## Ready for binary (kermit) download ...

## Start Addr      = 0x00100000
```

Unlike other images we have downloaded to the target, you cannot use the *imi* command to check the image, since the U-Boot image downloaded was not packaged on the host using the *mkimage* command. You can, however, use *crc32* before and after copying the image to flash to verify proper copying.

Now, unprotect the flash region where U-Boot is located so you can erase it (in this case, U-Boot occupies the flash region from 0x40000000 to 0x4003FFFF):

```
=> protect off 40000000 4003FFFF
Un-Protected 5 sectors
```

Erase the previous bootloader image:

```
=> erase 40000000 4003FFFF
Erase Flash from 0x40000000 to 0x4003ffff
... done
Erased 5 sectors
```

Copy the new bootloader to its final destination:

```
=> cp.b 00100000 40000000 $(filesize)
Copy to Flash... done
```

Erase the `filesize` environment variable set during the download:

```
=> setenv filesize
```

Save the environment variables:

```
=> saveenv
Saving Enviroment to Flash
Un-Protected 1 sectors
Erasing Flash...
. done
Erased 1 sectors
Writing to Flash... done
Protected 1 sectors
```

At this stage, the new bootloader image has been installed and is ready to be used. Until you issue the *reset* command, however, you can still use the old U-Boot currently running to fix any problems that may have occurred during the update. Once you are satisfied that every step of the update has gone through cleanly, you can go ahead and restart the system:

```
=> reset


U-Boot 0.2.0 (Jan 27 2003 - 20:20:21)
```

```
CPU:    XPC860xxZPnnD3 at 80 MHz: 4 kB I-Cache 4 kB D-Cache FEC present
Board:  TQM860LDB0A3-T80.201
DRAM:   16 MB
FLASH:   8 MB
In:     serial
Out:    serial
Err:    serial
Net:    SCC ETHERNET, FEC ETHERNET
PCMCIA:   No Card found
Hit any key to stop autoboot: 5
```

If you can see the U-Boot boot message again, U-Boot has been successfully updated. Otherwise, there has been a problem with the replacement of the firmware and you need to reprogram the flash device using the appropriate hardware tools.

Sometimes, kernel images that used to boot with the older bootloader version will fail to boot with newer versions. When upgrading from a PPCBoot version prior to 1.0.5 to Version 1.0.5 or later, for example, kernels prior to 2.4.5-pre5 may fail to boot. In that case, the reason behind the problem is in the way U-Boot passes the clock speed to the kernel. Prior to kernel 2.4.5-pre5, kernels expected to receive the speed in MHz, while later kernels expect to receive the speed in Hz. To this end, PPCBoot 1.0.5 passes the clock speed to kernels in Hz. Kernels that expect to receive it in MHz, however, fail to boot. In practice, the boot process will start as it would normally, but the system will freeze right after U-Boot finishes uncompressing the images for startup. You will, therefore, see something like:

```
...
Entry Point:  00000000
Verifying Checksum ... OK
Uncompressing Kernel Image ... OK
```

Nothing will be output after that, and there will be no responses to any input from the terminal. To solve the problem, you need to tell the newer version of U-Boot to keep passing the clock speed in MHz to the older kernels. This is done by setting the clocks_in_mhz environment variable to 1:

```
=> setenv clocks_in_mhz 1
=> saveenv
```

Though this sort of problem does not occur for every upgrade, changes in the kernel sometimes require significant changes to the tools that interface with it. Given that such problems are difficult to figure out if you are not involved in the actual development of each project, I strongly encourage you to keep in touch with the rest of the U-Boot users by subscribing to the U-Boot users mailing list from the project's web site and to read announcements of new versions carefully.

## CHAPTER 10

Setting Up Networking Services

Increasingly, embedded system designers are called upon to include networking capabilities in their products. An embedded system may, for example, include a web server to enable web-based configuration. It may also enable remote login for maintenance and upgrading purposes. Because the Linux kernel, and the networking software that run on it, are often the preferred software for running networking services that require high reliability and high availability, you will find Linux particularly well suited for networking applications.

In this chapter, we will discuss the setup and configuration of the networking services most commonly found in embedded Linux systems. This discussion will include instructions on how to cross-compile each networking package and how to modify the target's root filesystem to run the services provided by each package. In particular, I will cover the use of the internet super-server (*inetd*), remote administration with SNMP, network login through Telnet, secure communications with SSH, serving web content through HTTP, and dynamic configuration through DHCP.

There are, of course, many other networking services that can run on top of Linux. Though I couldn't realistically cover all of them in a single chapter, the explanations included here should provide you with some hints as to how to install and use other networking packages. Also, I will not cover the setup, configuration, and use of actual networking hardware. If you need information regarding these issues, have a look at *Running Linux* and *Linux Network Administrator's Guide*, both published by O'Reilly. I will not provide in-depth coverage, either, of the configuration and use of the various networking packages, since many already have entire books dedicated to them. For more information regarding Linux networking in general, look at books such as the ones mentioned earlier that discuss the issue from the perspective of a server or a workstation.

This chapter builds on the material presented in Chapter 6. The operations presented here are done as part of building the target's root filesystem described in Chapter 6. Though these operations are supplemental, we discuss them here because they are not essential to the creation of the target's root filesystem.

The Internet Super-Server

As in most other Unix systems, networking services are implemented as daemons in Linux. Each networking daemon responds to requests on a particular port. The Telnet service, for example, operates on port 23. For networking services to function properly, some process must be alive and listening on each corresponding port. Instead of starting all the networking daemons so that each would listen to its own port, however, most systems make use of an internet "super-server." This super-server is a special daemon that listens to the ports of all the enabled networking services. When a request comes in from a particular port, the corresponding networking daemon is started, and the request is passed on to it for service.

There are two main benefits to this scheme. First, only the minimal set of needed daemons is active at all times, and therefore, no system resources are wasted. Second, there is a centralized mechanism for managing and monitoring network services.

Though many networking services can be managed by the internet super-server, some services such as an HTTP server or an SNMP agent are almost always set up to have direct control of their ports for reasons of scalability and reliability. In fact, the daemons providing such services will not require an internet super-server to operate properly. For each networking service discussed in the following sections, we will consider whether the service depends on the super-server.

There are two main internet super-servers available for Linux, *inetd* and *xinetd*. Though *inetd* used to be the standard super-server for most Linux distributions, it is gradually being replaced by *xinetd*, which contains more features. But because *inetd* contains fewer features than *xinetd*, it is also smaller and may be better for an embedded Linux system.

inetd

inetd is part of one of the netkit packages available from *ftp://ftp.uk.linux.org/pub/linux/Networking/netkit/*. Netkit is a set of packages that provide various networking capabilities. *inetd* is part of the netkit-base package, which also contains *ping*. Like other netkit packages, netkit-base is distributed under the terms of a BSD license. In this section and throughout this chapter, I will use an ARM-based system as my system management (SYSM) module[*] to present the operations you need to carry out.

First, download netkit-base and extract it into your *${PRJROOT}/sysapps* directory. For my SYSM module, I used netkit-base Version 0.17. Now, move to the directory where netkit-base was extracted:

```
$ cd ${PRJROOT}/sysapps/netkit-base-0.17
```

---

[*] See "Example Multicomponent System" in Chapter 1 for details about the components in my example system.

Before you begin configuring netkit-base, you need to modify the *configure* script to prevent it from trying to run test programs on your host. Because you are instructing it to use the compiler you built for the target, the test programs it compiles will be fit only for your target. Hence, these test programs will fail to run on the host, and the *configure* script fails to complete if it is not modified. To avoid these problems, edit the *configure* script and comment all the lines that attempt to execute the compiled binary by adding a # symbol at the beginning of each line. The actual test programs *configure* tries to run are all called *__conftest*. Here is an example commented line:

```
# ./__conftest || exit 1;
```

To build, *inetd* requires either glibc or uClibc. To link it against uClibc, however, you need to make sure that RPC support was enabled in uClibc. If uClibc was built with RPC disabled, which is the default, you must reinstall uClibc.

Once the *configure* script has been properly edited, configure and compile netkit-base:

```
$ CC=arm-linux-gcc ./configure --prefix=${TARGET_PREFIX}
$ make
```

Netkit-base builds quite rapidly. The binary generated is 24 KB in size when linked dynamically with glibc and stripped. When linked statically with glibc and stripped, the size of the binary is around 460 KB. With uClibc, the stripped binary is 24 KB when linked dynamically and 85 KB when linked statically. Regardless of the actual link method you choose, the resulting *inetd* binary is much smaller than the *xinetd* binary, as we shall see in the next section.

> The file sizes provided throughout this chapter correspond to my own setup and you are likely to obtain slightly different sizes. Use the numbers provided here as an indication only, because your actual binaries are likely to have different sizes from mine. ARM code, for instance, and RISC code in general, is usually larger than x86 code.

In contrast with other packages we've built in other chapters, don't use *make install*, because the Makefiles were not properly built for cross-platform development. Among other things, they attempt to use the host's *strip* command to strip the binaries of their symbol tables.

To install *inetd*, copy the *inetd* binary and the sample configuration file manually to your target's root filesystem:

```
$ cp inetd/inetd ${PRJROOT}/rootfs/usr/sbin
$ cp etc.sample/inetd.conf ${PRJROOT}/rootfs/etc
```

Edit the *inetd.conf* file according to your own setup. In addition to *inetd.conf*, the *etc.sample* directory contains other file samples that may be used in your target's */etc* directory, such as *resolv.conf* and *services*. For my SYSM module, for example, here's the *inetd.conf* entry for the Telnet daemon discussed in "Network Login Through Telnet":

```
telnet   stream  tcp     nowait  root     /usr/sbin/telnetd
```

Once *inetd* is copied and configured, edit your target's */etc/inittab* file to add a line for *inetd*. Here is an example line for my SYSM module that uses BusyBox's *init*:

```
::respawn:/usr/sbin/inetd -i
```

The *-i* option instructs *inetd* not to start as a daemon. Hence, *init* can respawn *inetd* if it dies for some unexpected reason.[*]

Because netkit-base also includes *ping*, you will find a *ping* binary in the *ping* directory. You don't need to use this binary if you are already using BusyBox, however, since BusyBox includes a *ping* command.

For more information regarding the use of *inetd*, have a look at the man pages included in the netkit-base package under the *inetd* directory.

xinetd

xinetd is preferable to *inetd* on some systems, because it allows some secure authorization, provides extensive logging abilities, and can prevent denial-of-access attacks, among other things. Though the FAQ available from the *xinetd* project web site contains a complete list of advantages over *inetd*, suffice it to say that you should use the *xinetd* super-server if your embedded system is designed to provide extensive networking services or live in a hostile networking environment such as the Internet.

xinetd is distributed at *http://www.xinetd.org/* under a BSD-like license. For my SYSM module, I used *xinetd* Version 2.3.9. Download and extract the *xinetd* package into your *${PRJROOT}/sysapps* directory, and move into the package's directory for the rest of the manipulations:

```
$ cd ${PRJROOT}/sysapps/xinetd-2.3.9
```

As with *inetd*, *xinetd* can't be compiled with uClibc if it lacks certain features. In particular, *xinetd* will fail to build with uClibc if it doesn't support RPC and C99. In addition to the C library, *xinetd* depends on the math library (libm) and the cryptography library (libcrypt).

Configure, compile, and install *xinetd*:

```
$ CC=arm-linux-gcc ./configure --host=$TARGET --prefix=${TARGET_PREFIX}
$ make
$ make install
```

xinetd builds quite rapidly. The stripped dynamically linked binary itself is quite large, being 130 KB in size with either uClibc or glibc. When statically linked and

---

[*] The super-server is not normally subject to crashing. The reliance on *init* is therefore just an extra precaution.

stripped, the binary's size is 615 KB with glibc and 210 KB with uClibc. The *xinetd* package installs its components in the *${TARGET_PREFIX}* directory. The build also installs manpages. The *xinetd* binary itself is installed in *${TARGET_PREFIX}*. Copy it from that directory to your target's root filesystem and strip it:

```
$ cp ${TARGET_PREFIX}/sbin/xinetd ${PRJROOT}/rootfs/usr/sbin
$ arm-linux-strip ${PRJROOT}/rootfs/usr/sbin/xinetd
```

A sample configuration file is provided with *xinetd*, *xinetd/sample.conf*. Use this sample as the basis for configuring your target. Copy it to your target's root filesystem and edit it according to your needs:

```
$ cp xinetd/sample.conf ${PRJROOT}/rootfs/etc/xinetd.conf
```

Here is the entry in my SYSM module's *xinetd.conf* for the Telnet daemon discussed in "Network Login Through Telnet":

```
service telnet
{
        socket_type             = stream
        wait                    = no
        user                    = root
        server                  = /usr/sbin/telnetd
        bind                    = 127.0.0.1
        log_on_failure          += USERID
}
```

Finally, edit your target's */etc/inittab* file to add a line for *xinetd*. As for *inetd*, I had to add a line for *xinetd* in my SYSM module's *inittab*:

```
::once:/usr/sbin/xinetd
```

Unlike *inetd*, *xinetd* can be started only as a daemon. Therefore, it cannot be respawned by *init* if it dies.

For more information regarding the use and configuration of *xinetd*, look at the manpages included in the *xinetd* directory of the *xinetd* package. The project's web site also includes an FAQ and a mailing list.

Remote Administration with SNMP

The *Simple Network Management Protocol* (SNMP) allows the remote management of devices on TCP/IP networks. Though networking equipment, such as routers and switches, is the most likely to be SNMP-enabled, almost any device that connects to a TCP/IP network can be equipped with an SNMP *agent*.* An SNMP agent allows you to monitor the target remotely and automatically. In other words, you don't need to have an operator stand by the system and make sure it's still alive and watch over its current performance. The SNMP agent allows you to automatically query the

---

* Basically, an agent is the SNMP software component that runs in the networked device to enable it to be managed remotely.

device for its status using an SNMP *manager*[*] application running on a separate system. The agent running in your target can also be configured to send SNMP *traps* to the SNMP manager to inform it of software or hardware failure. If your target is part of a complex network or if you need to be able to constantly monitor its status remotely, you should think about including an SNMP agent in it.

There are quite a few SNMP agents and packages that enable interaction with SNMP-enabled devices, many of them are quite expensive. In the open source world, Net-SNMP is the standard package for building and managing SNMP-enabled systems. Net-SNMP is distributed at *http://net-snmp.sourceforge.net/* under a composite license that is similar to the BSD license.[†]

The Net-SNMP package is relatively large and contains many software components. For most targets, however, we will be interested only in the SNMP agent, since this is the software component that will allow our device to be remotely managed. Start by downloading and extracting the Net-SNMP package to your *${PRJROOT}/sysapps* directory. For my SYSM module, for example, I used Net-SNMP Version 5.0.6. Now, move to the package's directory for the rest of the manipulations:

```
$ cd ${PRJROOT}/sysapps/net-snmp-5.0.6
```

The Net-SNMP package can be compiled with both uClibc and glibc. There are a few requirements when using uClibc, however, as we'll see. In addition to the C library, Net-SNMP depends on the shared object dynamic loading library (libdl) and the math library (libm).

To configure Net-SNMP for building with glibc enter:

```
$ CC=arm-linux-gcc ./configure --host=$TARGET --with-endianness=little
```

To link Net-SNMP against uClibc, uClibc must be configured with IPv6 support. If it isn't, you can add the *--disable-ipv6* option to Net-SNMP's configuration command line to disable IPv6 support within Net-SNMP. Also, you will need to fix the *agent/mibgroup/ucd-snmp/disk.c* file so that it compiles properly with uClibc. Edit the file and look for the following declaration:

```
#if HAVE_FSTAB_H
        endfsent( );
#endif
```

Replace that declaration with the following one:

```
#if !defined HAVE_GETMNTENT && defined HAVE_FSTAB_H
        endfsent( );
#endif
```

Finally, issue the *configure* command using *arm-uclibc-gcc* instead of *arm-linux-gcc*.

---

[*] A manager is an SNMP software component that runs on a normal workstation or server and that is responsible for monitoring remote systems running SNMP agents.

[†] See the *COPYING* file in the Net-SNMP package for the complete details about the license.

Note that we avoid using the *--prefix* option when configuring Net-SNMP. If we used it, the resulting SNMP agent would always look for its files in the directory provided in the option. Instead, we want the SNMP agent to take its configuration from the default */usr/local/share/snmp* directory. To control the directory where the SNMP components are installed, we will set the values of prefix and exec_prefix when issuing the *make install* command.

During its execution, the configuration script will prompt you for certain information regarding the functionality of the SNMP agent, including the SNMP version to use, the contact information for the device, and the system's location. The instructions provided by the configuration script are usually sufficient to understand the purpose of the information requested. If you need more information regarding the configuration process of the Net-SNMP agent, look at the *Essential SNMP* book by Douglas Mauro and Kevin Schmidt (O'Reilly).

Once the configuration script has completed, build and install the Net-SNMP components:

```
$ make
$ make prefix=${TARGET_PREFIX} exec_prefix=${TARGET_PREFIX} install
```

The values we provide for the prefix and exec_prefix variables determine the main directory where the Net-SNMP components are installed. By avoiding the use of the *--prefix* option during the configuration earlier and by setting the prefix and exec_prefix variables here, we ensure that the SNMP agent runs from the target's */usr/local/share/snmp* directory even though its components are initially installed in the *${TARGET_PREFIX}* directory on the host. If you forget to set exec_prefix, the installation will fail, because the scripts will try to install components into your host's */usr* directory.

The SNMP agent built by Net-SNMP is a very large binary. If you compile it against glibc and strip it, it will measure 650 KB when linked dynamically and 1.1 MB when linked statically. If you compile it against uClibc and strip it, it will measure 625 KB when linked dynamically and 680 KB when linked statically. Because the figures for the unstripped binaries all exceed 1.7 MB, I strongly encourage you to strip the agent binary.

The complete build and installation will take around 10 minutes, depending on your hardware, because Net-SNMP is quite a large package. In addition to copying binaries, the installation copies manpages and headers into the *${TARGET_PREFIX}* directory. The SNMP daemon (*snmpd*), which is the actual SNMP agent, is installed in *${TARGET_PREFIX}/sbin*. The other SNMP utilities, such as *snmpget*, are installed in *${TARGET_PREFIX}/bin*. The SNMP trap daemon is also installed in *${TARGET_PREFIX}/sbin* (this daemon is used to monitor incoming traps). The MIB information required by the SNMP daemon is installed in *${TARGET_PREFIX}/share/snmp*.

With all the Net-SNMP components installed in your development workspace on the host, copy the SNMP daemon to your target's root filesystem:

```
$ cp ${TARGET_PREFIX}/sbin/snmpd ${PRJROOT}/rootfs/usr/sbin
```

Copy the relevant components found in *${TARGET_PREFIX}/share/snmp* to the */usr/local/share/snmp* directory of your target's root filesystem:

```
$ mkdir -p ${PRJROOT}/rootfs/usr/local/share
$ cp -r ${TARGET_PREFIX}/share/snmp ${PRJROOT}/rootfs/usr/local/share
```

The SNMP MIB information weighs in at around 1.3 MB. Added with the stripped binary, this brings the minimum cost of the total SNMP package to a little over 2 MB in storage. This is a fairly large package for most embedded Linux systems.

To run properly, the SNMP agent requires a configuration file. An *EXAMPLE.conf* example configuration has been created during the build of the Net-SNMP package in the package's root directory. Customize that file and copy it to your *${PRJROOT}/ rootfs/usr/local/share/snmp* directory:

```
$ cp EXAMPLE.conf ${PRJROOT}/rootfs/usr/local/share/snmp/snmpd.conf
```

Finally, edit your target's */etc/inittab* file to add a line for snmpd. Here is the line I add for *snmpd* in my SYSM module's *inittab*:

```
::respawn:/usr/sbin/snmpd -f
```

The *-f* option instructs *snmpd* not to fork from the calling shell. In other words, *snmpd* will not become a daemon and *init* will respawn it if it dies.

For more information regarding SNMP, including the configuration and use of Net-SNMP, look at the *Essential SNMP* book mentioned earlier. The Net-SNMP project's web site contains quite a few resources, including an FAQ, various documents, and a mailing list. The manpages installed by Net-SNMP are also informative.

Network Login Through Telnet

The Telnet protocol is one of the simplest ways to log in to a remote network host. Consequently, it's the easiest way to access your target system once it is connected to a network. To enable remote login, your target must run a Telnet daemon. There are two main Telnet daemons available for use in embedded Linux systems, *telnetd*, which is part of the netkit packages mentioned earlier, and *utelnetd*, which is maintained by Robert Schwebel of Pengutronix. In terms of size, the binary generated by the *utelnetd* package is clearly smaller than the one generated by the netkit Telnet package. In addition, *utelnetd* does not require an internet super-server, while *telnetd* does. If your system has very limited resources and does not include other network services managed by an internet super-server, use *utelnetd*.

Though Telnet is a convenient, lightweight communications mechanism for managing your device on a dedicated network, it's not a secure protocol and is, therefore, not fit for use on the Internet. If you need to remotely log in to a device that resides on the Internet, use SSH instead. We will discuss SSH in detail in "Secure Communication with SSH."

netkit-telnetd

As with other netkit packages, netkit-telnet, which contains *telnetd*, is distributed at *ftp://ftp.uk.linux.org/pub/linux/Networking/netkit/* under a BSD license. For my SYSM module, I used netkit-telnet Version 0.17.

Download and extract the netkit-telnet package into your *${PRJROOT}/sysapps* directory and move to the package's directory for the rest of the manipulations:

```
$ cd ${PRJROOT}/sysapps/netkit-telnet-0.17
```

As in the case of the netkit-base package described earlier, the *configure* script included in netkit-telnet package attempts to run some test programs. Because these test programs are compiled using the target's compiler, they will fail. To avoid this, edit the *configure* script and comment out all the lines that attempt to execute test binaries. As earlier, here is an example commented line:

```
# ./__conftest || exit 1;
```

Once the script has been modified, you are ready to configure and compile the Telnet daemon. To link with glibc, type:

```
$ CC=arm-linux-gcc ./configure --prefix=${TARGET_PREFIX}
$ touch ${TARGET_PREFIX}/include/termcap.h
$ make -C telnetd
```

To build with uClibc, type:

```
$ CC=arm-uclibc-gcc ./configure --prefix=${TARGET_PREFIX}
$ touch ${PREFIX}/uclibc/include/termcap.h
$ make -C telnetd
```

As you can see, we compile only *telnetd*. The package also includes the *telnet* client, but the Makefile for that client doesn't allow cross-compilation. Even if it did, you'll find it better to use the miniature *telnet* client included in BusyBox. We used *touch* to create a *termcap.h* file in the appropriate header directory because *telnetd*'s source files include this header file. We don't need the termcap library, however. The build process requires only the termcap header file to be present, and the file can be empty.

The complete build process for *telnetd* is fairly short. The resulting binary is quite small. When built with uClibc and stripped, the binary is 30 KB if linked dynamically and 65 KB if linked statically. When built with glibc and stripped, the binary is 30 KB if linked dynamically and 430 KB if linked statically.

Don't use *make install*, because the Makefile was not properly built for cross-platform development and attempts to use the host's *strip* command instead of the version we built earlier for the target.

Instead, copy the *telnetd* binary by hand to your target's root filesystem:

```
$ cp telnetd/telnetd ${PRJROOT}/rootfs/usr/sbin
```

You need to have a properly configured copy of either the *inetd* or *xinetd* internet super-server that allows Telnet connections to your target. Alternatively, you could edit your target's */etc/inittab* to start the Telnet daemon using the *-debug* option so that it doesn't need to rely on any super-server. However, *telnetd* wasn't meant to be used this way.

In addition to the C library, *telnetd* depends on the login routines library (libutil). Hence, do not forget to copy this library to your target's */lib* directory if you link *telnetd* dynamically.

For further information regarding the use of *telnetd*, have a look at the manpage included in the *telnetd* directory of the netkit-telnet package, or the manpage installed on your host for your workstation's native *telnetd*.

utelnetd

The *utelnetd* package is distributed at *http://www.pengutronix.de/software/utelnetd_en.html* under the terms of the GPL. *utelnetd* depends on the C library and can be built using uClibc. For my SYSM module, I used *utelnetd* 0.1.3.

Download and extract the *utelnetd* package into your *${PRJROOT}/sysapps* directory and move to that package's directory for the rest of the installation:

```
$ cd ${PRJROOT}/utelnetd-0.1.3
```

utelnetd does not require any configuration before compilation. To compile the package against glibc, type:

```
$ CC=arm-linux-gcc make
```

The compilation time is very short, since the entire daemon is contained in a single source file. The resulting *utelnetd* binary is around 10 KB in size when linked dynamically with either glibc or uClibc and stripped. When linked statically, the binary is 375 KB if linked against glibc and stripped, and 25 KB if linked against uClibc and stripped.

There are no configuration files required for *utelnetd*. All you need is to copy the binary to your target's root filesystem and modify the system's initialization to start a copy of *utelnetd* at startup. Unlike *telnetd*, *utelnetd* is standalone and doesn't rely on an internet super-server such as *inetd* or *xinetd*. First, copy the file to your target's root filesystem:

```
$ cp utelnetd ${PRJROOT}/rootfs/usr/sbin
```

Now, edit your target's */etc/inittab* file to start *utelnetd* at startup. As an example, here is the line I add for *utelnetd* in my SYSM module's */etc/inittab*:

```
::respawn:/usr/sbin/utelnetd
```

Though there is little documentation on the use of *utelnetd*, the package is simple enough that a quick glance at the source code should provide you with all the information you need.

Secure Communication with SSH

Though you can easily communicate with your target using Telnet, it is a very insecure protocol and its vulnerabilities are widely documented. The user password, for instance, is transmitted in clear text from the client to the server. It would therefore be rather unprudent, and in most cases downright dangerous, to include a Telnet daemon in your product in the hopes of being able to remotely fix problems once the product is at the client's site. Instead, it would be much preferable to use a protocol that relies on strong encryption and other mechanisms to ensure the communication's confidentiality. The best way to do this currently is to use the SSH protocol and related tool suite. SSH uses public-key cryptography to guarantee end-to-end communication encryption while being fairly easy to use and deploy.

Because SSH is an IETF standard, there are a few competing implementations, some of which are proprietary commercial products. The main open source implementation is OpenSSH. Although there are other open source implementations, they are either very difficult to cross-compile or have dependencies that make them impractical for use in embedded Linux systems. I will therefore devote most of this section to discussing OpenSSH. We will briefly review the other open source implementations, because they may eventually become usable in embedded Linux systems.

An embedded system that can be accessed through SSH runs the same SSH server software usually run on a traditional server. Our discussion will therefore concentrate on the compilation of the SSH server for the target, and its setup, configuration, and use on the target. I will not cover aspects of how to set up and use any of the other SSH components.

If you are seriously considering using an SSH package in your target, I suggest you take a look at *SSH, The Secure Shell: The Definitive Guide* by Daniel Barrett and Richard Silverman (O'Reilly). It provides the in-depth coverage I cannot undertake here.

OpenSSH

OpenSSH is developed and maintained as part of the OpenBSD project. It is available from *http://www.openssh.org/* under a composite BSD license (see the *LICENSE* file for the complete details) along with ample documentation and quite a few other resources. To use OpenSSH in your target, you also need two libraries: OpenSSL and zlib. OpenSSL is an open source implementation of the *Secure Socket Layer* (SSL) protocol and is available from *http://www.openssl.org/* under a BSD-like license. The zlib compression library is the same as the one we discussed earlier in "MTD-Supported Devices" in Chapter 7. Before building and installing OpenSSH, you must first build and install both these libraries in your host's cross-platform development framework. In addition, OpenSSH, OpenSSL, and zlib need to exist natively on your host. If you intend to link OpenSSH with uClibc, uClibc must be installed natively on your host. Before you go any further, make sure that the required components are properly installed on your workstation, since they are needed for compiling OpenSSH for the target.

For my example SYSM module, I used OpenSSH 3.5p1, OpenSSL 0.9.6g, and zlib 1.1.4. Because vulnerabilities are found from time to time in some of these packages, it is important to keep track of the versions you are using and to have upgrade plans, in case serious vulnerabilities are found in one of the versions you are using.

The OpenSSH package is hostile to cross-compilation. Among many other things, its configuration script attempts to run test samples it builds using the compiler specified with CC=. Because the applications built using the cross-compiler can't run on the host, the script stops and emits an error. As you'll see, we need to resort to a number of tricks to force the package's configuration scripts and Makefiles to build the software. The headers and libraries installed natively on the host are used extensively, for example, in fooling the package into compiling for the target. Though the instructions that follow try to be as complete as possible, you may need to put some effort into figuring out a few modifications for your own setup.

In the following, I discuss both OpenSSL and OpenSSH. Because the names of both packages differ by only one letter, it is easy to confuse the names while reading the text. Pay close attention to the last letter of each package name to avoid any confusion.

We will discuss how to build and install OpenSSL shortly. First, however, refer to "MTD-Supported Devices" in Chapter 7 for instructions on how to build zlib. In contrast to these earlier instructions, you need to build zlib as a static library instead of a shared library. To do so, don't set the value of LDSHARED and don't use the -- shared option, as we did earlier, on the *configure* command line.

In the rest of this section, I will assume that you are building OpenSSH against glibc. If you would rather use uClibc, replace all references to *${TARGET_PREFIX}* with references to *${PREFIX}/uclibc* and all references to *arm-linux-gcc* with references to *arm-uclibc-gcc*. If you had not enabled shadow password support and C99 support when installing uClibc, you will need to reinstall uClibc with support for these features enabled. Also, you will need to install zlib in uClibc's directory. To do so, set the value of prefix to *${PREFIX}/uclibc* instead of *${TARGET_PREFIX}* when issuing the *make install* command for zlib.

With zlib properly built and installed, download and extract OpenSSL in your *${PRJROOT}/build-tools* directory. Move to the package's directory to configure, compile, and install it:

```
$ ./config --prefix=${TARGET_PREFIX} compiler:arm-linux-gcc
$ make
$ make install
```

Here, the compiler is specified using the *compiler:* option instead of setting the value of CC. Once completed, all the components installed are found under the *${TARGET_PREFIX}* directory. The compilation takes around 10 minutes on my hardware setup.

Once OpenSSL is installed, download and extract OpenSSH into your *${PRJROOT}/ sysapps* directory. Now move to OpenSSH's directory to proceed:

```
$ cd ${PRJROOT}/sysapps/openssh-3.5p1
```

To trick OpenSSH's *configure* script into successfully creating useful Makefiles, we need to pretend that we are actually configuring it for the host. We then use the Makefiles created by *configure* to build OpenSSH for the target. For this scheme to succeed, we must use a few fake file links. Mainly, we need to:

1. Create a symbolic link to the host's C compiler bearing the same name as the C compiler we generated for the target.
2. Create a symbolic link to the host's native OpenSSL headers.
3. Create a symbolic link to the host's native OpenSSL libraries.

On my development host, for example, the native OpenSSL headers and libraries are located in the */usr/local/ssl* directory, and the C compiler is located in */usr/bin*. Here are the preliminary steps I use for preparing the build of OpenSSH for my SYSM module:

```
$ export PATH=./:$PATH
$ which gcc
/usr/bin/gcc
$ ln -s /usr/bin/gcc ./arm-linux-gcc
$ ln -s /usr/local/ssl/include ./fake-include
$ ln -s /usr/local/ssl/lib ./fake-lib
```

I modified the PATH to force *configure* to start looking in the current directory first for all binaries. This enables me to trick it into using a compiler called *arm-linux-gcc* when this is really the host's own compiler. I can now run the *configure* script itself using the fake links:

```
$ CC=arm-linux-gcc CFLAGS=-I./fake-include LDFLAGS=-L./fake-lib \
> ./configure --host=$TARGET
```

The line above generates Makefiles that build dynamically linked binaries. To link the binaries statically, change the value of LDFLAGS to "-L./fake-lib -static".

The script's output resembles the output of other *configure* scripts we've seen before. At the end, however, it prints a summary of the configuration it has found:

```
OpenSSH has been configured with the following options:
                     User binaries: /usr/local/bin
                   System binaries: /usr/local/sbin
               Configuration files: /usr/local/etc
                  Askpass program: /usr/local/libexec/ssh-askpass
                     Manual pages: /usr/local/man/manX
                         PID file: /var/run
  Privilege separation chroot path: /var/empty
              sshd default user PATH: /usr/bin:/bin:/usr/sbin:/sbin:...
                   Manpage format: doc
                      PAM support: no
               KerberosIV support: no
                KerberosV support: no
                Smartcard support: no
                      AFS support: no
                    S/KEY support: no
             TCP Wrappers support: no
             MD5 password support: no
        IP address in $DISPLAY hack: no
            Use IPv4 by default hack: no
             Translate v4 in v6 hack: yes
                 BSD Auth support: no
             Random number source: OpenSSL internal ONLY

                             Host: arm-unknown-linux-gnu
                         Compiler: arm-linux-gcc
                   Compiler flags: -I./fake-include -Wall -Wpointer-arith -Wno-un...
               Preprocessor flags:
                     Linker flags: -L./fake-lib
                        Libraries:   -lutil -lz -lnsl  -lcrypto -lcrypt
```

This output indicates that the SSH software expects to operate through the root */usr* and */var* directories, which is fine since it will be running as root on the target. The most important parts, however, are the Compiler and the various *flags* fields at the bottom. In the output shown, the compiler name is the right one, and the include and library paths point to the fake entries I created earlier. Hence, I have succeeded in fooling *configure* into creating Makefiles that use filenames that I can control. To finish the trick, I can now remove the fake links I created earlier and create appropriate ones for my target:

```
$ rm arm-linux-gcc fake-include fake-lib
$ ln -s ${TARGET_PREFIX}/include ./fake-include
$ ln -s ${TARGET_PREFIX}/lib ./fake-lib
```

By removing the *arm-linux-gcc* file link, I am forcing the Makefiles to use the *arm-linux-gcc* command found in the PATH, which is the actual cross-compiler I built earlier for my target. Similarly, the library and header file path links I just created will force the Makefiles to use my target's actual libraries and header files. All is set now for building OpenSSH.

Before you issue the *make* command, you may need to hand-tweak some header files if the C library version you are using for your target is not the same as the one used on your host or if the sizes of the various C types on the target differ from those on the host. In my case, for example, I had to edit *defines.h* and *config.h*. In *defines.h*, I had to add an #if 0 and #endif around the definitions of __ss_family. In *config.h*, I had to do the same with the #define of HAVE_GETGROUPLIST. You will probably need to modify those files in your own way to get OpenSSH to compile. If you get errors at link time about missing symbols, this probably means you have to edit *config.h* and comment out the appropriate HAVE_ definition. Note that any modification to *config.h* will be lost if you run the *configure* script again.

With the headers having been properly modified, everything is ready for building OpenSSH:

```
$ make
```

The complete compilation takes less than five minutes on my hardware. The resulting SSH daemon—which is the binary we are most interested in for our target, as I said earlier—is fairly large. When compiled against glibc and stripped, the binary is around 1 MB in size if linked dynamically and 1.4 MB if linked statically. When compiled with uClibc and stripped, the binary is around 1 MB when linked dynamically and 1.1 MB when linked statically.

Copy the SSH daemon to your target's root filesystem and strip it:

```
$ cp ./sshd ${PRJROOT}/rootfs/usr/sbin
$ arm-linux-strip ${PRJROOT}/rootfs/usr/sbin/sshd
```

To run the daemon, you need a configuration file and a set of private and public keys. An example configuration file is already provided as part of the OpenSSH package, *sshd_config*. Copy this file to your target's root filesystem and customize it according to your needs:

```
$ mkdir -p ${PRJROOT}/rootfs/usr/local/etc
$ cp sshd_config ${PRJROOT}/rootfs/usr/local/etc
```

Also, you need to generate the keys for your target. There are three types of keys to generate, RSA1, RSA, and DSA, and each has a private and a public component. All keys will be located in the same directory as the daemon's configuration file, in the target's */usr/local/etc/* directory. Using your host's native OpenSSH tools, create the keys for your target:

```
$ ssh-keygen -t rsa1 -f ${PRJROOT}/rootfs/usr/local/etc/ssh_host_key
$ ssh-keygen -t rsa -f ${PRJROOT}/rootfs/usr/local/etc/ssh_host_rsa_key
$ ssh-keygen -t dsa -f ${PRJROOT}/rootfs/usr/local/etc/ssh_host_dsa_key
```

In addition, create */var* entries on your target's root filesystem for OpenSSH:

```
$ mkdir -p ${PRJROOT}/rootfs/var/run ${PRJROOT}/rootfs/var/empty
$ su -m
Password:
```

```
# chown root:root ${PRJROOT}/rootfs/var/run ${PRJROOT}/rootfs/var/empty
# chmod 755 ${PRJROOT}/rootfs/var/empty
# exit
```

Finally, you need to have a "privilege separation" user on your target. This user isolates the connection to the outside world from the brain of the SSH daemon. Thus, if the connection is compromised, the remote party does not obtain root access to the system. To add the privilege separation user, first edit your target's */etc/group* file and add the following line:

```
sshd:x:255:
```

Replace the 255 value with a group ID that is still available on your target. If you are using CRAMFS, remember that this number must be below 256. Now, edit your target's */etc/passwd* file and add the privilege separation user:

```
sshd:x:501:255:sshd privsep:/var/empty:/bin/false
```

Also, edit your target's */etc/shadow* file and add an entry for the privilege separation user:

```
sshd:*:11880:0:99999:7:-1:-1:0
```

Furthermore, you need to copy all the libraries *sshd* depends on to your target's root filesystem, if you had used dynamic linking. Use *arm-uclibc-ldd* to find the complete list of dependencies.

As with the earlier networking packages, edit your target's */etc/inittab* file to start the *sshd* process:

```
::respawn:/usr/sbin/sshd -D
```

The -D flag is used to tell *sshd* not to fork from the shell and become a daemon. Hence, *init* can respawn it if it dies. This, however, is not a common occurrence, and any failure of *sshd* should be considered a serious bug and be properly investigated.

For further information on how to configure and operate OpenSSH, see the *SSH, The Secure Shell: The Definitive Guide* book mentioned earlier.

A Word on Other SSH Implementations

Apart from OpenSSH, there are a few other open source SSH implementations; most notably LSH and FreSSH. At the time of this writing, however, neither is fit for use in production embedded Linux systems.

LSH, for example, depends on packages that have their own dependencies. In particular, it depends on the GNU MP library, zlib, and liboop. The first two dependencies are tolerable. The problem is that liboop depends on glib, which in turn requires pkg-config. Moreover, the glib package doesn't lend itself well to cross-compiling. If you are using a host of the same architecture as the target, you may to consider compiling LSH statically and then using it on your target. If, as in most cases, your target isn't of the same architecture as your host, LSH isn't a practical choice at this time.

FreSSH, on the other hand, is a relatively new package that isn't as mature as the other open source SSH packages. Among other things, it lacks a *configure* script and requires extensive Makefile modifications to build. In addition, it can be built only against glibc. The compilation against uClibc requires a number of source code modifications. When compiled against glibc, the resulting SSH daemon's size is around 850 KB, which is very close to the size of the SSH daemon generated by OpenSSH.

Serving Web Content Through HTTP

One of the biggest trends in network-enabling embedded systems is the inclusion of a web (HTTP) server. The added HTTP server can then be used for enabling remote administration or remote data viewing. In the case of my SYSM module, for example, the HTTP server enables my users to configure and monitor various aspects of the control system.

Though the open source Apache HTTP server is the most widely used HTTP server in the world, it is not necessarily fit for embedded systems. Mainly, it is very difficult to cross-compile and tends to be rather large in terms of required storage space. There are, nevertheless, other open source HTTP servers that are much more adapted to embedded systems. In particular, Boa and *thttpd* are small, lightweight, fast servers and are a perfect fit for embedded Linux systems.

There does not seem to be a clear set of characteristics to help in choosing between Boa and *thttpd*. The only really notable difference is that Boa is distributed under the terms of the GPL while *thttpd* is distributed under the terms of a BSD-like license. The size of the resulting binaries are, however, quite comparable. Both packages also support CGI scripting. Therefore, I suggest you have a look at both to decide which one you prefer.

Boa

Boa is available from *http://www.boa.org/* and is distributed under the terms of the GPL. Boa requires only a C library and can be compiled both against glibc and uClibc. For my SYSM module, I used Boa 0.94.13.

Download and extract Boa in your *${PRJROOT}/sysapps* directory. With the package extracted, move to the appropriate directory:

```
$ cd ${PRJROOT}/sysapps/boa-0.94.13/src
```

Configure and compile Boa:

```
$ ac_cv_func_setvbuf_reversed=no CC=arm-linux-gcc ./configure \
> --host=$TARGET
$ make
```

The command line above generates a dynamically linked binary. If you would rather have a statically linked binary when compiling with uClibc, add LDFLAGS="-static" to the *make* command line. To statically link against glibc, use the following *make* command line instead:

```
$ make \
> LDFLAGS="-static -Wl --start-group -lc -lnss_files -lnss_dns \
> -lresolv -Wl --end-group"
```

 If you are trying to statically link Boa against glibc but you didn't use the *--enable-static-nss* option when configuring the build of the library, the command line above will fail because of missing files.

If you try to avoid this error by using only LDFLAGS="-static" with a glibc not built for enabling static NSS linking, the resulting binary will not function properly on the target, as I said in Chapter 4. Mainly, the binary attempts to load its dynamic NSS libraries from *${TARGET_ PREFIX}* on the target. Since this directory doesn't exist, Boa always fails to find the libraries it needs and stops. Though it may complain about a different sort of problem, such as an unknown user, you can see the files it tries to open using *strace*.

To avoid these problems altogether, you must recompile glibc with the *--enable-static-nss* option. Once the library is recompiled and installed, you will be able to link a real static binary that includes the appropriate NSS libraries.

Note that you won't encounter this type of problem with uClibc, since it doesn't implement glibc-style NSS.

The compilation time is short. When linked against uClibc and stripped, the resulting binary is 60 KB in size when linked dynamically and 90 KB when linked statically. When linked against glibc and stripped, the resulting binary is 60 KB in size when linked dynamically and 520 KB when linked statically.

Once the binary is ready, copy it to your target's root filesystem and strip it:

```
$ cp boa ${PRJROOT}/rootfs/usr/sbin
$ arm-linux-strip ${PRJROOT}/rootfs/usr/sbin/boa
```

For Boa to run, it needs a *boa/* subdirectory in the target's */etc* directory and a configuration file in that same directory. Create Boa's directory and copy the sample configuration file to it:

```
$ mkdir -p ${PRJROOT}/rootfs/etc/boa
$ cp ../boa.conf ${PRJROOT}/rootfs/etc/boa
```

At runtime, Boa will need a user account to run. This user account is specified in the *boa.conf* file. Edit this file and your target's */etc/passwd* and */etc/groups* files to add a user for Boa to use. Boa also needs a */var/log/boa* directory on your target's root filesystem to log accesses and errors:

```
$ mkdir -p ${PRJROOT}/rootfs/var/log/boa
```

Remember that log files can be a problem in an embedded system if their growth is not restricted. Having a script that runs periodically to reinitialize such files, for example, is a simple way to ensure they don't use up the available storage space.

When running, Boa finds its web content from the target's */var/www* directory. This is where you should put any HTML files, including *index.html*. Create the directory and copy your content to it:

```
$ mkdir -p ${PRJROOT}/rootfs/var/www
$ cp … ${PRJROOT}/rootfs/var/www
```

Finally, add a line in your target's */etc/inittab* for Boa. On my SYSM module, for example, here is the line I add for Boa:

```
::respawn:/usr/sbin/boa
```

For more information on how to use Boa, see the documentation included in the Boa package and on the project's web site.

thttpd

thttpd is available from *http://www.acme.com/software/thttpd/* and is distributed under a BSD-like license. In addition to the C library, *thttpd* also depends on the cryptography library (libcrypt). Download and extract *thttpd* in your *${PRJROOT}/ sysapps* directory. For my SYSM module, for example, I used *thttpd* 2.23beta1. Move to the package's directory for the rest of the instructions:

```
$ cd ${PRJROOT}/sysapps/thttpd-2.23beta1
```

Now, configure and compile *thttpd*:

```
$ CC=arm-linux-gcc ./configure --host=$TARGET
$ make
```

This command line generates a dynamically linked binary. As with Boa, to generate a statically linked binary with uClibc, add LDFLAGS="-static" to the *make* command line. To statically link against glibc, you must use a *make* command similar to that used for Boa:

```
$ make \
> LIBS="-static -Wl --start-group -lc -lnss_files -lnss_dns \
> -lcrypt -lresolv -Wl --end-group"
```

As with Boa, if you are trying to statically link *thttpd* against a version of glibc that wasn't built to enable static NSS linking, the command line above will fail. Even if bypassed using LDFLAGS="-static", the resulting binary will not function properly on the target. See the note in the previous section for details.

As with Boa, the compilation ends quickly. When linked against uClibc and stripped, the resulting binary is 70 KB in size when linked dynamically and 115 KB when linked statically. When linked against glibc and stripped, the resulting binary is 70 KB when linked dynamically and 550 KB when linked statically.

Copy the resulting binary to the target's root filesystem and strip it:

```
$ cp thttpd ${PRJROOT}/rootfs/usr/sbin
$ arm-linux-strip ${PRJROOT}/rootfs/usr/sbin/thttpd
```

Unlike Boa, you can configure *thttpd* either by using a configuration file or by passing the appropriate command-line options. Use the -C option to provide a configuration file to *thttpd*. An example configuration file is provided in *contrib/redhat-rpm/thttpd.conf*. If you wish to use a configuration file, edit this file to fit your target's configuration after having copied it to your target's root filesystem:

```
$ cp contrib/redhat-rpm/thttpd.conf ${PRJROOT}/rootfs/etc
```

Like Boa, *thttpd* operates with a special user account. By default, it uses the nobody account. Create this account using procedures outlined earlier, or set *thttpd* to use an account of your choice. The configuration file copied earlier specifies the use of the httpd user. It also identifies the target's */home/httpd/html* directory as the location for source HTML files:

```
$ mkdir -p ${PRJROOT}/rootfs/home/httpd/html
```

Finally, edit your target's */etc/inittab* file. Here is the line I add for *thttpd* in my SYSM module's *inittab*:

```
::respawn:/usr/sbin/thttpd -C /etc/thttpd.conf
```

For more information on how to install and run *thttpd*, see the manpage included in the package and the project's web site.

A Word on Apache

Apache is available from *http://www.apache.org/* and is distributed under the Apache license.* As I said earlier, Apache does not lend itself well to cross-compiling. If you are not deterred by this warning and would still be interested in attempting to cross-compile Apache, have a look at the procedure outlined by David McCreedy in his posting to the Apache development mailing list: *http://hypermail.linklord.com/new-httpd/2000/May/0175.html*. If you succeed, you'll probably want to take peek at *Apache: The Definitive Guide* by Ben Laurie and Peter Laurie (O'Reilly) for more information regarding the configuration and use of Apache.

---

* This license is BSD-like. See the *LICENSE* file included with the package for the complete licensing details.

Dynamic Configuration Through DHCP

The *Dynamic Host Configuration Protocol* (DHCP) allows for the automatic network configuration of hosts. Automatic configuration usually involves assigning IP addresses but can include other configuration parameters, as we saw in Chapter 9. On a network that uses DHCP, there are two sorts of entities: clients that request a configuration and servers that provide the clients with functional configurations.

An embedded Linux system can easily be used as a DHCP server. In my example system, for instance, the SYSM module can provide dynamic configurations to the UI modules. Conversely, an embedded Linux system may need to obtain its own configuration from a DHCP server. My UI modules, for example, may obtain their configurations from the SYSM module.

The standard DHCP package used in most Linux distributions is the one distributed by the *Internet Software Consortium* (ISC). Although the package may seem to be a good candidate for use in embedded Linux systems because of its widespread use and the fact that it includes both the client and the server, its Makefiles and configuration scripts do not allow cross-compilation in any way.

There is, nevertheless, another open source package that provides both a DHCP server and a DHCP client, and that can be used in an embedded Linux system: udhcp. The udhcp project is maintained as part of the BusyBox project, and its web site is located at *http://udhcp.busybox.net/*. The package is available from that web site and is distributed under the terms of the GPL. udhcp depends only on the C library and can be compiled both with glibc and uClibc.

Begin by downloading and extracting the udhcp package in your *${PRJROOT}/ sysapps* directory. For my SYSM module, for example, I used udhcp 0.9.8. Move to the package's directory for the rest of the operations:

```
$ cd $(PRJROOT}/sysapps/udhcp-0.9.8
```

There is no configuration needed with this package. Hence, compiling the package is all that needs to be done:

```
$ make CROSS_COMPILE=arm-uclibc-
```

Here, too, the compilation time is short. If you want to build statically, add `LDFLAGS="-static"` to the *make* command line. Also set `CROSS_COMPILE` to `arm-linux-` if you would prefer to build with glibc instead of uClibc. When linked against glibc and stripped,[*] the server and the client are around 16 KB in size when linked dynamically. The client is 375 KB in size and the server 450 KB in size when linked statically against glibc and stripped. Note that udhcp uses glibc's NSS and will require Makefile modifications in order to pass the link options at the end of the compile lines, not in the middle as it does by default. You will also need to set `LDFLAGS` to values similar

---

[*] The udhcp Makefile automatically strips the binaries once they are built.

as the ones we used earlier to build Boa and *thttpd* statically against glibc. When linked against uClibc and stripped, the server and the client are around 15 KB in size when linked dynamically and 40 KB in size when linked statically.

If you are using the server in your system, copy it to your target's */usr/sbin* directory:

```
$ cp udhcpd ${PRJROOT}/rootfs/usr/sbin
```

If you are using the client, copy it to your target's */sbin* directory:

```
$ cp udhcpc ${PRJROOT}/rootfs/sbin
```

Both server and client need configuration files and runtime files to store information regarding lease status.

For the server, create a */var/lib/misc* directory and a lease file, and copy the sample configuration file to your target's root filesystem:

```
$ mkdir -p ${PRJROOT}/rootfs/var/lib/misc
$ touch ${PRJROOT}/rootfs/var/lib/misc/udhcpd.leases
$ cp samples/udhcpd.conf ${PRJROOT}/rootfs/etc
```

If you forget to create the lease file, the server will refuse to start.

For the client, create a */etc/udhcpc* directory and a */usr/share/udhcpc* directory, and copy one of the sample configuration files to */usr/share/udhcpc/default.script*:

```
$ mkdir -p ${PRJROOT}/rootfs/etc/udhcpc
$ mkdir -p ${PRJROOT}/rootfs/usr/share/udhcpc
$ cp samples/sample.renew \
> ${PRJROOT}/rootfs/usr/share/udhcpc/default.script
```

Also, edit your target's */etc/inittab* file to start the daemon you need. For instance, here is the line for the DHCP server I use in my SYSM module:

```
::respawn:/usr/sbin/udhcpd
```

For a complete discussion on the configuration and use of udhcpd and udhcpc, read the manpages included with the package and look at the project's web site.

Debugging Tools

In the previous chapters, we've discussed how to set up, configure, and use various preexisting free and open source software components. Now that you are ready to work with your system, you'll need some powerful debugging tools.

In this chapter, we discuss the installation and use of the main software debugging tools used in the development of embedded Linux systems. This discussion covers debugging applications with *gdb*, tracing applications and system behavior, performance analysis, and memory debugging. In addition, I briefly review some of the hardware tools often used in developing embedded Linux systems. Because the particular operating system on the target makes little difference in the way the hardware debugging tools are used, we do not discuss how to use them. I will, nevertheless, suggest ways that you can use hardware tools to facilitate debugging the software running in your embedded Linux system.

To best use the tools discussed in this chapter, I strongly recommend the use of an NFS-mounted root filesystem for your target. Among other things, this enables you to rapidly update your software once you've identified and corrected a bug. In turn, this speeds up debugging, because you can continue debugging the updated software much sooner than if you had to transfer the updated binary manually to your target first. In essence, an NFS-mounted root filesystem simplifies the updating and debugging process and, therefore, reduces development time. In addition, NFS allows for performance data generated on the target to be available immediately on the host.

Though I cover the most important free and open source debugging tools in this chapter, I do not cover all the debugging tools available in Linux. The material covered in this chapter should, nevertheless, help you make the best use of any additional Linux debugging tools you may find on the Web or in your distribution. Among the debugging tools I do not discuss are all the tools used for kernel debugging. If you need to debug a kernel, have a look at Chapter 4 of *Linux Device Drivers*.

Debugging Applications with gdb

The *GNU debugger* (*gdb*) is the symbolic debugger of the GNU project and is arguably the most important debugging tool for any Linux system. It has been around for over 10 years, and many non-Linux embedded systems already use it in conjunction with what is known as *gdb* stubs to debug a target remotely.[*] Because the Linux kernel implements the `ptrace( )` system call, however, you don't need *gdb* stubs to debug embedded applications remotely. Instead, a *gdb* server is provided with the *gdb* package. This server is a very small application that runs on the target and executes the commands it receives from the *gdb* debugger running on the host. Hence, any application can be debugged on the target without having the *gdb* debugger actually running on the target. This is very important, because as we shall see, the actual *gdb* binary is fairly large.

This section discusses the installation and use of *gdb* in a host/target configuration, not the actual use of *gdb* to debug an application. To learn how to set breakpoints, view variables, and view backtraces, for example, read one of the various books or manuals that discuss the use of *gdb*. In particular, have a look at Chapter 14 of *Running Linux* (O'Reilly) and the *gdb* manual available both within the *gdb* package and online at *http://www.gnu.org/manual/*.

Building and Installing gdb Components

The *gdb* package is available from *ftp://ftp.gnu.org/gnu/gdb/* under the terms of the GPL. Download and extract the *gdb* package in your *${PRJROOT}/debug* directory. For my control module, for example, I used *gdb* Version 5.2.1. As with the other GNU toolset components I described in Chapter 4, it is preferable not to use the package's directory to build the actual debugger. Instead, create a build directory, move to it, and build *gdb*:

```
$ mkdir ${PRJROOT}/debug/build-gdb
$ cd ${PRJROOT}/debug/build-gdb
$ ../gdb-5.2.1/configure --target=$TARGET --prefix=${PREFIX}
$ make
$ make install
```

These commands build the *gdb* debugger for handling target applications. As with other GNU toolset components, the name of the binary depends on the target. For my control module, for example, the debugger is *powerpc-linux-gdb*. This binary and the other debugger files are installed within the *$PREFIX* directory. The build process proper takes from 5 to 10 minutes on my hardware, and the binary generated is fairly large. For a PPC target, for example, the stripped binary is 4 MB in size when

---

[*] *gdb* stubs are a set of hooks and handlers placed in a target's firmware or operating system kernel in order to allow interaction with a remote debugger. The *gdb* manual explains the use of *gdb* stubs.

linked dynamically. This is why the *gdb* binary can't be used as-is on the target and the *gdb* server is used instead.

 At the time of this writing, the *gdb* built for the target cannot handle target *core* files. Instead, the faulty program must be run on the target using the *gdb* server to catch the error as it happens natively. There has been discussion regarding adding cross-platform *core* file reading capabilities to *gdb* on the *gdb* mailing lists, and a few patches are already available. Support for reading cross-platform *core* files in *gdb* may therefore be available by the time your read this.

The *gdb* server wasn't built earlier because it has to be cross-compiled for the target using the appropriate tools. To do so, create a directory to build the *gdb* server, move to it, and build the *gdb* server:

```
$ mkdir ${PRJROOT}/debug/build-gdbserver
$ cd ${PRJROOT}/debug/build-gdbserver
$ chmod +x ../gdb-5.2.1/gdb/gdbserver/configure
$ CC=powerpc-linux-gcc ../gdb-5.2.1/gdb/gdbserver/configure \
> --host=$TARGET --prefix=${TARGET_PREFIX}
$ make
$ make install
```

The *gdb* server binary, *gdbserver*, has now been installed in your *${TARGET_PREFIX}/bin* directory. The dynamically linked *gdbserver* is 25 KB in size when stripped. Compared to *gdb*, the size of *gdbserver* is much more palatable.

Once built, copy *gdbserver* to your target's root filesystem:

```
$ cp ${TARGET_PREFIX}/bin/gdbserver ${PRJROOT}/rootfs/usr/bin
```

There are no additional steps required to configure the use of the *gdb* server on your target. I will cover its use in the next section.

Using the gdb Components to Debug Target Applications

Before you can debug an application using *gdb*, you need to compile your application using the appropriate flags. Mainly, you need to add the *-g* option to the *gcc* command line. This option adds the debugging information to the object files generated by the compiler. To add even more debugging information, use the *-ggdb* option. The information added by both debugging options is thereafter found in the application's binary. Though this addition results in a larger binary, you can still use a stripped binary on your target, granted you have the original unstripped version with the debugging information on your host. To do so, build your application on your host with complete debugging symbols. Copy the resulting binary to your target's root filesystem and use *strip* to reduce the size of the binary you just copied by removing all symbolic information, including debugging information. On the target, use the stripped binary with *gdbserver*. On the host, use the original unstripped

Debugging Information, Symbol Tables, and strip

Most modern Linux binaries are in the ELF format. As with binaries of other formats, ELF binaries contain a number of sections, each with a different name and role. The actual executable code for the binary is usually in the .text section. There are also other sections such as .data for initialized data and .bss for uninitialized data. Debugging information is usually in the .stab and .stabstr sections. These sections are formatted according to the *Stabs* (short for symbol table) debug format and contain information such as line numbers, paths to source files, paths to include files, variables declarations, types declarations, and so on.

Both *objdump* and *readelf* can be used to view the sections of an ELF binary. Here is a sample output generated by running *readelf* on the unstripped *gdbserver* binary:

```
$ powerpc-linux-readelf -S gdbserver
There are 32 section headers, starting at offset 0x1aca4:

Section Headers:
  [Nr] Name            Type          Addr      Off    Size   ES Flg Lk Inf Al
...
  [12] .text           PROGBITS      10000b48 000b48 003008 00  AX   0   0 4
...
  [17] .data           PROGBITS      10015470 005470 000914 00  WA   0   0 4
...
  [25] .bss            NOBITS        10016114 005e54 00236c 00  WA   0   0 16
  [26] .stab           PROGBITS      00000000 005e54 00798c 0c      27   0 4
  [27] .stabstr        STRTAB        00000000 00d7e0 00d1d5 00       0   0 1
  [28] .comment        PROGBITS      00000000 01a9b5 0001ee 00       0   0 1
  [29] .shstrtab       STRTAB        00000000 01aba3 0000ff 00       0   0 1
  [30] .symtab         SYMTAB        00000000 01b1a4 000f40 10      31  6e 4
  [31] .strtab         STRTAB        00000000 01c0e4 000d19 00       0   0 1
Key to Flags: W (write), A (alloc), X (execute), M (merge), S (strings)
              I (info), L (link order), O (extra OS processing required)
              o (os specific), p (processor specific) x (unknown)
```

When the *strip* command is used, the sections containing the debugging information, .stab and .stabstr, are removed from the binary along with .symtab and .strtab, while the rest of the sections, except .shstrtab, remain unchanged. The only section that changes is the section header string table, .shstrtab, which shrinks in size since there are fewer sections in the binary. Here is the output generated by running *readelf* on the stripped *gdbserver* binary:

```
$ powerpc-linux-readelf -S gdbserver
There are 28 section headers, starting at offset 0x6134:

Section Headers:
  [Nr] Name            Type          Addr      Off    Size   ES Flg Lk Inf Al
...
  [12] .text           PROGBITS      10000b48 000b48 003008 00  AX   0   0 4
...
```

—continued—

```
   [17] .data          PROGBITS     10015470 005470 000914 00  WA   0  0 4
...
   [25] .bss           NOBITS       10016114 005e54 00236c 00  WA   0  0 16
   [26] .comment       PROGBITS     00000000 005e54 0001ee 00       0  0 1
   [27] .shstrtab      STRTAB       00000000 006042 0000f0 00       0  0 1
Key to Flags: W (write), A (alloc), X (execute), M (merge), S (strings)
              I (info), L (link order), O (extra OS processing required)
              o (os specific), p (processor specific) x (unknown)
```

For more information on binary formats, including ELF, have a look at John Levine's *Linkers & Loaders* (Morgan Kaufmann). For information on the Stabs format, have a look at the *The "stabs" debug format* manual provided in the *gdb/doc* directory of the *gdb* package and available online at *http://sources.redhat.com/gdb/current/onlinedocs/stabs.html*.

binary with *gdb*. Though the two *gdb* components are using different binary images, the target *gdb* running on the host is able to find and use the appropriate debug symbols for your application, because it has access to the unstripped binary.

Here are the relevant portions of my command daemon's Makefile that changed (see Chapter 4 for the original Makefile):

```
...
DEBUG          = -g
CFLAGS         = -O2 -Wall $(DEBUG)
...
```

Though *gcc* allows us to use both the *-g* and *-O* options in the same time, it is often preferable not to use the *-O* option when generating a binary for debugging, because the optimized binary may contain some subtle differences when compared to your application's original source code. For instance, some unused variables may not be incorporated into the binary, and the sequence of instructions actually executed in the binary may differ in order from those contained in your original source code.

There are two ways for the *gdb* server running on the target to communicate with the *gdb* debugger running on the host: using a crossover serial link or a TCP/IP connection. Though these communication interfaces differ in many respects, the syntax of the commands you need to issue is very similar. Starting a debug session using a *gdb* server involves two steps: starting the *gdb* server on the target and connecting to it from the *gdb* debugger on the host.

Once you are ready to debug your application, start the *gdb* server on your target with the means of communication and your application name as parameters. If your target has a configured TCP/IP interface available, you can start the *gdb* server and configure it to run over TCP/IP:

```
# gdbserver 192.168.172.50:2345 command-daemon
```

In this example, the host's IP address[*] is 192.168.172.50 and the port number used locally to listen to *gdb* connections is 2345. Note that the protocol used by *gdb* to communicate between the host and the target doesn't include any form of authentication or security. Hence, I don't recommend that you debug applications in this way over the public Internet. If you need to debug applications in this way, you may want to consider using SSH port forwarding to encrypt the *gdb* session. The book *SSH, The Secure Shell: The Definitive Guide* (O'Reilly) explains how to implement SSH port forwarding.

As I said earlier, the *command-daemon* being passed to *gdbserver* can be a stripped copy of the original *command-daemon* built on the host.

If you are using a serial link to debug your target, use the following command line on your target:

```
# gdbserver /dev/ttyS0 command-daemon
```

In this example, the target's serial link to the host is the first serial port, */dev/ttyS0*.

Once the *gdb* server is started on the target, you can connect to it from the *gdb* debugger on the host using the *target remote* command. If you are connected to the target using a TCP/IP network, use the following command:

```
$ powerpc-linux-gdb command-daemon
(gdb) target remote 192.168.172.10:2345
Remote debugging using 192.168.172.10:2345
0x10000074 in _start ( )
```

In this case, the target is located at IP 192.168.172.10 and the port number specified is the same one we used above to start the *gdb* server on the target. Unlike the *gdb* server on the target, the *command-daemon* used here has to be the unstripped copy of the binary. Otherwise, *gdb* will be of little use to try debugging the application.

If the program exits on the target or is restarted, you do not need to restart *gdb* on the host. Instead, you need to issue the *target remote* command anew once *gdbserver* is restarted on the target.

If your host is connected to your target through a serial link, use the following command:

```
$ powerpc-linux-gdb progname
(gdb) target remote /dev/ttyS0
Remote debugging using /dev/ttyS0
0x10000074 in _start ( )
```

Though both the target and the host are using */dev/ttyS0* to link to each other in this example, this is only a coincidence. The target and the host can use different serial ports to link to each other. The device being specified for each is the local serial port where the serial cable is connected.

---

[*] At the time of this writing, this field is actually ignored by *gdbserver*.

With the target and the host connected, you can now set breakpoints and do anything you would normally do in a symbolic debugger.

There are a few *gdb* commands that you are likely to find particularly useful when debugging an embedded target such as we are doing here. Here are some of these commands and summaries of their purposes:

file

Sets the filename of the binary being debugged. Debug symbols are loaded from that file.

dir

Adds a directory to the search path for the application's source code files.

target

Sets the parameters for connecting to the remote target, as we did earlier. This is actually not a single command but rather a complete set of commands. Use *help target* for more details.

set remotebaud

Sets the speed of the serial port when debugging remote applications through a serial cable.

set solib-absolute-prefix

Sets the path for finding the shared libraries used with the binary being debugged.

The last command is likely to be the most useful when your binaries are linked dynamically. Whereas the binary running on your target finds its shared libraries starting from / (the root directory), the *gdb* running on the host doesn't know how to locate these shared libraries. You need to use the following command to tell *gdb* where to find the correct target libraries on the host:

```
(gdb) set solib-absolute-prefix ../../tools/powerpc-linux/
```

Unlike the normal shell, the *gdb* command line doesn't recognize environment variables such as ${TARGET_PREFIX}. Hence, the complete path must be provided. In this case, the path is provided relative to the directory where *gdb* is running, but we could use an absolute path, too.

If you want to have *gdb* execute a number of commands each time it starts, you may want to use a *.gdbinit* file. For an explanation on the use of such files, have a look at the "Command files" subsection in the "Canned Sequences of Commands" section of the *gdb* manual.

To get information regarding the use of the various debugger commands, you can use the *help* command within the *gdb* environment, or look in the *gdb* manual.

Interfacing with a Graphical Frontend

Many developers find it difficult or counter-intuitive to debug using the plain *gdb* command line. Fortunately for these developers, there are quite a few graphical interfaces that hide much of *gdb*'s complexity by providing user-friendly mechanisms for setting breakpoints, viewing variables, and tending to other common debugging tasks. Examples include DDD (*http://www.gnu.org/software/ddd/*), KDevelop and other IDEs we discussed in Chapter 4. Much like your host's debugger, the cross-platform *gdb* we built earlier for your target can very likely be used by your favorite debugging interface. Each frontend has its own way for allowing the name of the debugger binary to be specified. Have a look at your frontend's documentation for this information. In the case of my control module, I would need to configure the frontend to use the *powerpc-linux-gdb* debugger.

Tracing

Symbolic debugging is fine for finding and correcting program errors. However, symbolic debugging offers little help in finding any sort of problem that involves an application's interaction with other applications or with the kernel. These sorts of behavioral problems necessitate the tracing of the actual interactions between your application and other software components.

The simplest form of tracing involves monitoring the interactions between a single application and the Linux kernel. This allows you to easily observe any problems that result from the passing of parameters or the wrong sequence of system calls.

Observing a single process in isolation is, however, not sufficient in all circumstances. If you are attempting to debug interprocess synchronization problems or time-sensitive issues, for example, you will need a system-wide tracing mechanism that provides you with the exact sequence and timing of events that occur throughout the system. For instance, in trying to understand why the Mars Pathfinder constantly rebooted while on Mars, the Jet Propulsion Laboratory engineers resorted to a system tracing tool for the VxWorks operating system.[*]

Fortunately, both single-process tracing and system tracing are available in Linux. The following sections discuss each one.

Single Process Tracing

The main tool for tracing a single process is *strace*. *strace* uses the ptrace( ) system call to intercept all system calls made by an application. Hence, it can extract all the

---

[*] For a very informative and entertaining account on what happened to the Mars Pathfinder on Mars, read Glenn Reeves' account at *http://research.microsoft.com/~mbj/Mars_Pathfinder/Authoritative_Account.html*. Glenn was the lead developer for the Mars Pathfinder software.

system call information and display it in a human-readable format for you to analyze. Because *strace* is a widely used Linux tool, I do not explain how to use it, but just explain how to install it for your target. If you would like to have more details on the usage of *strace*, see Chapter 14 of *Running Linux*.

strace is available from *http://www.liacs.nl/~wichert/strace/* under a BSD license. For my control module I used *strace* Version 4.4. Download the package and extract it in your *${PRJROOT}/debug* directory. Move to the package's directory, then configure and build *strace*:

```
$ cd ${PRJROOT}/debug/strace-4.4
$ CC=powerpc-linux-gcc ./configure --host=$TARGET
$ make
```

If you wish to statically link against uClibc, add `LDFLAGS="-static"` to the *make* command line. Given that *strace* uses NSS, you need to use a special command line if you wish to link it statically to glibc, as we did for other packages in Chapter 10:

```
$ make \
> LDLIBS="-static -Wl --start-group -lc -lnss_files -lnss_dns \
> -lresolv -Wl --end-group"
```

When linked against glibc and stripped, *strace* is 145 KB in size if linked dynamically and 605 KB if linked statically. When linked against uClibc and stripped, *strace* is 140 KB in size if linked dynamically and 170 KB when linked statically.

Once the binary is compiled, copy it to your target's root filesystem:

```
$ cp strace ${PRJROOT}/rootfs/usr/sbin
```

There are no additional steps required to configure *strace* for use on the target. In addition, the use of *strace* on the target is identical to that of its use on a normal Linux workstation. See the web page listed earlier or the manpage included with the package if you need more information regarding the use of *strace*.

System Tracing

The main system tracing utility for Linux is the *Linux Trace Toolkit* (LTT), which was introduced and continues to be maintained by this book's author. In contrast with other tracing utilities such as *strace*, LTT does not use the ptrace( ) mechanism to intercept applications' behavior. Instead, a kernel patch is provided with LTT that instruments key kernel subsystems. The data generated by this instrumentation is then collected by the trace subsystem and forwarded to a trace daemon to be written to disk. The entire process has very little impact on the system's behavior and performance. Extensive tests have shown that the tracing infrastructure has marginal impact when not in use and an impact lower than 2.5% under some of the most stressful conditions.

In addition to reconstructing the system's behavior using the data generated during a trace run, the user utilities provided with LTT allow you to extract performance data regarding the system's behavior during the trace interval. Here's a summary of some of the tasks LTT can be used for:

- Debugging interprocess synchronization problems
- Understanding the interaction between your application, the other applications in the system, and the kernel
- Measuring the time it takes for the kernel to service your application's requests
- Measuring the time your application spent waiting because other processes had a higher priority
- Measuring the time it takes for an interrupt's effects to propagate throughout the system
- Understanding the exact reaction the system has to outside input

To achieve this, LTT's operation is subdivided into four software components:

- The kernel instrumentation that generates the events being traced
- The tracing subsystem that collects the data generated by the kernel instrumentation into a single buffer
- The trace daemon that writes the tracing subsystem's buffers to disk
- The visualization tool that post-processes the system trace and displays it in a human-readable form

The first two software components are implemented as a kernel patch and the last two are separate user-space tools. While the first three software components must run on the target, the last one, the visualization tool, can run on the host. In LTT Versions 0.9.5a and earlier, the tracing subsystem was accessed from user space as a device through the appropriate */dev* entries. Starting in the development series leading to 0.9.6, however, this abstraction has been dropped following the recommendations of the kernel developers. Hence, though the following refers to the tracing subsystem as a device, newer versions of LTT will not use this abstraction and therefore will not require the creation of any */dev* entries on your target's root filesystem.

Given that LTT can detect and handle traces that have different byte ordering, traces can be generated and read on entirely different systems. The traces generated on my PPC-based control module, for example, can be read transparently on an x86 host.

In addition to tracing a predefined set of events, LTT enables you to create and log your own custom events from both user space and kernel space. Have a look at the *Examples* directory included in the package for practical examples of such custom events. Also, if your target is an x86-or PPC-based system, you can use the DProbes package provided by IBM to add trace points to binaries, including the kernel, without recompiling. DProbes is available under the terms of the GPL from IBM's web site at *http://oss.software.ibm.com/developer/opensource/linux/projects/dprobes/*.

LTT is available under the terms of the GPL from Opersys's web site at *http://www. opersys.com/LTT/*. The project's web site includes links to in-depth documentation and a mailing list for LTT users. The current stable release is 0.9.5a, which supports the i386, PPC, and SH architectures. The 0.9.6 release currently in development adds support for the MIPS and the ARM architectures.

Preliminary manipulations

Download the LTT package, extract it in your *${PRJROOT}/debug* directory, and move to the package's directory for the rest of the installation:

```
$ cd ${PRJROOT}/debug
$ tar xvzf TraceToolkit-0.9.5a.tgz
$ cd ${PRJROOT}/debug/TraceToolkit-0.9.5
```

The same online manual that provides detailed instructions on the use of LTT is included with the package under the *Help* directory.

Patching the kernel

For the kernel to generate the tracing information, it needs to be patched. There are kernel patches included with every LTT package in the *Patches* directory. Since the kernel changes with time, however, it is often necessary to update the kernel patches. The patches for the latest kernels are usually available from *http://www.opersys.com/ ftp/pub/LTT/ExtraPatches/*. For my control module, for example, I used *patch-ltt-linux-2.4.19-vanilla-020916-1.14*. If you are using a different kernel, try adapting this patch to your kernel version. Unfortunately, it isn't feasible to create a patch for all kernel versions every time a new version of LTT is released. The task of using LTT would be much simpler if the patch was included as part of the main kernel tree, something your author has been trying to convince the kernel developers of doing for some time now. In the case of my control module, I had to fix the patched kernel because of failed hunks.

Given that the binary format of the traces changes over time, LTT versions cannot read data generated by any random trace patch version. The -1.14 version appended to the patch name identifies the trace format version generated by this patch. LTT 0.9.5a can read trace data written by patches that use format Version 1.14. It cannot, however, read any another format. If you try opening a trace of a format that is incompatible with the visualization tool, it will display an error and exit. In the future, the LTT developers plan to modify the tools and the trace format to avoid this limitation.

Once you've downloaded the selected patch, move it to the kernel's directory and patch the kernel:

```
$ mv patch-ltt-linux-2.4.19-vanilla-020916-1.14 \
> ${PRJROOT}/kernel/linux-2.4.18
$ cd ${PRJROOT}/kernel/linux-2.4.18
$ patch -p1 < patch-ltt-linux-2.4.19-vanilla-020916-1.14
```

You can then configure your kernel as you did earlier. In the main configuration menu, go in the "Kernel tracing" submenu and select the "Kernel events tracing support" as built-in. In the patches released prior to LTT 0.9.6pre2, such as the one I am using for my control module, you could also select tracing as a module and load the trace driver dynamically. However, this option has disappeared following the recommendations of the kernel developers to make the tracing infrastructure a kernel subsystem instead of a device.

Proceed on to building and installing the kernel on your target using the techniques covered in earlier chapters.

Though you may be tempted to return to a kernel without LTT once you're done developing the system, I suggest you keep the traceable kernel, since you never know when a bug may occur in the field. The Mars Pathfinder example I provided earlier is a case in point. For the Pathfinder, the JPL engineers applied the *test what you fly and fly what you test* philosophy, as explained in the paper I mentioned in the earlier footnote about the Mars Pathfinder problem. Note that the overall maximum system performance cost of tracing is lower than 0.5% when the trace daemon isn't running.

Building the trace daemon

As I explained earlier, the trace daemon is responsible for writing the trace data to permanent storage. Though this is a disk on most workstations, it is preferable to use an NFS-mounted filesystem to dump the trace data. You could certainly dump it to your target's MTD device, if it has one, but this will almost certainly result in increased wear, given that traces tend to be fairly large.

Return to the package's directory within the *${PRJROOT}/debug* directory, and build the trace daemon:

```
$ cd ${PRJROOT}/debug/TraceToolkit-0.9.5
$ ./configure --prefix=${PREFIX}
$ make -C LibUserTrace CC=powerpc-linux-gcc UserTrace.o
$ make -C LibUserTrace CC=powerpc-linux-gcc LDFLAGS="-static"
$ make -C Daemon CC=powerpc-linux-gcc LDFLAGS="-static"
```

By setting the value of LDFLAGS to -static, we are generating a binary that is statically linked with LibUserTrace. This won't weigh down the target, since this library is very small. In addition, this will avoid us the trouble of having to keep track of an extra library for the target. The trace daemon binary we generated is, nevertheless, still dynamically linked to the C library. If you want it statically linked with the C library, use the following command instead:

```
$ make -C Daemon CC=powerpc-linux-gcc LDFLAGS="-all-static"
```

The binary generated is fairly small. When linked against glibc and stripped, the trace daemon is 18 KB in size when linked dynamically and 350 KB when linked statically. When linked against uClibc and stripped, the trace daemon is 16 KB in size when linked dynamically and 37 KB when linked statically.

Once built, copy the daemon and the basic trace helper scripts to the target's root filesystem:

```
$ cp tracedaemon Scripts/trace Scripts/tracecore Scripts/traceu \
> ${PRJROOT}/rootfs/usr/sbin
```

The trace helper scripts simplify the use of the trace daemon binary, which usually requires a fairly long command line to use adequately. Look at the LTT documentation for an explanation of the use of each helper script. My experience is that the *trace* script is the easiest way to start the trace daemon.

At the time of this writing, you need to create the appropriate device entries for the trace device on the target's root filesystem for the trace daemon to interface properly with the kernel's tracing components. Because the device obtains its major number at load time, make sure the major number you use for creating the device is accurate. The simplest way of doing this is to load all drivers in the exact order they will usually be loaded in and then *cat* the */proc/devices* file to get the list of device major numbers. See *Linux Device Drivers* for complete details about major number allocation. Alternatively, you can try using the *createdev.sh* script included in the LTT package. For my control module, the major number allocated to the trace device is 254:*

```
$ su -m
Password:
# mknod ${PRJROOT}/rootfs/dev/tracer c 254 0
# mknod ${PRJROOT}/rootfs/dev/tracerU c 254 1
# exit
```

As I said earlier, if you are using a version of LTT that is newer that 0.9.5a, you may not need to create these entries. Refer to your package's documentation for more information.

Installing the visualization tool

The visualization tool runs on the host and is responsible for displaying the trace data in an intuitive way. It can operate both as a command-line utility, dumping the binary trace data in a textual format, or as a GTK-based graphical utility, displaying the trace as a trace graph, as a set of statistics, and as a raw text dump of the trace. The graphical interface is most certainly the simplest way to analyze a trace, though you may want to use the command-line textual dump if you want to run a script to analyze the textual output. If you plan to use the graphical interface, GTK must be installed on your system. Most distributions install GTK by default. If it isn't installed, use your distribution's package manager to install it.

We've already moved to the LTT package's directory and have configured it in the previous section. All that is left is to build and install the host components:

```
$ make -C LibLTT install
$ make -C Visualizer install
```

---

* I obtain this number by looking at the */proc/devices* file on my target after having loaded the trace driver.

The visualizer binary, *tracevisualizer*, has been installed in the *${PREFIX}/bin* directory, while helper scripts have been installed in *${PREFIX}/sbin*. As with the trace daemon, the helper scripts let you avoid typing long command lines to start the trace visualizer.

Tracing the target and visualizing its behavior

You are now ready to trace your target. As I said earlier, to reduce wear, avoid using your target's solid-state storage device for recording the traces. Instead, either write the traces to an NFS-mounted filesystem or, if you would prefer to reduce polluting the traces with NFS-generated network traffic, use a TMPFS mounted directory to store the traces and copy them to your host after tracing is over.

Here is a simple command for tracing the target for 30 seconds:

```
# trace 30 outt
```

The outt name specified here is the prefix the command should use for the names of the output files. This command will generate two files: *outt.trace*, which contains the raw binary trace, and *outt.proc*, which contains a snapshot of the system's state at trace start. Both these files are necessary for reconstructing the system's behavior on the host using the visualization tool. If those files are stored locally on your target, copy them to your host using your favorite protocol.

It is possible that your system may be generating more events than the trace infrastructure can handle. In that case, the daemon will inform you upon exit that it lost events. You can then change the size of the buffers being used or the event set being traced to obtain all the data you need. Look at the documentation included in the package for more information on the parameters accepted by the trace daemon.

Once you've copied the files containing the trace to the host, you can view the trace using:

```
$ traceview outt
```

This command opens a window that looks like Figure 11-1.

In this case, the graph shows the interaction between the BusyBox shell and another BusyBox child. On the left side of the visualizer display, you see a list of all the processes that were active during the trace. The Linux kernel is always the bottom entry in that list. On the right side of the display, you see a graph that characterizes the behavior of the system. In that graph, horizontal lines illustrate the passage of time, while vertical lines illustrate a state transition. The graph portion displayed here shows that the system is running kernel code in the beginning. Near the start, the kernel returns control to the *sh* application, which continues running for a short period of time before making the wait4( ) system call. At that point, control is transferred back to the kernel, which runs for a while before initiating a scheduling change to the task with PID 21. This task starts executing, but an exception occurs, which results in a control transfer to the kernel again.

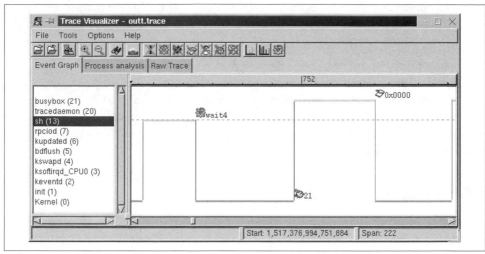

Figure 11-1. Example LTT trace graph

The graph continues in both directions, and you can scroll left or right to see what happened before or after this trace segment. You can also zoom in and out, depending on your needs.

Using this sort of graph, you can easily identify your applications' interaction with the rest of the system, as I explained earlier. You can also view the same set of events in their raw form by selecting the "Raw Trace" thumbnail, as seen in Figure 11-2.

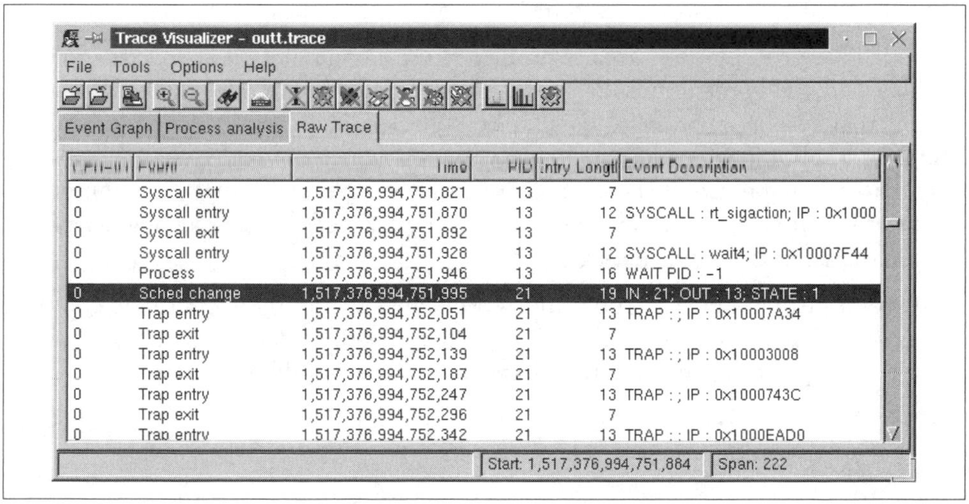

Figure 11-2. Example LTT raw event list

If you would prefer not to use the graphic tool at all, you can use the *tracevisualizer* on the command line. In that case, the *tracevisualizer* command takes the two input files and generates a text file containing the raw event list. This list is the same as the one displayed in the "Raw Trace" thumbnail of the graphic interface. To dump the content of the trace in text, type:

```
$ tracevisualizer outt.trace outt.proc outt.data
```

The first two parameters of this command, *outt.trace* and *outt.proc*, are the input files I described earlier, and the last parameter, *outt.data*, is the output file to where the trace's content is dumped in text. You can also use one of the facilitating scripts such as *tracedump* or *traceanalyze*. We discuss LTT's analysis capabilities and the "Process analysis" thumbnail later in this chapter.

Performance Analysis

Obtaining in-depth data regarding various aspects of your target's performance is crucial for making the best use out of the target's capabilities. Though I can't cover all aspects of performance analysis, I will cover the most important ones. In the following sections, we will discuss process profiling, code coverage, system profiling, kernel profiling, and measuring interrupt latency.

Process Profiling

Process profiling is a mechanism that helps understanding the intricate behavior of a process. Among other things, this involves obtaining information regarding the time spent in each function and how much of that time the function spent on behalf of each of its callers, and how much time it spent in each of the children it called.

A single process in Linux is usually profiled using a combination of special compiler options and the *gprof* utility. Basically, source files are compiled with a compiler option that results in profiling data to be collected at runtime and written to file upon the application's exit. The data generated is then analyzed by *gprof*, which displays the call graph profile data. Though I will not cover the actual use of *gprof* and the interpretation of its output, since it is already covered in the GNU *gprof* manual, I will cover its cross-platform usage specifics.

First, you must modify your applications' Makefiles to add the appropriate compiler and linker options. Here are the portions of the Makefile provided in Chapter 4 that must be changed to build a program that will generate profiling data:

```
CFLAGS      = -Wall -pg
...
LDFLAGS     = -pg
```

Note that the *-pg* option is used both for the compiler flags *and* for the linker flags. The *-pg* compiler option tells the compiler to include the code for generating the performance data. The *-pg* linker option tells the linker to link the binary with *gcrt1.o* instead of *crt1.o*. The former is a special version of the latter that is necessary for profiling. Note also that we aren't using the *-O2* compiler optimization option. This is to make sure that the application generated executes in exactly the same way as we specified in the source file. We can then measure the performance of our own algorithms instead of measuring those optimized by the compiler.

Once your application has been recompiled, copy it to your target and run it. The program must run for quite a while to generate meaningful results. Provide your application with as wide a range of input as possible to exercise as much of its code as possible. Upon the application's exit, a *gmon.out* output file is generated with the profiling data. This file is cross-platform readable and you can therefore use your host's *gprof* to analyze it. After having copied the *gmon.out* file back to your application's source directory, use *gprof* to retrieve the call graph profile data:

```
$ gprof command-daemon
```

This command prints the call graph profile data to the standard output. Redirect this output using the > operator to a file if you like. You don't need to specify the *gmon.out* file specifically, it is automatically loaded. For more information regarding the use of *gprof*, see the GNU *gprof* manual.

Code Coverage

In addition to identifying the time spent in the different parts of your application, it is interesting to count how many times each statement in your application is being executed. This sort of coverage analysis can bring to light code that is never called or code that is called so often that it merits special attention.

The most common way to perform coverage analysis is to use a combination of compiler options and the *gcov* utility. This functionality relies on the gcc library, libgcc, which is compiled at the same time as the *gcc* compiler.

Unfortunately, however, gcc versions earlier than 3.0 don't allow the coverage functions to be compiled into libgcc when they detect that a cross-compiler is being built. In the case of the compiler built in Chapter 4, for example, the libgcc doesn't include the appropriate code to generate data about code coverage. It is therefore impossible to analyze the coverage of a program built against unmodified gcc sources.

To build the code needed for coverage analysis in versions of gcc later than 3.0, just configure them with the *--with-headers=* option.

To circumvent the same problem in gcc versions earlier than 3.0, edit the *gcc-2.95.3/gcc/libgcc2.c* file, or the equivalent file for your compiler version, and disable the following definition:

```
/* In a cross-compilation situation, default to inhibiting compilation
   of routines that use libc.  */

#if defined(CROSS_COMPILE) && !defined(inhibit_libc)
#define inhibit_libc
#endif
```

To disable the definition, add #if 0 and #endif around the code so that it looks like this:

```
/* gcc makes the assumption that we don't have glibc for the target,
   which is wrong in the case of embedded Linux. */
#if 0

/* In a cross-compilation situation, default to inhibiting compilation
   of routines that use libc.  */

#if defined(CROSS_COMPILE) && !defined(inhibit_libc)
#define inhibit_libc
#endif

#endif /* #if 0 */
```

Now recompile and reinstall gcc as we did in Chapter 4. You don't need to rebuild the bootstrap compiler, since we've already built and installed glibc. Build only the final compiler.

Next, modify your applications' Makefiles to use the appropriate compiler options. Here are the portions of the Makefile provided in Chapter 4 that must be changed to build a program that will generate code coverage data:

```
CFLAGS       = -Wall -fprofile-arcs -ftest-coverage
```

As we did before when compiling the application to generate profiling data, omit the *-O* optimization options to obtain the code coverage data that corresponds exactly to your source code.

For each source file compiled, you should now have a *.bb* and *.bbg* file in the source directory. Copy the program to your target and run it as you would normally. When you run the program, a *.da* file will be generated for each source file. Unfortunately, however, the *.da* files are generated using the absolute path to the original source files. Hence, you must create a copy of this path on your target's root filesystem. Though you may not run the binary from that directory, this is where the *.da* files for your application will be placed. My command daemon, for example, is located in */home/karim/control-project/control-module/project/command-daemon* on my host. I had to create that complete path on my target's root filesystem so that the daemon's *.da* files would be properly created. The *-p* option of *mkdir* was quite useful in this case.

Once the program is done executing, copy the *.da* files back to your host and run *gcov*:

```
$ gcov daemon.c
 71.08% of 837 source lines executed in file daemon.c
Creating daemon.c.gcov.
```

The *.gcov* file generated contains the coverage information in a human-readable form. The *.da* files are architecture-independent, so there's no problem in using the host's *gcov* to process them. For more information regarding the use of *gcov* or the output it generates, look at the *gcov* section of the gcc manual.

System Profiling

Every Linux system has many processes competing for system resources. Being able to quantify the impact each process has on the system's load is important in trying to build a balanced and responsive system. There are a few basic ways in Linux to quantify the effect the processes have on the system. This section discusses two of these: extracting information from */proc* and using LTT.

Basic /proc figures

The */proc* filesystem contains virtual entries where the kernel provides information regarding its own internal data structures and the system in general. Some of this information, such as process times, is based on samples collected by the kernel at each clock tick. The traditional package for extracting information from the */proc* directory is procps, which includes utilities like *ps* and *top*. There are currently two procps packages maintained independently. The first is maintained by Rik van Riel and is available from *http://surriel.com/procps/*. The second is maintained by Albert Cahalan and is available from *http://procps.sourceforge.net/*. Though there is an ongoing debate as to which is the "official" procps, both packages contain Makefiles that are not cross-platform development friendly, and neither is therefore fit for use in embedded systems. Instead, use the *ps* replacement found in BusyBox. Though it doesn't output process statistics as the *ps* in procps does, it does provide you with basic information regarding the software running on your target:

```
# ps
  PID  Uid      VmSize Stat Command
    1 0          820 S    init
    2 0              S    [keventd]
    3 0              S    [kswapd]
    4 0              S    [kreclaimd]
    5 0              S    [bdflush]
    6 0              S    [kupdated]
    7 0              S    [mtdblockd]
    8 0              S    [rpciod]
   16 0          816 S    -sh
   17 0          816 R    ps aux
```

If you find this information insufficient, you can browse */proc* manually to retrieve the information you need regarding each process.

Complete profile using LTT

Because LTT records crucial system information, it can extract very detailed information regarding the system's behavior. Unlike the information found in */proc*, the statistics generated by LTT are not sampled. Rather, they are based on an exact accounting of the time spent by processes inside the kernel. LTT provides two types of statistics: per-process statistics and system statistics. Both are provided in the "Process analysis" thumbnail.

The per-process statistics are display by LTT when you select a process in the process tree displayed in the "Process analysis" thumbnail. Figure 11-3 illustrates the data that can be extracted for a single process.

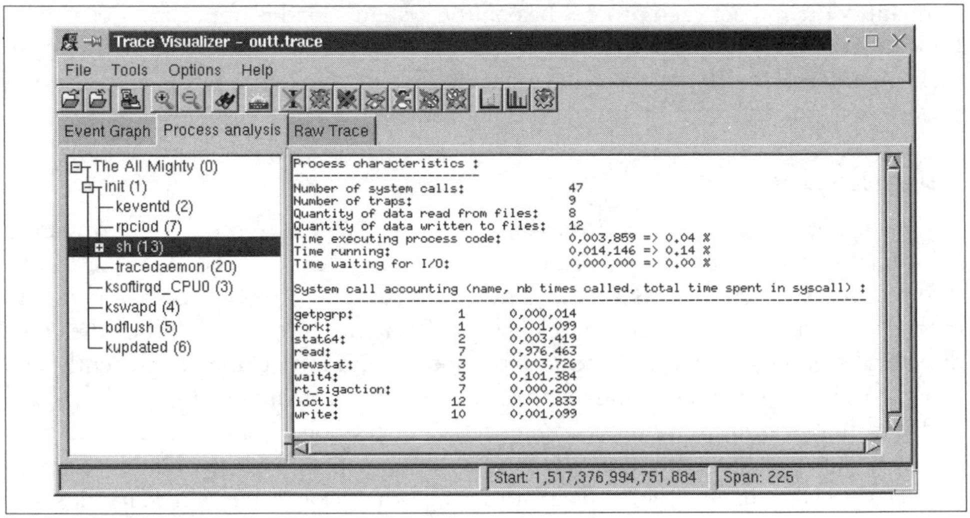

Figure 11-3. Single process statistics

Among other things, the data tells you how much time your task was scheduled by the kernel ("Time running") versus how much time was spent running actual application code ("Time executing process code"). In this case, the task wasn't waiting for any I/O. But if it did, the "Time waiting for I/O" line would give you a measure of how much time was spent waiting. The times and percentages given depend on the time spent tracing. In this case, tracing lasted 10 seconds.

LTT also provides information regarding the system calls made by an application. In particular, it gives you the number of times each system call was made and the total time the kernel took to service all these calls.

The system-wide statistics are displayed by LTT when you select the topmost process entry in the process tree, which is called "The All Mighty (0)." Figure 11-4 illustrates the system data extracted by LTT.

The system statistics start with a few numbers regarding the trace itself. In this case, the trace lasted almost 10 seconds and the system was idle for over 98% of that time. Next, the number of times a few key events have happened are provided. On 7467 events, LTT says that 1180 were traps and 96 were interrupts (with 96 IRQ entries and 96 IRQ exits.) This sort of information can help you pinpoint actual problems with the system's overall behavior. The screen also displays a cumulative summary of the system calls made by the various applications running on the system.

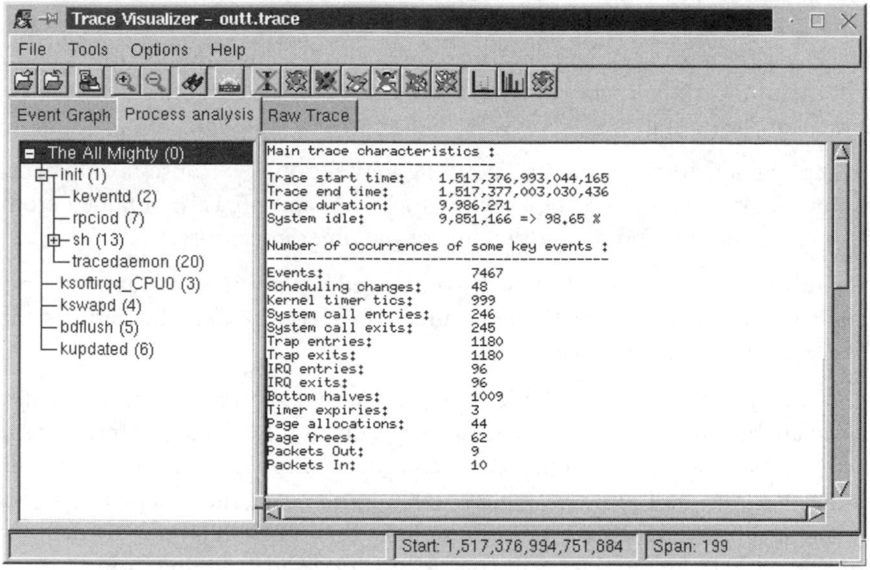

Figure 11-4. Overall system statistics

As with the actual trace information, the statistics displayed in the "Process analysis" thumbnail can be dumped in text form to file from the command line. Look at the LTT documentation for more information on how this is done.

Kernel Profiling

Sometimes the applications are not the root of performance degradation, but are rather suffering from the kernel's own performance problems. In that case, it is necessary to use the right tools to identify the reasons for the kernel's behavior.

There are quite a few tools for measuring the kernel's performance. The most famous is probably LMbench (*http://www.bitmover.com/lmbench/*). LMbench, however, requires a C compiler and the Perl interpreter. It is therefore not well adapted for use in embedded systems. Another tool for measuring kernel performance is kernprof (*http://oss.sgi.com/projects/kernprof/*). Though it can generate output that can be fed to *gprof*, it involves the use of a kernel patch and works only for x86, ia64, sparc64, and mips64. As you can see, most embedded architectures are not supported by kernprof.

There remains the sample-based profiling functionality built into the kernel. This profiling system works by sampling the instruction pointer on every timer interrupt. It then increments a counter according to the instruction pointer. Over a long period of time, it is expected that the functions where the kernel spends the greatest amount of time will have a higher number of hits than other functions. Though this is a crude kernel profiling method, it is the best one available at this time for most embedded Linux systems.

To activate kernel profiling, you must use the `profile=` boot parameter. The number you provide as a parameter sets the number of bits by which the instruction pointer is shifted to the right before being used as an index into the sample table. The smaller the number, the higher the precision of the samples, but the more memory is necessary for the sample table. The value most often used is 2.

The sampling activity itself doesn't slow the kernel down, because it only occurs at each clock tick and because the counter to increment is easily obtained from the value of the instruction pointer at the time of the timer interrupt.

Once you've booted a kernel to which you passed the `profile=` parameter, you will find a new entry in your target's */proc* directory, */proc/profile*. The kernel's sample table is exported to this */proc* entry.

To read the profile samples available from */proc/profile*, you must use the *readprofile* utility available as an independent package from *http://sourceforge.net/projects/minilop/* or as part of the util-linux package from *http://www.kernel.org/pub/linux/utils/util-linux/*. In the following explanations, I will cover the independent package only since util-linux includes a lot more utilities than just *readprofile*. Download the *readprofile* package and extract it in your *${PRJROOT}/debug* directory. Move to the package's directory and compile the utility:

```
$ cd ${PRJROOT}/debug/readprofile-3.0
$ make CC=powerpc-uclibc-gcc
```

To compile the utility statically, add `LDFLAGS="-static"` to the *make* command line. The binary generated is fairly small. When statically linked with uClibc and stripped, for example, it is 30 KB in size.

Once *readprofile* is built, copy it to your target's */usr/bin*:

```
$ cp readprofile ${PRJROOT}/rootfs/usr/bin
```

For *readprofile* to operate adequately, you must also copy the appropriate *System.map* kernel map file to your target's root filesystem:

```
$ cp ${PRJROOT}/images/System.map-2.4.18 ${PRJROOT}/rootfs/etc
```

With your target root filesystem ready, change the kernel boot parameters and add the `profile=2` boot parameter. After the system boots, you can run *readprofile*:

```
# readprofile -m /etc/System.map-2.4.18 > profile.out
```

The *profile.out* file now contains the profiling information in text form. At any time, you can erase the sample table collected on your target by writing to your target's */proc/profile*:[*]

```
# echo > /proc/profile
```

---

[*] There is nothing in particular that needs to be part of that write. Just the action of writing erases the profiling information.

When done profiling, copy the *profile.out* file back to your host and have a look at its contents:

```
$ cat profile.out
    ...
    30 __save_flags_ptr_end         0.3000
    10 __sti                        0.1250
     8 __flush_page_to_ram          0.1053
     7 clear_page                   0.1750
     3 copy_page                    0.0500
     1 m8xx_mask_and_ack            0.0179
     2 iopa                         0.0263
     1 map_page                     0.0089
    ...
     1 do_xprt_transmit             0.0010
     1 rpc_add_wait_queue           0.0035
     1 __rpc_sleep_on               0.0016
     1 rpc_wake_up_next             0.0068
     1 __rpc_execute                0.0013
     2 rpciod_down                  0.0043
    15 exit_devpts_fs               0.2885
 73678 total                        0.0618 0.04%
```

The left column indicates the number of samples taken at that location, followed by the name of the function where the sample was taken. The third column is a number that provides an approximation of the function's load, which is calculated as a ratio between the number of ticks that occurred in the function and the function's length. See the *readprofile* manpage included with the package for in-depth details about the utility's output.

Measuring Interrupt Latency

One of the most important metrics for real-time embedded systems is the time it takes for them to respond to outside events. Such systems, as I explained in Chapter 1, can cause catastrophic results if they do not respond in time.

There are a few known ad-hoc techniques for measuring a system's response time to interrupts (more commonly known as *interrupt latency*). These measurement techniques can be roughly divided into two categories:

Self-contained
> In this case, the system itself triggers the interrupts. To use this technique, you must connect one of your system's output pins to an interrupt-generating input pin. In the case of a PC-based system, this is easily achieved by connecting the appropriate parallel port pins together, as is detailed in the *Linux Device Drivers* book. For other types of systems, this may involve using more elaborate setups.

Induced
> Using this technique, the interrupts are triggered by an outside source, such as a frequency generator, by connecting it to an interrupt-generating input pin on the target.

In the case of the self-contained method, you must write a small software driver that initiates and handles the interrupt. To initiate the interrupt, the driver does two things:

1. Record the current time. This is often done using the do_gettimeofday( ) kernel function, which provides microsecond resolution. Alternatively, to obtain greater accuracy, you can also read the machine's hardware cycles using the get_cycles( ) function. On Pentium-class x86 systems, for example, this function will return the content of the TSC register. On the ARM, however, it will always return 0.

2. Toggle the output bit to trigger the interrupt. In the case of a PC-based system, for example, this is just a matter of writing the appropriate byte to the parallel port's data register.

The driver's interrupt handler, on the other hand, must do the following:

1. Record the current time.

2. Toggle the output pin.

By subtracting the time at which the interrupt was triggered from the time at which the interrupt handler is invoked, you get a figure that is very close to the actual interrupt latency. The reason this figure is not the actual interrupt latency is that you are partly measuring the time it takes for do_gettimeofday( ) and other software to run. Have your driver repeat the operation a number of times to quantify the variations in interrupt latency.

To get a better measure of the interrupt latency using the self-contained method, plug an oscilloscope on the output pin toggled by your driver and observe the time it takes for it to be toggled. This number should be slightly smaller than that obtained using do_gettimeofday( ), because the execution of the first call to this function is not included in the oscilloscope output. To get an even better measure of the interrupt latency, remove the calls to do_gettimeofday( ) completely and use only the oscilloscope to measure the time between bit toggles.

Though the self-contained method is fine for simple measurements on systems that can actually trigger and handle interrupts simultaneously in this fashion, the induced method is usually the most trusted way to measure interrupt latency, and is closest to the way in which interrupts are actually delivered to the system. If you have a driver that has high latency and contains code that changes the interrupt mask, for example, the interrupt driver for the self-contained method may have to wait until the high latency driver finishes before it can even trigger interrupts. Since the delay for triggering interrupts isn't measured, the self-contained method may fail to measure the worst-case impact of the high latency driver. The induced method, however, would not fail, since the interrupt's trigger source does not depend on the system being measured.

The software driver for the induced method is much simpler to write than that for the self-contained method. Basically, your driver has to implement an interrupt handler to toggle the state of one of the system's output pins. By plotting the system's response along with the square wave generated by the frequency generator, you can measure the exact time it takes for the system to respond to interrupts. Instead of an oscilloscope, you could use a simple counter circuit that counts the difference between the interrupt trigger and the target's response. The circuit would be reset by the interrupt trigger and would stop counting when receiving the target's response. You could also use another system whose only task is to measure the time difference between the interrupt trigger and the target's response.

However efficient the self-contained and the induced methods or any of their variants may be, Linux is not a real-time operating system. Hence, though you may observe steady interrupt latencies when the system is idle, Linux's response time will vary greatly whenever its processing load increases. Simply increase your target's processing load by typing *ls -R /* on your target while conducting interrupt latency tests and look at the flickering oscilloscope output to observe this effect.

One approach you may want to try is to measure interrupt latency while the system is at its peak load. This yields the maximum interrupt latency on your target. This latency may, however, be unacceptable for your application. If you need to have absolute bare-minimum bounded interrupt latency, you may want to consider using one of the real-time derivatives mentioned in Chapter 1.

Memory Debugging

Unlike desktop Linux systems, embedded Linux systems cannot afford to let applications eat up memory as they go or generate dumps because of illegal memory references. Among other things, there is no user to stop the offending applications and restart them. In developing applications for your embedded Linux system, you can employ special debugging libraries to ensure their correct behavior in terms of memory use. The following sections discuss two such libraries, Electric Fence and MEM-WATCH.

Though both libraries are worth linking to your applications during development, production systems should not include either library. First, both libraries substitute the C library's memory allocation functions with their own versions of these functions, which are optimized for debugging, not performance. Secondly, both libraries are distributed under the terms of the GPL. Hence, though you can use MEM-WATCH and Electric Fence internally to test your applications, you cannot distribute them as part of your applications outside your organization if your applications aren't also distributed under the terms of the GPL.

Electric Fence

Electric Fence is a library that replaces the C library's memory allocation functions, such as `malloc( )` and `free( )`, with equivalent functions that implement limit testing. It is, therefore, very effective at detecting out-of-bounds memory references. In essence, linking with the Electric Fence library will cause your applications to fault and dump core upon any out-of-bounds reference. By running your application within *gdb*, you can identify the faulty instruction immediately.

Electric Fence was written and continues to be maintained by Bruce Perens. It is available from *http://perens.com/FreeSoftware/*. Download the package and extract it in your *${PRJROOT}/debug* directory. For my control module, for example, I used Electric Fence 2.1.

Move to the package's directory for the rest of the installation:

```
$ cd ${PRJROOT}/debug/ElectricFence-2.1
```

Before you can compile Electric Fence for your target, you must edit the *page.c* source file and comment out the following code segment by adding `#if 0` and `#endif` around it:

```
#if ( !defined(sgi) && !defined(_AIX) )
extern int          sys_nerr;
extern char *       sys_errlist[ ];
#endif
```

If you do not modify the code in this way, Electric Fence fails to compile. With the code changed, compile and install Electric Fence for your target:

```
$ make CC=powerpc-linux-gcc AR=powerpc-linux-ar
$ make LIB_INSTALL_DIR=${TARGET_PREFIX}/lib \
> MAN_INSTALL_DIR=${TARGET_PREFIX}/man install
```

The Electric Fence library, *libefence.a*, which contains the memory allocation replacement functions, has now been installed in *${TARGET_PREFIX}/lib*. To link your applications with Electric Fence, you must add the *-lefence* option to your linker's command line. Here are the modifications I made to my command module's Makefile:

```
CFLAGS        = -g -Wall
...
LDFLAGS       = -lefence
```

The *-g* option is necessary if you want *gdb* to be able to print out the line causing the problem. The Electric Fence library adds about 30 KB to your binary when compiled in and stripped. Once built, copy the binary to your target for execution as you would usually.

By running the program on the target, you get something similar to:

```
# command-daemon

  Electric Fence 2.0.5 Copyright (C) 1987-1998 Bruce Perens.
Segmentation fault (core dumped)
```

Since you can't copy the *core* file back to the host for analysis, because it was generated on a system of a different architecture, start the *gdb* server on the target and connect to it from the host using the target *gdb*. As an example, here's how I start my command daemon on the target for Electric Fence debugging:

```
# gdbserver 192.168.172.50:2345 command-daemon
```

And on the host I do:

```
$ powerpc-linux-gcc command-daemon
(gdb) target remote 192.168.172.10:2345
Remote debugging using 192.168.172.10:2345
0x10000074 in _start ()
(gdb) continue
Continuing.

Program received signal SIGSEGV, Segmentation fault.
0x10000384 in main (argc=2, argv=0x7ffff794) at daemon.c:126
126             input_buf[input_index] = value_read;
```

In this case, the illegal reference was caused by an out-of-bounds write to an array at line 126 of file *daemon.c*. For more information on the use of Electric Fence, look at the ample manpage included in the package.

MEMWATCH

MEMWATCH replaces the usual memory allocation functions, such as `malloc( )` and `free( )`, with versions that keep track of allocations. It is very effective at detecting memory leaks such as when you forget to free a memory region or when you try to free a memory region more than once. This is especially important in embedded systems, since there is no one to monitor the device to check that the various applications aren't using up all the memory over time. MEMWATCH isn't as efficient as Electric Fence, however, to detect pointers that go astray. It was unable, for example, to detect the faulty array write presented in the previous section.

MEMWATCH is available from its project site at *http://www.linkdata.se/ sourcecode.html*. Download the package and extract it in your *${PRJROOT}/debug* directory. MEMWATCH consists of a header and a C file, which must be compiled with your application. To use MEMWATCH, start by copying both files to your application's source directory:

```
$ cd ${PRJROOT}/debug/memwatch-2.69
$ cp memwatch.c memwatch.h ${PRJROOT}/project/command-daemon
```

Modify the Makefile to add the new C file as part of the objects to compile and link. For my command daemon, for example, I used the following Makefile modifications:

```
CFLAGS       = -O2 -Wall -DMEMWATCH -DMW_STDIO
...
OBJS         = daemon.o memwatch.o
```

You must also add the MEMWATCH header to your source files:

```
#ifdef MEMWATCH
#include "memwatch.h"
#endif /* #ifdef MEMWATCH */
```

You can now cross-compile as you would usually. There are no special installation instructions for MEMWATCH. The *memwatch.c* and *memwatch.h* files add about 30 KB to your binary once built and stripped.

When the program runs, it generates a report on the behavior of the program, which it puts in the *memwatch.log* file in the directory where the binary runs. Here's an excerpt of the *memwatch.log* generated by running my command daemon:

```
============= MEMWATCH 2.69 Copyright (C) 1992-1999 Johan Lindh =====...
...
unfreed: <3> daemon.c(220), 60 bytes at 0x10023fe4          {FE FE FE ...
...
Memory usage statistics (global):
 N)umber of allocations made: 12
 L)argest memory usage      : 1600
 T)otal of all alloc() calls: 4570
 U)nfreed bytes totals      : 60
```

The unfreed: line tells you which line in your source code allocated memory that was never freed later. In this case, 60 bytes are allocated at line 220 of *daemon.c* and are never freed. The T)otal of all alloc() calls: line indicates the total quantity of memory allocated throughout your program's execution. In this case, the program allocated 4570 bytes in total.

Look at the *FAQ*, *README*, and *USING* files included in the package for more information on the use of MEMWATCH and the output it provides.

A Word on Hardware Tools

Throughout this chapter we have mainly concentrated on software tools for debugging embedded Linux software. In addition to these, there are a slew of hardware tools and helpers for debugging embedded software. As I said earlier in this chapter, the use of a particular operating system for the target makes little difference to the way you would normally use such hardware tools. Though hardware tools are sometimes more effective than software tools to debug software problems, one caveat of hardware tools is that they are almost always expensive. A good 100 Mhz oscilloscope, for example, costs no less than a thousand dollars. Let us, nevertheless, review some of the hardware tools you may use in debugging an embedded target running Linux.

 Although brand-new hardware tools tend to be expensive, renting your tools or buying secondhand ones can save you a lot of money. There are actually companies that specialize in renting and refurbishing hardware tools.

The most basic tool that can assist you in your development is most likely an oscillo-scope. As we saw in "Measuring Interrupt Latency," it can be used to measure interrupt latency. It can, however, be put to many other uses both for observing your target's interaction with the outside world and for monitoring internal signals on your board's circuitry.

Though an oscilloscope is quite effective at monitoring a relatively short number of signals, it is not adapted for analyzing the type of transfers that occur on many wires simultaneously, such as on a system's memory or I/O bus. To analyze such traffic, you must use a logic analyzer. This allows you to view the various values being trans-mitted over a bus. On an address bus, for example, the logic analyzer will enable you to see the actual addresses transiting on the wires. This tool will also enable you to identify glitches and anomalies.

If the problem isn't at a signal level, but is rather caused by faulty or immature oper-ating system software, you need to use either an In-Circuit Emulator (ICE), or a BDM or JTAG debugger. The former relies on intercepting the processor's interac-tion with the rest of the system, while the latter rely on functionality encoded in the processor's silicon and exported via a few special pins, as described in Chapter 2. For many reasons, ICEs have been gradually replaced by BDM or JTAG debuggers. Both, however, allow you to debug the operating system kernel using hardware-enforced capabilities. You can, for instance, debug a crashing Linux kernel using such tools. As a matter of fact, the Linux kernel is usually ported to new architectures with the help of BDM and JTAG debuggers. If you are building your embedded system from scratch, you should seriously consider having a BDM or JTAG interface available for developers so that they can attach a BDM or JTAG debugger, even though it may be expensive. Most commercial embedded boards are already equipped with the appro-priate connectors.

There is at least one open source BDM debugger available complete with *gdb* patches and hardware schematics. The project is called BDM4GDB and its web site is located at *http://bdm4gdb.sourceforge.net/*. This project supports only the MPC 860, 850, and 823 PowerPC processors, however. Though this is quite a feat in itself, BDM4GDB is not a universal BDM debugger.

The LART project (*http://www.lart.tudelft.nl/*) provides a JTAG dongle for program-ming the flash of its StrongARM-based system. This dongle's schematics and the required software are available from *http://www.lart.tudelft.nl/projects/jtag/*. Though this dongle can be used to reprogram the flash device, it cannot be used to debug the system. For that, you still need a real JTAG debugger.

If you are not familiar with the subject of debugging embedded systems with hard-ware tools, I encourage you to look at Arnold Berger's *Embedded Systems Design* (CMP Books), and Jack Ganssle's *The Art of Designing Embedded Systems* (Newnes). If you are actively involved in designing or changing your target's hardware, you are likely to be interested by John Catsoulis' *Designing Embedded Hardware* (O'Reilly).

Worksheet

Though embedded Linux systems differ greatly, the method outlined in this book should readily apply to building any sort of embedded Linux system. It follows from this that it is possible to lay out a set of rules for specifying the particularities of each embedded Linux system. The worksheet presented in this appendix does just that. Once completed, any developer can use a worksheet in conjunction with the explanations in this book to recreate an embedded Linux system without any assistance from the original designers. During development, the worksheet can be used by members of the development team to obtain detailed information regarding each component of the system.

The worksheet contains one section for detailing each aspect of an embedded Linux system. Each section contains a set of attributes pertaining to the aspect of the embedded Linux system it describes. The sections are:

- Project identification
- Hardware summary
- Development tools
- Kernel
- Root filesystem
- Storage device organization
- Bootloader configuration and use
- Networking services
- Custom project software
- Debug notes
- Additional notes

Most sections include a "Main contact" field. This field should be used to specify the name of the person responsible for this particular aspect of the embedded system during development. The person in charge of a certain aspect of the system is expected to be aware of the various caveats and keep up to date with the recent developments of the relevant open source and free software packages. The person responsible for the kernel, for example, should ideally be subscribed to the Linux kernel mailing list and the kernel development list for the architecture the system is based on.

Though the worksheet attempts to be as exhaustive as possible, you may need to modify it and extend it for your project's purposes. The number of entries for listing some system components, such as the "Peripherals" list in the "Hardware summary" section for example, may be insufficient to describe your system. Feel free to add more pages to leave more space for detailing your system's characteristics.

A copy of the blank worksheet is available for download in PDF and OpenOffice format from the book's web site at *http://www.embeddedtux.org/*. Alternatively, you can photocopy the worksheet included in this appendix. Avoid writing directly in this book, however, as you may want to make changes to your worksheet and use the book across different projects.

The rest of this chapter describes each section of the worksheet in detail. Though the meaning of most fields should be apparent, some fields may require some explanation. Whenever appropriate, references the relevant chapters are provided.

Project Identification

This section contains high-level information regarding your embedded system. Most of the information required for this section can be found in Chapter 1. Table A-1 describes each field in the "Project identification" section.

Table A-1. Description of "Project identification" fields

Field	Description
Name	The name of the project.
Internal ID	The number or string uniquely identifying this project in your organization.
Project leader	The main person in charge of the project.
Start date	The date at which the project started.
Expected completion date	The date at which the project is expected to be finished.
Project description	A high-level description of your project.
Type of system	The type of the system as presented in Chapter 1.

Table A-1. Description of "Project identification" fields (continued)

Field	Description
Size	One of: small, medium, or large. See Chapter 1 for the complete description of each embedded Linux system type.
Time constraints	One of: mild or stringent. See Chapter 1 for the discussion regarding each type of time constraint.
Degree of user interaction	A qualitative measure of how elaborate the system's user interface is. See Chapter 1 for examples.
Are networking services offered or used?	One of: yes or no.

Hardware Summary

This section contains detailed information regarding your hardware from the software perspective. The information required for this section is most likely found in your embedded system's specifications, which are available either from your hardware department or from your board and processor vendors. This hardware information is crucial for many aspects of building the embedded Linux system. Table A-2 describes each field in the "Hardware summary" section. As I said earlier, feel free to extend the number of entries related to "Peripherals" so there's one for each of your system's peripherals.

Table A-2. Description of "Hardware summary" fields

Field	Description
Processor family	One of the processor families discussed in Chapter 3.
Processor model	The processor model within a processor family. If the processor is part of the PowerPC family, for example, its model could be 450, 750, 860, etc.
Board type	Manufacturers usually have board families or types that have similar characteristics. You can leave this field empty if there is no such characteristic for your board.
Board model	The model or part number for your board.
RAM size	The size of system RAM.
RAM start and end addr	The location of the RAM in the physical address space.
ROM/Flash size	The size of system ROM or flash.
ROM/Flash start and end addr	The location of the ROM/Flash in the physical address space.
ROM/Flash model	The ROM or flash chip model.
Processor startup address	The address from which the processor fetches its first instruction.
Disk storage type	Fill this field if you are using an IDE or SCSI device or a device that acts as one, such as a CompactFlash device.
Disk storage size	The storage space available on the disk device.

Field	Description
Peripherals: Type	The kind of peripheral device: Ethernet controller, video controller, CAN interface, etc.
Peripherals: Model	The model or part number for the peripheral chip.
Peripherals: Description	A description of the peripheral's characteristics.
Peripherals: Mem location	The physical address space window used to access the peripheral.
Peripherals: ID	Some peripherals have unique IDs. If the peripheral is an Ethernet device, for example, write the device's MAC address, if there's only one such device being produced, or the MAC address range used for the production run, if there are many units produced.

Development Tools

This section describes the developments tools used for building the embedded system and how these tools are themselves created. Most of the information in this section pertains to the setup of the development tools as described in Chapter 4. You should record this information as you build the tools so you don't lose the information. Table A-3 describes each field in the "Development tools" section. Many of the fields are identical for all development tools.

Table A-3. Description of "Development tools" fields

Field	Description
Host type	The type of host used for development. See Chapter 2 for the types of hosts that can be used for embedded Linux development.
Tool: version	The official version of the tool as downloaded from its project's web site.
Tool: Special build flags	Any build flags used to build the tool that are not listed in Chapter 4.
Tool: Special configuration flags	Any configuration flags used to configure the tool that are not listed in Chapter 4.
Tool: Configuration summary	A summary of the way the tool's build was configured. This applies to uClibc only, as discussed in Chapter 4.
Tool: Patches/Changes	A description of the patches or changes applied to the tool.
Editor/IDE	The editor or IDE used by the members of the development team for this project.
Terminal emulator	The terminal emulator used by the members of the development team for this project.
Notes	Any additional notes regarding the setup and use of the development tools.

Kernel

This section contains complete details regarding the kernel used in the embedded system. This information is to be used in conjunction with the explanations provided in Chapter 5. Table A-4 describes each field in the "Kernel" section.

Table A-4. Description of "Kernel" fields

Field	Description
Version	The official kernel version as obtained from the primary download site for your architecture.
Download location	The URL from which you obtained the kernel.
Patches: Description	A description of the patch you applied.
Patches: Download location	The URL from which you obtained the patch.
Configuration file location	The complete path on your internal servers or repository to the configuration file used to build the system's kernel.
Configuration summary	A detailed list of the most important configuration options enabled for the system's kernel.
Kernel failure handler description	A description of the kernel panic handler implemented for your system. See "In the Field" in Chapter 5 for details.

Root filesystem

This section contains complete details of the target's root filesystem. This information is to be used in conjunction with the explanations provided in Chapter 6. Table A-5 describes each field in the "Root filesystem" section. The "*/dev* device entries" part of this section lists the */dev* entries created in addition to those discussed in Chapter 6. The "System applications" part of this section lists the system applications used to provide basic Unix services, such as BusyBox, TinyLogin, and Embutils. The "System initialization" part of this section lists the services started by *init* and the fashion in which they are started.

Table A-5. Description of "Root filesystem" fields

Field	Description
C library	The C library used in the embedded system: glibc, uClibc, or diet libc.
C library components	The C library components copied to the target's */lib* directory as discussed in Chapter 6.
/dev device entries: Name	The name of the entry.
/dev device entries: Major nbr	The device major number for this entry.
/dev device entries: Minor nbr	The device minor number for this entry.
/dev device entries: Used by	The applications that use this entry.
System applications: Package	The name of the system application package.
System applications: Version	The package version
System applications: Build config	A summary of the package's configuration. For BusyBox, for example, list the configuration changes to the configuration default.

Field	Description
System applications: Config file location	The complete path on your internal servers or repository to the configuration file used to build this package.
System initialization: Service	The service or binary being started.
System initialization: Type of activation	The type of *init* activation. Examples include: askfirst, wait, and once. See Chapter 6 for the complete list.

Storage Device Organization

This section describes the content of the system's storage device. The primary storage device is expected to be a ROM or flash storage chip, whereas the secondary storage device is either a disk or additional solid-state storage devices. The contents of this section should be used in conjunction with the explanations in Chapters 7 and 8. Table A-6 describes each field in the "Storage device organization" section.

Table A-6. Description of "Storage device organization" fields

Field	Description
Development setup	The setup used for transferring software components from the host to the target as described in Chapter 2.
Storage device[a] content: Component	The type of component stored. This can be a bootloader, a kernel, boot parameters, or any sort of filesystem, including a root filesystem.
Storage device content: Size	The storage size allocated to this component.
Storage device content: Location	The location of the component within the storage device. In the case of a solid-state storage device, such as ROM or flash, this is the physical start and end addresses. In the case of a disk storage device, this is the start and end sectors.
Storage device content: Dependency	The other components that load or use this component. A root filesystem, for example, depends on a kernel, and a kernel depends on a bootloader.
Storage device content: Format	The format in which the component is stored. For a filesystem, for instance, this is the filesystem type, such as ext2 or JFFS2.

[a] Though the entries listed here are generic, the are many possible types of storage devices, as I said earlier.

Bootloader Configuration and Use

This section contains detailed information on the bootloader's configuration and use. This information is to be used in conjunction with the explanations in Chapter 9. Table A-7 describes each field in the "Bootloader configuration and use" section.

Table A-7. Description of "Bootloader configuration and use" fields

Field	Description
Package	The bootloader used in the system.
Version	The package version.
Build configuration	A description of the build configuration.
Setup procedure	The manner in which the bootloader is installed in the target's storage device. This can include both software and hardware manipulations.
Boot options: Option	One of the boot options configured into the bootloader.
Boot options: Description	A description of the result of selecting this boot option.
Default boot option	The boot option activated if no other option is selected.
Security	The security procedure for locking and unlocking the bootloader to avoid user tampering.

Networking services

This section provides details regarding the networking services offered by the embedded system. This information is to be used in conjunction with the explanations provided in Chapter 10. Table A-8 describes each field in the "Networking services" section.

Table A-8. Description of "Networking services" fields

Field	Description
Main network service	The main network service provided by the system.
Service	The networking service being offered
Package	The package used to offer the networking service.
Version	The package version.
Configuration summary	A summary of the package's configuration.

Custom Project Software

This section provides information regarding your custom software project. This information can be obtained only by analyzing your own software. This isn't meant to be a complete description of such software. It is expected that your team has its own internal documentation regarding the project's architecture and internals. This worksheet section is really just a summary meant to provide a bird's eye view of how your custom software interacts with the rest of the system. Table A-9 describes each field in the "Custom project software" section.

Table A-9. Description of "Custom project software" fields

Field	Description
Main source repository	The main repository where your project's source code is stored.
Code maintainer	The main person in charge of the project's source code.
Location in target root filesystem	The complete path to the final location of the project's components on your target's root filesystem.
Binary size	The total size of all binaries in your project.
Data size	The total maximum size occupied by your project's data.
Dependencies	The other software packages on which your project depends. The C library is likely to be one of the dependencies listed here.
Initialization procedure	The way in which the software is started by the other system components. If your software is launched by *init*, say it here.

Debug Notes

This section contains information about debugging your project. The information in this section is to be used in conjunction with the explanations provided in Chapter 11. Debugging is a creative process, and it is done differently by each developer. This worksheet section is, therefore, only meant to be a summary. It is very likely that your team will need to maintain its own up-to-date bug list during project development. Table A-10 describes each field in the "Debug notes" section.

Table A-10. Description of "Debug notes" fields

Field	Description
Tools used	The detailed list of tools used to debug the system.
Summary of major bugs found	A summary of the most important bugs found in your system.
System's fragilities	Every system has its weaknesses. Listing these explicitly will help you, and others that work on this system, keep an eye out for problems that may be caused by these fragilities.

Additional Notes

Use this worksheet section to add any additional details about your embedded system you think would be helpful for anyone that works on the project or that may need to understand how the project components are assembled. Depending on your actual system, you may also prefer to create an additional worksheet section to enter details about other aspects of your embedded system not covered by the current version of the worksheet.

Embedded Linux Systems Worksheet

Project identification

Name:

Internal ID:

Project leader:

Start date:

Expected completion date:

Project description:

Type of system: Size:

Time constraints: Degree of user interaction:

Are networking services offered or used?:

Hardware summary

Processor family: Main contact:

Processor model:

Board type:

Board model:

RAM size: Start addr: End addr:

ROM/Flash size: Start addr: End addr:

ROM/Flash model: Processor startup address:

Disk storage type: Disk storage size:

Peripherals

Type	Model	Description	Mem location	ID
			Start:	
			End:	
			Start:	
			End:	
			Start:	
			End:	

Development tools	
Host type:	Main contact:

binutils version:

Special build flags:

Patches / Changes:

Patch location / Change description:

gcc version:

Special configuration flags:

Patches / Changes:

Patch location / Change description:

glibc version:

Special configuration flags:

Patches / Changes:

Patch location / Change description:

uClibc version:

Configuration summary:

Patches / Changes:

Patch location / Change description:

diet libc version:

Special build flags:

Patches / Changes:

Patch location / Change description:

Editor / IDE:

Terminal emulator:

Notes:

Kernel		
Version:		**Main contact:**
Download location:		
	Patches	
Description	*Download location*	

Configuration file location:

Configuration summary:

Kernel failure handler description:

Root filesystem	
C library:	Main contact:
C library components:	

/dev device entries			
Name	*Major nbr*	*Minor nbr*	*Used by*

System applications			
Package	*Version*	*Build config*	*Config file location*

System initialization	
Service	*Type of activation*

Storage device organization

Development setup:			Main contact:		

Primary storage device content

Component	Size	Location	Dependency	Format
		Start:		
		End:		
		Start:		
		End:		
		Start:		
		End:		
		Start:		
		End:		
		Start:		
		End:		
		Start:		
		End:		
		Start:		
		End:		

Secondary storage device content

Component	Size	Location	Dependency	Format
		Start:		
		End:		
		Start:		
		End:		
		Start:		
		End:		
		Start:		
		End:		
		Start:		
		End:		
		Start:		
		End:		
		Start:		
		End:		

Bootloader configuration and use

Package: **Main contact:**

Version:

Build configuration:

Setup procedure:

Boot options

Option	Description

Default boot option:

Security:

Networking services

Main network service: **Main contact:**

Service	Package	Version	Configuration summary

Custom project software

Main source repository:

Code maintainer:

Location in target root filesystem:

Binary size:

Data size:

Dependencies:

Initialization procedure:

Debug notes

Tools used:

Summary of major bugs found:

System's fragilities:

Additional notes

Resources

This book refers to external material when appropriate. The following references point to material that parallels this book or is in the periphery of the issues discussed.

Online

With the ever-increasing popularity of "embedded Linux," many sites have been created to help potential users and adopters. Here is a list of such sites in alphabetical order:

All Linux Devices (http://alllinuxdevices.com/)
> Contains links to stories and news items related to embedded Linux. Maintained as part of Internet.com's Linux resources.

Embedded-Linux.de (http://embedded-linux.de/)
> German-language site providing updates about the releases of some of the main open source packages used in embedded Linux systems, such as BusyBox and uClibc.

LinuxAutomation (http://www.linux-automation.de/)
> Contains a well-organized set of links to various resources related to the use of Linux in automation applications. Though the site's main page is in German, a link is provided to an English version of the same site. Maintained by Robert Schwebel.

LinuxDevices.com (http://www.linuxdevices.com/)
> Contains lots of industry-related news items. Also contains articles about open source and free software community developments, but clearly has a commercial perspective. This site provides many introductory guides and is frequently updated. Likely the most visible embedded Linux site around.

Linux Documentation Project (http://www.tldp.org/)
> The main repository for HOWTOs, FAQs, and other guides about open source and free software packages. Probably one of the most important Linux resources given the breadth and depth of issues covered by its documents. This site is community maintained.

SiliconPenguin.com (http://www.siliconpenguin.com/)
> Contains a collection of links to embedded Linux-related material.

uCdot (http://www.ucdot.org/)
> A news and community site for uClinux users.

Though this list includes sites that specialize in providing information about embedded Linux, there are many other sites that provide general Linux information which you may find useful. Consult *Running Linux* for such sites.

Books

There are quite a few books out there about Linux and about embedded systems in general. Here are a few titles that you may find useful:

Advanced Programming in the UNIX Environment, by Richard Stevens (Addison Wesley)
> Considered by many as the most important Unix programming book available. If you need understand how to think and program in the Unix mindset, this is the book you need. Stevens' books are, in general, highly recommended.

The Art of Designing Embedded Systems, by Jack Ganssle (Newnes Press)
> This book's style is different from most other technical books in that it uses a mix of technical explanations and practical advice about real-life issues. It captures the essence of the experiences most embedded system designers have in their day-to-day work. Jack Ganssle has regular columns in *Embedded Systems Programming* magazine and is a frequent speaker at embedded systems conferences.

Embedded Systems Design, by Arnold S. Berger (CMP Books)
> An introductory text to embedded system design from both the hardware and the software perspective. If you are not familiar with the process of developing embedded systems, you will find this book helpful.

Linux Device Drivers, by Alessandro Rubini and Jonathan Corbet (O'Reilly)
> The classic text book for understanding how Linux device drivers are developed. Written by two respected members of the open source and free software community. A must read for any Linux device driver developer.

Running Linux, by Matt Welsh, Lar Kaufman, Terry Dawson, and Matthias Kalle Dalheimer (O'Reilly)
> This book provides you with all that you need to learn how to install and use Linux without requiring any prior knowledge of either Linux or Unix. I've owned a copy of this book's first edition and have come back to it every time I forgot how something was done in Linux. A terrific book that covers much of

the background material required to make the best out of the use of Linux in embedded systems.

Programming Embedded Systems in C and C++, by Michael Barr (O'Reilly)
This introductory book covers the basics of embedded software development and offers insight into many of the software tricks used in developing embedded systems.

Understanding the Linux Kernel, by Daniel Bovet and Marco Cesati (O'Reilly)
There have been a number of books on the Linux kernel's internals over the years. This one is particularily well researched and structured, and has been updated to cover the current stable version of Linux, 2.4.

Publications

Though there aren't any embedded Linux–centric publications at the time of this writing, there are many publications that discuss the use of Linux in embedded systems as part of the other issues they cover:

Embedded Systems Programming (http://www.embedded.com/mag.html)
The main magazine for embedded software programmers. Contains many very interesting and in-depth articles about specific issues. Subscription to this magazine is free for qualified readers. I strongly encourage you to take the time to subscribe to this publication.

Linux Journal (http://www.linuxjournal.com/)
The oldest of the Linux publications and the most well-established. The publishers of *Linux Journal* also started an *Embedded Linux Journal* publication that specialized in covering the use of Linux in embedded systems, but it was later discontinued. Instead, there is a regular "Embedded" section in every *Linux Journal* issue.

Linux Magazine (http://www.linuxmagazine.com/)
Another well-established Linux publication. Covers various aspects of Linux's use in a range of applications.

Linux Magazine France (http://www.linuxmag-france.org/)
A French-language publication that provides thorough articles about various open source and free software packages. Articles often provide a lot of programming examples and tips on how to use and configure various commands and services.

Organizations

As discussed in Chapter 1, there are a number of organizations who's activities are relevant to the use of Linux in embedded systems:

- Embedded Linux Consortium (*http://www.embedded-linux.org/*)
- Emblix (*http://www.emblix.org/*)

- Filesystem Hierarchy Standard Group (*http://www.pathname.com/fhs/*)
- Free Software Foundation (*http://www.fsf.org/*)
- Free Standards Group (*http://www.freestandards.org/*)
- Linux Standard Base (*http://www.linuxbase.org/*)
- OpenGroup (*http://www.opengroup.org/*)
- Real-Time Linux Foundation (*http://www.realtimelinuxfoundation.org/*)
- TV Linux Alliance (*http://www.tvlinuxalliance.org/*)

Linux and Open-Source-Oriented Hardware Projects

FreeIO (http://www.freeio.org/)
> FreeIO (Free Hardware Resources for the Free Software Community) is an effort to develop and distribute hardware schematics and designs under the terms of the GNU GPL. The web site already hosts a number of hardware designs along with the relevant Linux drivers.

LART (http://www.lart.tudelft.nl/)
> This project's goal is to develop a StrongARM-based embedded board that runs Linux. The board schematics and lots of extension modules and software are available from the project's web site.

MyLinux (http://www.azpower.com/mylinux/)
> This project aims to develop a SuperH-based PDA-like embedded system that runs Linux. The project's details along with pictures are available from the project's web site.

Opencores.ORG (http://www.opencores.org/)
> A collection of projects that develop Intellectual Property (IP) cores and distribute them under the terms of the GNU GPL. Quite a few building blocks are already available.

Simputer (http://www.simputer.org/)
> An effort to develop an inexpensive reference hardware platform that runs Linux.

TuxScreen (http://www.tuxscreen.net/)
> Originally a Philips product, TuxScreen is a StrongARM-based platform that includes a phone set, a screen, and a full keyboard. Though no more units are available for purchase, the site includes schematics that may be useful to other projects.

uClinux boards (http://www.uclinux.org/)
> One of the first hardware projects specifically aimed at building an embedded system capable of running Linux. The MMU-less port of Linux originates from this project.

Important Licenses and Notices

The use and distribution of open source and free software is subject to a few well-known and widely advertised licenses, as we discussed in Chapter 1. There are, nevertheless, some issues surrounding Linux's licensing that keep resurfacing and seem to cause confusion. These uncertainties revolve around the fact that the Linux kernel is itself distributed under the terms of the GNU GPL.

Over time, Linus Torvalds and other kernel developers have helped shed some light on the limits and reaches of the kernel's licensing. This appendix presents some of the messages published by Linus and other kernel developers regarding three aspects of the kernel's licensing: the use of non-GPL applications, the use of binary-only modules, and the general licensing issues surrounding the kernel's source code.

Exclusion of User-Space Applications from Kernel's GPL

To avoid any confusion regarding the status of applications running on top of the Linux kernel, Linus Torvalds added the following preamble to the kernel's license:

```
   NOTE! This copyright does *not* cover user programs that use kernel
services by normal system calls - this is merely considered normal use
of the kernel, and does *not* fall under the heading of "derived work".
Also note that the GPL below is copyrighted by the Free Software
Foundation, but the instance of code that it refers to (the Linux
kernel) is copyrighted by me and others who actually wrote it.

Also note that the only valid version of the GPL as far as the kernel
is concerned is _this_ license (ie v2), unless explicitly otherwise
stated.

                    Linus Torvalds
```

Notices on Binary Kernel Modules

Recurring controversy has erupted over loadable kernel modules not distributed under the terms of the GPL. Many companies already ship such binary modules and many industry players contend that such modules are permitted. Yet many Linux kernel developers have come out rather strongly against this practice. Here are some messages sent to the Linux kernel mailing list by Linus Torvalds and Alan Cox that provide some insight as to the use of binary modules.

First Posting by Linus in Kernel Interface Thread

```
From:     torvalds@transmeta.com (Linus Torvalds)
Subject:  Re: Kernel interface changes (was Re: cdrecord problems on
Date:     1999-02-05 7:13:23

In article <36bab0c7.394438@mail.cloud9.net>,
John Alvord <jalvo@cloud9.net> wrote:
>On Thu, 4 Feb 1999 22:37:06 -0500 (EST), "Theodore Y. Ts'o"
><tytso@MIT.EDU> wrote:
>>
>>And as a result, I've seen more than a few MIT users decide to give up
>>on Linux and move over to NetBSD.  I think this is bad, and I'm hoping
>>we can take just a little bit more care in the 2.2 series than we did in
>>the 2.0 series.  Is that really too much to ask?

Yes.  I think it is.  I will strive for binary compatibility for
modules, but I _expect_ that it will be broken.  It's just too easy to
have to make changes that break binary-only modules, and I have too
little incentive to try to avoid it.

If people feel this is a problem, I see a few alternatives:
 - don't use stuff with binary-only modules. Just say no.
 - work hard at making a source-version of the thing available (it
   doesn't have to be under the GPL if it's a module, but it has to be
   available as source so that it can be recompiled).
 - don't upgrade
 - drop Linux

>I suggest we treat binary compatibility problems as bugs which need to
>be resolved during the 2.2 lifetime. Even with all care, some changes
>will occur because of mistakes... if we cure them, there will be
>limited impact to users.

It's often not mistakes.  Things sometimes have to change, and I
personally do not care for binary-only modules enough to even care.  If
people want to use Linux, they have to live with this.  In 2.2.x, the
basics may be stable enough that maybe the binary module interface won't
actually change.  I don't know.  That would be good, but if it is not to
be, then it is not to be.
```

I _allow_ binary-only modules. I allow them because I think that
sometimes I cannot morally require people to make sources available to
projects like AFS where those sources existed before Linux. HOWEVER,
that does not mean that I have to _like_ AFS as a binary-only module.

Quite frankly, I hope AFS dies a slow and painful death with people
migrating to better alternatives (coda, whatever). Or that somebody
makes an AFS client available in source form, either as a clone or
through the original people.

As it is, what has AFS done for me lately? Nothing. So why should I
care?

> Linus

Second Posting by Linus in Kernel Interface Thread

From: torvalds@transmeta.com (Linus Torvalds)
Subject: Re: Kernel interface changes (was Re: cdrecord problems on
Date: 1999-02-07 8:15:24

In article <79g5buspd1@palladium.transmeta.com>,
H. Peter Anvin <hpa@transmeta.com> wrote:
>
>* Linus Torvalds has no interest whatsoever in developing such a
> plug-in ABI. Someone else is welcome to do it.

No, it's even more than that.

I _refuse_ to even consider tying my hands over some binary-only module.

Hannu Savolainen tried to add some layering to make the sound modules
more "portable" among Linux kernel versions, and I disliked it for two
reasons:

  - extra layers decrease readability, and sometimes make for performance
    problems. The readability thing is actually the larger beef I had
    with this: I just don't want to see drivers start using some strange
    wrapper format that has absolutely nothing to do with how they work.

  - I _want_ people to expect that interfaces change. I _want_ people to
    know that binary-only modules cannot be used from release to release.
    I want people to be really really REALLY aware of the fact that when
    they use a binary-only module, they tie their hands.

Note that the second point is mainly psychological, but it's by far the
most important one.

Basically, I want people to know that when they use binary-only modules,
it's THEIR problem. I want people to know that in their bones, and I
want it shouted out from the rooftops. I want people to wake up in a
cold sweat every once in a while if they use binary-only modules.

Why? Because I'm a prick, and I want people to suffer? No.

Because I _know_ that I will eventually make changes that break modules. And I want people to expect them, and I never EVER want to see an email in my mailbox that says "Damn you, Linus, I used this binary module for over two years, and it worked perfectly across 150 kernel releases, and Linux-5.6.71 broke it, and you had better fix your kernel".

See?

I refuse to be at the mercy of any binary-only module. And that's why I refuse to care about them - not because of any really technical reasons, not because I'm a callous bastard, but because I refuse to tie my hands behind my back and hear somebody say "Bend Over, Boy, Because You Have It Coming To You".

I allow binary-only modules, but I want people to know that they are _only_ ever expected to work on the one version of the kernel that they were compiled for. Anything else is just a very nice unexpected bonus if it happens to work.

And THAT, my friend, is why when somebody complains about AFS, I tell them to go screw themselves, and not come complaining to me but complain to the AFS boys and girls. And why I'm not very interested in changing that.

> Linus

Post by Alan Cox in Kernel Hooks Thread

This is a response to a posting by *Theodore Ts'O*.

From: Alan Cox <alan@lxorguk.ukuu.org.uk>
Subject: Re: [ANNOUNCE] Generalised Kernel Hooks Interface (GKHI)
Date: 2000-11-09 14:26:33

> Actually, he's been quite specific. It's ok to have binary modules as
> long as they conform to the interface defined in /proc/ksyms.

What is completely unclear is if he has the authority to say that given that there is code from other people including the FSF merged into the tree.

I've taken to telling folks who ask about binary modules to talk to their legal department. The whole question is simply to complicated for anyone else to work on.

> Alan

First Post by Linus in Security Hooks License Thread

From: Linus Torvalds <torvalds@transmeta.com>
Subject: Re: [PATCH] make LSM register functions GPLonly exports
Date: 2002-10-17 17:08:19

Note that if this fight ends up being a major issue, I'm just going to remove LSM and let the security vendors do their own thing. So far

- I have not seen a lot of actual usage of the hooks
- seen a number of people who still worry that the hooks degrade performance in critical areas
- the worry that people use it for non-GPL'd modules is apparently real, considering Crispin's reply.

I will re-iterate my stance on the GPL and kernel modules:

There is NOTHING in the kernel license that allows modules to be non-GPL'd.

The _only_ thing that allows for non-GPL modules is copyright law, and in particular the "derived work" issue. A vendor who distributes non-GPL modules is _not_ protected by the module interface per se, and should feel very confident that they can show in a court of law that the code is not derived.

The module interface has NEVER been documented or meant to be a GPL barrier. The COPYING clearly states that the system call layer is such a barrier, so if you do your work in user land you're not in any way beholden to the GPL. The module interfaces are not system calls: there are system calls used to _install_ them, but the actual interfaces are not.

The original binary-only modules were for things that were pre-existing works of code, ie drivers and filesystems ported from other operating systems, which thus could clearly be argued to not be derived works, and the original limited export table also acted somewhat as a barrier to show a level of distance.

In short, Crispin: I'm going to apply the patch, and if you as a copyright holder of that file disagree, I will simply remove all of he LSM code from the kernel. I think it's very clear that a LSM module is a derived work, and thus copyright law and the GPL are not in any way unclear about it.

If people think they can avoid the GPL by using function pointers, they are WRONG. And they have always been wrong.

> Linus

Second Post by Linus in Security Hooks License Thread

From: Linus Torvalds <torvalds@transmeta.com>
Subject: Re: [PATCH] make LSM register functions GPLonly exports
Date: 2002-10-17 17:25:12

On Thu, 17 Oct 2002, Linus Torvalds wrote:
>
> If people think they can avoid the GPL by using function pointers, they
> are WRONG. And they have always been wrong.

Side note: it should be noted that legally the GPLONLY note is nothing but
a strong hint and has nothing to do with the license (and only matters
for the _enforcement_ of said license). The fact is:

 - the kernel copyright requires the GPL for derived works anyway.

 - if a company feels confident that they can prove in court that their
   module is not a derived work, the GPL doesn't matter _anyway_,
   since a copyright license at that point is meaningless and wouldn't
   cover the work regardless of whether we say it is GPLONLY or not.

   (In other words: for provably non-derived works, whatever kernel
   license we choose is totally irrelevant)

So the GPLONLY is really a big red warning flag: "Danger, Will Robinson".

It doesn't have any real legal effect on the meaning of the license
itself, except in the sense that it's another way to inform users about
the copyright license (think of it as a "click through" issue - GPLONLY
forces you to "click through" the fact that the kernel is under the GPL
and thus derived works have to be too).

Clearly "click through" _has_ been considered a legally meaningful thing,
in that it voids the argument that somebody wasn't aware of the license.
It doesn't change what you can or cannot do, but it has some meaning for
whether it could be wilful infringement or just honest mistake.

                    Linus

Legal Clarifications About the Kernel by Linus Torvalds

This is a fairly long explanation by Linus Torvalds regarding the kernel's licensing
and how this licensing applies to foreign code:

Feel free to post/add this. I wrote it some time ago for a corporate
lawyer who wondered what the "GPL exception" was. Names and companies
removed not because I think they are ashamed, but because I don't want
people to read too much into them.

                    Linus

Date: Fri, 19 Oct 2001 13:16:45 -0700 (PDT)
From: Linus Torvalds <torvalds@transmeta.com>
To: Xxxx Xxxxxx <xxxxx@xxx.xxxx.com>
Subject: Re: GPL, Richard Stallman, and the Linux kernel

[This is not, of course, a legal document, but if you want to forward it
  to anybody else, feel free to do so. And if you want to argue legal
  points with me or point somehting out, I'm always interested. To a
  point ;-]

On Fri, 19 Oct 2001, Xxxx Xxxxxx wrote:
>
> I've been exchanging e-mail with Richard Stallman for a couple of
> weeks about the finer points of the GPL.

I feel your pain.

> I've have spent time pouring through mailing list archives, usenet,
> and web search engines to find out what's already been covered about
> your statement of allowing dynamically loaded kernel modules with
> proprietary code to co-exist with the Linux kernel. So far I've
> been unable to find anything beyond vague statements attributed to
> you. If these issues are addressed somewhere already, please refer
> me.

Well, it really boils down to the equivalent of "_all_ derived modules
have to be GPL'd". An external module doesn't really change the GPL in
that respect.

There are (mainly historical) examples of UNIX device drivers and some
UNIX filesystems that were pre-existing pieces of work, and which had
fairly well-defined and clear interfaces and that I personally could not
really consider any kind of "derived work" at all, and that were thus
acceptable. The clearest example of this is probably the AFS (the Andrew
Filesystem), but there have been various device drivers ported from SCO
too.

> Issue #1
> ========
> Currently the GPL version 2 license is the only license covering the
> Linux kernel. I cannot find any alternative license explaining the
> loadable kernel module exception which makes your position difficult
> to legally analyze.
>
> There is a note at the top of www.kernel.org/pub/linux/kernel/COPYING,
> but that states "user programs" which would clearly not apply to
> kernel modules.
>
> Could you clarify in writing what the exception precisely states?

Well, there really is no exception. However, copyright law obviously
hinges on the definition of "derived work", and as such anything can
always be argued on that point.

I personally consider anything a "derived work" that needs special hooks
in the kernel to function with Linux (ie it is _not_ acceptable to make a
small piece of GPL-code as a hook for the larger piece), as that obviously
implies that the bigger module needs "help" from the main kernel.

Similarly, I consider anything that has intimate knowledge about kernel
internals to be a derived work.

What is left in the gray area tends to be clearly separate modules: code
that had a life outside Linux from the beginning, and that do something
self-containted that doesn't really have any impact on the rest of the

kernel. A device driver that was originally written for something else, and that doesn't need any but the standard UNIX read/write kind of interfaces, for example.

> Issue #2
> ========
> I've found statements attributed to you that you think only 10% of
> the code in the current kernel was written by you. By not being the
> sole copyright holder of the Linux kernel, a stated exception to
> the GPL seems invalid unless all kernel copyright holders agreed on
> this exception. How does the exception cover GPL'd kernel code not
> written by you? Has everyone contributing to the kernel forfeited
> their copyright to you or agreed with the exception?

Well, see above about the lack of exception, and about the fundamental
gray area in _any_ copyright issue. The "derived work" issue is obviously
a gray area, and I know lawyers don't like them. Crazy people (even
judges) have, as we know, claimed that even obvious spoofs of a work that
contain nothing of the original work itself, can be ruled to be "derived".

I don't hold views that extreme, but at the same time I do consider a
module written for Linux and using kernel infrastructures to get its work
done, even if not actually copying any existing Linux code, to be a
derived work by default. You'd have to have a strong case to _not_
consider your code a derived work..

> Issue #3
> ========
> This issue is related to issue #1. Exactly what is covered by the
> exception? For example, all code shipped with the Linux kernel
> archive and typically installed under /usr/src/linux, all code under
> /usr/src/linux except /usr/src/linux/drivers, or just the code in
> the /usr/src/linux/kernel directory?

See above, and I think you'll see my point.

The "user program" exception is not an exception at all, for example, it's
just a more clearly stated limitation on the "derived work" issue. If you
use standard UNIX system calls (with accepted Linux extensions), your
program obviously doesn't "derive" from the kernel itself.

Whenever you link into the kernel, either directly or through a module,
the case is just a _lot_ more muddy. But as stated, by default it's
obviously derived - the very fact that you _need_ to do something as
fundamental as linking against the kernel very much argues that your
module is not a stand-alone thing, regardless of where the module source
code itself has come from.

> Issue #4
> ========
> This last issue is not so much a issue for the Linux kernel
> exception, but a request for comment.
>

> Richard and I both agree that a "plug-in" and a "dynamically
> loaded kernel module" are effectively the same under the GPL.

Agreed.

The Linux kernel modules had (a long time ago), a more limited interface,
and not very many functions were actually exported. So five or six years
ago, we could believably claim that "if you only use these N interfaces
that are exported from the standard kernel, you've kind of implicitly
proven that you do not need the kernel infrastructure".

That was never really documented either (more of a guideline for me and
others when we looked at the "derived work" issue), and as modules were
more-and-more used not for external stuff, but just for dynamic loading of
standard linux modules that were distributed as part of the kernel anyway,
the "limited interfaces" argument is no longer a very good guideline for
"derived work".

So these days, we export many internal interfaces, not because we don't
think that they would "taint" the linker, but simply because it's useful
to do dynamic run-time loading of modules even with standard kernel
modules that _are_ supposed to know a lot about kernel internals, and are
obviously "derived works"..

> However we disagree that a plug-in for a GPL'd program falls
> under the GPL as asserted in the GPL FAQ found in the answer:
> http://www.gnu.org/licenses/gpl-faq.html#GPLAndPlugins.

I think you really just disagree on what is derived, and what is not.
Richard is very extreme: _anything_ that links is derived, regardless of
what the arguments against it are. I'm less extreme, and I bet you're even
less so (at least you might like to argue so).

> My assertion is that plug-ins are written to an interface, not a
> program. Since interfaces are not GPL'd, a plug-in cannot be GPL'd
> until the plug-in and program are placed together and run. That is
> done by the end user, not the plug-in creator.

I agree, but also disrespectfully disagree ;)

It's an issue of what a "plug-in" is - is it a way for the program to
internally load more modules as it needs them, or is it _meant_ to be a
public, published interface.

For example, the "system call" interface could be considered a "plug-in
interface", and running a user mode program under Linux could easily be
construed as running a "plung-in" for the Linux kernel. No?

And there, I obviously absolutely agree with you 100%: the interface is
published, and it's _meant_ for external and independent users. It's an
interface that we go to great lengths to preserve as well as we can, and
it's an interface that is designed to be independent of kernel versions.

But maybe somebody wrote his program with the intention to dynamically
load "actors" as they were needed, as a way to maintain a good modularity,

and to try to keep the problem spaces well-defined. In that case, the
"plug-in" may technically follow all the same rules as the system call
interface, even though the author doesn't intend it that way.

So I think it's to a large degree a matter of intent, but it could
arguably also be considered a matter of stability and documentation (ie
"require recompilation of the plug-in between version changes" would tend
to imply that it's an internal interface, while "documented binary
compatibility across many releases" implies a more stable external
interface, and less of a derived work)

Does that make sense to you?

> I asked Richard to comment on several scenarios involving plug-ins
> explain whether or not they were in violation of the GPL. So far he
> as only addressed one and has effectively admitted a hole. This is
> the one I asked that he's responded to:
>   [A] non-GPL'd plug-in writer writes a plug-in for a non-GPL'd
>   program. Another author writes a GPL'd program making the
>   first author's plug-ins compatible with his program. Are now
>   the plug-in author's plug-ins now retroactively required to be
>   GPL'd?
>
> His response:
>   No, because the plug-in was not written to extend this program.
>
> I find it suspicious that whether or not the GPL would apply to the
> plug-in depends on the mindset of the author.

The above makes no sense if you think of it as a "plug in" issue, but it
makes sense if you think of it as a "derived work" issue, along with
taking "intent" into account.

I know lawyers tend to not like the notion of "intent", because it brings
in another whole range of gray areas, but it's obviously a legal reality.

Ok, enough blathering from me. I'd just like to finish off with a few
comments, just to clarify my personal stand:

 - I'm obviously not the only copyright holder of Linux, and I did so on
   purpose for several reasons. One reason is just because I hate the
   paperwork and other cr*p that goes along with copyright assignments.

   Another is that I don't much like copyright assignments at all: the
   author is the author, and he may be bound by my requirement for GPL,
   but that doesn't mean that he should give his copyright to me.

   A third reason, and the most relevant reason here, is that I want
   people to _know_ that I cannot control the sources. I can write you a
   note to say that "for use XXX, I do not consider module YYY to be a
   derived work of my kernel", but that would not really matter that much.
   Any other Linux copyright holder might still sue you.

   This third reason is what makes people who otherwise might not trust me
   realize that I cannot screw people over. I am bound by the same

agreement that I require of everybody else, and the only special status
I really have is a totally non-legal issue: people trust me.

(Yes, I realize that I probably would end up having more legal status
than most, even apart from the fact that I still am the largest single
copyright holder, if only because of appearances)

- I don't really care about copyright law itself. What I care about is my
  own morals. Whether I'd ever sue somebody or not (and quite frankly,
  it's the last thing I ever want to do - if I never end up talking to
  lawyers in a professional context, I'll be perfectly happy. No
  disrespect intended) will be entirely up to whether I consider what
  people do to me "moral" or not. Which is why intent matters to me a
  lot - both the intent of the person/corporation doign the infringement,
  and the intent of me and others in issues like the module export
  interface.

  Another way of putting this: I don't care about "legal loopholes" and
  word-wrangling.

- Finally: I don't trust the FSF. I like the GPL a lot - although not
  necessarily as a legal piece of paper, but more as an intent. Which
  explains why, if you've looked at the Linux COPYING file, you may have
  noticed the explicit comment about "only _this_ particular version of
  the GPL covers the kernel by default".

  That's because I agree with the GPL as-is, but I do not agree with the
  FSF on many other matters. I don't like software patents much, for
  example, but I do not want the code I write to be used as a weapon
  against companies that have them. The FSF has long been discussing and
  is drafting the "next generation" GPL, and they generally suggest that
  people using the GPL should say "v2 or at your choice any later
  version".

  Linux doesn't do that. The Linux kernel is v2 ONLY, apart from a few
  files where the author put in the FSF extension (and see above about
  copyright assignments why I would never remove such an extension).

The "v2 only" issue might change some day, but only after all documented
copyright holders agree on it, and only after we've seen what the FSF
suggests. From what I've seen so far from the FSF drafts, we're not likely
to change our v2-only stance, but there might of course be legal reasons
why we'd have to do something like it (ie somebody challenging the GPLv2
in court, and part of it to be found unenforceable or similar would
obviously mean that we'd have to reconsider the license).

                    Linus

PS. Historically, binary-only modules have not worked well under Linux,
quite regardless of any copyright issues. The kernel just develops too
quickly for binary modules to work well, and nobody really supports them.
Companies like RedHat etc tend to refuse to have anything to do with
binary modules, because if something goes wrong there is nothing they can
do about it. So I just wanted to let you know that the _legal_ issue is
just the beginning. Even though you probably don't personally care ;)

Index

We'd like to hear your suggestions for improving our indexes. Send email to *index@oreilly.com*.

ARM (Advanced RISC Machine) processor
  architecture overview, 59, 60
  bootloader comparison, 248
  diet libc support, 139
  embedded system survey, 12
  embutils, 190
  GNU toolchain, 111
  kernel considerations, 157, 160, 162, 166
  U-Boot and, 249
  UI modules and, 35
ARMBoot project, 252
As, 179, 286
as (GNU assembler) utility, 120, 129
ASCII
  Modbus messaging format, 104
ATA (ARCnet Trade Association), 103
ATA (AT Attachment), 91
ATA-ATAPI (IDE) hardware support, 91–93
ATAPI (ATA Packet Interface), 91
Attached Resource Computer NETwork
      (ARCnet), 103, 104
ATV (Automatic Transfer Vehicle), 10
authentication, 312
authorization, secure, 288

B

.bb files, 324
.bbg files, 324
BBT (Bad Block Table), 212, 213, 216
BDM debugger, 40, 48, 335
BDM4GDB project, 335
/bin directory, 129, 173, 174, 191
binaries
  downloading to flash, 275–277
  sections for debugging, 309
  strip command, 311
  U-Boot, 272–273
BIN_GROUP variable (make
      command), 193
BIN_OWNER variable (make
      command), 193
binutils (binary utilities)
  gcc cautions, 130
  GPL license, 22
  resources, 116
  setting up, 120–122
  Unix systems and, 44
  version considerations, 110
BIOS
  interrupt handlers and, 263
  LILO and, 260
  ROM chips and, 250

system startup process, 216
  TSR program and, 262
Blackdown project, 59, 142, 143
blob bootloader, 248, 251
block devices, 228, 234
BlueCat (LynuxWorks), 19
BlueDrekar stack, 99
Bluetooth, 98
  Ericsson blip and, 9
  hardware support, 98–101
  kernel support options, 160
  unlisted features, 161
BlueZ stack, 99, 100
Boa, 301–303
book resources, 354, 355
boot configuration, 52–54
/boot directory, 172
boot scripts, 271
bootable DOS diskette, 212, 213
booting
  basics of, 52
  BOOTP/DHCP, TFTP, NFS, 274–275
  CF devices, 279–282
  diskless systems, 250
  from DOC, 217
  hard disks and, 223
  network boot, 249, 253–257
  RAM disk, 278–279
  from ROM, 250
  system reboot, 169, 195
  U-Boot and, 267–269
bootldr bootloader, 248, 251
bootloaders
  ATA-IDE limitations, 92
  boot configurations, 52–54
  comparison, 247–249
  DOS method installation, 213
  example, 56
  GRUB and DOC devices, 262–266
  importance of, 246
  installing, 216, 217
  LILO with disk and CF devices, 258–261
  minicom constraints, 152
  mounting filesystem, 257–258
  partitions and, 212
  server setup for network boot, 253–257
  setting up, 37, 39
  SPL as, 216
  system startup component, 51
  worksheet, 342
  (see also specific bootloaders)
bootm command, 281

H

hard real-time system, 6, 33
hardware support
    ARM processor, 59, 60
    buses and interfaces, 64–75
    debugging tools, 48, 334, 335
    IBM/Motorola PowerPC, 60, 61
    industrial grade networking, 101–105
    input/output, 75–85
    kernel configuration options, 160
    kernprof and, 327
    Linux and, 15, 26, 43
    MIPS processor, 61–62
    Motorola 68000, 64
    networking, 94–101
    open source projects, 356
    processor architectures, 57
    storage, 85–93
    SuperH, 63
    U-Boot, 252
    x86 processor, 58, 59
HCI (Host Controller Interface), 99, 100
hcidump tool (BlueZ), 100
hdparm utility, 92
header files, 162, 164
help command, 280
HelpPC shareware, 59
Here, 33
hexadecimal format, 269
HEYU! project, 81
high-availability, 69
Hitachi SuperH (see SuperH processor)
home automation, 80, 81
/home directory, 172
Host Controller Interface (HCI), 99, 100
host systems
    automatic network configuration, 305
    byte ordering considerations, 230, 231
    debug setups, 47, 48
    defined, 4
    development setups, 44–47
    GNU toolchain, 110, 111
    installing MTD utilities, 204–205
    testing connections, 40
    types of, 42–44
Hot Swap specification (CompactPCI), 68
HTTP
    SYSM module and, 34
    web content and, 301–304

I

I^2C (Inter-Integrated Circuit) bus, 74, 75
i386 platform
    embutils, 190
    GNU toolchain, 111
    hardware support, 58
    PCMCIA support, 66
    target build example, 112
i386-linux directory, 129
IAP (Information Access Protocol), 96
IAS (Information Access Service), 94
IBM/Motorola PowerPC (see PowerPC)
ICE (In-Circuit Emulator), 48, 335
ide commands, 280, 282
IDE drives (see also ATA-ATAPI)
    CF cards and, 221
    CompactFlash devices as, 89
    LILO and, 259, 260
    U-Boot and, 252
IDEs (integrated development environments)
    availability, 150
    listed, 149
    using, 40
    worksheet, 339
IEEE1284 standard, 70
IEEE1394 (Firewire) standard, 72, 73, 160
IEEE488 (GPIB) standard, 73
IEEE 802.11 (wireless) standard, 97, 98
IETF standard, 295
If, 205
iminfo command, 274, 276
implementation methodology, 37–41
In, 206
In-Circuit Emulator (ICE), 48, 335
include directory, 119, 129
index.html files, 303
Industry Standard Architecture (ISA), 65, 67
inetd super-server, 256, 286–288, 294
info directory, 129
Infrared Data Association (see IrDA)
init program
    BusyBox init, 194–197
    kernel and, 191
    Minit, 197
    respawning cautions, 300
    standard System V init, 192, 194
    start_kernel( ) function, 51
    system startup component, 51
Initial Program Loader (IPL), 216, 262

V

value-added packages, 28
/var directory, 172, 173, 174
VDC (Venture Development Corporation), 12
vendor support
  ARM, 59, 60
  CAN, 101
  CompactPCI bus, 70
  DAQ packages, 78
  distributions and, 28
  I2C bus, 74
  independence, 16
  IrDA, 94
  MIPS, 62
  Motorola 68000 processors, 64
  PowerPC architecture, 60
  process control, 79
  VME bus, 68
Venture Development Corporation (VDC), 12
versions
  EXTRAVERSION variable, 163
  firmware, 213, 214
  kernels, 156, 157, 158
  LILO, 259
  naming conventions, 163
  NTFL formatting, 219
  tracking, 296
  worksheet, 340
VFIR (very fast infrared), 95
vi (IDE), 149
ViewML, 19
virtual addresses, 55, 56
virtual machines, 143
visualization tool, 317, 319, 320
VME bus, 64, 67, 68
vmlinux file, 166
VxWorks (WindRiver), 11, 314

W

watchdog timers, 105, 106
wear leveling, 89, 227
web content, 301–304
Windows workstations, 44
WindowsCE, 62

WinModem, 77, 78
wireless technologies (see Bluetooth; IEEE 802.11; IrDA)
worksheet, embedded Linux systems, 337–344
workspace, 107–109, 114–115
workstations, 42, 43, 44

X

X terminals, 36, 250
X Window System
  graphical interface, 83
  JDK and JRE, 142
  kernel configuration, 162
  xconfig script, 118
X10 corporation, 80
X10 Power Line Carrier (PLC) protocol, 80, 81
x86 processor
  architecture overview, 58, 59
  bootloader comparison, 248
  bzImage target, 165
  diet libc support, 139
  DiskOnChip devices, 212
  embedded system survey, 12
  GRUB and, 264
  ISA support, 65
  kernel, 157, 160
  system startup process, 216
xconfig command, 118
XEmacs (IDE), 149
XFS journalling filesystem, 234
xinetd super-server
  features, 288, 289
  Red Hat-based, 256
  telnetd and, 294
  TFTP service, 256
XIP (eXecute In Place), 89

Y

Yellow Dog Linux, 60

Z

zImage file, 166
zlib compression library, 206, 295, 296, 300

About the Author

Karim Yaghmour is the founder and president of Opersys Inc. (*http://www.opersys.com*), a company providing expertise and courses on the use of open source and free software in embedded systems. As an active member of the open source and free software community, Karim has firmly established Opersys's services around the core values of knowledge sharing and technical quality that are promoted by this community. As part of his community involvement, Karim is the maintainer of the Linux Trace Toolkit and the author of a series of white papers that led to the implementation of the Adeos nanokernel, which allows multiple operating systems to exist side by side.

Karim's quest for understanding how things work started at a very young age when he took it upon himself to break open all the radios and cassette players he could lay his hands on in order to "fix" them. Very early, he developed a keen interest in operating system internals and embedded systems. He now holds a B.Eng. and an M.A.Sc. from the École Polytechnique de Montréal. While everyone was hacking away at Linux, Karim took a detour to write his own distributed microkernel to get to the bottom of operating system design and implementation. When not working on software, Karim indulges in his passion for history, philosophy, sociology, and humanities in general. He's especially addicted to essays and novels by Umberto Eco and Gerald Messadié.

Colophon

Our look is the result of reader comments, our own experimentation, and feedback from distribution channels. Distinctive covers complement our distinctive approach to technical topics, breathing personality and life into potentially dry subjects.

Linley Dolby was the production editor and copyeditor for *Building Embedded Linux Systems*. Claire Cloutier, Phil Dangler, Matt Hutchinson, and Darren Kelly provided quality control. Derek Di Matteo and Jamie Peppard provided production assistance. Lucie Haskins wrote the index.

The image on the cover of *Building Embedded Linux Systems* is a windmill. Emma Colby designed the cover of this book, based on a series design by Hanna Dyer and Edie Freedman. The cover image is a 19th-century engraving from the Dover Pictorial Archive. Emma Colby produced the cover layout with QuarkXPress 4.1 using Adobe's ITC Garamond font.

Bret Kerr designed the interior layout, based on a series design by David Futato. The chapter opening images are from the Dover Pictorial Archive, *Marvels of the New West: A Vivid Portrayal of the Stupendous Marvels in the Vast Wonderland West of the Missouri River*, by William Thayer (The Henry Bill Publishing Co., 1888), and *The Pioneer History of America: A Popular Account of the Heroes and Adventures*, by Augustus Lynch Mason, A.M. (The Jones Brothers Publishing Company, 1884). This book was converted by Joe Wizda to FrameMaker 5.5.6 with a format conversion tool created by Erik Ray, Jason McIntosh, Neil Walls, and Mike Sierra that uses Perl and XML technologies. The text font is Linotype Birka; the heading font is Adobe Myriad Condensed; and the code font is LucasFont's TheSans Mono Condensed. The illustrations that appear in the book were produced by Robert Romano and Jessamyn Read using Macromedia FreeHand 9 and Adobe Photoshop 6. The tip and warning icons were drawn by Christopher Bing.